The Music of
Berlioz

Julian Rushton

The Music of
Berlioz

OXFORD
UNIVERSITY PRESS

OXFORD

UNIVERSITY PRESS

Great Clarendon Street, Oxford OX2 6DP

Oxford University Press is a department of the University of Oxford.
It furthers the University's objective of excellence in research, scholarship,
and education by publishing worldwide in

Oxford New York

Athens Auckland Bangkok Bogotá Buenos Aires Cape Town
Chennai Dar es Salaam Delhi Florence Hong Kong Istanbul Karachi
Kolkata Kuala Lumpur Madrid Melbourne Mexico City Mumbai Nairobi
Paris São Paulo Shanghai Singapore Taipei Tokyo Toronto Warsaw
and associated companies in Berlin Ibadan

Oxford is a registered trade mark of Oxford University Press
in the UK and in certain other countries

Published in the United States
by Oxford University Press Inc., New York

British Library Cataloguing in Publication Data

Data available

Library of Congress Cataloging in Publication Data

Rushton, Julian.
The music of Berlioz / Julian Rushton.
p. cm.
Includes bibliographical references and indexes.
1. Berlioz, Hector, 1803–1869—Criticism and interpretation. I. Title.
ML410.B5 R87 2001   780′.92—dc21   00-045299
ISBN 0–19–816690–7
ISBN 0–19–816738–5 (pbk.)

10 9 8 7 6 5 4 3 2 1

Typeset by Hope Services (Abingdon) Ltd.
Printed in Great Britain
on acid-free paper by
Biddles Ltd.,
Guildford & King's Lynn

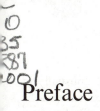

Preface

This book was originally conceived as a sequel to my *The Musical Language of Berlioz* (1983). A review by the late Philip Friedheim expressed the wish that I had included more about the meaning of the music, and considered works more as wholes, precisely the aspects I hoped to cover in 'Volume 2', which might have been called *Berlioz's Musical Works*.[1] *The Music of Berlioz* is certainly not the chronological, work-by-work study I once expected to write, and for which today there seems no compelling necessity. Nevertheless, this book is about the music first, including associated texts and, I hope, 'meanings'; it is not a biography, nor is it a work of musical philosophy.

Since 1983, the understanding of Berlioz has benefited from a number of fine biographical studies, and several studies of his works, including hand-books on *Les Troyens* and *Roméo et Juliette*; three issues of *L'Avant-scène opéra*, several new volumes of the New Berlioz Edition (hereafter NBE), which is now nearing completion; monographs and dissertations in French, English, and German, and volumes of essays. I have tried to consult as many of these as possible, but there are certainly gaps, and to the neglected authors I can only apologize. The time elapsed since 1983 enables me to take into consideration the startling discovery, in 1991, of Berlioz's *Messe solennelle*. This early work may be discussed more than its intrinsic merits warrant, but these discussions contribute to an agenda which I will not deny, which is to continue the revaluation of a composer whose music, or nearly all of it, I love, and who still appears to be undervalued in some quarters—or evaluated unevenly, with excessive emphasis on symphonic music, a point I will return to in conclusion.

The first section (Chapters 1 to 3) is a biography of Berlioz's music—not of his life. To establish the order of his compositions may appear redundant, and these chapters are frankly dependent upon modern biographical and other scholarship, including the NBE and Holoman's thematic

---

[1] *Journal of the American Musicological Society*, 38 (1985), 178–83.

catalogue.[2] But they form a chronological narrative which, unusually in Berlioz biography, refrains from looking ahead at the subsequent uses he made of dramatic concepts and actual musical themes. When Berlioz as a teenager published his romance 'Le Dépit de la bergère', he did not know that he would use the same tune in his last work, *Béatrice et Bénédict*; even with *Huit scènes de Faust*, published in 1829, withdrawn, and built into *La Damnation de Faust* in 1845–6, there is no evidence that his first use of a particular musical invention was, at the time, provisional, or that he could foresee its later incarnation. A qualified exception to this statement may be his Prix de Rome cantatas, works which he wrote to win the prize, and which contain striking ideas familiar from their appearance in later masterpieces. These works have since become known through published scores and recordings, and have an independent existence within today's musical culture (see Chapter 4); and since the Prix de Rome mattered a great deal to Berlioz, there is every reason to suppose that he presented the best work of which he felt himself capable, within the limitations imposed by the genre. Thus the biography of works (Chapters 1–3) is presented as far as possible parallel to real time, which includes knowledge of the past, but not the future.

Interpretation of musical data begins with Chapters 4–6, although I would argue that it was not absent from *The Musical Language of Berlioz*, even when I was subjecting the music to the discipline of post-Schenkerian analysis. In these chapters I hope to have cleared up some loose ends relating to Berlioz's technique, and to consider his musical language as a signifying system. Musical analysis appears in these chapters and in the last four. There is no question of discussing every section of every work in equivalent detail; I particularly wished to avoid writing a series of miniature handbooks. I also did not want to repeat arguments I have made elsewhere; accordingly the footnotes contain what may seem an inordinate number of references to my own publications. The notes use short titles, which are explained below, and refrain from repeating details which appear in the bibliography. In tables, lower-case letters imply minor keys. Where there is possible ambiguity, pitch notation conforms to the Helmholtz system, in which the octave below middle C is c–b, the octave from middle C is c′–b′; otherwise letters are used (e.g. 'a leap from a′–a‴; but 'the dominant seventh on A').

I am particularly grateful to Bruce Phillips, who encouraged this project when he was at Oxford University Press, to Helen Peres da Costa at OUP, my present editor, and Mary Worthington. The Leverhulme foundation supported me for a semester of sabbatical leave to complete research and write

---

[2] D. Kern Holoman, *Catalogue of the Works of Hector Berlioz*, New Berlioz Edition (NBE), 25. Other works extensively used are Berlioz, *Correspondance générale*; Jacques Barzun, *Berlioz and the Romantic Century*; Berlioz, *Memoirs of Hector Berlioz*, ed. and trans. David Cairns; Hugh Macdonald, *Berlioz*; D. Kern Holoman, *Berlioz*; David Cairns's two-volume biography, *Berlioz: The Making of an Artist*, and *Berlioz: Servitude and Greatness*; Peter Bloom, *The Life of Berlioz*; forewords and critical apparatus of the NBE.

the book; I am eternally grateful for this, and for the additional semester granted by the Faculty of Arts research leave scheme at the University of Leeds. I thank those who have already heard parts of this book as live presentations, and for their feed-back, including listeners at the Universities of Cambridge, Columbia, North Texas, Oxford, Western Ontario, Bar-Ilan, and York; The Royal Musical Association Conference and its Irish Chapter; the British Conference on Nineteenth-Century Music; and the City University Music Analysis Conference, 1991. I am grateful to the libraries whose collections support my work, sometimes on projects for which even this long book has insufficient space, and which I hope to develop later. Besides the Brotherton Library in Leeds, these include the Bibliothèque nationale, Paris; the British Library; Cambridge University Library; and the Goethe-Schiller Archiv, Weimar. I thank Barry Millington of *BBC Music Magazine* for sending most of Berlioz's output on CD for review. For loan of material, and many friendly consultations, I am grateful to David Charlton, David Lloyd-Jones, Diana Bickley, D. Kern Holoman, Hugh Macdonald, Ian Kemp, Ian Rumbold of the New Berlioz Edition, Katharine Ellis, Peter Bloom, Ralph Locke, Roger Parker, and Simon McGuire of Sotheby's; for permission to cite unpublished material, Annegret Fauser, Paul Banks, Janet L. Johnson, and Benjamin Walton; to Miriam Lensky, so far my only Berliozian research student; and for the constant inspiration of his wonderful biography, David Cairns.

JULIAN RUSHTON

Leeds, December 1999

Contents

List of Tables   xii

List of Abbreviations   xiii

I. A BIOGRAPHY OF BERLIOZ'S MUSIC   1

1. Provincial to Prize-Winner   3
   Sources   3
   La Côte-Saint-André   4
   Paris   7
   Compositions to 1825   8
   The Ferrand era   11
   The Prix de Rome   14
   Opus 1   24

2. The Romantic Decade   28
   Symphonie fantastique   28
   Italie!   30
   Le retour de l'artiste d'Italie   34
   Italian music   36
   The artist as hero   37
   Grande messe des morts   40
   Roméo et Juliette   41
   End of the romantic decade   44

3. Damnation and After   47
   Les années mystérieuses   47
   The salvaging of Faust   50
   Purgatory   52
   Writing a Te Deum   55
   Empire and religion   58
   Les Troyens   61
   Swan songs   65

Contents

II. TECHNIQUES AND MEANINGS   69

4. Implications of a Musical Biography   71
   Intertextuality and the musical work   71
   A typology of borrowing   73
   Hermeneutics   82
   Words and music   84

5. Techniques of Composition   98
   Musical language   98
   Compositional process   101
   The *Messe solennelle* and counterpoint   107
   Harmony revisited   112
   Harmony and expression   118
   The outré: 'Le Ballet des ombres'   121

6. Signs and Evocations   125
   Introduction   125
   Topics and rhetoric   126
   The grotesque, the supernatural, the sublime   133
   Death and life, heaven and hell   139
   Exoticism, eroticism, and love   143
   Programmes   155

III. THE WORKS   163

7. The Lyric Berlioz   165
   Romance, ballad, and 'Gothic Song'   165
   After *Irlande*: romance to *mélodie*   178
   The mature *mélodie*   179
   Small choral works   185
   Arias in dramatic works   187

8. Architecture, Patriotism, and the End of the World   192
   'Paris vaut une messe'   192
   A second vision of judgement: *Grande messe des morts*   203
   Architecture and patriotic fervour   216
   Te Deum   220

9. A Fantastic Symphonist   237
   Orchestral rhetoric: first essays   237
   Symphonie fantastique   251
   Brigands in the mountains: *Harold en Italie*   266
   Italian Liebestod: 'Roméo au tombeau'   269
   Genre: the last symphonic works   275

10. Berlioz Dramatist   281
    Introduction   281
    Benvenuto Cellini, 'petit opéra semi-seria'   291
    Concert opera: dramatic legend   303
    L'Enfance du Christ: Oratorium einer Zukunftsmusiker?   315
    Les Troyens, Tragédie lyrique   324

Postscript   339
    Béatrice et Bénédict   339
    Posterity   340
    Berlioz conservative or radical? success or failure?   344

Select Bibliography   348

Index of Berlioz's works   355

General index   361

List of Tables

4.1	Borrowings: the principal sources	74
5.1	Invertible counterpoint in the Kyrie	111
7.1	Design of 'Une amoureuse flamme' (*Huit scènes de Faust*)	183
8.1	*Messe solennelle*: list of movements	195
8.2	Use of the *Messe solennelle* in later works of Berlioz	201
8.3	Evolution of the Resurrexit: changes in the version of *c*.1828	202
8.4	Design of *Grande messe des morts*	204
8.5	Text of the Te Deum	222
8.6	Overall form of the Te Deum	223
8.7	Comparison of Agnus Dei with 'Te ergo quæsumus'	228
9.1	Chronological list of beginnings	242
9.2	Varieties of monodic opening	243
9.3	Form of *Symphonie fantastique*: the 'Pastoral' perverted	253
9.4	The *ad astra* narrative perverted	253
9.5	*Symphonie fantastique*, 'Songe d'une Nuit du Sabbat'	255
9.6	Sources of *Symphonie fantastique*	265
9.7	Comparison of *Roméo* with Beethoven, Op. 131	276
10.1	Nine scenes from *Faust*	305
10.2	Simultaneity in *La Damnation*, Part III	307

Abbreviations

If full bibliographical information is not given in a note, full details appear in the bibliography. The following standard references are used in the notes.

A travers chants	Berlioz, *A travers chants*, ed. Léon Guichard (Paris: Gründ, 1971)
Bloom, *Studies*	Peter Bloom (ed.), *Berlioz Studies* (Cambridge University Press, 1992)
Cairns, *Making of an Artist*	David Cairns, *Berlioz*. vol. i: *The Making of an Artist* (London: Deutsch, 1989; 2nd rev. edn. London: Allen Lane, the Penguin Press, 1999) (page numbers: first edition/second edition)
Cairns, *Servitude*	David Cairns, *Berlioz*, vol. ii: *Servitude and Greatness* (London: Allen Lane, the Penguin Press, 1999)
Holoman, *Catalogue*	D. Kern Holoman, *Catalogue of the Works of Hector Berlioz*, NBE vol. 25 (Kassel: Barenreiter, 1987)
CG	*Correspondance générale de Hector Berlioz* (Paris: Flammarion), i: *1803–32* (1972); ii: *1832–42* (1975); iii: *1842–50* (1978); iv: *1851–5* (1983); v: *1855–9* (1989); vi: *1859–63*; followed by volume number and page (not letter) number
Condé	*Hector Berlioz. Cauchemars et passions*, ed. Gérard Condé (Paris: J.-C. Lattès, 1981)
Critique musicale	Berlioz, *Critique musicale 1823–1863*, ed. H. Robert Cohen and Yves Gérard (Paris: Buchet/Chastel), i: *1823–34* (1996); ii: *1835–6* (1998), followed by volume number and page number

Dömling, *Zeit*	Wolfgang Dömling, *Hector Berlioz und seine Zeit* (Laaber: Laaber-Verlag, 1986)
F-Pn	Bibliothèque nationale, Paris
Grotesques	Berlioz, *Les Grotesques de la musique* (Paris: Bourdillat, 1859); critical edn., ed. Léon Guichard (Paris: Gründ, 1969)
H numbers	Holoman numbers, applied to musical works
HC numbers	Holoman numbers applied to Berlioz's critical writings.
Holoman, *Creative Process*	D. Kern Holoman, *The Creative Process in the Autograph Documents of Hector Berlioz c.1818–1840* (Ann Arbor: UMI Studies in Musicology, 1980)
Holoman, 'Conservatoire'	D. Kern Holoman, 'Berlioz au Conservatoire: Notes biographiques', *Revue de Musicologie*, 62 (1976), 289–92
Holoman, 'Sketchbook'	D. Kern Holoman, 'The Berlioz Sketchbook Recovered', *19th-Century Music*, 7 (1984), 282–317
Kemp, *Les Troyens*	Ian Kemp, *Hector Berlioz: Les Troyens* (Cambridge Opera Handbook) (Cambridge University Press, 1988)
Macdonald, *Berlioz*	Hugh Macdonald, *Berlioz (The Master Musicians)* (London: Dent, 1982)
Macdonald, '*Messe solennelle*'	Hugh Macdonald, 'Berlioz's *Messe solennelle*', *19th-Century Music*, 16 (Spring, 1973), 267–85
Memoirs	*Mémoires d'Hector Berlioz* (Paris: Michel Lévy, 1870); critical edn. ed. Pierre Citron (Paris: Flammarion, 1969; repr. 1991 with addenda and corrigenda); trans. David Cairns as *The Memoirs of Hector Berlioz* (London: Gollancz, 1969). References are to the chapter, not the page, to accommodate all editions
MLB	Julian Rushton, *The Musical Language of Berlioz* (Cambridge Studies in Music) (Cambridge University Press, 1983)
Mongrédien, *Le Sueur*	Jean Mongrédien, *Jean-François Le Sueur, contribution à l'étude d'un demi-siècle de musique française (1780–1830)*, 2 vols. (Berne: Peter Lang, 1980)

NBE	Hector Berlioz: *New Edition of the Complete Works* (Kassel: Bärenreiter, 1969–[2003])
OBE	Hector Berlioz: *Werke*, ed. Malherbe and Weingartner (Leipzig: Breitkopf & Härtel, 1900–7)
'Overture'	Julian Rushton, 'The Overture to *Les Troyens*', *Music Analysis*, 4 (1985), 119–44
Roméo	Julian Rushton, *Berlioz: Roméo et Juliette* (Cambridge Music Handbook) (Cambridge University Press, 1994)
Soirées	Berlioz, *Les Soirées de l'Orchestre*, ed. Léon Guichard (Paris: Gründ, 1968)
Traité	Berlioz, *Grande Traité d'Instrumentation et d'Orchestration modernes*, 1st edn. (Paris: Schonenberger, 1843); 2nd edn. (1855); trans. M. Cowden Clarke as *A Treatise Upon Modern Instrumentation and Orchestration* (London: Novello, 1856). References are to the article, to accommodate all editions.

PART I

A Biography of Berlioz's Music

1 Provincial to Prize-Winner

SOURCES

Berlioz worked within a composing tradition founded on notated scores. The earliest surviving trace of this activity is usually an autograph, the basis for copies, manuscript performing material, and publication. Berlioz destroyed much of the paper mountain generated by his musical activities. We know from letters and memoirs that he sketched extensively, but little survives; had he had any conception of the value—financial, aesthetic, and scholarly—that posterity places on such things, he might have been still more ruthless.[1] Survival of informal documents depends on the accidents of economy. Berlioz wrote corrections on the blank sides of sketch-paper; thus fascinating sketches of Faust's 'Invocation à la nature' survive glued into the autograph of *Harold en Italie*.[2] Even complete scores had limited sentimental value, for Berlioz apparently did not always trouble to retrieve smaller autographs from the publishers, and many are lost.

Berlioz's squirrel-like habit of burying good material for use in later works is well known, and provides much information about his compositional development.[3] The Resurrexit from the *Messe solennelle*, composed in 1824, was revised in 1825 and again in 1828, then withdrawn; but ideas from it reappeared in later works, up to 1849. In other cases a still longer period elapses between the first and final destinations of a musical idea. From an early stage, Berlioz destroyed works that did not satisfy him; yet enough rejected music has survived for Tovey to remark unkindly that for Berlioz 'destroyed' meant 'carefully preserved'. The notion of Berlioz as a habitual liar dies hard, but Tovey may be forgiven for not understanding the limits of Berlioz's control over his own works.[4] In fact he retained scores until he was sure their usefulness was

---

[1] On Berlioz's compositional process see Holoman, *Creative Process*; *MLB* 12–14.

[2] See *MLB* 243–53; Rushton, 'The Genesis of Berlioz's "La Damnation de Faust"'.

[3] Hugh Macdonald, 'Berlioz's Self-borrowings', *Proceedings of the Royal Musical Association*, 92 (1965–6), 27–44. Details are given work by work in Holoman, *Catalogue*, and in NBE forewords.

[4] Tovey, *Essays in Musical Analysis*, iv: *Illustrative Music* (London: Oxford University Press, 1937), 74, the context being *Rob Roy* and *Harold en Italie*. The notion of Berlioz as a liar surfaces again, through misreading the evidence, in Charles Rosen, *The Romantic Generation*, 543.

3

exhausted. The manuscript of the fragmentary duet from *La Nonne sanglante* bears his note: 'à consulter et non à brûler', later altered to 'à consulter—à brûler après ma mort'.[5] Other works survived in manuscript copies Berlioz no longer owned by the time he decided they were no longer representative: those which fetched up with his friend Humbert Ferrand include the only sources of *La Mort d'Orphée* and the first version of *Scène héroïque*, as well as a revised version of the Resurrexit.[6] Without these survivals our knowledge of his early works would be severely restricted.

Part of the reason for this frequent transfer of material between works is that Berlioz's ability to invent memorable phrases, and whole tunes, ran ahead of his self-belief in matters of harmony, instrumentation, and form. Despite an obviously outstanding ability in aural conceptualization, he often found it necessary to revise compositions following the experience of hearing them performed, and from 1830 to 1850 his works were seldom published before undergoing surgery. As he said of *Roméo et Juliette*: 'If I have failed to find and remove other faults, I have at least made every possible effort to hunt them down, and exerted what little wisdom I possess to deal with them. After that, what can one do, other than frankly admit that one could not do better, and learn to accept any remaining imperfections?'[7] Most of this surgery consists of cutting, to effect better proportions, rather than changing melodies, harmonies, or instrumentation. Berlioz's difficulty was a by-product of his originality, not least in reinterpretation of genre.[8] The first three chapters tell the story of Berlioz's use and reuse of ideas alongside the conception and elaboration of new material. If more attention is paid to short works than would be expected in a synoptic account, this is because larger works receive more attention in later chapters.

LA CÔTE-SAINT-ANDRÉ

Berlioz was born on 11 December 1803 at La Côte-Saint-André in the Dauphiné, a few months after Beethoven completed his 'Eroica' Symphony and a few months before Napoleon proclaimed himself Emperor of the French. Berlioz preferred the organizational hierarchy of a well-run monarchy, more likely than a republic to offer patronage to a 'difficult' composer, although this hope was nevertheless usually disappointed. He had Bonapartist leanings; some of his finest music implicitly supports an imperialist agenda. He matured during the Bourbon restoration from 1814, when loss of empire stimulated French cultural development, including the upsurge of rebellious romanticism. Yet the restoration left many imperial institutions intact and several of its officers remained in post, including Berlioz's princi-

---

[5] F-Pn Rés Vm² 178. See Holoman, *Creative Process*, 353 (n. 11).
[6] On *Orphée*, see NBE 6; on the others, NBE 12a. 395 and 403–4.
[7] *Memoirs*, ch. 49.
[8] See Rushton, 'Genre in Berlioz', in Bloom (ed.), *The Cambridge Companion to Berlioz*, 41–52.

pal teacher Jean-François Lesueur at the royal chapel in the Palais des Tuileries.

Berlioz's youthful environment was largely free of the kind of music—choral, operatic, symphonic—to which he later attached the highest importance. The music of La Côte-Saint-André embraced the sounds of nature (bird-song enters some of his works) and the music of society. The household had no piano, but La Côte had its church and its National Guard, and music was made in the home. Berlioz took lessons in flute and guitar, and began to teach himself by writing accompaniments to songs and original vocal and chamber works. All this was encouraged by his father, later so ill-disposed towards his musical career.[9] Berlioz's early musical education was appropriate for an amateur expected to train as a doctor and inherit and manage his father's practice and property. The two visiting teachers at La Côte cannot have offered much useful criticism of his early compositions, nor help his struggle with d'Alembert's simplified version of Rameau's harmonic theory. He understood Catel's simpler harmony treatise better, but it contains no real music. He learned by example from the simple compositions in Devienne's flute tutor, quartets by Pleyel, and a considerable repertoire of songs and arias.[10]

Within a bourgeois home, music was not an affair of deep emotions, nor could it escape the clarity of the major and (more rarely) minor tonal system. Berlioz came to associate folk music with modes other than major or minor, but he never employed them systematically, only occasionally introducing unusual scale patterns and their resultant harmonies. The theory, once advanced, that he depended on memories of folk music for 'original' melodic invention, reads like a speech for the prosecution; for many musicians this could be a cause for congratulation. The evidence is in any case slender.[11] The band of the National Guard was bad enough to amuse the Berlioz children, but the continuity of such an institution from revolution and empire will have fixed the association, ingrained in European culture, between the signified—military, ceremonial, nationalistic—and the signifiers, wind and percussion. The provincial cousins of the great revolutionary ceremonies sowed the seeds of some of Berlioz's grandest music, as well as some we may take less seriously. Once Berlioz reached Paris he composed no more chamber music. Perhaps, despite his admiration for Beethoven's quartets, he was too much affected by memory of the domestic context in which he first heard and played such music; but in any case, there was no market for it. It is hard to imagine what his early quintets (H.2, 3) were like.[12] While we need not mourn the loss

---

[9] See David Cairns's masterly evocation of La Côte and his analysis of the family problem: *Making of an Artist*, *passim*.

[10] A more detailed account of Berlioz's education is in *MLB* 5–10 and 52–72.

[11] Léon Vallas, in *Grove's Dictionary of Music and Musicians*, 5th edn., vol. i, 664: see *MLB* 151.

[12] 'H' numbers are derived from Holoman's chronologically organized *Catalogue of the Works of Hector Berlioz* (henceforth *Catalogue*).

of *Potpourri concertant sur des thèmes italiens* (H.1), it would be fascinating to know what themes were used. But there is little evidence to support a picture of Berlioz as a salon or chamber composer manqué.

When Berlioz said his first musical experience came at his first communion, he did not mean that by the age of 11 he had heard no music. What he had previously heard was not truly a 'musical experience', because it was not emotionally significant. The impact of the virginal chorus as he knelt at the altar-rail never left him, even when he discovered, with amusement, that the music was 'Quand le bien-aimé reviendra', from Dalayrac's *Nina*, no doubt slowed down and curdled by the harmony. The first communion was *experience triggered by* music, rather than *of* music: an experience of the numinous, which later attained full expression in his own sacred music, particularly at the end of *L'Enfance du Christ*, where a perfect performance induced 'the religious ecstasy that I had dreamed of while writing it'.[13] Like Verdi, Berlioz had the power to realize religious feelings in art despite lacking orthodox, or any other, belief. In that first communion was born the composer of songs and dramatic music, including an autobiographical symphony, as well as of music to sacred texts. The genre most deeply ingrained in Berlioz's musical consciousness was the melody-dominated strophic song, the 'Romance'. The earliest surviving pieces in his hand, and his earliest publications, are guitar accompaniments for songs (H.5, 8) and original romances. Berlioz eventually moved away from the standard strophic romance towards more sophisticated designs, but the romance remains a perceptible influence in his finest songs and arias (see Chapter 7). Throughout his career he transferred music from one context to another, but whatever else he changed, the melodies were largely unaltered.

Berlioz's life, a triumph of will and artistic sensibility over all kinds of obstacle, can also be read as a worldly failure. Had he become a guitar virtuoso, or a successful composer of romances and operas, we might read his youthful experiences differently. Enjoying his music without suffering his difficulties, we may feel the benefit of his rejection of routine. Berlioz required strong internal motivation to conceive a substantial work, and disliked repeating himself. The few commissions which came his way were either flouted (Paganini's viola concerto became a symphony, *Harold en Italie*), or angled to fulfil an artistic dream (the Requiem). There was no formal commission for *Symphonie fantastique*, *Roméo et Juliette*, *La Damnation de Faust*, the Te Deum, *L'Enfance du Christ*, or *Les Troyens*; Berlioz had to master the art of self-promotion because his musical conceptions fitted no patterns of genre or patronage. Nor did he originate or develop genres to refine and transcend, like Chopin's Ballades or Schumann's special type of piano cycle. Berlioz's formal inventions are not patterns, since he seldom used them twice, and their status as genre depends on critical interpretation more than subse-

---

[13] *CG* vi. 463–5; see NBE 11, p. xi.

quent emulation by other composers. The mental basis for many of these peculiarities will have been laid down in his adolescent years; when he left La Côte-Saint-André for Paris, he will have had little idea of what making a musical career entailed, or of an audience, willing or needing to be wooed, for his music.

PARIS

On arrival in Paris in October 1821, Berlioz was not yet 18. But as an apprentice musician, we should note that he was *already* 18, an age by which many composers in preceding generations had reached a first maturity. He was hell-bent on making his way as a composer, for which Paris was a more difficult, but also a more stimulating environment than La Côte. He learned most by reading and hearing other composers' work, and hearing and revising his own. Now he had new and larger models to study, influences to absorb, and alternative, and grander, father-figures. Luigi Cherubini, director of the Conservatoire since 1822, was 61, the same age as Jean-François Lesueur, and Beethoven's contemporary Antonín Reicha, who taught Berlioz at the Conservatoire from 1826, was also older than Berlioz's father. A mingling of imitation and emulation governed Berlioz for the next few years, until he broke through and became himself.

In Paris, Berlioz plunged deep into an intoxicating world of orchestral and staged dramatic music. He already knew of Gluck, but his absolute devotion dates from this period; Berlioz came to recognize Gluck's peculiarities of technique, for which the dramatic force of his invention more than compensated.[14] He also lapped up works by Gluck's French and Italian contemporaries and followers, Piccinni, Sacchini, Salieri, Méhul, and Spontini. In the short time remaining before the music of Weber and Beethoven was heard in Paris, and just before Rossini came to dominate the Opéra, Berlioz acquired a taste for late eighteenth-century neo-classicism, an artistic evocation of the antique which in music, painting, and architecture persisted under the Revolution and whose last triumph is *Les Troyens*. It would have been natural for him to admire Cherubini, whose *Médée* (1797) is a masterpiece of this tendency; circumstances were to conspire against them becoming friendly, and mixed feelings about the man may have affected Berlioz's evaluation of Cherubini's music, but he studied it with care, as can be seen from his memorial tribute.[15] He seemed destined to be the disciple of Lesueur, once also an outsider and rebel, now a pillar of the establishment. Berlioz was introduced to him late in 1822 by an older student, Hyacinth Gerono, and showed him a dramatic cantata, subsequently destroyed, *Le Cheval arabe* (H.12), and a three-part canon (H.13).[16] Lesueur told Gerono to instruct Berlioz in the

---

[14] See the essays on *Orphée* and *Alceste* in *A travers chants*.
[15] *Journal des Débats*, 20 Mar. 1842 (HC 480); Condé, 141–4.
[16] See Holoman, *Berlioz*, 25; id., 'Conservatoire', 291–2.

rudiments of harmony according to Rameau's system (see Chapter 5) before he could be admitted as a private student.

Jean Mongrédien confirms that we know little of Lesueur's teaching except that, rather obviously, he commented on students' original work; nothing suggests that he set composition exercises by way of training.[17] Certainly he did not inhibit Berlioz, who over the next few years was remarkably prolific. No complete account is possible, as we do not know how long or complex were the lost works, but by the summer of 1827 he had written two operas (*Estelle et Némorin*, H.17, and *Les Francs-juges*, H.23); a Latin oratorio (*Le Passage de la mer rouge*, H.18); the fifty-minute *Messe solennelle* (H.20); and two cantatas (*Beverley, ou le joueur*, H.19, for solo bass and orchestra, and the twenty-minute *Scène héroïque*, inspired by the Greek war of independence, H.21, for soloists, full orchestra, and chorus). This amounts to five or six hours of vocal music with orchestra, of which only the Mass, *Scène héroïque*, and fragments of *Les Francs-juges* survive.

Berlioz formally entered the Conservatoire in late 1826, after a deserved failure in the preliminary test for the Prix de Rome, an exercise in strict counterpoint and fugue.[18] He was registered for composition classes (Lesueur) and studied counterpoint (Reicha) with the sole objective of passing this test. Students normally studied harmony, but Berlioz, enrolled as an occasional student by special favour, was exempted. Discovery of the *Messe solennelle* in 1991 revealed that by 1824 Berlioz already knew enough about counterpoint to include two fugues, both using invertible countersubjects (see Chapter 5). Yet in January 1827 Cherubini noted that 'he has only just enrolled . . . we must wait'; a year later the Director grudgingly allowed that his fugue was 'passable'.[19] But in the summer of 1827 Berlioz had already satisfied the examiners, as he did every year to 1830, and qualified for the competition proper, in which he had to compose a dramatic cantata. Nobody taught Berlioz rhythm or orchestration, in both of which his taste for experiment was particularly marked; he learned the capacities of the instruments and voices, and the effect of combinations, from reading scores, talking to instrumentalists, and hearing his music in performance.[20]

COMPOSITIONS TO 1825

The music that survives from before Berlioz met Lesueur is all strophic song, in which the music is repeated (not usually renotated) for each stanza of poetry. Berlioz's first publication, 'Le Dépit de la bergère' (H.7), is paradig-

[17] Mongrédien, 'Le Sueur et ses élèves', *Le Sueur*, from 977. While the spelling 'Le Sueur' is said to have been preferred by the composer, Berlioz uses 'Lesueur', as do many contemporary publications.

[18] Published in NBE 6. 3–5; *MLB* 117.

[19] Holoman, 'Conservatoire', 290.

[20] *Memoirs*, ch. 13. One of Berlioz's most distinguished predecessors had no public performances before winning the Prix de Rome. Ruth Jordan, *Fromental Halévy: His Life and Music* (London: Kahn & Averill, 1994), 14.

matic: a pretty tune with a clumsy accompaniment, and a slightly different musical setting for the fourth stanza.[21] At least three songs with texts by 'le doux Florian' were composed at La Côte. 'Je vais donc quitter pour jamais' (H.6) is unusual in that it alone supports Berlioz's assertion that 'Nearly all my songs were in the minor mode . . . a black drape was spread over my thoughts . . .'.[22] The major-mode 'Le Maure jaloux' (H.9) and 'Amitié, reprends ton empire' (H.10) were published after Berlioz went to Paris; autographs of earlier versions show that their accompaniments were revised for publication, but their melodies were left intact (see Chapter 5). Six of these early songs were published soon after Berlioz reached Paris, then quietly forgotten. Three of them (H.9–11) probably appeared in 1822, and the rest (H.14–16) before February 1823. That the title-pages of the latter group proclaim Berlioz 'Élève de Mr LESUEUR' tells us nothing about the dates of composition, which are likely to have been before he became Lesueur's pupil. Besides 'Le Maure' and 'Amitié', 'Pleure pauvre Colette' (H.11) was probably composed at La Côte; this and 'Canon libre à la quinte' (H.14) have texts by Bourgerie. Berlioz may have known Albert Du Boys slightly before reaching Paris, but the two songs to his poems, 'Le Montagnard exilé' (H.15) and 'Toi qui l'aimas' (H.16), which show increasing control of their material, were probably composed in 1822 (see also Chapters 5 and 7). Such unambitious and readily consumable music then disappears from Berlioz's surviving output for a few years.

The loss of early large-scale works may not be an aesthetic disaster, but it leaves a major gap in our knowledge of Berlioz's development. Four bars of *Beverley* were published many years later, from memory, by a friend. They are neutral in style, and do not bear out Berlioz's description of this cantata as 'musique violente'.[23] Of *Estelle et Némorin* we know nothing, not even whether Lesueur's influence was already to be felt. Hugh Macdonald suggests that the Offertory motet in the *Messe solennelle* 'Quis similis tui, Domine, in fortibus?', a thanksgiving for Israel's deliverance from Egypt, may have been transferred from *Le Passage de la mer rouge* (H.18).[24] If so, it is his earliest surviving choral and orchestral music, and in G major, one of his favourite orchestral keys; but it is devoid of orchestrational originality. Its opening and closing gestures, redolent of a stately Gluckian chaconne, feel regressive in relation to the Resurrexit which precedes it. The second phrase introduces rudimentary canon over a pedal but breaks off dramatically (bar 29) on a diminished seventh, which should resonate through the rests before being resolved, and the homophonic climax (from bar 90) is grandly resonant. The virtual absence of structural modulation (cadences in E minor and D are

---

[21] Analysis in *MLB* 61–3.

[22] *Memoirs*, ch. 4. The song has been lost; but see Ex. 7.1.

[23] *Memoirs*, ch. 7. The friend was Adolphe Laferrière, *Mémoires*, 1re série (Paris, 1876), 60–1; the music is printed in Cairns, *Making of an Artist*, 2nd edn., 148.

[24] NBE 23, p. viii.

immediately neutralized by returns to the tonic) suggests that Berlioz was indeed following Lesueur's precepts. In a letter to a student written shortly before he began to teach Berlioz, Lesueur offers a rare insight into what Berlioz later rejected as his 'system': discussing a motet, he says it lacks only

the art . . . of continually relating the secondary keys [tons] and modes to the tonic [ton principal]. It is not enough that motives connect well through rhythmic association; it is just as important that the hidden thread of harmonic succession links every part of an aria or chorus, not by mere juxtaposition of harmonic ideas, but by *threading* ideas which are born from one another . . . one alien key, unrelated to the first and last keys of the piece, ruptures the musical connections and ruins the effect which, however, will be very fine if you obey the natural laws of true harmonic progression.[25]

Berlioz's first attempt to conquer the French capital was the performance of the *Messe solennelle* on 10 July 1825. Its main benefit was self-education, however, since he had no particular audience in his sights. Whether he or Lesueur proposed this composition, he did not find it easy. In July 1824 he wrote to Lesueur from La Côte: 'when I wanted to get to work on the mass I told you about, I found myself so cold, even icy, when reading the Credo and Kyrie that I decided I could never write anything half-decent in this state of mind, and gave up.'[26] Back in Paris in the autumn, he found the touch he wanted, and made full use of the chance to try out ideas on a grand scale. The title 'Messe solennelle' implies music intended for a major church festival, for soloists and chorus with orchestra. Berlioz was asked to produce it at the feast of the Holy Innocents (27 December 1824); but at that time only his music was sacred, and the first performance took place the following summer.

Berlioz records the destruction of the Mass, alongside *Beverley* and the oratorio, with marked self-deprecation: 'This mass, with its unevenness of style and somehow arbitrary colouring, was nothing but a clumsy imitation of Lesueur.'[27] His published tributes to Lesueur, which include an obituary (1837) and a review of the *Troisième Messe solennelle*, concentrate more on sacred than on dramatic music.[28] The Kyrie is partly modelled on, and com-

---

[25] Lesueur's letter to his student J. F. J. Janssens, 7 May 1822, in Jean Mongrédien, *Jean-François Le Sueur*, 980 and 1005: 'l'art . . . de rendre constamment les *tons* et *modes secondaires* parents du ton principal. Il ne suffit pas que le *motif* se suive bien quant au dessin rhythmique; il faut en outre que le lien secret de la série harmonique unisse tout le corps d'un *air* ou d'un chœur, non pas par un simple voisinage d'idées harmoniques, mais par une *filiation* de ces idées qui naissent l'une de l'autre . . . un seul *ton étranger* qui n'a plus de rapport avec le ton premier et dernier du morceau casse tous les ressorts musicaux et détruit l'effet qui, au contraire, serait très grand en obéissant aux lois naturelles d'une véritable *série harmonique*.'

[26] *CG* i. 60 ('je suis demeuré si froid, si glacé, en lisant le *Credo* et le *Kyrie* que bien convaincu que je ne pourrai jamais rien faire de supportable dans un pareille disposition d'esprit, j'y ai renoncé').

[27] 'Cette messe, dont le style, avec sa coloration inégale et en quelque sorte accidentale, ne fut qu'une imitation maladroite du style de Lesueur' (*Memoirs*, ch. 7).

[28] HC 282 (obituary), and HC 318 (review of *Troisième Messe solennelle*), partly reused in *Memoirs*. See also Klaus Heinrich Kohrs, '*La Veillée de David*. Hector Berlioz über Jean-François Lesueur'.

prehensively outstrips, the Kyrie of Lesueur's *Oratorio de Noël*.[29] Lesueur's example clearly lies behind other features, but cannot account for its melodic and rhetorical originality. An almost abrasive vigour pervades the Credo and 'Crucifixus', real tenderness the 'O salutaris'. The Sanctus is more conventionally brusque, like the Offertory, but the Agnus, for which there may have been no example by Lesueur to serve as model, has a particularly incisive melodic profile and is beautifully punctuated by choral responses, successively in one, two, and three parts (bars 42, 63, 75). Sheer energy also informs the closing 'Domine salvum', which like the Kyrie breaks through from D minor to a radiant D major conclusion. The rediscovery of the Mass in 1991 was astonishing; its vivid inventiveness, which compensates for its lack of sophistication, is even more so. It alters the visible landscape of Berlioz's career, as well as supplying a previously unsuspected source of ideas over a twenty-five-year period.[30] This is not surprising in itself; should the oratorio or *Beverley* resurface, we may recognize more old friends.

THE FERRAND ERA

Humbert Ferrand collaborated on several projects with his friend Berlioz, before the latter fatally discouraged him, on failing to finish a composition, by telling him 'you are too much the poet for a musician'.[31] Usually it was Ferrand who failed to finish a poem. Work on *Les Francs-juges* in 1825–6 was interrupted for a cantata on the fashionable topic of the Greek war of independence, in which Ferrand, as devout as Berlioz was free-thinking, used Constantine's victory over paganism as a model for the contemporary struggle against the Turks. The opera too concerns a struggle against tyranny, but defends monarchical legitimacy by an intrigue like those of *opera seria*; the heroine agrees to marry the usurper Olmerick if the life of her lover, the legitimate heir, is spared. This plot-archetype is spiced with the menace of the secret court and an active double agent.

Unfortunately we cannot say which surviving parts of *Les Francs-juges* were written before the cantata, and the autograph of the latter has disappeared.[32] *Les Francs-juges* was originally an *opéra comique*, with spoken dialogue, now lost; the surviving libretto dates from 1829 and may have been meant for a continuously sung opera.[33] The first version was complete by October 1826. Four vocal numbers survive in an autograph full score, with

---

[29] See Rushton 'Ecstasy of Emulation: Berlioz's *Messe solennelle* and his Debt to Lesueur', *Musical Times*, 140/1868 (Autumn 1999), 11–18.

[30] See Berlioz, *Memoirs*, ch. 7; Macdonald, '*Messe solennelle*'; NBE 23; and below.

[31] Letter of 27 Dec. 1829, *CG* i. 291 ('vous êtes trop poète pour le musicien').

[32] The surviving MS of the *Scène héroïque* is a copy made for Ferrand, probably from the period of the performance, 1828. The close correspondence with the printed libretto suggests that it was not much, if at all, revised. Holoman, *Creative Process*, 32–3; NBE 12a, pp. x, 396.

[33] The 1829 libretto, possibly in the hand of Thomas Gounet, is in F-Pn, papiers divers de Berlioz, no. 45. It is published in Holoman, *Creative Process*, 291–325; see also *Catalogue*, 38. In 1829 the hero is called 'Lenor' but in 1826 'Arnold'.

many pages torn away, leaving more music decipherable near the binding.[34] The 'trio-nocturne' and overture exist in later, possibly revised versions. The overture was Berlioz's first work to enter the repertoire, and he performed it as late as his final visit to Russia (28 December 1867). Other parts of the opera are known to have been used in later works, and more may have survived without being identified. Perhaps what remains exists only because Berlioz did not think it worth recycling.

In 1829, the opera underwent major revisions. The libretto is annotated by Berlioz with 'musique à faire' and 'musique faite'. No comment can be made on the larger musical design of either version.[35] More was intended for musical setting than Berlioz's annotation implies; eventually there would have been over twenty formal numbers or music cues, besides (in 1829) the recitatives.[36] In the two surviving choruses, of oppressed people and sinister Francs-juges, both in C minor, Berlioz attained a cohesive vigour, and in the first, which follows the overture, the late change from defiance to terrified subservience when the tyrant enters could have real theatrical impact (see Ex. 4.7). The style is reminiscent of Lesueur's 'Scandinavian death song' (in *Ossian, ou les Bardes*). The villains' duet, considerably revised in the autograph, is surely too long, possibly the result of trying to out-do predecessors such as Méhul in constructing an image of fanatical hatred represented by obsessive orchestral repetition; the use of solo oboe in connection with mercy, however, harks back directly to Gluck. In the pastoral chorus 'L'ombre descend dans la vallée', echo effects using off-stage brass anticipate other spatial configurations in Berlioz, but they derive from a well-established theatrical tradition; indeed, the rural scenes (all country people are good-hearted and loyal) are a frank bid for the city's sentimental approval.

Two passages in Act III are identifiable from the torn pages. The hero's soliloquy included a recitative, a slow aria ('Descends et viens rendre à mes songes'), and a nightmare ('His sleep is restless and difficult. The principal scenes of the previous acts are mingled in his dreams'), and enough survives to identify a reminiscence of a theme from the 'Marche des gardes'.[37] The traditional operatic dream scene, related to the mad scene, may have brought out something special from Berlioz; to represent a nightmare without using voices seems particularly original and is the opera's main hint, after the overture, of what Berlioz was to achieve in *Symphonie fantastique*. In the closing scene the hero meekly presents himself before the secret court. The 1829

---

[34] F-Pn Rés. Vm² 177. See Holoman, *Creative Process*, 215–36; id., 'Les Fragments de l'Opéra "perdu" de Berlioz', *La Revue de Musicologie*, 63 (1977), 78–88 (incidentally I did not ask the questions attributed to me in the discussion); Paul Banks, 'Berlioz's "Marche au supplice" and *Les Francs-juges*: A Re-examination', *Musical Times*, 130 (Jan. 1989), 16–19.

[35] Reicha asserts that such planning is relatively unimportant in opera with spoken dialogue; *L'Art du compositeur dramatique* (Paris, 1833), 77.

[36] Holoman (*Catalogue*) lists the fourteen numbers Berlioz said had been composed.

[37] 'Son sommeil est agité et pénible. Les principales scènes des actes précédents lui apparaissent confusément en songe.'

libretto prescribes 'un bruit terrible et toujours croissant' from off-stage, and the dénouement includes a brief 'Chœur général', marked neither 'faite' nor 'à faire'. Parts of the final chorus are visible from the torn pages. Lost music that Berlioz marked 'faite' includes a scena for Conrad, the double agent, classically patterned as an orchestral recitative and double aria; the cantabile ('douloureuse rêverie') praises friendship, and the allegro (Conrad 'se ranime et s'enflamme') is a call to action. Berlioz intended to include it in a concert (November 1829), but it was not performed and unless the music is identified in a later work, its style can only be guessed at. The same applies to Amélie's elegy, where two ten-line strophes mainly of classical twelve-syllable verses were surely resistant to music. Verses of three or four syllables, perhaps modelled on Victor Hugo, must have presented Berlioz with the opposite problem in the quartet, which merges into a choral finale as the gypsies (Bohémiens) draw the hero away from the sinister castle.[38]

Where, in 1826, did Berlioz stand in relation to operatic traditions? In *Les Francs-juges* David Cairns claims to see 'no sign of the Romantic Orchestra', although a case might be made for Spontini and Méhul as more than mere forerunners of romanticism in their expressive deployment of orchestral timbres.[39] Berlioz learned from Spontini (*Fernand Cortez*) the trick of muting the clarinet by wrapping a bag round it (in the dream sequence). With its blend of the political and bucolic, of heroism, sentiment, and the grotesque, *Les Francs-juges* is a child of its time, falling within a tradition of French opera initiated in the 1790s, and which influenced Weber. Castil-Blaze's version of *Der Freischütz* (*Robin des bois*) reached Paris in 1824, and of *Euryanthe* (*Le Forêt de Sénart*) in 1826, powerfully influencing Berlioz in their turn. Yet it seems that major influences took their time to work on him; his first surviving operatic music does not suggest that the influence of Weber had yet penetrated to the core.

The cantata *Scène héroïque: La Révolution grecque* is Berlioz's first romantic and political manifesto, and shows greater technical assurance. It is designed like an intermezzo, for Berlioz to make his first (vain) assault upon an established platform, the Concert spirituel at the Opéra. He attributed to this work an ancestry by then already more respected than Lesueur: 'every page breathes the vital influence of Spontini'.[40] Berlioz had encountered *La Vestale* in 1822, before meeting Lesueur. Spontini's rhetoric is more Italian than Gluckian, but his command of the grandiose, his long lines, and his orchestration, expressive and sumptuous, directed towards dramatic ends in the Gluck tradition, aroused Berlioz's lifelong admiration.[41] *Scène héroïque* is essentially a double crescendo, separated by an interlude. Vigorous if

---

[38] Such lines fill Hugo's libretto *Esmerelda*, composed by Louise Bertin.
[39] Cairns, *Making of an Artist*, 219/233; see also Edward J. Dent, *The Rise of Romantic Opera*, (Cambridge: Cambridge University Press, 1976). Méhul and Spontini are both cited in *Traité*.
[40] 'l'on sentait à chaque page l'énergique influence de Spontini' (*Memoirs*, ch. 11).
[41] See 'Un suicide par enthousiasme' in *Soirées*. Cairns, 'Spontini's Influence on Berlioz'.

13

under-characterized gestures introduce a recitative (Ex. 4.6) and a short aria for 'a Greek hero' (Ex. 1.1), the simplest of ternary forms in which the dignified opening is imaginatively destabilized by a push towards the subdominant, only to end in the tonic minor, while the simplified reprise has not a single accidental. Within the first section, the reckless orchestral response to the word 'splendour' includes a scale which is developed in the turbulent middle section, an early example of Berlioz piling up diminished sevenths in sequence; the climax on a supertonic seventh, unrolling into a slow cadence, is effective and characteristic. Joined by a Greek priest, the hero urges the armies to action; this choral rodomontade has a grand harmonic adventure for climax.[42] The central prayer introduces female voices, and makes characteristic use of parallel § chords, a signifier of the sacred inherited from Gluck.[43] The finale begins like a rerun of the first chorus, but is interrupted by bardic harps, 'en approchant insensiblement', providing another associative layer with the remote epoch of Greek heroism. At the top of a 'crescendo extrêmement ménagé', female voices enter and Berlioz combines two previously independent melodies. Rather than emulate the first chorus's chromatic progression, Berlioz leaps into an unrelated key, the flat mediant (E flat for C); would Lesueur have accepted this within 'natural laws of true harmonic progression'? This stirring music is a little blunted by the neutrality of the actual ideas, but their deployment shows both imagination and skill.

THE PRIX DE ROME

During 1827 to 1830, Berlioz carried on a running battle with the establishment, measured by his annual entry for the Prix de Rome, and by his self-promotion in three grand concerts in the Salle du Conservatoire, on 26 May 1828, 1 November 1829, and, on the eve of his departure for Italy, 5 December 1830. During 1826–7, while studying counterpoint with Reicha, Berlioz scraped a living by teaching, proof-reading, and singing in the chorus of Théâtre des Nouveautés. Time spent copying parts of *Les Francs-juges* in the hope of a trial rehearsal may have slowed his original productivity, but the documentation of the period January to September 1827 is 'particularly meagre' and some dates remain uncertain.[44] In 1827 Berlioz passed the tests in counterpoint and fugue, and competed for the Prix de Rome with his cantata *La Mort d'Orphée* (H.25); the undated *Grande Ouverture de Waverley* (H.26), eventually his Op. 1, was probably composed soon afterwards. It was not performed until 1828. *Waverley* has a slow introduction, a sonata-form allegro with little development, and a coda, like overtures by Rossini and Weber; it approaches the freshness and originality of the latter's best work.

The requirements of the Prix de Rome cantata are entertainingly satirized in Berlioz's memoirs, but as a test of skill and imagination in dramatic com-

---

[42] See *MLB* 43–4.
[43] For instance, the priestesses' music in *Iphigénie en Tauride* (*MLB* 108–9).
[44] Cairns, *Making of an Artist*, 195/207.

Ex. 1.1 Aria (*Scène héroïque*)

des hé - ros, ter - re, ter - re ché - ri - e.

position they are fair enough, and were taken seriously by his less rebellious rivals.[45] The texts comprised three (in 1829, for *Cléopâtre*, two) sequences of recitatives and arias, the first aria being a cantabile and the last displaying the energy born of desperation (the protagonist is about to die, or rush into battle). A well-behaved student would set one aria in the minor, and use at least one recitative figure related to an aria. The voice part is designed for an experienced opera singer, capable of a thrilling high note, but also of dramatic and rhetorical delivery. The exercise also tested mastery of the orchestra. Most composers took advantage of the occasion to write for 'grand orchestre', with two extra horns and three trombones added to the usual pairs of woodwind, horns, and trumpets, plus timpani and strings. The *Orpheus* cantatas require a harp, standing for the lyre, and cymbals for the Bacchanal.

Berlioz adopted many of the appropriate clichés, particularly in *Herminie* (H.29, 1828), in which he tried hard to behave. The cantabile often starts over a tonic pedal—the whole of *Herminie* begins this way—and a fast aria may begin on dominant harmony, with an upward chromatic surge, crescendo, the voice entering on the crest of a wave, as in the second aria of *Herminie*. But in *Cléopâtre* (H.36, 1829), confident of the prize, he was reluctant to observe stylistic conventions. The beginning of an aria should be securely diatonic, but Berlioz started his cantabile with a disturbing modulation (Ex. 4.1*a*). He closed all his cantatas with an instrumental representation of the end of the drama. In this he was undeniably eccentric, although his rivals took care to represent such features as the Bacchanal (*Orphée*, 1827) and the fire (*Sardanapale*, 1830) in the orchestral material of their final arias. In recitative, where his rivals were generally content with rhetorical figures and vocal patterns which would not have been out of place at the Paris Opéra of the 1780s, Berlioz introduced some dangerous *verismo*, not only when letting himself go at the end of *Cléopâtre*, but even in *Herminie*. The second aria sweeps to high

---

[45] The poems of the cantatas from 1827 to 1830 inclusive, in their original forms, are in NBE 6. 238–41. In formulating these remarks I have examined the following: 1826, *Herminie* by Jean-Baptiste Guiraud; 1827, *Orphée* by Alphonse Gilbert and Guillaume Ross-Despréaux; 1828, *Herminie* by Ross-Despréaux (the winning entry), and Pierre-Julien Nargeot; 1829, *Cléopâtre* by Eugène Prosper Prévost; 1830, *Sardanapale* by Gilbert and Edouard Millault; 1831, *Bianca Capello* by Prévost (the winning entry). To these may be added comments by A. E. F. Dickinson on Guiraud's *Orphée*; 'Berlioz's Rome Prize Works', *Music Review*, 25 (1964), 179–85.

b♭", but then chokes with emotion at its cadence (Ex. 1.2, bar 180).[46] In the following recitative, the opening gestures are conventional, including attractive sighing motives (bars 185, 190–2). Extended tremolo is a cliché, but not the grinding dissonance at each entry of the striking bass motive (bars 196–8), nor the glorious major ninth on 'Chrétiens'. The horn call, prepared by 'horn fifths' in the strings (bar 200), reminds of the danger of war, and as if hearing it, Herminie hesitates ('que dis-je?'). A citation from the middle section of the previous aria, where the text is 'j'exhale en vain ma plainte fugitive', convinces her that she must go to Tancredi's rescue. Berlioz visits E flat and F between the aria's D minor and A (bar 195); a flatward move to D brings the melodic reminiscence, preparing for the double sharpward manœuvre to E for the next aria. Note how the last motive (bars 209–11) appears at three-beat intervals. Berlioz prescribes no fewer than thirteen directions, almost one every two bars, concerning mood, style (measured or free, 'récit.'), and tempo, including nine metronome marks, although it is far from clear why, unless Berlioz planned a performance of which there is no trace.[47] The citation from the aria is at half-speed, with doubled note-values, so that it should sound exactly the same.

Berlioz was humiliated in 1827, when his cantata was declared 'unplayable', and 1829, when no first prize was awarded. But he did not fail because he took the texts seriously (as one might infer from his memoirs). The Orpheus cantatas by his rivals also fade away with plaintive cries of 'Euridice'. In *Herminie* Berlioz says that he was criticized for replacing the middle section of the fast third aria with a prayer.[48] But the other composers, by slowing the harmonic rhythm, reducing the orchestral texture, and introducing a new cantabile melody, represent the prayer-like character of these lines ('Dieu des Chrétiens') without recourse to a new tempo or metre; and they do not, like Berlioz (somewhat dubiously in *Herminie* and *Cléopâtre*), bring back the words already set to slow music during the fast finale. In the first aria of *Sardanapale*, Alphonse Gilbert risked a change of metre at 'Venez, aimable bayadères', where Edouard Millault continued his cantabile aria; Berlioz may have done the same as Gilbert (this part of Berlioz's score is lost), but he won nevertheless. There seems no difference in approach between pupils of Lesueur and of Berlioz's enemy Henri-Montan Berton.

It is hard to assess Berlioz's motivation in 1827. If Ferrand's MS copy of *Orphée* represents what was submitted, Berlioz was either downright ignorant of what he was meant to do, or wilful. The result is beautiful, and despite its immaturity the most consistently satisfying conception of the four cantatas, perhaps because it is so concise; but if Berlioz knew what he was about, he must have expected rejection. He turned the second part of the opening

---

[46] Bar numbers correspond to NBE 6.

[47] This profusion is not shared by other Prix de Rome cantatas. See Hugh Macdonald, 'Berlioz and the Metronome', in Bloom, *Studies*, 17–36.

[48] *Memoirs*, ch. 23.

Ex. 1.2 *Herminie*, end of second aria; third recitative

bats De son sexe ab-ju-rant la fai-bles-se crain-ti - ve; Le cou-

Allegretto

ra - ge gui-de ses pas. Que je lui porte en-

mesuré

ff

vi - e!

mesuré, un peu lent

plus vite

A ces murs sus-pen-

p

ff

débit de plus en plus rapide

du - e, Son ar-mu-re frap-pe ma vu - e. Si j'o-sais m'en cou-vrir!... Si, trom-pant tous les

Andante

p

f > **p**

cresc.

yeux, Sous cette ar-mure aux pé-rils con-sa-cré-e, Je fuy-ais d'A-la-din le pa-lais o-di-

cresc. sempre

f > **p**

f > **p**

eux, Et du camp des Chré-tiens al - lais ten-ter l'en-tré - e!

Maestoso mesuré

Récit Lent

Mais, que dis-je? Que dis - je? Mon fai - ble bras Pour-rait-il sou-te-nir sa re-dou-ta-ble

Adagio

lan-ce? *plus vite* Tan-

Moderato

crè - de va mou-rir peut - ê - tre, et je ba-lan - ce! C'est trop tar -

der, je cours l'ar-ra-cher au tré-pas. *Allegro impetuoso vivace*

21

recitative into his cantabile ('O seul bien qui me reste') and omitted the first aria ('Art séduisant'). The aesthetic rightness of this decision may not have been obvious to the judges. The cue for bird-song (the text alludes to the nightingale, duly imitated by the other composers) precedes the second aria, which Berlioz also cut. This cavalier treatment of the text is barely credible, and one wonders whether the surviving score, a presentation copy made some months later with autograph inscription, is to be trusted. Did Berlioz really add, during the competition, a chorus of Bacchantes, writing his own words?[49] The institute would have provided only a solo singer for the trial; Berlioz reports that the pianist broke down in the Bacchanal, which could have happened with or without a chorus. Whatever version he handed in, no doubt he was honestly doing his best to make dramatic music from tawdry verses, and the possibility that he revised the cantata while planning its performance in May 1828 remains open.

Orphée was probably affected by Weber's alliance of colour and lyricism, particularly in the solos for woodwind, horn, and cello. Berlioz joked that all prize cantatas begin with sunrise, and in *Orphée*, although nothing in the opening text suggests it, he imitated the dawn chorus of bird-song, striking a note of mystery by an enharmonic modulation as early as bar 5.[50] His middle-range melody anticipates cello melodies from Gilbert (1830) and Eugène Prosper Prévost (1831), the latter also reminiscent of Berlioz's *Waverley*. After the cantabile, the approaching Maenads are signalled by a dominant minor ninth, the harshest dissonance academicians allowed without preparation. This licence may not normally have extended to chords scored for brass, isolated by silence, immediately repeated with mutes, and obliquely resolved onto another dissonance, part of a slow harmonic progression from D major to C minor. Orpheus calls the sound 'affreux'; the examiners may have agreed. Berlioz used the minor ninth to open the second aria in *Herminie*, but more conventionally scored, and immediately resolved. Besides adding a chorus, Berlioz completed *Orphée* with an instrumental movement. As the Maenads leave Orpheus dead, the tonic pedal and descending chromatic line form the first of many such cadential dissolves (pre-echoing the endings of Part II of *La Damnation de Faust* and Act III of *Les Troyens*). The woodwind echo the poet's cry of 'Euridice'; after isolated bass notes, silence. There follows a 'Tableau Musical', in which 'the wind [tremolo strings] moans sadly and occasionally stirs the strings of Orpheus's half-broken lyre [harp]. In the distance, a shepherd of the Thracian mountains who has heard Orpheus's original song [the cantabile], tries to reproduce it on his flute [clarinet]. The wind dies down gradually with the sounds it brought, the harps give out only a few disconnected vibrations. Calm . . . silence . . . solitude.'[51]

---

[49] See NBE 6 (the original and Berlioz's texts, 238–9) and Cairns, *Making of an Artist*, 205–6/218–19.   [50] *MLB* 67–9.

[51] See Peter Bloom, 'Orpheus's Lyre Resurrected: A *Tableau musical* by Berlioz', *Musical Quarterly*, 61 (1975), 189–211. This programme seems to anticipate the 'Scène aux champs'.

Convinced that the musicians of the jury awarded the prize on time-honoured principles of mutual back-scratching, Berlioz next strove to present himself as a major composer whom not even sculptors, painters, and other non-musicians could overlook. Berlioz will also have had Harriet Smithson in his sights, not to mention his sceptical family, on 26 May 1828, when he presented an ambitious programme of which only the *Resurrexit*, extracted from the *Messe solennelle*, had been heard before.[52] Unfortunately, although Berlioz wrote on the score of *Orphée* that it was performed although 'declared unplayable by the music section of the Institute', it was cancelled because the singer was ill. The rehearsals, however, justified Berlioz in refuting the institute's verdict.[53] Berlioz must have benefited immensely from hearing his work in rehearsal; and although *Scène héroïque* went badly, he did not yet set it aside. The *Marche religieuse des Mages* (H.27), now lost, was presumably an emulation of Cherubini's Communion March for the 1825 coronation, which Berlioz admired.[54] The most significant aspect of this concert was the inclusion of two overtures, *Waverley* and *Les Francs-juges*, alongside vocal extracts from the opera, a clear but bootless hint to theatre managers that there was a major talent waiting to enrich them. This was the first time Berlioz appeared in public as the composer of the large-scale instrumental music which remains central to the general understanding of his work. The timing is significant, for in March Habeneck had begun his Beethoven symphony series at the Société des concerts du Conservatoire with the 'Eroica'. Berlioz had already written these overtures, although he may later have revised them; but by May 1828, he was well aware of what in 1830 he called 'the *expressive* genre of instrumental music [genre *instrumental expressif*]'. He went on to explain:

In former times instrumental music seems to have had no other aim than to please the ear or to engage the intellect, just as modern Italian cantilena evokes a kind of voluptuous sensation in which the heart and imagination have no part; but in Beethoven's and Weber's works, one cannot miss the poetic thought, for it is ubiquitous.[55]

Both overtures are remarkably effective, and entirely different, syntheses of lessons from Weber and Rossini, and hardly at all from Lesueur, who regarded instrumental music as an inferior genre, until the impact of Beethoven's Fifth Symphony drove him to unwilling recognition that instrumental music can embody the emotive vitality he believed confined to vocal music.[56] The impact of Beethoven on Berlioz emerges with greater clarity in works written from 1830–4.

---

[52] Holoman (*Berlioz*, 612) lists 'Credo and Resurrexit', which could imply two movements or four, but he (p. 51) and other writers elsewhere mention only the Resurrexit.

[53] The score states that the performance was on 22 July, when there was no concert and Berlioz was writing *Herminie*.

[54] See Berlioz's obituary of Cherubini, Condé, 141–2.

[55] 'Aperçu sur la musique classique et la musique romantique', in *Le Correspondant*, 22 Oct. 1830. *Critique musicale*, i. 63–8; translation, *Roméo*, 90.

[56] *Memoirs*, ch. 20; Mongrédien, *Le Sueur*, 989; Cairns, *Making of an Artist*, 245/262.

In July 1828, Berlioz won the second prize with *Herminie*, the first cantata to be preserved in autograph. The necessary good behaviour entailed in setting all the text did not compromise his urge to rhetorical truth. He imposed a thematic pattern on the cantata by using a melodic phrase (see Ex. 1.2) for the introduction which recurs in two recitatives, and begins the extended cantabile in the middle of the second aria. In the third aria, after the controversial prayer, which is cunningly prepared by anticipatory slowing of the harmonic rhythm, the reprise reaches an impeccably correct (and powerful) climax on top b″ at the cadential ⁶₄. Berlioz added a lingering instrumental diminuendo, repeating the prayer in long note-values over a throbbing continuation of the allegro, as if Herminie's prayer to the Christian god echoed in her head as she went forth to battle. This passage foreshadows many effects of simultaneity in later works. It is not known whether the best ideas in these cantatas occurred to Berlioz under examination conditions, or whether he took them with him as a legitimate aid to speedy composition. Some ideas might have been intended for lost or unrealized projects, such as the opera *Richard en Palestine* (on Scott's *The Talisman*) which he planned in detail with Léon Compaignon during 1826–7; *Herminie* is also about crusaders.[57] Given all the futile effort put into *Les Francs-juges*, because the Odéon failed to obtain permission to mount new operas, he may have written nothing of *Richard*. Less original than *Orphée*, *Herminie* nevertheless represents an advance in techniques not to be despised because of their conventionality; and it is strikingly more original than its rivals.

OPUS 1

From late 1827, Berlioz endured writing-blocks brought about by his love for Harriet Smithson. He earned a living by guitar-teaching, and he is recorded as publishing pedagogical variations (H.30), unimaginable in relation to his mature style; they have disappeared (an unknown composer could only expect a short print-run).[58] The undatable 'Nocturne à deux voix', accompanied by guitar (H.31), belongs in spirit with the early Romances which it resembles in its simplicity, effete ornamentation, and silly anonymous poem on the virtues of inconstancy, sentiments the passionate admirer of Harriet could not have shared.[59] But from the end of 1828 until his departure for Italy, Berlioz surpassed all his previous work; and he also prepared, without completing, a new version of *Les Francs-juges*.

[57] *CG* i. 113–51; Cairns, *Making of an Artist*, 210–12/223–5.

[58] Only one copy exists of 'Le Dépit de la bergère', and none of 'Le Ballet des ombres', the copy which served for the OBE being no longer extant.

[59] 'The calligraphy suggests a date before *c*.1830; the work is placed here, adjacent to the variations . . . for convenience' (Holoman, *Catalogue*, 56). Its authorship might be questioned: the score, an unsigned fair copy, could be a revision or an arrangement for teaching purposes. What might suggest a later date is that there is only one serious 'fault', consecutive octaves between bass and treble (bars 8–9), arising legitimately from using the best guitar sonority for a B major seventh chord.

The work he published as 'Œuvre 1', *Huit scènes de Faust* (H.33), was begun in September 1828 with the ballad 'Le Roi de Thulé', and published early in 1829. Berlioz was wading deep in the literature of romanticism—Byron, Moore, Scott, Hugo, and Goethe as well as Shakespeare—and loved to have his heroes work together: mottoes from Moore appear on the copy of *Orphée* and the engraved score of *Huit scènes*, where each scene is also headed by a quotation from *Hamlet* or *Romeo and Juliet*. Goethe is similarly used in the Moore settings, *Irlande*, and it was he, in Gérard de Nerval's translation, who was the first to inspire Berlioz to a musical setting (another Goethe setting, 'Chanson du pêcheur', may have been written about this time: see Chapter 2). He quickly withdrew *Huit scènes*, perceiving their immaturity on a technical level, and he no doubt realized that so miscellaneous a collection of pieces, with different instrumentation, had no public. Yet he must also have recognized a maturity of dramatic aptitude, characterization, and economy in evoking atmosphere, for he never adapted the music to another subject. The neutral material which he used to build the Mass and the cantatas is replaced by a portraitist's sharpness. The stuttering Rat song, interrupted by hiccups, could never be sung by Mephistopheles, whose Flea song leaps, teases, itches. In each stanza the third bar, originally a tonic arpeggio, is lowered a semitone, and the sneering escape from this harmonic conundrum, which gets more remote from the tonic each time, is thicker and rougher. Berlioz later used these songs in *La Damnation de Faust*. A few harmonic modifications in the second verse are the only change of substance in the Flea song, and much else required only cosmetic alteration to fit into one of Berlioz's ripest works. The choruses needed more alteration than the solos; equally bold in conception, they required greater experience (including that of the Requiem and *Roméo*) before their realization matched their freshness of invention. *Huit scènes* has little to do with Lesueur, Spontini, or Beethoven, but is surely affected by Weber; the mingled bucolic and demonic in *Der Freischütz* lies behind the Rat and Flea songs and the dancing peasants. The contrast between Weber's Ännchen and Agathe suggests the Marguerite of the ballad and the haunting Romance. Only Mendelssohn, whom Berlioz did not yet know, and Weber's *Oberon* contain magic like that of Berlioz's sylphes. He also found his own way of handling a sacred text (the Easter Hymn), freed from Lesueur's restrictions on modulation.

Emboldened by the compliments of musicians such as Onslow and Meyerbeer, and perhaps hoping to benefit from a fashion for German opera, Berlioz turned back to *Les Francs-juges*.[60] At some point, the overture was rewritten for larger forces than those of the Odéon, and the MS of the 'Marche des gardes', one of his greatest exercises in the monumental grotesque, is dated 1829. Its conception is earlier, since the main theme is

---

[60] 'Die Deutsche Oper macht hier Furore', as Berlioz's words appeared in the *Berliner Allgemeine Musikalische Zeitung*, 6 June 1829; *Critique musicale*, i. 18.

visible on the 1826 fragment (see above), and there is no way of telling whether the 1829 work was a rearrangement for larger forces or a new composition using an existing theme; nor is it clear where it should appear in the opera.[61] Another leap forward, to the consternation of the jury, came in his 1829 cantata, *Cléopâtre* (H.36). One may mock the 'symbolically named poetaster' Vieillard.[62] But some of Berlioz's inspiration must have been drawn from his words; the final modulation in the recitative before the wonderful 'Meditation' yields little to the best recitatives of *Les Troyens*. Other ideas depend for their potency on the subject, if not the words: the frenzied introduction represents the Queen's escape from her interview with conquering Octavius Caesar, and her pause to control her raging thoughts before opening with 'C'en est donc fait!'; the searing violin passage before the first aria;[63] the coda with its vivid representation of the effect of snakebite. The central Meditation was probably supposed to be a fast aria (Prévost, the best of Berlioz's rivals, treated the last four quatrains as a single aria text). It is Berlioz's first sustained attempt at supernatural evocation through unpredictable chromatic progressions (see Ex. 6.5). Writing to Ferrand, Berlioz described it as Juliet's horror of awakening among the dead; but this and the epigraph ('What if when I am laid into the tomb') do not prove that Berlioz was already planning work on *Romeo and Juliet*—unless, that is, the Moore and Shakespeare epigraphs to *Huit scènes* in some way qualify their inspiration from Goethe.

The supernatural haunts most of Berlioz's music from 1829–30, with the exception of *Neuf mélodies irlandaises*. 'Le Ballet des ombres' (H.37; see Ex. 5.8) is a piece of grotesquerie with a characteristically raw piano accompaniment. Berlioz printed it as Op. 2, but may not have offered it for sale; the opus number was reassigned to *Neuf mélodies* (later known as *Irlande*, H.38: separate numbers H.39–47). For this less daring enterprise he used mainly new, and free, verse translations by Thomas Gounet. *Irlande* includes four strophic songs and four useful concert-fillers for vocal ensemble, all in rondo form: the artless ballad 'Hélène' (H.40) and three choruses, warlike (H.41), drinking (H.43), and sacred (H.44). The main section of 'Chant sacré' is unusual, in that a small work was extracted from a larger one; it is Herminie's prayer, with new episodes to complete the rondo form. Three pieces were later orchestrated, but not the song which would have benefited most, 'Élégie en prose' (H.47), which is neither strophic nor a rondo, but an intoxicating declamation written under severe emotional pressure.[64] The essence of *Irlande* lies in the clearly phrased but rhythmically free melodies of the solo

[61] David Cairns, 'Reflections on the *Symphonie Fantastique* of 1830', in Bloom, *Music in Paris in the Eighteen-Thirties*, 82–6.

[62] Barzun, *Berlioz and the Romantic Century*, i. 94. Vieillard also wrote the libretto of *Herminie*.

[63] See *MLB* 70.

[64] *Memoirs*, ch. 18; Berlioz implicitly pre-dates the composition by two years.

songs, particularly those where striking harmonic progressions are subsumed by the melodic interest, 'Le Coucher du soleil' (H.39) and 'La Belle Voyageuse' (H.42, later turned into a duet). 'L'Origine de la harpe' (H.45) and 'Adieu Bessy' (H.46) are not far behind in interest, and Berlioz rewrote the latter as strophic variations years later. The piano-writing is traditional but neatly laid out, and more effective on the lighter-touch instruments of the period.

During the July revolution of 1830, Berlioz composed his prize cantata on the downfall of the lascivious tyrant Sardanapalus, and rejoiced at the fall of the reactionary Charles X. Sardanapalus consigns himself, his concubines, and his wealth to the sword and to fire rather than submit to his enemies. Determined not to put a foot wrong, Berlioz withheld a fiery orchestral coda (he called it the 'incendie') until the prize had been secured; a letter to his father describes the effect of the 'incendie' at rehearsal, and its disastrous performance.[65] Only a part of the third aria (with additional choral parts added later) and the 'incendie' survive, so that no full comparison can be be made with his rivals or his own previous cantatas. Berlioz himself had mixed feelings about *Sardanapale*. His faith in its melodies is clear, since several appear in later works. He wrote to Ferrand of the contribution made by the July revolution raging outside: 'The noise of cannon and shooting was favourable to my last number', which must refer to the third aria rather than the 'incendie'.[66] But to a fellow musician, Adolphe Adam, whose inveterate hostility to Berlioz was not yet manifest, he called it 'a mediocre piece which doesn't at all represent my innermost musical thoughts; there isn't much in it that I acknowledge; this score . . . is full of commonplace things, trivial orchestration, which I was forced to write in order to win the prize'.[67] Nevertheless, it was the only prize cantata he included in his own concerts after returning from Italy; by then the others had been partially recycled.[68] The coda begins with fragments of the first two arias; the fire itself is quickly burned out, and the nostalgic ending, based on the third aria, ends with a ravishing clarinet solo. As they stand, the reminiscences are unarticulated, lacking context; musicology can tell us what is being recalled, but we do not actually hear it. But before writing *Sardanapale* Berlioz had already completed the first version of the masterpiece by which he is still most widely known, *Symphonie fantastique*.

---

[65] Ibid., ch. 30; *CG* i. 379.

[66] 'Le bruit de canon et de la fusillade a été favorable à mon dernier morceau'. *CG* i. 352.

[67] 'un ouvrage fort médiocre qui ne représente pas du tout ma pensée musicale intime; il y a fort peu de choses que j'avoue; cette partition . . . est pleine de lieux communs, d'instrumentations triviales, que j'ai été forcé d'écrire pour avoir le prix' (*CG* i. 375).

[68] Berlioz performed *Sardanapale* on 14 Nov. 1833 and 14 Dec. 1834. On the fate of the manuscript, see NBE 6. 228.

2 The Romantic Decade

SYMPHONIE FANTASTIQUE

On 1 November 1829 Berlioz presented his second grand concert. More cautious this time, he did not confine it to his own music, but included vocal items by other composers and the first French performance of Beethoven's Fifth Piano Concerto played by Ferdinand Hiller. Berlioz's two overtures were repeated. The Resurrexit resurfaced as *Le Jugement dernier*, and the only new work was the sylphes' scene from *Huit scènes de Faust*.[1] He withdrew the scenes shortly afterwards, but the grip Goethe's *Faust* exerted had led to an unsuccessful attempt, in 1828, to obtain the commission for a ballet; more significant, during 1829, was his idea for a 'descriptive symphony' on *Faust*.[2] The hypothesis that much of *Symphonie fantastique*, composed early in 1830, was conceived with *Faust* in mind is certainly tempting (see Chapter 9). Jacques Barzun well says that the 'skill and substance' of *Symphonie fantastique* represent 'the sum of Berlioz's inward and outward experience' to this point.[3] It is also a culminating work in that many of the finest ideas of the preceding decade found their final home here. The opening is the Florian song (H.6), which Berlioz may have associated with his first love, Estelle Dubœuf; the only evidence is his own word, which there seems no reason to doubt. The demolition of *Herminie* was completed when, with a little alteration to make a stronger cadence, the long melody in the middle of its second aria became the *idée fixe* (see Exx. 1.2 and 4.4). The contrapuntal handling of the first motive of this melody, and its development over a chromatically ascending sequence, are foreshadowed in the cantata.[4] The main theme of the third movement is the earliest known borrowing from the Mass ('Gratias agimus'), and *Les Francs-juges* was fatally wounded when the symphony incorporated

---

[1] A plan to perform the Rat and Flea songs may be inferred from the survival of unused orchestral parts. See Rushton, 'Berlioz's *Huit Scènes de Faust*: New Source Material', *Musical Times*, 115 (1974), 471–3; Cairns, *Making of an Artist*, 313–16/339–42.

[2] *CG* i. 217, 232; see also NBE 5, p. ix, NBE 8b. 455.

[3] Barzun, *Berlioz and the Romantic Century*, i. 166. Yet Barzun was sceptical about earlier sources, even doubting the evidence concerning the March.

[4] See Bockholdt, 'Die idée fixe der Phantastischen Symphonie', 195–8; *MLB* 99–102.

its savage 'Marche des gardes'. Except for the latter, all these ideas were subjected to new and striking developments. Berlioz did not recycle material merely to save time; using an old melody would hardly accelerate the compositional process, and textural and developmental elaboration would take just as long as with new ideas. In any case, he had no commission, and no deadline, the pressure to complete the work being internal and emotional.

Not only was it daring of Berlioz to base an orchestral work on his own experiences; it was daring to write a symphony at all. The average output of French symphonies since 1800 had been fewer than one a year.[5] As eventually devised, the programme evokes several literary parallels.[6] But it was probably a crisis in Berlioz's one-sided relation with Harriet Smithson that unlocked something new in his creativity. The quasi-autobiographical plan was first set down on paper in a letter to Ferrand on 16 April 1830, after the music was written, but it presumably existed earlier.[7] The music itself was extensively revised and the version heard in 1830 is lost beyond recall; the original, longer form of the outer movements cannot be reconstructed, and the second and third movements were completely recopied, the 1830 MS being lost.[8] The revisions followed experience of the work in performance, and in so far as their impact can be assessed, they tightened its structure and set its radical qualities into higher relief.

Despite the Herculean effort of completing the symphony and copying the orchestral parts, Berlioz triumphed in the 1830 Prix de Rome with *Sardanapale*. He then composed his first Shakespearean work, *Ouverture de la Tempête* (H.52) for chorus and large orchestra, based on a play he had not seen, a single movement unrestrained by the formal and generic expectations of its title. It is ebullient, uncomplicated programme music, partly inspired by Berlioz's love-affair with Camille Moke. He provided titles for each section (Introduction, Storm, Action, Dénouement). The spirits (a plural Ariel) are evoked by the novel colouristic use of a piano in the orchestra (two players, always above middle C). As with the fire in *Sardanapale*, the chaos of the storm is short-lived and merges into a reprise of the magical opening, notated in longer values in a fast tempo. 'Action' is framed by a loose sonata-allegro,

[5] Barry S. Brook, *La Symphonie en France*, cited in Locke, 'Paris: Centre of Intellectual Ferment', 63.

[6] Besides Goethe, Temperley suggests Chateaubriand's *René*, de Quincey's *Confessions*, and Hugo's *La Ronde du Sabbat* (NBE 16. 191–3); Cairns discusses Hugo's *Le Dernier Jour d'un condamné* ('Reflections on the *Symphonie Fantastique* of 1830', in Bloom *Music in Paris in the Eighteen-Thirties*, 86–7), and the Preface to *Cromwell*; see also Arnaud Laster, 'Berlioz et Victor Hugo', in *Romantisme*, 12 (1976). The title 'fantastique' is probably taken from E. T. A. Hoffmann, whose stories appeared in France as *Contes fantastiques* and were enjoyed by Berlioz late in 1829; *CG* i. 293, 301.

[7] *CG* i. 318–20. For alternative forms of the programme, see NBE 16. 168–70.

[8] The second movement was rewritten in Italy (the paper is Italian), but the third, which is on French paper, may have been revised later. On revisions and omitted material in the first movement, see Holoman, *Creative Process*, 264–75, and NBE 16. 195–210; see also the source description, NBE 16. 171–2.

its two themes representing the lovers. The Miranda theme is taken from *Cléopâtre* (do any Shakespeare heroines have less in common?), but transformed with bubbling Rossinian decoration. Rather than a development, there are interludes in the central section, Caliban's dance in quintuple metre, and an authoritarian Prospero theme. The Miranda theme comes three times, finally achieving a triple synthesis: previously instrumental, it is now sung, the magic texture returns as accompaniment, and tonic harmony is finally stabilized. In Berlioz's other overtures the coda is a sonata peroration, thematically pertinent to the end. Here a coarsely triumphal 'dénouement' seems connected neither to the rest of the music, nor to the play. *La Tempête* was later called *Fantaisie dramatique*. The generic title Tchaikovsky applied to his Shakespearean works, 'fantasy-overture', would suit it perfectly. In *Lélio*, the artist-hero introduces it as his own composition: 'Let us choose an original subject, in which dark colours are ruled out . . . let the spirits sing and frolic! Let the storm grow, flash, and rage! Let Ferdinand sigh! Let Miranda smile tenderly! Let the monster Caliban dance and groan! Let Prospero threaten and command! And may Shakespeare protect me!'

ITALIE!

During the reign of Louis-Philippe d'Orléans (1830–48), Berlioz was at his most prolific as composer and critic. His Italian visit (1831–2) encouraged compositions with an Italian setting, but only after his return home; the main exception in the 1830s, his Requiem (*Grande messe des morts*, 1837), resulted from a government commission. The rebellious romanticism of the 1820s moved centre-stage in French culture, and he partook in its triumph, especially with *Harold en Italie* and *Roméo et Juliette*, symphonies based on literature in English, but with Italian settings. Only his assault on the Paris Opéra was a failure.

While in Italy, however, Berlioz kept away from Italian subjects. His Italian exile (1831–2), for that was how he perceived it, tore him from the combats and opportunities of Paris; yet the most uninhibitedly lively section of his memoirs deals with this period. Despite his complaints of being rendered compositionally impotent by the backwardness of Italian musical life, he remained active, but only his last composition before returning home, 'La Captive', evokes a Mediterranean atmosphere, and the context is Spanish and Turkish, not Italian. At first, he maintained his allegiance to British literature with two overtures, *Le Roi Lear* and *Rob Roy*, and expended compositional energy on revising *Symphonie fantastique* and compiling its sequel, *Le Retour à la vie*. The latter was too provocative for an *envoi* (work sent to the Institute to demonstrate the scholar's diligence). Instead Berlioz had his Resurrexit, already performed four times in Paris, freshly copied on Italian paper, in a crude hand totally unlike his own. He gleefully reported that it was welcomed as an indication of progress away from 'unfortunate tendencies'—by which were presumably meant *Cléopâtre* and *Symphonie fantastique*.[9] He also sent *Rob Roy* and *Quartetto et coro dei maggi*, of which the manuscripts are similar.

Le Roi Lear (H.53) outlasted even *Symphonie fantastique* in Berlioz's performing repertoire; he conducted it in Moscow in 1867. More governed by sonata form than a programme, its exposition and crisp development move away from Beethoven's model by the length of the lyrical second theme, part-repeated in the development and fully recapitulated. Berlioz's response to Beethoven was more rhetorical than architectural; the thematic breakdown from bar 384 owes a debt to the end of *Coriolan*, but Berlioz's hero picks himself up, possibly reflecting the existence of texts of *King Lear* with a happy ending. Berlioz's second overture inspired by Scott, *Rob Roy* (H.54), takes its pseudo-authenticity from 'Scots wha hae', which Berlioz subjected to resourceful development.[10] This is the only one of Berlioz's overtures with a slow middle section (the Italian eighteenth-century form), a cor anglais solo of artless character, artfully made. Its later phrases yield unexpected extensions from the simple premiss of its opening, a gentle yodelling which has no known vocal origin, but might have been one of Berlioz's more sophisticated Romances.[11] He withdrew *Rob Roy* after one performance (14 April 1833), and but for the Institute's copy we would know nothing of it.

Le Retour à la vie: 'mélologue' (H.55), the second part of 'Episode in the life of an artist' in which an actor plays the composer-hero of *Symphonie fantastique*, is usually known as *Lélio*, a title dating from its revision and publication in 1855, when several changes were made to words and music.[12] Berlioz adopted the term 'mélologue' from Thomas Moore. Its speeches reveal his ideals and aesthetics, holding romantic rodomontade at bay by irony, even in the implicit self-identification with Hamlet. He may have written texts for some of the musical sections as well. In a letter of 14 June he says: 'The music is also done, I have only to copy it out.'[13] Since *Lear* was finished in May, his rapid progress tends to confirm that all the music of *Lélio* was taken from

---

[9] *Memoirs*, ch. 39. The story is confirmed by the report of the Académie des beaux-arts of the French Institute (Cairns, *Making of an Artist*, 500/554). On the Resurrexit see NBE 12b. The Académie may have been put off its guard by its expectation that laureates would send liturgical music with a Latin text; several of Berlioz's contemporaries (and rivals) did so.

[10] It is uncertain where he found this melody, whose first bars are melodically different in various contemporary publications. One where the opening corresponds to Berlioz's, although in dotted rhythms rather than 6/8 and with minor differences later on, is in Matthias [von] Holst, *A Selection of The Most Favourite Scottish Melodies, Arranged for the Voice, with Symphonies and Accompaniments for the Spanish Guitar* (London, Bedford Musical Repository, c.1825–7). Conceivably Berlioz, then teaching guitar, found this when on the look-out for pedagogical material.

[11] David Cairns connects this melody with Huber's 'Sur les Alpes, quel délice', which Berlioz sang in Italy and later arranged in three parts (H.64, transcribed in Holoman, *Creative Process*, 284). Cairns, *Making of an Artist*, 453/500. Berlioz was probably unaware that the hills of Rob Roy country are not exactly Alps.

[12] The 1855 title is '*Lélio, ou le Retour à la vie:* monodrame lyrique'. On the name 'Lélio' see NBE 7, p. xiv; for the 1831 and 1855 librettos, 232–40.

[13] *CG* i. 456–7; NBE 7, p. ix.

earlier works, as is usually supposed. Yet up to three of its six numbers *may* have been composed in Italy. The hero, awakened from the nightmare (the symphony), hears (1831) or remembers (1855) one of his own songs, sung by his friend (whose name, Horatio, strengthens the *Hamlet* connection). He says: 'c'est la ballade du pêcheur de Goëthe, qu'Horatio traduisit, et dont je fis la musique il y a quatre ou cinq ans.'[14] This is probably fiction; it implies 1826–7, but a later date (1828–9), when Berlioz was exploring *Faust*, is more plausible, and quite possibly Du Boys sent Berlioz the translation in Italy and he composed it there.[15] When the Byronic hero invokes the ghost from Hamlet, we hear No. 2, the Meditation from *Cléopâtre* adapted for unison chorus singing nonsense-language ('ancient Nordic dialect': French words were substituted later). Berlioz added a bar to the introduction and extended the coda, but despite its sonorous impact, the effect is weaker without its dramatic context.[16] In the cantata we hear this supernatural frisson directly from the mind and voice of Cleopatra, whereas the fantasy in Lélio's mind is distanced, since after the introduction (in which he speaks over the music) he takes no further part in it.

Lélio's rebellious mood induces a longing for brute freedom, expressed by 'Chanson de brigands'. This is usually thought to be Berlioz's own text, replacing Victor Hugo's 'Chanson des pirates' (H.34, 1829), but this hypothesis seems unconvincing; having used Goethe and invoked Shakespeare, why should Berlioz not enrol his great compatriot in this poetic League of David against the Philistines? Berlioz's personal acquaintance with brigands dates from after the composition of the mélologue, and his hero might just as properly have consorted with pirates. Peter Bloom suggests that the original was Ferrand's 'Chant du brigand', which Berlioz began setting early in 1830 but probably never completed, but if so it is still less clear why he needed new words.[17] This rough-and-tumble piece, strikingly original in rhythm, harmony, and orchestration, formed with 'Le Pêcheur' the substance of an elaborate concertante fantasia by Liszt (c.1835).[18]

In No. 4, 'Chant de bonheur', perhaps lacking confidence to write introspective poetry, Berlioz wrote what he called 'prose cadencée', with some internal rhyme. The music was written in Rome, but is adapted from Orpheus's *aria cantabile*, probably from memory. One altered harmony (*Orphée*, bar 109: root position vi; *Lélio*, bar 3: first inversion IV) could be an inaccurate recall or a conscious revision, but the first phrase is new, and the borrowed material seems to arise spontaneously from it. Berlioz did not rely on memory for No. 5; he wrote to Ferrand on 3 July 1831, asking for a copy

[14] 'Horatio' may be the translator of Goethe, Albert Du Boys, or Thomas Gounet, the translator of Thomas Moore.

[15] NBE 7, p. xi.

[16] One harmonic revision weakens the climax; see *MLB* 34; NBE 7. 211.

[17] NBE 7, pp. xi–xii. A year before (Jan. 1831) he wrote to Ferrand: 'if I succeed in setting your chanson de Brigands' (*CG* i. 301).

[18] A detailed analysis of 'Chanson de brigands' is in *MLB* 14–22.

of the instrumental coda to *Orphée*, a work now to be 'sacrificed': 'I can't remember it well enough to write it out without a score, and I mustn't change a single note.'[19] This reminiscence of the preceding song was called 'The last sighs of the harp', in tribute to Moore; in 1855 it was renamed 'La Harpe éolienne'. Again, however, it makes a stronger impression in its original dramatic context. The music was copied a semitone higher (A not A flat), with the interesting result that the clarinet solo, now for an instrument in A rather than B flat, is necessarily notated up a whole tone; the raised tessitura adds an eloquent intensity even in pianissimo.[20] No. 6, *La Tempête*, being the large composition next after *Symphonie fantastique*, is an apt symbol of the artist's recovery from love-fever, and his renewed ability to compose. After the 1832 performance of the symphony and its sequel, Berlioz finally met Harriet Smithson, and quite soon they were married. More than confessions or a mere anthology, and effective against the odds in performance, *Lélio* may not be Berlioz's most fruitful experiment, nor, by using music from *Orphée* and *Cléopâtre* out of context but essentially unchanged, does it fully validate ideas rejected with the Prix de Rome cantatas. The progress of the monologue seems determined by these musical selections, but fortunately *Lélio* does not so much lack musical form as treat it as an irrelevance.

Berlioz's Italian portfolio contained three more short items, and one unfinished project. 'Méditation religieuse' (H.56), like 'Chanson du pêcheur', might have originated during Berlioz's intense preoccupation with Moore in 1829–30; he quoted its text early in 1829 (*CG* i. 167–8). But one sacred song was enough for *Irlande*. This gentle music is the most moving Berlioz wrote in Italy, but its eloquence owes much to its subtle orchestration, elaborated much later, before its publication as No. 1 of *Tristia* (H.119); the 1831 version, with wind accompaniment, is lost.[21] Berlioz showed no further interest in *Quartetto e coro dei Maggi* (H.59), a bland cousin to the Easter Hymn from *Faust*. The title is inexplicable; there are no soloists and it is not a chorus of Magi but of angels proclaiming the birth of Christ. There is no reason to connect this misleading autograph title-page with the lost *Marche religieuse des Mages*.[22] The unfinished work is typical of the difficulties Berlioz sometimes encountered in setting simple texts. For him, the subject of Pierre-Jean Béranger's poem on the death of Napoleon, *Le cinq mai* (H.74), had a stronger appeal than the actual words. Berlioz said that he had struggled to

---

[19] *CG* i. 466–7.

[20] In *Orphée* the B flat clarinet is notated in B flat, sounding A flat. In *Lélio* the A clarinet is notated in C and thus sounds in A natural. The A clarinet is generally considered 'warmer' in tone, and C a brighter key, but the instrument is muted in a cloth or leather bag. The importance for Berlioz of using the right clarinet, emphasized in *Traité*, is noted by José A. Bowen, 'Finding the Music in Musicology', in Nicholas Cook and Mark Everist (eds.), *Rethinking Music* (Oxford: Oxford University Press, 1999), 428.

[21] On the complex history of this and the special significance of the text for Berlioz, see NBE 12b, p. x; on the orchestration, *MLB* 76–80.

[22] H.59 may actually be the 'lost' 'Chœur des anges', H.58, in which case it is the *Quartetto e coro dei maggi* that is lost; see NBE 12a, p. xii.

find music for the refrain for a long time (one account says two months, another two years). One day he fell into the Tiber, from which he emerged singing 'Pauvre soldat, tu reverrais la France'.[23] But he did not immediately finish the setting. On the other hand, 'La Captive' (H.60), from Hugo's *Les Orientales*, was composed in the mountains, with a guitar to hand; the first notation, for the benefit of friends in Rome who took the melody to their hearts, was for voice and piano. This simple romance soon acquired a solo cello, providing strophic variation for the more sophisticated Parisian audience; this version was published in 1833, and in 1834 Berlioz made a first orchestral version, now lost.

LE RETOUR DE L'ARTISTE D'ITALIE

Berlioz's impressions of Italy were not all of *couleur locale* and the corruption of a once-great culture. The grandeur of the distant past was reflected in the immediate, Napoleonic past, and although Berlioz never completed his proposed commemoration of the Emperor, his mind buzzed with projects related to it. In the early 1830s he was also fruitlessly obsessed with eschatological visions, laying plans for a Last Judgement oratorio, *Le Dernier Jour du monde*, with overtones of Saint-Simonism, in which, no doubt, the Resurrexit fanfare would have found a home. So might *Sardanapale*, since the conception included a tyrant laying on a special orgy complete with a parody of the last judgement, interrupted by the real thing; the oratorio could have exploited the voluptuous elements of the cantata, as well as its 'Incendie'.[24] A more practical notion, for which sketches exist, was a 'Military Symphony', *Le Retour de l'armée d'Italie*, in two parts: a lament for the fallen heroes of Napoleon's Italian campaigns, and the army's triumphal entry into Paris. The first part may have been redirected towards the *Fête musicale funèbre à la mémoire des hommes illustres de la France*, a project for which he even planned a performance in 1835.

From this period a single sketchbook (H.62) is a precious relic, covering 1832 to 1836 without identifiable notations for 1833.[25] Pocket-sized with ruled staves, it reveals much through its informality. If this lone survivor is representative, Berlioz used such booklets sporadically and for different purposes. The more elaborate sketches are comparable to the surviving later sketches (not in books) for *La Damnation de Faust* and *Les Troyens*. In the sketchbook, Berlioz wasted music paper on noting his travel expenses, and sketching a review. Some musical notations relate to compositions never

---

[23] See *CG* ii. 259; *A travers chants*, 343; NBE 12a, p. xiii.

[24] See *CG* i. 467 and 520; *CG* ii. 105, 113. Cairns, *Making of an Artist*, 458/505; Ralph P. Locke, 'Autour de la lettre à Duveyrier: Berlioz et les Saint-Simoniens', *Revue de Musicologie*, 63 (1977), 55–77; id., *Music, Musicians, and the Saint-Simonians* (Chicago: University of Chicago Press, 1986), 114–21.

[25] It has been fully described by D. Kern Holoman, 'The Berlioz Sketchbook', *19th-Century Music*, 7 (1984), 282–317, including diplomatic transcriptions and a facsimile; further comment and selected facsimiles in Holoman, *Berlioz*, 213–19; see also Chapter 5.

realized, including *Le Retour de l'armée d'Italie*. Most promising is a setting of Hugo ('Dans l'alcôve sombre'), for which all the words are written and different melodies underlaid to three of the nine stanzas. There are no notations for *Le cinq mai*, but it might have been associated with a poem on Napoleon's death which Berlioz drafted. When he returned to Paris, most of the pages were still blank; they contain sketches for *Harold*, *Benvenuto Cellini*, and two romances.

On returning home, Berlioz drew renewed attention to himself by concert-giving. Having revived the modified *Symphonie fantastique*, and presented its controversial sequel, he needed new works to retain momentum, and into these he naturally unleashed his Italian experiences. But there were other markets to cultivate; from an economic as well as an artistic viewpoint, his main objective was to write an opera. A successful career in the theatre was the best means of support for a composer who was not an instrumental virtuoso, and Berlioz was eager to prove himself in the arena favoured by such heroes as Gluck and Spontini, and now disputed by Auber, Halévy, the Italians, and Meyerbeer, about whom Berlioz's feelings were equivocal. While waiting for the breakthrough that never came, he developed virtuosity as a conductor, and he became one of the capital's leading art journalists in a period when such people counted. But he preferred where possible to exercise his true *métier*, and in default of opera, there was a market for songs. Building on the success of *Irlande* and 'La Captive', he tried more varied kinds of local colour. For a concert on 6 June 1833 he arranged hunting choruses by Weber ('La Chasse de Lützow', H.63, lost: see *CG* ii. 182) and Huber ('Sur les Alpes, quel délice'). His next finished composition refers to France's Celtic fringe. 'Le Jeune Pâtre breton' (H.65, originally 'Le Paysan breton') is a good example of modestly charming material continually reworked for better effect, by orchestration and the addition of an evocative solo horn (in the piano-accompanied version published in 1835); but no amount of polish could make this a second 'Captive'. Another Hugo setting ('Romance de Marie Tudor') is lost. A Béranger romance 'Les Champs' (H.67) and Léon Guérin's 'Je crois en vous' (H.70, developed in the sketchbook) were intended to be sold for publication in periodicals, for which he also offered three pieces from *Faust*.[26] Songs published in this way occupied two facing pages, the music being underlaid with the first stanza, and the remaining stanzas written out as poetry, an economical method already used for *Irlande*.

In the early 1830s Berlioz sought for acceptable opera librettos while keeping himself before the public in other ways. His music was played at seven concerts in 1833 and four more at the end of 1834, including the first performances of *Harold en Italie* (in which Berlioz, a willing percussionist, played the cymbals). Most were his own promotions, but other opportunities arose from political commemorations. In 1833 Berlioz rescored two movements of

---

[26] *CG* ii. 172.

Scène héroïque for wind band for the third anniversary of the July revolution.[27] He tried resuscitating *Les Francs-juges*, but without the 'Marche des gardes', by now inextricably part of *Symphonie fantastique*, and without Ferrand, turning instead to Gounet to make a one-act intermezzo for theatre performance called *Le Cri de guerre de Brisgaw* (1833–4, H.23C). Besides music from the opera, it was to include 'Le Jeune Pâtre breton' and the finale of *Scène héroïque*.[28] Such a piece (like *Scène héroïque*) could have been fitted into those theatrical evenings which mingled ballet and vocal music, but Berlioz's attempts to insinuate himself into the Paris Opéra in this way were uniformly unsuccessful. His relative success in the concert-hall, moreover, probably militated against his acceptance as a potential opera composer by helping to categorize him as a symphonist and eccentric.

ITALIAN MUSIC

Berlioz's Italian experiences were represented in music only after hesitation and changes of direction, yet they must have been bursting for expression by 1834. Berlioz contemplated another Scottish subject, a choral work on the death of Marie Stuart. His idea was to double it with a viola concerto for Paganini, whose views of this traditionally showy genre were never likely to coincide with Berlioz's artistic aims. In the event Berlioz shifted his attention to Italy, dispensed with the chorus, and changed the national signification of the themes from *Rob Roy*, which he had abandoned after one hearing (April 1833). The overture's cor anglais melody became the hero's (viola's) song in *Harold en Italie*, an *idée fixe* representing the partially Scottish Lord Byron and, at one remove, the composer himself. The piping melody from the overture became an important secondary theme in the first movement. As the third movement also reminds us, the Italians too have bagpipes, which Berlioz had heard and duly imitated.

Harold has the conventional four movements, but otherwise avoids any neo-classical pattern. The first movement's slow section, as in *Lear*, has two themes. After a sombre fugato, the *idée fixe* is formed into a lyrical period with a repetition still more lush than in *Rob Roy*. The *idée fixe* is woven into the later stages of the Allegro, combined with each theme in turn, a process adumbrated in *Waverley*. Reworking the Allegro after Paganini's rejection, Berlioz removed several virtuoso flourishes, matching the unique texture with an individual form, neither concerto nor sonata.[29] The first two movements are indebted to Beethoven's Seventh, the first in rhythm, the second in mood, but the form of 'Marche des pèlerins' is mainly strophic, regularly punctuated by bells: Berlioz systematically begins each ten-bar 'stanza' in the tonic, but the successive cadences form an ascending pattern: bars 23, 33, 43, d♯, E, f♯ (but bar 53, E); bars 111, 121, 131, 141, 151, 161: d♯, E, f♯, g♯, A, B. Each time

---

[27] The performance was cancelled: NBE 12a, p. xi.
[28] See Holoman, *Creative Process*, and NBE 4 (forthcoming).   [29] See *MLB* 196–200.

a low C♮, dissonant to the immediately preceding harmony, is resolved obliquely to a high B, the dominant, preparing for the next strophe. This movement could conceivably be based on the lost *Marche religieuse des Mages*, but may simply be new. The mountaineer's serenade (third movement) is one of Berlioz's comparatively rare brushes with folk music, and one of his most enchanting miniatures. The finale pays Beethoven's Ninth Symphony an awkward tribute; its opening recalls, then rudely brushes aside, the main themes of the previous movements.[30] The viola, unlike Beethoven, is unable to think of a new theme, and is eloquently silent through most of the 'Orgie des brigands'—equally an orgy of rhythmic inventiveness. Without apparent irony, Berlioz drew his ebullient second theme from a sketch for the triumphal return of Napoleon's army.

On its richly coloured surface, *Harold* is a picturesque, rather than programmatic, symphony, like Mendelssohn's 'Italian' (with which it shares the topic of a pilgrims' march). The intricacy of its relationship to Byron remains a subject for speculation. The solo viola is a musical analogue to the detached, ironic Byron of a stanza from the Swiss canto: 'I live not in myself, but I become|Portion of that around me; and to me|High mountains are a feeling, but the hum|Of human cities torture: I can see|Nothing to loathe in nature, save to be|A link reluctant in a fleshly chain,|Class'd among creatures, when the soul can flee,|And with the sky, the peak, the heaving plain|Of ocean, or the stars, mingle, and not in vain.'[31]

Some of Berlioz's shorter works are potboilers, but others are jewels, among them 'Sara la baigneuse' (H.69), setting a delicately erotic 'Orientale' by Victor Hugo. The first two versions, for male quartet (1834) and mixed chorus (*c*.1838), are lost (the work was orchestrally conceived; the duet version with piano is a later reduction). Shortly afterwards, Berlioz produced the modestly forgettable 'Le Chant des Bretons' (H.71), and in 1835 he finally completed *Le cinq mai* (H.74).[32] Despite many finely crafted details, this substantial orchestral ballad is over-dependent on the refrain which Berlioz discovered in the Tiber, and whose gentle curve underlines the dog-like devotion of the soldier to his leader. Nevertheless, this expression of imperial decline won considerable success in concerts over several years.

THE ARTIST AS HERO

Berlioz composed *Benvenuto Cellini* (H.76) over an extended period, rethinking its form from *opéra comique* to through-composed opera with recitatives, and partly shaping the libretto, while employing three people to produce the words.[33] Although Berlioz understandably felt poorly treated by the main opera theatres, the fact is that no other Prix de Rome laureate from Berlioz's first entry (1826) until Ambroise Thomas (who won in 1832) ever had a work

---

[30] See Mark Evan Bonds, 'Sinfonia anti-eroica: Berlioz's *Harold en Italie*' in *After Beethoven*.
[31] Byron, *Childe Harold's Pilgrimage*, canto III, st. 72.   [32] NBE 12a, p. xiii.
[33] Auguste Barbier, Léon de Wailly, and Alfred de Vigny. See NBE 1a, pp. xi–xiii.

mounted at the Opéra, although several wrote for the Opéra-Comique. The overtly political subject triggered some of his freshest musical ideas, and a previously unexplored gift for comedy illuminates the roistering opening, the sarcastic antics of the carnival, and an ironic portrayal of the Pope. Berlioz reached a new peak in the technical ease of his polyphony, the wealth of instrumental colour, and a startling rhythmic vitality. But fertile as he was in this period, Berlioz nevertheless cashed a good proportion of what Peter Bloom calls his 'musical savings account'.[34] 'Chansonette de M. de Léon de Wailly' (H.73), a song to words by one of the librettists, becomes the off-stage serenade in scene 1, and its development holds together one of opera's liveliest comic openings.[35] Not the least remarkable aspect of the first layer of the score is the way it points ahead towards an almost symphonic approach to opera. The leaping figure from the serenade, the bumbling motive of Balducci, and a flashing triplet figuration derived from the main theme of the overture, all function like personal motives; the simplifications required for Paris, and other later revisions, whittled away this proto-Wagnerian element. 'Je crois en vous', reconfigured in harmony and texture, becomes a song without words for cor anglais, accompanying Harlequin's mime: it was also worked into the slow section of the overture. The second theme of the overture's allegro derives from the Act I trio, but is made idiomatically instrumental.[36] The overture is no pot-pourri, but a symphonic poem without a programme in which elements of the opera's narrative may be reflected in the handing of the Pope's theme.[37] The kernel of the first tableau is a love duet, in which Cellini and Teresa are overheard by the hero's concealed rival Fieramosca (see Chapter 10). This includes a rapturous descending sequence from *Cléopâtre*, made to arise as if spontaneously from a new beginning (Ex. 4.1*a*), and leads to a whispered and wonderfully funny tarantella, as confidently worked as if Berlioz had been composing comic ensembles for years.

The Carnival is a crowd scene of unprecedented colour, variety, and spontaneity, yet to generate something of this length Berlioz had recourse to five older thematic ideas. 'Laudamus te' from the Mass, accelerated and rewritten in 3/8 (later 6/8), becomes the explosive secondary motive of the saltarello, and typifies Berlioz's method of borrowing a theme when a movement needed regeneration by new material. All the borrowings are from choral music, but no earlier version is known for the first theme of the saltarello.[38] The scene was extended by a motive from 'Le Ballet des ombres', presented in canon; this section was cut before the first performance.[39] The 'Galop des moccoli' is enlivened by a second theme from the original finale to *Les Francs-juges* (vis-

[34] Bloom, *Life of Berlioz*, 37. On the compositional history of *Benvenuto Cellini*, see NBE 1a, pp. xi–xv; *L'Avant-scène opéra*, 142 (*Benvenuto Cellini*).

[35] The Chansonette was published for the first time in Holoman, *Creative Process*, 286–8.

[36] See *MLB* 147–8.   [37] For an extended analysis of the overture, see *MLB* 202–27.

[38] Holoman suggests a possible origin in the 'Scène des bohémiens' composed for the later versions of *Les Francs-juges*; *Creative Process*, 232.

[39] This material is to be found in NBE 1b. 607–10.

ible on the torn pages); this theme reappears during the contretemps among the principals, shortly before Cellini kills Pompeo. From the Mass, the energetic second setting of 'Et iterum venturus est', a curiously explosive sequel to the Resurrexit fanfare, acquires a self-righteous air when the crowd accuses Cellini of the murder; then the often-repeated unison 'Cujus regni' functions as a theatrical freeze when the Fort St Angelo cannon announces Lent and all lights are extinguished, permitting Cellini's escape. These borrowings are not crudely pasted in; they are repeated less often than in their original contexts, and are freshly developed. Berlioz finds a simple alteration to the 'Cujus regni' which enhances its effect through a stronger climactic harmony (bar 1029: iii substituted for the tonic).[40]

Of course borrowing is heavily outweighed by new invention, some of it jettisoned before the first performance to shorten the action and accommodate the singers. Berlioz excised Balducci's aria 'Ne regardez jamais la lune', already a replacement for a lost original.[41] Teresa's aria 'Ah, que l'amour une fois dans le cœur' is a strikingly original piece in two alternating tempos. Perhaps during the prolonged rehearsal period Berlioz learned lessons about the sheer difficulty of his own music, for this tricky piece was replaced by a more traditional double aria ('Entre l'amour et le devoir'). The strophic romance for Cellini, added too late for the printed libretto, is simple enough to be considered weak by some critics, but Berlioz retained it in later revisions.[42] Berlioz announced for a concert in 1834 a 'Chœur des Ciseleurs', presumably the hymn to the craft practised by Cellini and his fellow goldsmiths ('Si la terre aux beaux jours'). Its repetition forms the second tableau into a larger structure; a minor-key version sets the harsh atmosphere of the final act, taking place on Ash Wednesday; and a reprise brilliantly crowns the final scene. Berlioz chose an unusual metre for a hymn, 3/8, and orchestrated it sumptuously, with emphasis on the still relatively new chromatic brass instruments. As a paean to the nobility and significance of the arts, it certainly embodied his feelings about his own sacred mission. As he wrote it, he must have believed himself to be surfing a wave; but it broke on the rocks of inadequate performance, managerial and critical hostility, and public indifference which caused him to withdraw his opera in March 1839.[43] Berlioz described the fall of *La Damnation de Faust* as the cruellest rejection he ever suffered,

---

[40] Bar numbers of NBE 1b; these passages are compared in Holoman, *Berlioz*, 35.

[41] Balducci's aria and Teresa's original aria are published for the first time in NBE 1a. 127 and 168.

[42] Analysis in *MLB* 175–8; see also Joël-Marie Fauquet, 'Les Voix de Persée', in *L'Avant-scène opéra*, 142, 84–93.

[43] See *Memoirs*, ch. 48; NBE 1a, p. xv; below, Ch. 10. Peter Bloom suggests that after its single London performance in 1853, Berlioz gave in and withdrew *Benvenuto* prematurely, rather than fight the Italian cabal (*Life of Berlioz*, 129). The same may have been true in 1839; he would not accept performance of Act I within a mixed programme as a gesture of faith from the management. Years later he resisted any revival of *Les Troyens à Carthage*; it should be given complete, or not at all. On the critical reception, see Bloom, *Hector Berlioz, Benvenuto Cellini. Dossier de Presse parisienne*.

but this earlier disaster was one from which he never fully recovered. The Opéra remained closed to him for the remainder of his career. Schlesinger nevertheless published the overture in full score and a handsome vocal score of selections, including a duet movement which Berlioz later omitted.

GRANDE MESSE DES MORTS

Although conceived later than the opera, the *Grande messe des morts* (H.75) was commissioned for the commemoration of the July revolution, composed quickly, and performed the same year, 1837. The distance could hardly be greater between the marmoreal qualities of the Requiem and the opera which still awaited performance. As publication was part of the deal, Schlesinger issued a score almost at once; Berlioz's habitual revisions necessitated a new edition (by Ricordi) in 1853.[44] The Requiem text offered Berlioz the chance to control his dramatic instincts within a hieratic framework. Like the *Messe solennelle*, it is intended for concert rather than liturgical performance, but its vast structure enacts a ritual rather than a drama; a better analogy would be a series of frescoes. Berlioz had clear models for Requiem setting, including Cherubini and Mozart, which he both recognized and eschewed. In the cruel choral writing, the cavalier approach to the text, and in obtaining length by enhanced repetition of enormous paragraphs, this is his greatest tribute to Lesueur, who died shortly before the first performance.

One borrowing from the Mass is in the second section of the Sequence ('Dies irae'), the setting of 'Tuba mirum spargens sonum' adapted from the relatively uninspired declamation of 'Et iterum venturus est' in the Resurrexit. The preceding fanfare was not borrowed, but replaced by a longer, harmonically more developed, equivalent; instead of nine brass instruments (1825) or eleven (1828), it disposes a minimum of eighteen into five groups: horns in the middle of the orchestra, and four groups of heavier instruments at its corners. The numbers in the score propose doublings amounting to fifty brass players. When the acres of timpani come into play, the graves do indeed seem to open and the melodic poverty of the declamation hardly matters. The hushed 'Mors stupebit' is of course new. The Requiem is famous (or infamous) for its loudness, but Berlioz explored the quietest sonorities with equal fervour, imagining their hushed projection in a vast acoustic space. The first performance was at the Invalides, huge enough and domed, but not Gothic; the building was subsequently reconfigured internally to create a tomb for Napoleon, so that the 'authentic' ambience of the first performance is no longer fully available.

The most successful adaptation from the Mass is the conversion of the Kyrie into the instrumental Offertoire fugue, with added choral chant. Although Berlioz was under severe pressure, most of the Requiem is original. He avoided the 'Dies irae' plainchant which he had savagely parodied in

[44] NBE 9, pp. ix–x.

Symphonie fantastique, instead devising a plainchant-like melody of his own, developed with a deliberately harsh series of counterpoints. Acoustic architecture is reflected in the breadth of the musical architecture, with the first movement (Introit and Kyrie) partly recapitulated in the closing Agnus Dei, which also begins with a varied reprise of the 'Hostias', and ends after a reference to the central 'Rex tremendae'. Two magnificent fugal sections, the Introit and 'Lacrimosa', show Berlioz at the height of his powers. Both are rhythmically forceful, but the arpeggio melody of the Introit continually plunges into unexpected harmonic depths, while the 'Lacrimosa' proceeds with a stark inevitability towards its gruelling climax. The unaccompanied choral fugue ('Quaerens me') shows that Berlioz was not merely dependent upon instrumental effects; throughout, the application of huge forces and multiplication of resources is calculated, not wanton. Three pairs of cymbals played pianissimo *do* sound different from one (see Chapter 8).

ROMÉO ET JULIETTE

Erigone (H.77), subtitled 'intermède antique', was another attempt at an intermezzo for the Opéra which Berlioz probably abandoned in 1838. It is a curiously frustrating fragment, since Greek antiquity seems otherwise remote from Berlioz's interests in the 1830s; the subject overlaps with *Orphée*, but Pierre-Simon Ballanche's mingling of Catholicism with antique ritual has vaster pretensions than the picturesque Prix de Rome libretto.[45] A lively female chorus (over 200 bars) survives, in what appears to be a fair copy of the voice parts, without bass or instrumentation. Berlioz's hopes, or his motivation, for this piece cannot have been great; when an opportunity for sustained creative work appeared, thanks to Paganini's gift of 20,000 francs, he turned instead to Shakespeare. Temporarily free of debt, he concentrated his efforts during 1839 on *Roméo et Juliette* (H.79), the final triumph of the romantic decade, interrupting himself only to write 'Aubade' (text by Musset, H.78), a *jeu d'esprit* with a melody in which every interval bar one is a major or minor third, adding a brass accompaniment decidedly lavish for a piece of twenty-one bars.

Whether, and to what extent, Berlioz seriously considered writing a symphony on *Romeo and Juliet* soon after he encountered the play in 1827 is unlikely to be established with certainty.[46] Nevertheless, the project must have matured over some years, and was planned as a definitive romantic tribute to Shakespeare. In constructing this 'Dramatic Symphony', Berlioz tried to balance the demands of music and representation by selecting vocal and instrumental forms appropriate to different scenes. No major nineteenth-century composition, even by him, takes such risks with generic blending. In his own concert programmes, Berlioz sometimes performed three instrumental

[45] Pierre-Simon Ballanche, 'Terpsichore—Erigone', bk. V of *Orphée*, in *Essais de Palingénésie sociale*, ii (Paris, 1829).
[46] On the genesis of *Roméo et Juliette*, see NBE 18, pp. viii–xi; *Roméo*, 7–20.

41

movements (No. 2: Ball scene; No. 3: Love scene, without its choral introduction; No. 4: Scherzo), to avoid the expense of soloists and chorus, and these movements have been privileged to this day.[47] The whole work is in seven parts, four of which require voices; the vocal forces increase in size and importance towards the end when Friar Lawrence steps forward as an individual, taking upon him the authority of Church and State, to reconcile the families over the bodies of their children. Romeo and Juliet themselves are 'sung' by instruments, acquiring a different kind of reality which, because the imagination is freed by the absence of sung texts and human voices, is more readily accommodated to individual readings of the story.

Berlioz's use of earlier music leads to speculation about when in fact he decided to treat Shakespeare's play symphonically. Cleopatra's meditation could not be used, having been incorporated into *Lélio*, and it is hardly a symphonic piece. Its original association with Juliet's soliloquy about being buried alive may be revived by a thematic resemblance noted by Ian Kemp, but the connection is with the recitative of the Prince of Verona rather than Juliet.[48] The symphony omits Juliet's soliloquy, but includes the next stage in her ordeal, a funeral procession (No. 5), whose material is apparently new. But *Roméo* spelled the end of *Sardanapale* (last performed in 1833) as a viable work. The oboe solo in No. 2 ('Roméo seul . . . Grande fête chez Capulet') must have been the (lost) first aria from the cantata; the context, male erotic fixation, is unchanged (see Ex. 4.3). In the cantata the concubine plays a lyre, presumably the source of the pizzicato cello arpeggios in the symphony. In the cantata's 'incendie', this melody reappears in expanded note-values within a faster tempo, as it does in the 'Grande fête'. The dance theme of this movement was probably the middle section of the same aria, as it too appears in the 'incendie' (Ex. 2.1). In the symphony, these melodies are combined at the height of the festivities; there is no sign of this in the cantata fragment. The ball music is recalled by the Capulet chorus in No. 3 ('Scène d'amour'), in 6/8 metre equivalent to two bars of the *Sardanapale* reminiscence; given other changes of metre in Berlioz's borrowings (notably from the Mass), the 3/4 version may well be the original, and the familiar duple metre of the ball music may have been new in 1839. Perhaps most remarkable is Berlioz's ability to fashion (probably) three different melodies from the same incipit.

The quantity of fugue in the Requiem might be attributed to its being a sacred work, but no such conventional explanation serves for *Roméo*. The fugal imitation in five out of the seven movements displays Berlioz's resourcefulness in exploiting linear accumulation of texture. The fast, brittle opening fugato is part of the exposition of a sonata form which is destroyed by the dramatic context, street fighting. The massive augmentation of the subject to form a brass recitative pays tribute to Beethoven's Ninth, and introduces

---

[47] Note that Berlioz performed them in the order they appear in the symphony. Conductors sometimes crassly place the ball last, presumably because it has the noisiest ending.

[48] '*Romeo and Juliet* and *Roméo et Juliette*', in Bloom, *Studies*, 37–79; see 53–5.

Ex. 2.1 Three versions of the 'ball theme'

wordless dramatis personae (here the Prince). The choral prologue was a striking novelty. It functions as a sung programme and, besides the plot, it introduces the main themes, or at least the ambience, of the next four movements. This section was later completely overhauled and a second prologue, after the Scherzo, was eliminated. No. 2 substitutes for a symphony's first movement; the double slow section and Allegro (which is decidedly not in sonata form) represents Romeo's *mal d'isolement*, his love song, and Capulet's ball.[49] The difference from the waltz in *Symphonie fantastique* demonstrates Berlioz's symphonic maturity. The 1830 waltz is very much a genre piece; the 1839 ball, in emphatic duple metre, corresponds to no particular dance-type, and forms a sustained metaphor for the giddy, hollow brilliance of the event against which the lovers' meeting, represented by the oboe melody in augmentation, has permanence and human reality. The programme, however, given Berlioz's reticence, may be open to alternative interpretations.[50]

The 'Scène d'amour' (No. 3), widely considered his finest movement, eludes analytical categories more completely than anything Berlioz wrote—factors which may be related.[51] Berlioz may not have had Shakespeare's Queen Mab

[49] On the form of this movement see Berger, *Phantastik als Konstruktion*, 170–4; *MLB* 74–6 and 194–6.

[50] Ian Kemp takes a more severely programmatic view than other interpreters: '*Romeo and Juliet*', 54–9 and 63. See also *Roméo*, 26–34.

[51] Analyses in Jacques Chailley, *La Revue de Musicologie*, 63 (1977), 115–22; Kemp, '*Romeo and Juliet*', 64–8; *Roméo*, 35–42; Rosen, *The Romantic Generation*, 556–68; Vera Micznik, 'Of

in mind when he withdrew 'Le Ballet des ombres', or when he excised a quotation from it in the Carnival Scene in *Benvenuto*. But this motive forms an episode in the Scherzo, 'La Reine Mab' (No. 4, from bar 615), restoring its original sinister connotation; Kemp notes a thematic connection with the main Scherzo theme.[52] In a rare near-repetition of a formal idea, Berlioz composed the beautiful 'Convoi funèbre' (No. 5) on the pattern of the Requiem Offertoire; a choral pedal irregularly punctuates an instrumental fugue with a chromatic subject. In a new twist, of formal and textural significance, voices and orchestra exchange roles at the mid-point.[53] Berlioz followed advice from friendly critics and cut out some literal, ritualistic psalmody. The programme of No. 6, 'Roméo au tombeau' ('Romeo at the Capulets' tomb'), explains the fragmentary recollections and frenzied reworkings of the love scene, using techniques developed from the handling of the *idée fixe*. Critical reception persuaded Berlioz that this movement would rarely be understood, and although he retained it in the published score, he suggested it should be omitted in performance (see Chapter 9). The finale, however, was no doubt welcomed by the audience as a frankly theatrical scena: idealized or covert opera yields to real opera. Berlioz shows how feuding will always recur unless checked by a higher power. He includes a reference to the opening fugue and, as in the Requiem, a final change of mode to B major for the culminating oath which outdoes its ostensible model in *Les Huguenots*. Those who regard the finale as stylistically regressive may be tempted to suggest that some of this music originated earlier, but there is no evidence for this (see Chapter 10).[54]

END OF THE ROMANTIC DECADE
At the end of the decade Berlioz contemplated putting his musical house in order by publishing his most important works. Publication for him was essentially the last stage in compositional activity, following what he hoped would be the final revisions. In 1839, ten years after *Huit scènes de Faust*, he published a second 'Opus 1', *Waverley*. Op. 2 was already assigned to *Irlande* and Op. 3 to the *Francs-juges* overture, published in 1836 in orchestral score and piano reduction. Op. 4, published in 1840, was *Lear*. The Requiem, published precipitately in 1837, became Op. 5; Opp. 6 and 7 were *Le cinq mai* and *Les Nuits d'été*. Thus Berlioz's opus numbers have no connection with the order of composition; none of the symphonies was published until 1843, and then the last was published first.

Ways of Telling, Intertextuality, and Historical Evidence in Berlioz's *Roméo and Juliette*', *19th-Century Music*, 24 (2000), 21–61.

[52] Kemp, '*Romeo and Juliet*', 69–73. [53] *Roméo*, 47–52.
[54] The first phrase of Lawrence's 'Pauvres enfants' could be sung to 'Noble amitié', the opening of Conrad's aria (*Les Francs-juges*). Berlioz intended to perform it in November 1829, a year in which he may also have been preoccupied with *Romeo and Juliet*. But although, as Holoman observes, 'Berlioz found it relatively easy to work words into a pre-existing musical context' (*Creative Process*, 354), Ferrand's long lines (averaging twelve syllables) could not have produced this melody, which is fitted to eight-syllable verses.

In retrospect, the first movement of *Grande symphonie funèbre et triomphale* (H.80) is an elegy for the decade of romanticism, and its finale, ostensibly celebrating the tenth anniversary of July 1830, commemorates a false dawn of populism. In practice it celebrated a decade of the Orléans monarchy, and is Berlioz's closest approach to a Napoleonic *sinfonia eroica*, and to realizing the more grandiose seven-movement project of five years earlier, the *Fête musicale funèbre*. The opening 'Marche funèbre', despite a weakly sequential middle section, is among his greatest instrumental movements, a sublime combination of passionate lyricism and ritualistic and military order.[55] The second movement, a funeral elegy ('Oraison funèbre'), is derived from the hero's invocation in *Les Francs-juges*, 'sung' by a solo trombone; the imitative echo from bar 28 can be read on the torn pages of the opera. The final march ('Apothéose') includes a motive used in crescendo (from bars 116 and 148), taken from the first chorus of *Scène héroïque*, with the common theme of glorification of past heroes. The Apothéose came to have a separate existence, with piano accompaniment, among those patriotic works of Berlioz which have understandably faded from the repertoire: in its symphonic form it remains a source of almost pagan excitement.

The other work of 1840 is *Les Nuits d'été* (H.81), neglected for a century or more but now among Berlioz's best-loved works, and often cited as a forerunner of the orchestral song cycles by composers such as Mahler.[56] But the orchestrations followed several years later; the 1840 version is for mezzo-soprano (or tenor) with piano accompaniment. The poems are by Théophile Gautier, perhaps the most distinguished literary figure, with De Vigny, among those Berlioz knew well. These lovely verses, which proved attractive to other composers (David, Bizet, Fauré, Duparc), freed Berlioz from the constraints of strophic form, lightly disguised with pert variations in 'Villanelle' (H.82). The outer songs are fast and cheerfully ironic, notably the last, 'L'Île inconnue' (H.87), called 'Barcarole' by the poet and set by Berlioz with a Venetian swing, in through-composed form: it roams in imagination over the planet looking for an imaginary island where love endures. Berlioz's achievement in the four central slow songs, which are performed consecutively without a hint of monotony, comes close to matching Haydn's in the eight slow movements of his *Seven Last Words*. Two starkly contrasted laments, 'Sur les lagunes' (H.84) and 'Au Cimetière' (H.86), were the last to be composed.[57] 'Le Spectre de la rose' (H.83) is a through-composed scena with elements of rondo form and a wonderfully varied tonal plan. 'Absence' ('Reviens, reviens, ma bien-aimée!', H.85) is the only song not essentially

[55] For analysis of the melodies, see Rushton, 'Berlioz through the Looking-Glass', 54–8, and *MLB* 164–7.
[56] This view is questioned by Annegret Fauser, in Bloom (ed.), *The Cambridge Companion to Berlioz*, 121.
[57] Cairns, *Servitude*, 247. Composition of *Sur les Lagunes* after *L'Île inconnue* if anything strengthens the hypothesis that they are thematically connected: see Rushton, '*Les Nuits d'été*: Cycle or Collection?', in Bloom, *Studies*, 130–2.

faithful to Gautier's verse structure; its refrain form (ABAB′A) is Berlioz's own, and he omitted several stanzas. This curious circumstance is explained by the manuscript libretto of *Erigone,* which includes a lyrical section ('Reviens, reviens, sublime Orphée') clearly designed for the music which became 'Absence'. It seems likely that Berlioz selected from and manipulated Gautier's poem to fit the existing music.[58]

[58] Even if the chronological relation of *Erigone* and 'Absence' cannot be proved, the handling of the poem would appear to contradict the assumption in Holoman, *Catalogue,* 190, 228, and NBE 13, pp. xi, 137, that 'Absence' preceded *Erigone* and was to be sacrificed for the larger work.

3 Damnation and After

LES ANNÉES MYSTÉRIEUSES

Early biographers identified a writing block between *Les Nuits d'été* and the major change in Berlioz's life brought about by the success of his first tour in Germany as an advocate for his own work. Adolphe Boschot called 1841–2 'les années mystérieuses'.[1] This period is treated cursorily in the memoirs, whereas the reprinted 'open letters' from Germany, supplied to the Paris press, cover the first two tours in as much detail as one could desire. Marital breakdown and his affair with the singer Marie Récio, whom he eventually married after Harriet's death, may explain his reticence about what, when he began to compile the memoirs, was still recent history. As he insisted, he was not writing confessions.

In fact, of course, Berlioz was busier than ever, completing several small compositions and advancing more substantial projects. He urgently desired another opera commission, and poured much of his energy into dramatic projects. But while his reputation was being established in Germany and Austria, it declined at home from the high point reached in *Roméo* and his second government commission, the *Symphonie funèbre*. Even the modest profit of *Roméo* caused him to complain that 'c'est la grande musique qui me ruine'.[2] The financial loss occasioned in 1846 by *La Damnation de Faust* may have upset him no less than the 'unexpected indifference' of its public reception; but the latter was unforeseen.[3]

The failed *démarche* towards opera began well with spin-offs from *Benvenuto Cellini*. Teresa's abandoned aria was revitalized in Berlioz's nearest approach to a concerto, *Rêverie et caprice* for violin and orchestra (H.88), which often featured in his concert programmes and was published in 1841 as Op. 8. In 1844 he revived memories of the opera with one of his most popular orchestral works, *Le Carnaval romain* (H.95), mainly transcribed from the Carnival saltarello. By this time he might have forgotten that it opens with the 'Laudamus te' from the Mass; it also includes a few bars which he had already

---

[1] Boschot, *Un Romantique sous Louis-Philippe*, 323.
[2] Letter to his sister Nanci, 29 Mar. 1841, *CG* ii. 684–5.   [3] *Memoirs*, ch. 54.

cut from the opera.[4] Reminiscences of a work of Italian orientation were soon outnumbered by projects with more northerly connections. For the Opéra, he composed stylish and expressive recitatives with French text for *Der Freischütz* (H.89), and orchestrated Weber's *Aufforderung zum Tanze* (*Invitation to the Dance*) for the obligatory ballet (H.90), firmly rejecting a proposal to use his own music.[5] He began work with Eugène Scribe, principal literary collaborator of Auber and Meyerbeer, on *La Nonne sanglante* (H.91), intended for the Opéra. The libretto is loosely derived from an episode in Matthew Lewis's gothic novel *The Monk*. Berlioz was well under way with the composition in 1841–2, but set it aside, not wishing to expend time where there was no definite commitment from the Opéra management; the project was not finally abandoned until 1848.[6] Berlioz says that he drafted two acts, including choruses and finales, but orchestrated only three movements. It is these which survive: a recitative and bass aria in D flat for the hermit Hubert (emphatically *not* the lascivious Monk of Lewis's novel); a tenor recitative and aria for Rodolphe, in E minor but with an idyllic middle section in A; and an incomplete duet during which Agnès narrates the legend of the bleeding nun. As the sceptical Rodolphe is trying to persuade her that the apparition can be used as cover for their elopement, the manuscript breaks off with a couple of torn folios which evidently contained music.[7] One can only speculate whether this passage was 'consulted' and recycled somewhere, such as *Les Troyens*; the possibility should not be excluded that the surviving movements themselves adapt music which once formed part of, perhaps, *Les Francs-juges*.

In 1842 Berlioz lost his best chance of royal patronage when the sympathetic Duc d'Orléans, heir to the throne, died in an accident. Soon afterwards, he undertook his first journeys of self-promotion, possibly with government assistance.[8] He first visited Brussels (September 1842), and two tours in Germany (1842–3 and 1845–6) took him as far as Vienna, Prague, Breslau (modern Wrocław), Dresden, and Berlin. Another stimulus to composition at this busy period came from the development of new musical resources. In 1843 he orchestrated 'Chant sacré', including two bass clarinets, and the next year he arranged it for six Sax instruments including saxophone. That this instrument was first considered by this acutely colour-sensitive composer in connection with sacred music is confirmed by signs in the MS of *La*

---

[4] *Le Carnaval romain*, from bar 276; compare NBE 1b. 603.

[5] See Bockholdt, *Berlioz-Studien*, 109–73; Olga Visentini, 'I recitativi di Berlioz per *Der Freischütz* di Weber: Sviluppi del recitativo francese tra settecento e ottocento', *Rivesta italiana di musicologia*, 28 (1993), 79–129.

[6] *Memoirs*, ch. 57.

[7] F-Pn Rés Vm² 178. See A. E. F. Dickinson, 'Berlioz's "Bleeding Nun"', *Musical Times*, 107 (1966), 584–8; Jacques Joly, 'La nonne sanglante tra Donizetti, Berlioz e Gounod', in *L'opera tra Venezia e Parigi* (Florence: Olschki, 1988), 193–252; Steven Huebner, *The Operas of Charles Gounod* (Oxford: Oxford University Press, 1990), 37–42; NBE 4 (forthcoming).

[8] Peter Bloom, 'La Mission de Berlioz en Allemagne: Un document inédit', *Revue de Musicologie*, 66/1 (1980), 70–85.

Damnation de Faust that he contemplated using two saxophones in the scene in heaven.[9] In 1844 he wrote three pieces (H.98–100) for Alexandre's 'orgue-mélodium' (a species of harmonium): a charming religious pastoral, 'Rustic serenade to the Madonna'; a slow fugue, 'Hymn for the Elevation'; and a rare and not very successful example of musical abstraction, 'Toccata'. In 1841–2 he published, first as sixteen articles, and in 1843 as a book, his most considered and, after the memoirs, his most important book, *Grand Traité d'instrumentation et d'orchestration modernes*; and in 1844 there appeared his longest work of prose fiction, 'Euphonia'.[10]

International success is reflected in many souvenir albumleaves, often quoting existing music (a favourite was the love scene from *Roméo*), but some with new, short, and usually trivial, pieces: 'Souvenirs', 'Bêtises', 'Improvisations' (H.93), a clumsy piano piece (H.96), a vocal serenade notated on hand-drawn staves (H.106), and a setting of cod Dante ('Nessun maggior piacere', H.114).[11] The 'abstract' pieces are negligible, but a poetic text guaranteed nothing: 'Hymne à la France' (H.97), written for a 'festival of Industry' in August 1844, is less strikingly Berliozian than its choral ancestors in *Irlande*. The more substantial *Chant des chemins de fer* (H.110) was performed at the opening of the railway line from Paris to Lille; within its conventional refrain structure it includes some effective energetic and lyrical passages (see Chapter 8).

The most personal works of this period are associated with *Hamlet* and *Faust*. An autograph catalogue of music manuscripts from 1845, for which there is no known purpose, lists prominently above the Requiem, 'Morceaux d'Hamlet: scène de la comédie [presumably the mousetrap scene], Ballade sur la mort d'Ophélie, Coronach'.[12] The first of these has not survived. The breakdown of Berlioz's marriage to 'Ophelia' is reflected in the peculiar intensity and despairing calm of the beautiful ballad, 'La Mort d'Ophélie' (H.92), one of his most impressive small-scale works. It was first published as a Romance with piano accompaniment, but a few years later, and not in a popular journal but as a supplement to *La Revue et gazette musicale*, in which Berlioz was editorially involved. About November 1844 a project to write incidental music to *Hamlet* stimulated the masterpiece variously called 'Coronach' and 'Marche funèbre' (H.103), for performance at the end of the play. It is a eulogy, rather than a portrait of Hamlet, a controlled response to the terror and waste of tragedy, its ritual dignity shattered by representation of Fortinbras's order 'Go, bid the soldiers shoot' (see Chapter 9).

[9] NBE 8b. 459.

[10] The articles 'De l'instrumentation' appeared in *Revue et Gazette musicale* between Nov. 1841 (HC 455) and July 1842 (HC 507).

[11] David Cairns draws attention to a setting of the original Dante ('Nessun maggior dolore') as an albumleaf, *c*.1841, found and lost in the 1960s, but of questionable authenticity. *Servitude*, 243.

[12] Holoman, *Catalogue*, 509.

The 'mysterious years' were productive, therefore, but not of 'la grande musique'—unless the Te Deum (H.118) was indeed composed at this time (see below). The somewhat unfocused picture of his creative activity is completed by a new overture and five further vocal works. Both the delicate 'Prière du matin' (H.112), subtitled 'Chœur d'enfants', and the witty 'Scherzo for two voices', 'Le Trébuchet' (H.113), can be dated only by their appearance in the so-called 'Labitte' catalogue of 1846, published (by Labitte) in the libretto of *La Damnation de Faust*. The dramatic Romance, with choral refrain, 'La Belle Isabeau' ('Conte pendant l'orage' H.94) was published in a periodical in December 1843, and unfortunately never orchestrated. Berlioz's concerts in Germany in 1845–6 were filled out by two strophic orchestral songs; 'Le Chasseur danois' is a domesticated cousin to 'Chanson de brigands', and the bolero 'Zaide' (H.107) is an engaging venture into picture-postcard exoticism. Berlioz commemorated his second visit to Nice in 1844 with an overture, *La Tour de Nice* (H.101), performed once on 19 January 1845. This is difficult if not impossible to reconstruct from the surviving autograph. Perhaps Berlioz found it diffuse, like *Rob Roy*, but this time he remained faithful to his conception, if not to his title. In the 'Labitte' catalogue it is called *Le Corsaire rouge*, from Fennimore Cooper's *Red Rover*; 'rouge' was later deleted, redirecting our attention to Byron's *The Corsair: A Tale*. These changes complicate programmatic interpretation, or simplify it by depriving the title of any hermeneutic significance. *Le Corsaire* is Berlioz's last work of programme music, or the last stage in his quest after a public for instrumental movements of totally original form, advertised by extra-musical allusions. It and *Le Carnaval romain* show Berlioz at the height of his powers and, with *La Nonne* on the back burner, ready for a larger challenge.

THE SALVAGING OF FAUST

Berlioz's letters of candidature for the Académie des Beaux-Arts of the Institute make the case for his election by lists of his works. The 1842 list, like the MS list already referred to, included *Huit scènes de Faust* as if it had never been withdrawn. Berlioz planned to perform the 'Romance' in 1844.[13] In 1845–6 he rescued the scenes by building a full-length work around them; the compatibility of music from 1829, albeit revised, with that of 1845–6, emphasizes the importance of his original Op. 1 to Berlioz's development. At first he called *La Damnation de Faust* 'Opéra de concert', an opera to be performed without being staged, freeing the imaginations of composer and listener from theatrical restrictions. He commissioned a libretto from Almire Gandonnière, to include the lyrics translated by Gérard de Nerval and set in *Huit scènes*, and took what was ready to Germany late in 1845.[14] The sextet of Sylphes was rewritten as a chorus, and is practically a new work; the glass harmonica

[13] Holoman, Catalogue, 504, 509; NBE 8b. 456.
[14] Berlioz necessarily ignored Nerval's 1835 revision, since the texts of the lyrics, particularly the Romance, were substantially changed.

is dropped along with fussy harp figuration and other details which had presumably been ineffective in the single performance in 1829. He reduced the original (and striking) introduction by sixteen bars, and completely rewrote the twelve-bar coda. Then he added two movements based on the same melody: Mephistopheles's aria 'Voici des roses', with a brass accompaniment at once unctuous and sinister, and the gossamer 'Ballet des sylphes'. He used nothing else from earlier works, although this same ballet, by way of the previous two movements, contains a reflection of the pastoral 'Christe' from the Mass (Ex. 3.1). The other choruses were also extensively revised, and Berlioz added a coda to the Serenade—an ingenious development of its motives which dilutes its vital naturalism. Amiably chuckling woodwind replace the grotesque orchestral representation of a huge guitar, and the musical sophistication impairs its diabolical raillery. The coda was quickly discarded,

Ex. 3.1 *Messe solennelle* and *La Damnation de Faust*: deployment of a melodic shape

possibly in response to a comment by a colleague, Maurice Bourges, who called it 'sterile'.[15]

Despite copious correspondence and the complex make-up of the manuscript, there are still gaps in our knowledge of *La Damnation*, notably the three-act ground plan Berlioz presumably agreed with Gandonnière (see Chapter 10).[16] Isolated from his collaborator, Berlioz exhausted the text supplied and began to write his own, starting with Faust's 'Invocation à la Nature'. The major change arose after Berlioz's visit to Vienna, where he composed a Hungarian March (*Marche de Rákóczy*, H.109) for his forthcoming visit to Budapest. Clearly it merited a hearing in Paris, so he incorporated it into his 'Concert Opera', which therefore opens 'on the plains of Hungary'. Such a formidable piece could conclude a Part I; the original Part I was presumably divided at this point and the work became a 'Dramatic Legend in Four Parts'. Faust's second monologue now opens Part II and leads to the Easter Hymn and the entrance of Mephistopheles; the rest follows, if not logically (*La Damnation* is not that kind of work) but in a sequence intelligibly related to Goethe's *Faust* (Part I).

Berlioz finished composing in early summer and planned performances for late November. Unfortunately the première had to be postponed; on 6 December the weather was poor; the King and Queen did not come and nor did the public; the Opéra-Comique was not 'fashionable', and nor were the soloists. Although his friends rallied round, Berlioz felt defeated, and again ruined by 'la grande musique'.[17] The reputation of *La Damnation* was rebuilt by performances (usually of the first two parts only) in Russia, Germany, and England. Berlioz revised it extensively prior to publication in 1854, and revivals of the whole work in Dresden, Weimar, and Vienna anticipated its posthumous success in Paris under Pasdeloup and Colonne from the late 1870s. For many years, but after Berlioz's death, it disputed with *Symphonie fantastique* the distinction of being his best-known work. But in early 1847, as he prepared to recoup his finances in Russia, the outlook appeared grim; the heroic age of romanticism was over.

PURGATORY

For the next few years Berlioz's conducting activity in Germany and England increased, and his recording of it for the press diminished to vanishing point. The only composition dated 1847 is the Dante albumleaf, written in England in November. In February 1848, revolution broke out in Paris, arousing fear of cultural collapse; Berlioz stayed in London until July; Dr Berlioz died on

---

[15] Maurice Bourges, *Revue et gazette musicale*, 13 (1846), 394. The coda is in NBE 8b. 520–1. Berlioz had also responded to criticisms of *Roméo et Juliette* (see *Roméo*, 71–2), but he was not over-suggestible; Bourges said he should not ouch a note of Mephistopheles' 'Invocation' before the 'Menuet des follets', but Berlioz made a cut, some of the original music being lost (NBE 8b. 514–17).

[16] On the authorship of the libretto, see NBE 8b. 501; Rushton, 'The Genesis of Berlioz' "La Damnation de Faust"'.

[17] *Memoirs*, ch. 54.

the 28th. While still in London, but lacking feasible musical projects, Berlioz started his brilliant, generally honest, but naturally biased and often bitter *Mémoires*. The project was dropped and resumed over many years, and its later stages lack detail, personal and artistic, compared to the thoroughness of the account of his first forty years (fortunately the documentation of his later years is otherwise far richer). Even before abandoning *La Nonne*, he thought of salvaging *La Damnation* by turning it into an opera with Scribe.[18] He hoped to capitalize on the political situation in France by publishing (in London) the 'Apothéose' from the *Symphonie funèbre*, with new words, together with arrangements of revolutionary songs by Méhul and Rouget de Lisle (H.115 and 116), now lost. Another gesture towards a popular republicanism Berlioz hardly espoused is the short revolutionary chorus (with orchestra), 'La Menace des Francs' (H.117). And a major project, the Te Deum, with more monarchical than republican resonance, was completed in 1849, well before Louis Napoleon's assumption of power and restoration of order.

Unfortunately Napoleon III did not emulate his uncle's support of Lesueur by bestowing favours on a once-rebellious composer. During the 1850s Berlioz had his greatest triumphs in Germany, including Berlioz festivals organized by Liszt in Weimar at which *Benvenuto Cellini* came into its own. Independently of political events, he decided to further his project of ordering his estate, even proposing publication of his complete works. He established a solid relationship with the publisher Richault, successor to Brandus, who in 1852 published yet another catalogue of Berlioz's works.[19] This stock-taking entailed polishing and improving the presentation of pieces he valued. 'Sara la baigneuse' was published, probably in 1849, its vocal palette enlarged to three diverse choral groups without compromising its transparency. The exquisite orchestrations of five of *Les Nuits d'été* cannot be dated exactly, but they belong to a later period (except 'Absence', orchestrated in 1843 for Marie Récio). Pieces of this kind could have been intended to refresh the repertoire of smaller works on the concert-tours which became increasingly important to Berlioz as a means of generating income, establishing and confirming his reputation outside Paris, and cultivating musical friendships.

The final version of 'La Captive' was published in 1849; it bore no dedication but was advertised as 'chantée par Madame [Pauline] Viardot Garcia'.[20] The sixth version listed in Holoman's catalogue, it marks an extreme point in generic transformation, showing Berlioz's increasing dissatisfaction with the Romance. In its original form, its folkloric air suited the bourgeois drawing-room. In this orchestral elaboration, Berlioz blurred the strophic outline: Tom Wotton compared the result to a miniature symphonic poem.[21] Instead

---

[18] NBE 8b. 457; *CG* iii. 444–5, 466, 473, 484–5.   [19] Holoman, *Catalogue*, 495, 512.

[20] It appears that she sang it in E, rather than the published key, D. NBE 13, pp. ix–x; Holoman, *Catalogue*, 125.

[21] Wotton, *Hector Berlioz*, 82; see also Tom Wotton, *Berlioz: Four Works* (The Musical Pilgrim) (London: Oxford University Press, 1929), 40–4.

of a voice with simple accompaniment, reincarnating the composer and his guitar, Berlioz created a lavish sonic metaphor for the captive's homesickness. The supple melodic curve is elaborated and disguised by diminution (second stanza, from bar 25), relegation to muted cellos (fourth stanza), and broken rhythm (final stanza, from bar 89). The fourth stanza has a vocal counterpoint, and *couleur locale* in bolero rhythm, a complete analogue to the poem's 'bed of moss' and 'air espagnol' (Ex. 3.2). For the final stanza (bar 89) Berlioz added a second string orchestra (expected only 'in the event that this piece is performed at a musical festival with a very large orchestra'), which plays in twenty-three bars out of 129, nearly all pianissimo; its double-basses play three notes. One might prefer the directness of the original, but this last version has all the artifice of a musical Fabergé.

Ex. 3.2 'La Captive', from bar 60

Berlioz continued to rationalize his output by grouping smaller works for publication. The third edition of *Irlande*, with revisions, came out in 1849. Four more collections were issued by Richault in 1850–1, the finest being *Tristia*, Op. 18 (H.119). As the name implies, these works for quite different forces—'Méditation religieuse' and the two *Hamlet* pieces—are connected mainly by melancholy. *Vox populi*, Op. 20 (H.120, published 1851) unites 'La Menace des Francs' (H.117) and 'Hymne à la France' (H.97). Two other collections probably appeared earlier, in 1850. Op. 19 contains three disparate pieces under the dismissive title *Feuillets d'album* (H.121): 'Zaide' (H.107), 'Les Champs' (H.67), and *Chant des chemins de fer* (H.110) form a strange blend of industrial, mock-pastoral, and the Spanish 'other'. The engaging 'Les Champs', however, was converted from seven identical stanzas, each of thirty-nine bars' repeated music, to four stanzas through-composed over 146 bars of refined strophic variation (see Ex. 7.5). The five pieces in Op. 13, more seductively marketed as *Fleurs des Landes* (H.124), are all pastoral. 'Le Trébuchet' is flanked by two works with a common regional association ('Le Jeune Pâtre breton' and 'Le Chant des Bretons'). The collection is headed by two songs whose dates of composition are otherwise unknown, in which the composer met a probably self-imposed challenge by contrasted settings of the same mild lyric by Adolphe de Bouchon. The first, 'Le Matin' (subtitled 'Romance', H.125), is in a sophisticated drawing-room style. The second, dubbed 'Petit Oiseau' (H.126), is strophic in form and uses a folkloric idiom suited to the subtitle 'Chanson de paysan'. Since 'Le Matin' is heavily dependent on the kind of flowing piano-writing for which Berlioz had no particular gift, it is not surprising that 'Petit Oiseau' is affectively the more convincing.

Berlioz may have been depressed about future prospects for large works, and although there is more to this activity than generating income (he sold material outright to Richault rather than receiving royalties), he did not often perform this last group of works. It is sometimes uncertain which songs were performed in his concerts, as programmes often name only the singer and genre ('Romance', 'Air') without a title. Thus apart from 'Absence', a staple of Marie Récio's repertoire in the 1840s which was also performed by tenors in Berlioz's concerts, few performances of the songs are established, and Berlioz seems never to have performed the greatest work published in 1850–1, the *Hamlet* march.

WRITING A TE DEUM

The autograph score of the Te Deum (H.118) is undated, but Berlioz's letters make clear that it was finished in August 1849. Nevertheless, it is listed as complete, though not yet performed, in the 1846 'Labitte' catalogue.[22] The existence of a Te Deum sketch on the autograph of the first harmonium piece,

[22] NBE 10, p. viii; Holoman, *Catalogue*, 311, calls the Labitte catalogue 'inexplicable'. Kent W. Werth, 'Dating the Labitte Catalogue of Berlioz's Works', *19th-Century Music*, 1 (1977), 137–41, includes a transcription of the catalogue.

while it proves nothing, suggests work undertaken before 1846.[23] It is unlikely that Berlioz finished this gigantic composition in the early 1840s, without mentioning it in his correspondence or making any attempt to perform it; yet he would hardly be likely to list a work with no existence on paper. The explanation may be that it was planned to the point where he was confident of being able to complete it quickly should an occasion arise for its performance; public announcement of its existence may have been intended to induce someone in government circles to commission it.

What is puzzling about this extended gestation is that the final realization of a long-standing project came to a head during the short-lived Second Republic. Finishing the score had the dual purpose of realizing his musical assets, and honouring the great Napoleon; the Te Deum was traditionally used in France to celebrate military victories. In 1849, Berlioz could hardly foresee the empire of Napoleon III. Berlioz included several overtly military elements: an instrumental 'Prélude' to the third choral movement raps out the rhythm of the first movement on side-drums, the fourth choral movement ('Tu Christe, rex gloriae') is march-like, and the last ('Judex crederis') ends with a brilliant fanfare. Berlioz later added a 'March for the presentation of the colours'. The prelude was intended only for ceremonial performance, and Berlioz eventually cut it; performances routinely omit the March. Since both these instrumental movements use the main theme of the first movement, and no others do so, their removal also eliminates a characteristic cyclic element along with the military framework; and the Prélude would add variety to the succession of choral movements. Without the march, the blaze of trumpets at the end of the 'Judex crederis' is no longer a bridge to a military finale; instead it welcomes the redeemed to heaven after the terrors of Berlioz's grandest eschatological vision (see Chapter 8).

The Te Deum cleaned up other unfinished business, becoming the final repository of music originating in the Mass. A short passage borrowed from the Resurrexit in 'Tu Christe' (bar 95) regenerates the movement after a lyrical interlude; the Mass text 'Et ascendit in coelum, sedet ad dexteram Patri' becomes 'Tu ad dexteram Dei sedes in gloria'. As Denis McCaldin observes, 'the words of the *Te Deum* exactly restate the sentiments of the Resurrexit'.[24] Since the Te Deum was not performed until 1855, it would not be surprising if nobody noticed that the tenor solo ('Te ergo quæsumus') was largely the same as the Agnus Dei last heard in 1827. Both texts are prayers addressed to the Redeemer. Berlioz must have kept a manuscript of the Agnus, but we cannot tell how closely it corresponded to either version, nor whether it was an autograph or a copy.[25] The most remarkable aspect of this borrowing is its

[23] Facsimile in NBE 10. 169.

[24] NBE 10, p. viii. This rising phrase is strikingly anticipated in the opening bars (orchestral introduction) of the Mass.

[25] The manuscript catalogue of 1845 includes 'Agnus Dei de la messe solennelle' (Holoman, *Catalogue*, 509). As Macdonald affirms ('*Messe solennelle*', 275), Berlioz could not have prepared 'Te ergo quaesumus' without a score of the 'Agnus'.

fidelity to the melodic pattern, bass, and harmonic structure of the original, whose origin was never suspected before 1991. Yet the music is transformed by richer and more subtle instrumentation, the addition of a brass chorale to the choral monotone which responds to the passionate solo tenor line, and a significant coda in which the melody forms the bass, giving rise to unorthodox progressions Berlioz might not have conceived, or risked, in the 1820s.

Berlioz patterned the Te Deum text (see Chapter 8) into choral movements called 'Hymn' and 'Prayer', connecting the first two (both 'Hymns') by a breathtaking modulation from F to B major. He scored the work for double chorus, to which he later added a unison choir of children; in 1851 he was deeply impressed by the concerts of charity children, singing 'The Old Hundredth' in perfect unison in the massy acoustic of St Paul's Cathedral, London (he also added children to the heavenly chorus in *La Damnation*). The Te Deum requires doubled wind, including bass clarinet, but less brass than the Requiem; exceptionally, Berlioz wrote a part for organ, despite his reservations about blending 'the Pope' with 'the Emperor' (the orchestra).[26] He wanted orchestra and organ at opposite ends of the performance space, again exploiting the musical effect of distance; for practical reasons this disposition is frequently ignored.

Further work-lists drawn up before elections to the Académie des Beaux-Arts are mainly in opus number order, so that little can be read into them. The 1842 list tried to impress by presenting the works hierarchically, leading with the Requiem, flagged as a government commission, followed by the symphonies, with *Lélio* linked to the *Fantastique* ('these pieces are equivalent in length to a two-act opera'; *Roméo* he optimistically equated with a three-act work). There follow *Benvenuto*, the *Freischütz* recitatives, larger vocal works and song cycles, four overtures, and extras ('Poësies diverses', *Grand Traité*). In 1845, though not for the Academy, Berlioz classified more precisely, starting with six Overtures, Symphonies (including *Lélio*), and 'Morceaux d'Hamlet', before the Requiem, *Benvenuto*, and the surprising 'Scènes de Faust', 'Agnus de la messe solennelle', and 'Psalmodie' (the last quite unknown). All the shorter vocal works are given by name, and the list ends with fragments: *Les Francs-juges*, *Sardanapale*, *La Nonne sanglante*. In 1854, Berlioz again presented the Academy with his works listed hierarchically, leading with *Roméo et Juliette* and *La Damnation de Faust*; then came Requiem and Te Deum, *Benvenuto*, and *L'Enfance du Christ*, its three parts listed as separate compositions. *Harold* is listed above *Symphonie fantastique* and the remaining works. The *Grand Traité*, now in a second edition, is promoted above the laconically described 'Six grand overtures'; a 'large number' of songs; and, mysteriously, 'Diverse *poësies* de Victor Hugo' (what were these, besides 'La Captive' and 'Sara la baigneuse'?). This list implies a re-evaluation intended to draw attention to the dramatic pieces, *Roméo* and

---

[26] *Traité*, 'The organ'.

Faust, which had recently made waves in Germany. If so, it did not work; when Berlioz was finally elected, in 1856, it was with a list in opus-number order.

EMPIRE AND RELIGION

In the 1850s Berlioz produced two major works, one of them his largest. But he may have tried to renounce composition, first around 1850, then again after the success of *L'Enfance du Christ*. Neither *L'Enfance* nor *Les Troyens* is known to contain much borrowed material, but we cannot be sure what Berlioz may have lifted from the missing sections of *La Nonne sanglante*, and some of *Les Francs-juges* is not accounted for. Part II of *L'Enfance*, *La Fuite en Egypte* (H.128), was originally an independent work, in turn developed from its centrepiece, the popular 'Adieu des Bergers' (Shepherds' Farewell).[27] Berlioz preceded it with one of his serenely melancholic fugues, purely instrumental, comparable to the opening of Part II of *La Damnation* or the fugue for 'orgue-mélodium', *Hymne pour l'élévation*. It is developed by antiphonal use of strings and high woodwind, the second theme being homophonic. The 'Farewell' is followed by a tenor solo narrating the story of the holy family's repose by a desert oasis (a popular subject with painters). This perfect miniature triptych was given to Richault for publication in 1852.

Composition of the rest of *L'Enfance* was intermingled with a massive cantata for double chorus and large orchestra; the line-up suggests tripling the woodwind, thirty-three brass players and 148 strings. *L'Impériale* (H.129) is the largest work Berlioz devoted to nationalistic, political, or quasi-religious themes. Most of his admirers would gladly exchange it, along with *Vox populi* and other choruses, for a few more songs of the calibre of *Les Nuits d'été*. Berlioz found a better use for imperial bombast within larger conceptions; *L'Impériale* may even have whetted his appetite to compose *Les Troyens*. It is assembled, developed, and coloured with utter professionalism. Whatever we may think of the glutinous sycophancy of the text, the characteristic move to the supertonic in the refrain 'Dieu qui protèges la France' (bars 108–9: Ex. 3.3) is glorious; but he had done this before, at the very climax of *Roméo* (finale, bars 441–2). And despite being written for the new Napoleon, the cantata is stylistically retrospective. The swinging theme with which it begins and ends comes at least in part from *Sardanapale*.[28] The first entry of female

[27] Its conception at a party, and its being passed off as the work of 'Pierre Ducré', is a well-known story; letter to Ella, *CG* iv. 156–9; *Memoirs*, Postscript.

[28] An albumleaf dated 5 Dec. 1853, which contains this theme, surfaced only after publication of *L'Impériale* in NBE 12b (Sotheby's Catalogue, 1 Dec. 1995, 53). It has no title, but since Berlioz had finished *L'Impériale* by July 1854 he surely wrote the albumleaf with the future use of the theme in mind, rather than the withdrawn cantata. Berlioz sometimes wrote music from an unfinished work in an albumleaf (e.g. from 'Faust, drame de concert en 3 actes': NBE 8b. 485). David Gilbert shows that the melody on the albumleaf fits the *Sardanapale* words better than those of *L'Impériale*, but this may only indicate the provisional nature of the latter some months before completion (NBE 6, p. xv).

voices brings a moment of mystery and a modulation from the chorus of shades (bars 97–8 in Ex. 3.3; compare *Lélio*, No. 2, bars 26–7). A later episode is strongly reminiscent of the aria in *Scène héroïque* (basses, bar 154; compare Ex. 1.1); the new words, 'O race révérée, race auguste et sacrée' could well have suggested the reminiscence of the apostrophe to Greece, 'Mère des héros'. Berlioz described *L'Impériale* as 'en style *énorme*' and drew attention, at the climax, to the superimposition of a traditional drum tattoo, 'Les Champs'.[29]

Ex. 3.3 *L'Impériale*, from bar 94

[29] Holoman, *Catalogue*, 511; NBE 12b, p. xvi.

Berlioz completed *L'Enfance du Christ* (H.130) in July 1854, mirroring its central triptych (*La Fuite*) in the design of his 'Trilogie sacrée'. In the first part a measured silence of seven bars separates the grotesque malevolence of the political world of Herod from the transfiguring peace of Bethlehem. *L'Enfance* is nowhere deficient in instrumental colour but, as in *Les Nuits d'été*, Berlioz achieves the subtlest effects and highest spirituality with the slenderest of means. At the close, the instruments fall silent for some of the loveliest unaccompanied choral writing of the nineteenth century. Despite its apparently modest intentions, the stylistic range of the trilogy is impressive. *L'Enfance* is not generically straightforward; although it is not intended to be staged, and is held within a narrative frame by an evangelist (narrator), the score is filled with stage directions. In Part I (*Le Songe d'Hérode*), the evangelist sings a prologue; then the first dramatic scene, 'A street in Jerusalem', is introduced by an extended overture. This is the 'Marche nocturne' (a Lesueur title), a spooky piece whose opening tread recalls a phrase in 'Le Ballet des ombres'. Its main theme is presented in the first of several fugal sections, but it is a sonata-form structure, with a homophonic second theme (like the overture to Part II), and is fully cadenced, despite the interruption by a short dialogue for two Roman soldiers. One of these intrudes on Herod's sombre meditation to introduce the grotesque soothsayers who interpret the king's dream of a usurping child, and propose the massacre of the innocents as remedy. The completely separate scene in Bethlehem is a duet followed by the angels' warning that the family should escape into Egypt. As with *Roméo*

et Juliette, the overtly dramatic mode now goes underground; Part II consists of three static tableaux, with no dramatic roles. The opening narration of Part III (*L'Arrivée à Saïs*) is based on a transformation of the overture to Part II, after which dramatic representation resurfaces, in the scene of racially motivated rejection of the Jewish family, and its eventual rescue by Ishmaelites in Saïs. The action freezes again as the two families listen to a concert (trio for two flutes and the otherwise unused harp). From this cosy scene Berlioz simulates the passing centuries by a series of isolated notes in a middle register, as devoid of rhythm as of sensationalism. The evangelist interprets the events of the action; the orchestra gradually falls silent as he begins a final meditation, joined by the chorus.

It is possible that some of this music existed within earlier projects, but it is difficult to see how much of it, being so firmly based on the composer's own text, could have been completed by the contrafactum process used for the Te Deum's 'Te ergo quæsumus'. Berlioz's practice elsewhere might suggest that the contrasting strain of the Part I chorus ('La beauté, la grâce, ni l'âge') could have been borrowed, whereas the opening idea, and the sequel based on the place-names of Israel, are too declamatory to have existed before. Berlioz's intimate style of sacred music had been formed in the Easter Hymn of *Huit scènes de Faust* and nurtured in the fugal 'Quaerens me' of the Requiem; *L'Enfance* is its most attractive manifestation. Contemporary critics suggested that he had changed his style; he pointed out that 'The subject naturally induced a naive and gentle kind of music . . . I would have written *L'Enfance du Christ* in the same style twenty years ago.'[30]

What may have led to this misunderstanding was the almost unchallenged success of the work with the public. The generic 'problems' of *L'Enfance*, unlike those of *Roméo* and *La Damnation*, are not obtrusive; their reconciliation is more a critical poser than one of public perception (see Chapter 10). *Romeo and Juliet* was a play; to make it into a symphony was decidedly odd. *Faust* was a drama, but *La Damnation* was not intended for the theatre, and thus was likewise peculiar; a number of comments, to Berlioz's annoyance, referred to *La Damnation* as a symphony.[31] The immediate appeal of *L'Enfance du Christ* to Berlioz's contemporaries may have resulted less from any perceived simplification of style as from a readiness to accept a free-wheeling series of illustrations and commentaries on subject-matter regularly treated in that way; the New Testament story has constantly been reinterpreted by art of all kinds.

LES TROYENS

At some point in the 1850s, perhaps inspired by the success of his oratorio, Berlioz came off the generic fence. Very minor works aside, the remainder of

---

[30] *Memoirs*, Postscript.

[31] See NBE 8b. 458. *Dictionnaire universel des contemporains* (1858) called *La Damnation* 'légende symphonique'; Berlioz vigorously crossed out 'symphonique'. See Grunfeld, ' "Not two flutes, you scoundrels!" ', 106.

his creative life was devoted to opera. He continued his work of revision; in 1855 *Lélio* was performed in Weimar, acquiring its new title and one of its most original details, the slow unfolding of the tonic chord with flat seventh, G♮, at the end of 'La Harpe éolienne', imitating natural harmonics, and never resolved.[32] There were other important alterations, not all precisely datable but of considerable rhetorical impact. The Goethe ballad is interrupted by a speech and a citation of the *idée fixe*; after *La Tempête*, a short monologue is added, in which Lélio relapses, haunted again by the *idée fixe* ('Encore, et pour toujours!'). Berlioz also changed the programme of *Symphonie fantastique*, making the whole symphony, not just the last two movements, an opium dream. While the revised *Lélio* still cannot claim to be tightly constructed, the dominating narrative emerges more clearly; yet it is odd that a document emphatically of 1831–2 is normally heard in a version prepared nearly a quarter-century on, after Harriet Smithson's death. In 1856, Berlioz published the orchestrations of *Les Nuits d'été*, each dedicated to a different singer in Weimar; again, he seemed to be setting his affairs in order before abandoning composition.

Thanks to the persuasion of Princess Wittgenstein, probably exerted at Weimar that year, he nevertheless embarked on his largest work, without a commission or real likelihood of performance. *Les Troyens* (H.133) was indeed never given complete in Berlioz's lifetime, and this wound was salted when Wagner was called to produce *Tannhäuser* at the Opéra in 1861, for Berlioz hoped against hope for performance at the only theatre fully equipped to do his work justice. Yet *Les Troyens* is far from typical of the Opéra repertoire. Superficially it has the attributes of 'Grand Opéra', the genre which, alongside contributions from Rossini, Auber, and Halévy, we associate most readily with Meyerbeer: five acts, a challenging plot intertwining the fates of the collective and the individual; expensive demands on staging, lavish orchestration.[33] The crowd scenes, rituals, and processions, the military emphasis of Acts I and III, the ballets in Acts I and IV, and the tragedy of love, desertion, and suicide which reaches its climax in Act V, even the historical thread that takes Aeneas away from Dido and suggests developments beyond the fall of the curtain, support this interpretation.[34] And while use of a recurring theme, the Trojan March, in Acts I, III (in the minor mode), and V, might suggest the composer of the *idée fixe*, it comes across as more architectural and symbolic (thus operatic) than symphonic.

[32] See Peter Bloom's sensitive discussion, 'Orpheus's Lyre Resurrected: A *Tableau musical* by Berlioz', *Musical Quarterly*, 61 (1975), 189–211. This beautiful effect was anticipated by Chopin's F major Prelude, Op. 28, where a flat seventh is left unresolved.

[33] Anselm Gerhard remarks that '"Grand Opera" is a suspect expression'. Gerhard, trans. Mary Whittall, *The Urbanization of Opera* (Chicago: University of Chicago Press, 1998), 1. See also David Charlton, 'On the Nature of "Grand Opera"', in Kemp, *Les Troyens*, 94–105.

[34] See Robinson, 'The Idea of History', *Opera and Ideas from Mozart to Strauss*, 103–54; and further discussion in Chapter 10.

But within this general framework, *Les Troyens* is generically unique. Whereas grand opera cultivated political subject-matter from historical times, often implying parallels with the present, dealt with religious and national differences, sometimes in a context of failed revolution (*La Muette de Portici*, *La Juive*, *Les Huguenots*, *Le Prophète*), and used librettos (frequently by Scribe) with some relationship to contemporary spoken theatre, *Les Troyens* is mythological and takes its lead from the great Latin epic. Perceived unsympathetically, it is simply out of tune with its time. Unconventional elements include the moving pantomime of Act I (No. 6); Berlioz's Andromache differs from Auber's mute heroine in that she is silent from choice, and appears purely for her symbolic significance, having no role in any intrigue—an integral ingredient of opera seria and grand opera of which *Les Troyens* is uniquely free.[35] The royal hunt is claimed for the French tradition of picturesque operatic *symphonie*, but its internal references include fugue; folk-song, in the melody at bar 30; a hunting fanfare (bar 45) almost vocal in style; and imitative music (rain, wind, thunder, and lightning) which is not decorative but essential to the development of the story, for the scene covers the consummation of the love of Dido and Aeneas in a cave. In most operatic traditions such an action would follow, rather than precede, a love duet, and the principals would sing.

The deepest blue water between *Les Troyens* and the successful tradition of grand opera is a consequence of the composer designing his own libretto. Scribe's librettos are not alone in their combination of fantastic improbability with the grand themes of history; such splendid operas as *Il trovatore* and *Don Carlos* similarly stretch credulity and historical fact for a dramatic end. *Les Troyens* falls outside the historical genre because, with the divine interventions and ghosts typical of epic, it makes no pretence at naturalism. *Robert le diable*, the first Meyerbeer grand opera, exploits the supernatural, as does *La Nonne sanglante*, but neither of these scenarios requires us to suspend disbelief in the gods of classical mythology, and just as its plot is devoid of intrigue, so the supernatural in *Les Troyens* has no hint of devilry. Berlioz's dramatic ancestry is in the eighteenth century, or even the seventeenth, and anticipates the neo-classical preoccupations of the twentieth.[36] It is not surprising, despite the imperial destiny of Aeneas, that interest on the part of the Opéra (and the Emperor) was tepid. *Les Troyens* looks back with love and nostalgia to days of learning and brooding in the fields around La Côte, on Virgil, heroism, love and fate, and on Berlioz's models, Gluck and Spontini. The nineteenth century has few greater paradoxes than that the two 'advanced' composers most daringly promoted in the 1850s by a third, Franz

---

[35] The point is made by Ian Kemp, 'Les Troyens as "grand opera"', Kemp, *Les Troyens*, 89–93. See also Cairns, *Servitude*, 601.

[36] See for instance the works discussed in Michael Burden (ed.), *A Woman Scorn'd: Responses to the Dido Myth* (London: Faber & Faber, 1998).

Liszt, should simultaneously have composed *Les Troyens* and *Tristan und Isolde*.

One short passage in Cassandra's second aria, and possibly a couple more allusions, exhausted the resources of *Sardanapale* (see Chapter 4), after which Berlioz apparently forgot to burn the remaining fragment of his cantata.[37] Holoman notes two passages in *Les Troyens* adumbrated in the *Scène héroïque*, but these are not strictly borrowings.[38] It is certainly understandable that, in what he regarded as his last work, Berlioz should have gathered together the stylistic and musical preoccupations of the previous thirty years; but unless *La Nonne* is a source, the music of *Les Troyens* is nearly all new. Berlioz describes how he disciplined himself to compose the libretto, then the music, only to go out of order and compose parts of Act IV before anything else. The fact of his being fully in control of the design and poetic substance, as in *L'Enfance*, will have contributed to the flow of fresh musical ideas. The analogy with Wagner as both poet and composer is obvious, but implies no rapport between them. Surveying the middle of the century and the development of post-romantic art, we cannot see Berlioz's works as significant pointers to the future. Even as the Lisztian critic Richard Pohl, in the 1850s, enrolled Berlioz among 'musicians of the future', the Frenchman was clearly no longer in the avant-garde. Nowadays that is happily no longer a cause for dismissing him; one can allow that a great artist over the age of 50, without loss of creative power, may gather himself for a supreme effort on the basis of retrospection, like J. S. Bach. Not everyone can be like Rameau, changing his career orientation to produce his first opera at 50; even in Berlioz's time, the exception, throwing lances into the future almost to his dying day, is Liszt. Wagner had written *Tristan* and most of *Der Ring* before he was 50; there are massively retrospective elements in *Die Meistersinger* and *Parsifal*.

In so far as Berlioz sought to enlarge his technical means, it was in an experimental spirit whose results he was surely wise, for the most part, to leave in his sketches. *L'Enfance* contains his principal search, in the wake of Lesueur and Beethoven, for expressive nuance through mixing major and minor with church modes. Sketching *Les Troyens*, Berlioz fiddled with harmonizing what he called 'new major and minor modes', somewhat like Verdi's later 'scala enigmatica'. A song of this period, 'Au bord d'une rivière' (H.132), is a strophe in pure Phrygian mode.[39] But Berlioz never completed the texture, nor did he publish it, although the opportunity came when his *Collection de 32 mélodies* (H.139) was assembled in 1863. In Act II of *Les Troyens* the lamenting women sing in the Locrian mode ('Puissante Cybèle', No. 14), but it continually resolves onto its second degree, and hence onto a major triad.

---

[37] In the MS of *Sardanapale* ideas used in *Roméo* are crossed out, but not those used in *L'Impériale* (facsimile, NBE 6. 234) or *Les Troyens*. On these borrowings, see Kemp, *Les Troyens*, 52–62; NBE 6. p. xv.

[38] Holoman, *Berlioz*, 38.

[39] On these scales see Holoman, *Creative Process*, 127–8; *MLB* 50–1.

L'Enfance and *Les Troyens* contain a few passages in irrational metres, and others were sketched, but Berlioz continued to vary his means of dramatic and musical presentation to suit particular circumstances, rather than embark on any systematic development of his musical language.

SWAN SONGS

Les Troyens was not after all Berlioz's final work. Performance of the Carthaginian acts at the well-meaning but inadequate Théâtre Lyrique in 1863 followed the successful première of *Béatrice et Bénédict* in Baden in 1862; a slightly enlarged version was given the following April. A world apart conceptually, these two operas are separated only by a couple of short choruses and two excellent arrangements, Martini's 'Plaisir d'amour' (a song Berlioz presumably knew from his youth) and Schubert's 'Erlkönig' (H.134, 136). The choruses are slight, although they deal with issues in a manner faintly echoing the heady days of Saint-Simonism, with which Berlioz was once peripherally involved.[40] The text of 'Hymne pour la consécration du nouveau tabernacle' (H.135, composed by 1859) may be by the medico-mystic J.-H. Vriès, who planned a new temple of universal peace. This strophic hymn begins promisingly, in swinging unison followed by a crunching suspension, but its unusually square phrasing hardly suffices for eight identical strophes, each starting in E minor and ending in G. No doubt it was intended for amateurs, whereas 'Le Temple universel' (H.137, composed before 1861) is freer in texture, phrasing, and form, and makes greater demands on the performers, including enharmonic modulation (bars 30–7). J.-F. Vaudin's text celebrates the unity of Western Europe. Were the practice of singing in large male choruses not more or less extinct outside the sports stadium, it would now be topical. Its musical qualities, in any case, deserve notice, and it completes a series of pieces of political character which forms a neglected strand in Berlioz's output.

Like *Otello*, *Béatrice et Bénédict* (H.138) begins with a victory over a Muslim enemy, but this plays a less important role even than in Verdi's opera, for the heroic qualities of Benedick are scarcely pertinent in a version of *Much Ado about Nothing* which omits the contretemps of Hero's wedding to Claudio and Benedick's defence of her honour. 'Le More est en fuite' makes a brilliant opening chorus, following Berlioz's most sparkling overture; but with curious redundancy, it is then repeated a semitone lower. Musical interest revives with the elegant Sicilienne, whose melody comes from Berlioz's first published work, 'Le Dépit de la bergère'; this is also the only identifiable borrowing in the score, and it is totally reconceived as a plaintive dance, initially in the minor mode, with a new bass, and seductively orchestrated.

This opening sequence serves to unbalance the generic expectations of *opéra comique*, and in view of the sequel, this is just as well. Berlioz had

---

[40] Ralph P. Locke, 'Berlioz et les Saint-Simoniens', *Revue de Musicologie*, 63 (1977), 55–77.

contemplated a work on *Much Ado about Nothing* for some thirty years, and its obvious destination would have been the Opéra-Comique; its eventual realization was aimed at the fashionable audience of Baden, where Berlioz had conducted regularly since 1856. Whereas *Les Troyens* shows a certain momentum, especially in the second and final acts, from the tableau-like method of construction by discrete musical numbers towards a more flexible continuity, and an extensive pattern of musical cross-reference, *Béatrice* is entirely a number opera, although a few numbers follow on without intervening dialogue. The only element of musical recall is the erection of a sign ('Enseigne', chorus, No. 14) to mock Benedick the married man: text and music are derived from the men's trio, No. 5. The listener is continuously teased by recollections of the overture, for as usual we hear first what was written last. The overture's pellucid form ingeniously integrates a multitude of ideas and matches Weber's greatest achievement of this kind, *Oberon*; as a comedy overture it ranks with Mozart's, and a few select contemporaries such as *The Bartered Bride*.[41]

Berlioz never ceased experimenting within the parameters defined by his diatonic language, and by his subject-matter. Worlds away from Wagner's music-drama, chromatic saturation, or Brahmsian thematicism, he was still original in his development of rhythm; the opera is filled with one-in-a-bar music in which the macrorhythms are particularly intricate.[42] The glum modal passage in No. 5 for Don Pedro's mockery of Benedick ('I shall see there ere I die look pale with love') is delectably funny. Berlioz's gift for comedy had already been exercised in *Benvenuto Cellini* and the sentries' duet in *Les Troyens*, a mixture of comedy with tragedy which the composer considered marked his Virgilian opera as Shakespearean. Satire, prominent in *Benvenuto* and *La Damnation*, surfaces in a more endearing form in Berlioz's creation of the Kappelmeister Somarone. Clearly intended to provide comic relief, even within a comedy, his buffoonery sets off a more serious strand, which is the development of love and tenderness, expressed for the gentle Hero in Berlioz's last great hit, the Duo-Nocturne which ends the first act, and expressed for the more independent-minded heroine, Beatrice, in a magnificent aria which immediately follows Somarone's drinking song at the opening of Act II. As a whole the opera, which works surprisingly well in production, is a piece of legerdemain in which Berlioz as librettist and composer manages to disguise a near-absence of dramatic impetus.

The run of *Les Troyens à Carthage* in 1863 produced enough income for Berlioz to retire from journalism, but he did not use this leisure to compose.

---

[41] I say *Oberon* rather than other Weber overtures, excellent as they are, because *Abu Hassan* does not relate to so many numbers in the opera; *Der Freischütz* proceeds, at the end, rather artificially to reintroduce the theme of Agathe's aria which also ends the opera; and the magnificent *Euryanthe* overture is interrupted by the ghost music which is not integrated into its surroundings the way everything is in the Berlioz, even the citation from the Duo-Nocturne.

[42] See *MLB* 136–7.

Health and happiness declined: he outlived his siblings, two wives, and his only child, dying on 8 March 1869, mercifully in time to avoid the Franco-Prussian war of 1870, the fall of empire, and the Paris Commune. A further attempt to impose order on his legacy is the *Collection de 32 mélodies* published during 1863 by Richault. Unlike earlier and smaller collections, this contained no previously unpublished work except an arrangement of *La Mort d'Ophélie*. Despite its title, which implies a collection of solo songs, this publication contains a rich mixture of solo and choral pieces including the earlier collections, *Les Nuits d'été*, *Irlande*, *Vox populi*, *Feuillets d'Album*, and *Fleurs des landes*, together with the vocal pieces of *Tristia*. In addition there are songs not previously collected—'La Captive', 'Le Chasseur danois', 'La Belle Isabeau'—and the choruses 'Sara la baigneuse', and 'Prière du matin'. A second edition (*33 Mélodies*) the following year added *Le cinq mai*. A final albumleaf of 1865, to nonsense words ('en langue et en musique kanaques', H.140) may have made a frivolous end to his career; or his last works may have been three religious choruses, one an arrangement of a keyboard work by Couperin (H.141 to 143). There is no positive evidence for dating the original pieces, which were eventually published as late as in 1885.[43] The melody of 'Veni Creator' is somewhat Mozartian; Hugh Macdonald suggests that it lacks 'any Berliozian signature'.[44] It is a nicely balanced piece of choral writing (the accompaniment is optional), and its old-fashioned cadences could be matched by some passages in the Te Deum (e.g. 'Dignare Domine', bars 105–7). 'Tantum ergo', with obbligato harmonium or organ accompaniment, still has a Berliozian flavour, including a contrapuntal, but not fugal, 'Amen' in the best of taste. Still, it is ironic that such a piece, sacred, and with keyboard accompaniment, may be his last composition.

[43] A date in 1860s is most likely since they were commissioned by Prosper Sain d'Arod, choir-master of St Sulpice from 1860 to 1867.

[44] Macdonald, *Berlioz*, 176.

Part II

Techniques and Meanings

4 Implications of a Musical Biography

INTERTEXTUALITY AND THE MUSICAL WORK

In Part I, discussing Berlioz's transference of musical material from one work to another, I avoided the usual practice of describing, for example, *Cléopâtre* in terms of *Lélio* and *Benvenuto Cellini*, instead deferring talk of recycling until it actually happened. Berlioz's self-borrowings do more than offer insight into his compositional workshop. As if to confirm Liszt's perception of the hero-artist as Berlioz's self-portrait, Cellini, running out of metal, sacrifices his earlier works by casting them into the mould from which springs his masterpiece, *Perseus*.[1] But, unlike Cellini's, Berlioz's destruction of early works actually *preserved* them, or at least their best ideas. He cannot be blamed for our present sense of confused textual identity resulting from the preservation of the superseded works. Berlioz's failure to demand the return of scores held by the Institute or by Ferrand, or to ensure the destruction of fragmentary manuscripts, need not be attributed to any intention to prolong their existence; he probably forgot them once their musical potential was exhausted. He could hardly predict the archaeological preoccupations of the twentieth century.

That said, we cannot ignore the situation as we have it. Tracing the migration of ideas raises questions of a peculiar form of intertextuality, something normally detected when an author's work shows a complex relationship (which may, but need not, include quotation) with work from a different author. Related fields of enquiry are influence and modelling, where a later text is designed against the background of an earlier; appropriation of ideas which are fully reworked (not to be confused with plagiarism); explicit allusion or quotation, when knowledge of the earlier text becomes indispensable to full understanding of the later; and 'anxiety of influence', when a text seems partly to result from a reading, or creative misreading, of an earlier text

---

[1] Liszt was in Italy at the time of the first performances, but wrote of the link between Perseus, Cellini, and Berlioz in 'The Perseus of Benvenuto Cellini' (*Gazette musicale*, 13 Jan. 1839), 14–15, repr. in *Lettres d'un bachelier ès musique*, trans. Charles Suttoni as *An Artist's Journey*, 152–7.

perceived by the later author to possess high status (hence the anxiety).[2] Familiar examples of the first of these categories include modelling by Beethoven upon Mozart, and Schubert and Brahms upon Beethoven; of the second, Mozart's adaptation of Handel in his Requiem; and of the third, Schumann's allusion to Beethoven in his piano fantasy, Op. 17.[3] Except in overt homage or in ironic mode, such overt intertextuality is mildly repugnant to romantic ideals of originality and independence; Berlioz was hard on plagiarism when he detected it in others, even Gluck.[4] Anxiety is a subtler matter, and possible instances in Berlioz will be discussed elsewhere in relation to particular compositions.

With Berlioz, most cross-over occurs within his own output. But it works differently from such instances as Verdi's appropriation of material for *Stiffelio* into *Rigoletto*, or Elgar's reorientation of an idea for *The Apostles* to *The Dream of Gerontius*, as these were sketches, never heard in public.[5] Berlioz's earlier works had mostly been performed; but had he prepared a 'complete edition' of his music, *Rob Roy*, *Scène héroïque*, the prize cantatas, and the fragmentary operas would have been excluded—whereas the lists of works prepared in 1842 and 1845 (see above) suggest that a Complete Edition from that time would have included *Huit scènes de Faust*. It is our contemporary culture of revival, our determination to publish, perform, and record works rejected by the composer, if necessary (as with *Sardanapale*) in fragmentary form, which creates complex identities for most of the works Berlioz considered canonical. The situation grows increasingly complex with the NBE's publication of works excluded from the OBE—the Mass, *Orphée*, *Sardanapale*, the incomplete operas—together with hitherto unpublished alternatives within, and versions of, textually complicated works (notably *Benvenuto Cellini*).

Not all recycled material was expected to lose its earlier identity. Berlioz hoped for an independent life for *La Tempête* following its performance within *Lélio*.[6] Orchestral versions of songs do not invalidate versions with piano accompaniment, some of which were republished in *33 Mélodies*, although in some cases substantial revisions (such as 'Adieu Bessy' and 'Les Champs') supersede the originals. But when a whole song or part of a larger work, even something well received in performance, was incorporated into a

---

[2] Harold Bloom, *The Anxiety of Influence: A Theory of Poetry* (Oxford: Oxford University Press, 1973).

[3] See Joseph Kerman, *The Beethoven String Quartets* (Oxford: Oxford University Press, 1967), 54–64, and Charles Rosen, *The Classical Style* (London: Faber, 1971), 455–8; Christoph Wolff, trans. Mary Whittall, *Mozart's Requiem* (Berkeley and Los Angeles: California University Press, 1994), 74–85; Nicholas Marston, *Schumann, Fantasy Op. 17* (Cambridge: Cambridge University Press, 1992), 35–7.

[4] *A travers chants*, 150–4. But Berlioz was aware of Gluck's extensive self-borrowings, and apparently regarded them as normal.

[5] Philip Gossett, 'New Sources for *Stiffelio*', *Cambridge Opera Journal*, 5 (1993), 222; Roger Parker, *Leonora's Last Act* (Princeton: Princeton University Press, 1997), 149–67; Jerrold N. Moore, *Edward Elgar* (Oxford: Oxford University Press, 1984), 294–5, 312–13.

[6] NBE 7, p. xii.

new conception, the original was effectively banished. *Cléopâtre*, which Berlioz never performed (although the circumstances of its rejection might have tempted him to do so), has acquired repertoire status through numerous performances and recordings. Many other works Berlioz brought to performance (the Mass, *Scène héroïque*, *Sardanapale*, *Rob Roy*), or planned to perform (*Orphée*), were also withdrawn.[7] The first three Prix de Rome cantatas and the Mass provided whole sections, even movements, in later works, while the Mass, *Les Francs-juges*, and *Sardanapale* became productive quarries into which he dug over a long time-span. Table 4.1 excludes shorter works which contributed a single idea to a larger work, such as 'Le Ballet des ombres'. All these superseded works are in the record catalogues at the time of writing.

A TYPOLOGY OF BORROWING
A simple type of borrowing arises when a smaller unit, in David Cairns's phrase, 'yielded to the gravitational pull' of a larger contemporary composition.[8] The two songs drawn into *Benvenuto Cellini* present no interpretative problem although one of them, the unpublished 'Chansonette', was elaborately developed. But the 'Marche des Gardes', absorbed intact by *Symphonie fantastique* as 'Marche au supplice', required an added programmatic coda involving the *idée fixe*, and many critics have heard this as too obviously tacked on to be musically satisfactory. Later the *Marche de Rákóczy* changed the scenario and proportions of *La Damnation* (see Chapter 3). Berlioz's stylistic development could accommodate borrowing from works written many years earlier; the problems are not of stylistic fitness, such as arise with certain well-known revisions (Wagner's *Tannhäuser*, Verdi's *Macbeth*) but of a possible clash of meaning. Revival of the earlier works raises such questions in relation to movements from *Cléopâtre* and *Orphée* taken into *Lélio*, and the second movement of *Symphonie funèbre*, taken over from *Les Francs-juges*. 'Te ergo quæsumus' in the Te Deum is in part a cosmetically altered version of the Agnus, and it is only with hindsight that one might suggest that the music fits the original text better. This was the only solo from the Mass to be recycled. In choral textures, refined underlay has less impact on musical rhetoric than in solo music, and most borrowings from choral sections of the Mass are readily adaptable to their new contexts. But when Berlioz pillaged his first major achievement, it was mainly to seek out its best tunes; powerful movements like the 'Credo' and 'Crucifixus', in which declamation of the text took priority over independent musical invention, were discarded.

To transfer a complete piece is less common than to adopt a distinctive melody for new treatment, as with the *idées fixes* in *Symphonie fantastique* and *Harold*, the main melody of 'Scène aux champs', and borrowings from *Sardanapale* in *Roméo*. As a complete work, *Rob Roy* is unusual in that it was

---

[7] None of these is in Colin Davis's huge Berlioz discography, although he has recorded *Cléopâtre* (twice) and *Herminie*.

[8] Cairns, *Making of an Artist*, 327/355.

TABLE 4.1 Borrowings: the principal sources

Source	Use in 1830–1	Use in 1832–9	Use in 1840s	Use in 1850s
1824 Mass	*Symphonie fantastique* III	1837 Requiem 1838 *Benvenuto*, Carnival	1844 *Le Carnaval romain* 1849 Te Deum	
1826 *Scène héroïque*	↑	↑	1840 *Symphonie funèbre*	
1826 *Les Francs-juges*	↑	1838 *Benvenuto*, Carnival	1840 *Symphonie funèbre* II	
1827 *Orphée*	*Lélio*, Nos. 4 and 5	↑		
1828 *Herminie*	'Chant sacré' (*Irlande*)	↑	*Chant sacré* Orchestrated	1855 *Lélio* revision of Nos.1 and 6
	Symphonie fantastique (idée fixe)			
1829 *Cléopâtre*	*La Tempête*, *Lélio* No. 2 ('Chœur d'ombres')	1838 *Benvenuto*, Act I duet		
1829 *Les Francs-juges*	*Symphonie fantastique* IV			
1830 *Sardanapale*	↑	1839 *Roméo* II	↑	1854 *L'Impériale* 1858 *Les Troyens*
1838 *Benvenuto*	↑	↑	*Rêverie et caprice*	

quickly cannibalized by something similar in genre, also named after a male protagonist. It is hard to hear the overture without recalling *Harold en Italie*. Its open-air freshness encourages us, despite Berlioz's opinion, to retain it as an occasional concert piece. Fortunately, the themes are differently treated. A simple melodic statement in the overture becomes the *idée fixe* of the symphony, subjected to development and combination with other themes in the first three movements; the borrowed 'piping' theme of the overture is presented in far more interesting variants within the first movement.[9] Other obviously Scottish elements are unique to the overture.

Rejected large works usually contribute to more than one source, raising potentially trickier problems of interpretation. Sometimes borrowed principal themes remain the principal material of a new movement (Mass: Kyrie to Requiem: Offertoire; 'Gratias' to *Symphonie Fantastique*: 'Scène aux champs'; *Sardanapale* to 'Grand fête chez Capulet' and *L'Impériale*). But quite often borrowed material surfaces only when a movement is well under way, as a secondary idea or the continuation of an otherwise new idea. The borrowed idea becomes integral to the later composition, making it hard to believe that the beginning and continuation were not simultaneously conceived. The phrase from *Cléopâtre* (Ex. 4.1*a*) has a different structural role in the *Benvenuto* duet, appearing later, as a melodic climax, whereas in the cantata the text compelled Berlioz to dissipate its impact. But in the cantata, this phrase is highlighted because it appears first within the orchestral ritornello, whereas in *Benvenuto* it is sung on its first appearance (it is not used in the overture).

In Cassandra's second aria (Ex. 4.1*b*) a separate phrase, following a startling change of key and a three-bar rest in the voice part, is derived from the second quatrain of the third *Sardanapale* aria, eliminating the rest (as the surviving cantata fragment is the reprise, we cannot be sure whether the first statement included this detail). Noticeable in this instance, though not in Ex. 4.1*a*, is the striking similarity of sentiment which brought this phrase back to Berlioz after more than twenty-five years.

The practice of contrafactum, the application of new words to existing music, is applied with varying degrees of success. In Ex. 4.1*a*, one might criticize the word-repetition and spinning out of 'Si loin de vous', although the repetition of 'Teresa', the name of the beloved, seems to arise naturally within the new material. When he took charge of librettos himself, Berlioz had less difficulty fitting words to existing melodies; he could even arrange for the new text to employ the same word in strategic places, as when he adapted Orpheus's aria for *Lélio* (Ex. 4.1*c*). Noticeable here, as in Ex. 4.1*a*, is the reduction of ornamentation from levels thought suitable to a prize cantata to those, presumably, that Berlioz liked.

---

[9] See Berger, *Phantastik als Konstruktion*, 182; *MLB* 198–9.

Ex. 4.1*a* Borrowings

gloi - re, J'ap - pa - rus tri - om - phante aux ri - ves du Cyd - nus!

per - dre l'es - poir.

Ex. 4.1*b*

Jadis la gloire et les plai - sirs

Et voir s'é - va - nou - ir

Faisaient la dou-ceur de ma vi - e;

Du bon-heur le plus pur la sé-dui-sante i - ma - ge!

Ex. 4.1*c*

ra - ni - me mes ac -

Re - po - se dans mes

cents, se - con - de mon dé - li - re;

bras, re - po - se cet - te tê - te char - man - te.

77

Good tunes raided from vocal works are more easily deployed in instrumental music. In *Herminie*, the underlay of what became the *Symphonie fantastique idée fixe* is already somewhat artificial, as if the melody might have had a still earlier origin. Melodies transferred to the orchestra often acquire instrumentally idiomatic ornamentation. An example within a single dramatic context is the adaptation of a melody in 3/4 from the Act I duet of *Benvenuto Cellini* within the opera overture; another is the languid melody when Cleopatra recalls words of the recitative within her final aria ('Du destin qui m'accable, est-ce moi de me plaindre?'), an idea which reappears with a good deal of ornamentation in *La Tempête*.[10] The most extended example of such generic reconstitution of an idea is *Rêverie et caprice*, based on a rejected aria from *Benvenuto*, where Berlioz turns an already instrumental passage from an orchestral ritornello into a piece of virtuosic preening (Ex. 4.2). The aria has an eight-bar orchestral ritornello and bar of 'till ready' accompaniment; Berlioz uses all of this, but brings in the solo violin dramatically, in the fourth bar. This event is triggered by the harmony: four bars in the eventual relative minor, an abrupt shift on the second quaver of the 6/8 bar, then the same melody in the major tonic (in *Rêverie et caprice* the music is transposed to F sharp minor and A major from the aria's B minor and D major). The solo violin enters on the unexpected second-beat chord, signals its virtuosity with a trill, then soars up an octave for the major-key version of the melody, which is further expanded by a double echo. Thus the soloist immediately contrasts the highest with the lowest register; only at the entry of the cantabile melody does it correspond in register to the aria. Alterations of this kind continue throughout. We need not, however, distinguish the aria as

---

[10] See *MLB* 147–8; Rushton, 'Genre in Berlioz', in Bloom (ed.), *The Cambridge Companion to Berlioz*, 44–5

Ex. 4.2 Teresa's aria (*Benvenuto Cellini*) adapted for *Rêverie et Caprice*

'penny plain' and *Rêverie et caprice* as 'twopence coloured', for the virtuosity of the violin solo substitutes for the colour originally provided by the words.

Transfer of vocal to instrumental music has led to speculation about possible texts for melodies known only from instrumental works, such as the *idée fixe* in *Harold* or the slow second theme of *Lear*. Known examples, however, should make us cautious of reconstructing hypothetical or lost vocal originals, for instance when melodies from *Sardanapale* reappear in *Roméo et Juliette*. The melody whose definitive form is the oboe solo in 'Roméo seul . . .' appears in the instrumental coda to *Sardanapale*, in the long note-values of 'Grande fête chez Capulet', but cut off after eight notes (Ex. 4.3); presumably it was originally in 3/4, and formed the first aria of the cantata, to which its text can be fitted. But my reconstruction differs from those of Ian Kemp and David Gilbert, both of whom sacrifice some element of the verse or the music, and take the length of the *Roméo* melody as a given.[11] Its development, however, is far from being convincingly vocal. Berlioz was certainly capable of maltreating the verse, but was unlikely, like Gilbert, to omit the name of the beloved Néhala, which he introduced during the 'incendie', without the librettist's prompting, as the king's dying cry. He was also unlikely to have

Ex. 4.3 *Sardanapale*, first aria (hypothetical reconstruction, based on *Roméo et Juliette*, No. 2)

[11] Sardanapalus's final cry of 'Néhala' is accented in accordance with French prosody, on the last syllable (see below); Kemp accents the second syllable ('*Romeo and Juliet* and *Roméo et Juliette*', in Bloom, *Studies*, 58). At 'mèle à vos accents', Gilbert (NBE 6, p. xv) preserves the *Roméo* melody by omitting 'Néhala' but adds a first-beat dotted rhythm in bar 6. He transposes the melody because other surviving settings of *Sardanapale* have the first aria in A, but this is hardly evidence for what Berlioz might have done.

risked a high tenor c♯″ (Gilbert), let alone e″ (Kemp) in a piece destined to be tried over at short notice before a jury. Otherwise my version is less square, and thus more characteristic. I have retained the key of *Roméo* (though not the one-flat key-signature), although Berlioz often transposed borrowed material; and I have added a decorous and symmetrical ending based on the cadence of the oboe solo, in order to set the whole stanza without a premature extension of range or ornamentation (such as might occur in a cadenza in the recapitulation). In 1830 Berlioz was anxious to behave.

The survival of Berlioz's rejected works, by making it hard to consider one work except in the light of another, questions the autonomy of the musical text, just as it reflects the pressures which led him to reposition musical ideas, and those which have led us to privilege parts of his output over others. The privileged repertoire is *Symphonie fantastique*, the overtures, and *Harold*, to which might be added *Les Nuits d'été* and the Requiem. Not all the rest of his output is neglected; but at the time of writing, *Symphonie fantastique* has been recorded over fifty times, and *Benvenuto* twice (and only once in French), as lopsided a piece of reception as one could hope to find. *Cléopâtre* is heard more often today than the works to which it contributed, except *Le Carnaval romain*. It would be easy to argue that when we hear the latter, we are not *obliged* to consider its relationship to *Benvenuto Cellini*, let alone the 1829 cantata. But this attitude appropriates the mental condition of Berlioz's contemporaries, who might have heard it as an overture rescued from an operatic failure, but who never knew *Cléopâtre*. Such contextual aloofness is only possible nowadays when all but one of the relevant works is destroyed or at least neglected.

A composer's works are always interdependent; recycling is only the visible surface of a phenomenon which runs, concealed, through any sustained *œuvre*. So do the self-borrowings mean no more than that Berlioz's works, like (say) Mahler's songs and symphonies, are 'cut from the same cloth'?[12] The hunt for unmistakable borrowings, classified in Hugh Macdonald's definitive 1969 article and further stimulated by rediscovery of the Mass, has led to the identification of several less obviously intertextual references, tenuous enough to be considered accidental but not necessarily insignificant. Among these is the foretaste of the 'Ballet des sylphes' in the Mass ('Christe eleison', Ex. 3.1), and of the 'Marche nocturne' of *L'Enfance* in 'Le Ballet des ombres'. David Gilbert relates *Sardanapale* to 'the accompanying figure to Dido's air "Chers Tyriens"' (Ex. 4.1*b*). Other minor similarities may well be fortuitous, including one in Dido's 'Adieu fière cité', a sufficiently unconventional piece to have involved, conceivably, conscious musical reference to Sardanapalus's regret that glory has been stolen in his sleep, as well as from Dido's own love duet with Aeneas.[13] In musical rhetoric, is it the gesture alone that counts? Or, for a possibly chance resemblance to signify anything, must more than one

[12] Philip Friedheim, review of *MLB* (see Preface, n. 1), 181.　　　[13] NBE 6, pp. xv, 203.

parameter of the putative original reappear in the copy? In Ex. 4.1*b* the arrangement of semiquavers on the third staff outlines a motive specific to Dido: Berlioz differentiated the two heroines of *Les Troyens* not by obvious 'personal motives' but through saturation of their utterances with different configurations.[14] The *Sardanapale* figure rises a fifth from the dominant, but the Dido figure rises a minor sixth from the tonic, and this difference is at least as potent for musical rhetoric as the similarity. Fortunately this figure is not included in Cassandra's aria, and there is thus no problematic overlap within *Les Troyens* itself.

HERMENEUTICS

Berlioz did not shift music around with the insouciance of Rossini's choice of an overture from the serious opera *Aureliano in Palmira* for *Il barbiere di Siviglia*, or his conversion of *Il viaggio a Reims* into *Le Comte Ory*—for both of which the term 'intertextuality' appears inadequate. With Berlioz, the new context often differs sufficiently from the old for questions of signification to be pertinent. In general, moreover, one can rule out self-quotation, in which the original signification is intended to contribute signification of its own. If intertextual considerations reveal something about the original signification of a passage, they may guide, if they may not entirely control, interpreta-tion—through a programme or not—of later works.

A borrowing that occurs at a rather obvious seam in the musical fabric is the 'Ballet des ombres' figure in the 'Queen Mab' Scherzo; its status as a fresh musical image is underlined by a new instrumental colour, antique cymbals, and has affected formal understanding—it is proposed as a 'second trio'—as well as programmatic interpretation of the movement. But if the programme is considered, the extra-musical contexts are strikingly similar. Mab is inter-fering with a young girl's dream and leading her back to the ghostly dance; when the tune is sung, in the first and third stanzas of 'Le Ballet des ombres' (from bar 72), the text is: 'Formez vos rangs, entrez en danse, Ombres, prenez-vous par la main', and 'Pourquoi nous craindre, enfants des hommes? Ce que vous êtes nous l'étions'. It would be easy to say that any borrowing can be jus-tified by results; where the music flows with more continuity than at this point in 'Queen Mab', nothing would seem to require explanation.[15] If we had not recovered the Mass, we would never guess that the second theme of the *Benvenuto* saltarello, and the motive which opens *Le Carnaval romain*, origi-nated as 'Laudamus te', nor that a song of thanksgiving ('Gratias agimus') had served as basis for a pastoral adagio ('Scène aux champs'). But we do have the Mass; and without interpretation, these borrowings might serve only to illustrate the essential meaninglessness of music. Such a thesis might have appealed to Hanslick, but not, surely, to Berlioz, despite his awareness of the

---

[14] Rushton, 'Dido's Monologue and Air', in Kemp, *Les Troyens*, 161–80.

[15] *Roméo*, 42–6. For a different view of the programme, see Kemp, '*Romeo and Juliet* and *Roméo et Juliette*', in Bloom, *Studies*, 68–9.

limitations of music as an articulate language.[16] Alban Ramaut claims that 'Berlioz's music anticipates the thinking of Hanslick . . . music is expressive in itself, not by imitation but by the formal and purely musical relationships which create its autonomy and specificity'; but his second clause does not entirely follow from the first.[17] Critical enquiry should not be hampered by a dogma which would eliminate hermeneutic specificity, and airbrush out comparative exploration of the various contexts in which a musical idea appears.

In the majority of instances, connections are easily made. The ghost music of Cleopatra, invoking her dead ancestors, to which Berlioz added a motto from *Romeo and Juliet*, masquerades in *Lélio* as a musical response to the ghost in *Hamlet*. As already noted, ideas taken from the Mass scarcely change their liturgical significance when they reappear in the Requiem and Te Deum. The Offertory 'Domine Jesu Christe', like 'Kyrie eleison', is a prayer for mercy; given this relationship, one might wonder why Berlioz troubled to reconfigure theme, texture, and metre. He was certainly under pressure of time and might have taken an easier course, for the Introit includes the words 'Kyrie eleison', and there were precedents for a fugue at this point, most obviously in Mozart's Requiem. Borrowings in *Benvenuto Cellini* may seem more remote from the liturgy. The motives from the Resurrexit near the end of the Carnival scene, shortly after one from the joyous finale to *Les Francs-juges*, transfer sacred music into secular, monumental into dramatic; but with Lesueur's guidance and example, Berlioz clearly aimed to dramatize parts of the Creed relating to death and judgement.

More interesting questions of interpretation arise when vocal music reappears in an instrumental work. Are we justified in using the rejected vocal original as a hermeneutic tool, to render orchestral music articulate? With the opening of *Symphonie fantastique*, the feelings evoked, depending on the version of the programme consulted, begin (1830A) 'Vague des passions [a term acknowledged as Chateaubriand's]; rêveries sans but'; (1830B) 'rêverie mélancolique'; (1855) 'ce malaise de l'âme, *ce vague des passions*, ces mélancolies'.[18] Compare the adolescent agony of the Florian lyric which Berlioz says inspired this melody: 'Je vais donc quitter pour jamais|Mon doux pays, ma douce amie,|Loin d'eux je vais traîner ma vie|Dans les pleurs et dans les regrets!' (see Ex. 7.1). The first movement deals with mixed emotions, including jealousy; the song suggests that the symphony's protagonist is thinking of his beloved from a metaphorical place of exile.

[16] 'De l'imitation musicale', *Revue et Gazette musicale*, 1 and 8 Jan. 1837, HC 225–6; translation in Cone, *Fantastic Symphony*, 36–46; see also *A travers chants*, 175–7, where Berlioz reproves Gluck for saying that an overture can indicate the *subject* of a drama: 'l'expression musicale ne saurait aller jusque-là'.

[17] 'la musique de Berlioz annonce la pensée d'Eduard Hanslick . . . la musique est en soi expressive non par imitation mais par des relations formelles purement musicales qui font son autonomie et sa spécificité', Ramaut, *Hector Berlioz, compositeur romantique français*, 42.

[18] (1830A), programme outlined in a letter to Ferrand, 16 Apr.; (1830B), printed programme distributed and later published with the score; (1855) programme as revised for performance with *Lélio* (NBE 13. 169–70).

The *idée fixe* itself first appears as an instrumental introduction to *Herminie*, in which form it is an unarticulated sign. When it intervenes in the first recitative, it falls between the words 'auteur de mes maux' and '(*avec tristesse*) Oui, Tancrède, à tes lois en amante asservie'; this developmental version may be compared with what follows the double-bar in the symphony's Allegro (Ex. 4.4*b*). Herminia is obsessed with Tancredi, whom she ought to hate. In the second aria she fears that he will die in battle: the text supplied ('Arrête! cher Tancrède, arrête . . . Frémis du péril où tu cours!') was read by Berlioz as 'Je frémis du péril . . .', transferring the trembling from Tancredi to Herminia herself.[19] This aria was not intended to be ternary, but Berlioz decided otherwise, and for the middle section he took a text intended for recitative ('J'exhale en vain vers lui ma plainte fugitive'); but he omitted 'vers lui', once again focusing on the emotions of the heroine. This melody is nearly identical to the exposition of the *idée fixe* (Ex. 4.4*a*). Finally the melody reappears in the last recitative (Ex. 1.2) before 'Tancrède va mourir . . .'. The common factor of these passages is not an image of Tancredi, but an image of Herminia's feeling for him; the melody embodies her complaint, but also the yearning that spurs her to action. In the *Symphonie fantastique* programme, Berlioz makes it clear that the *idée fixe* does not represent the beloved, but the protagonist's perception of her, because it invariably comes to his mind with her image. Its character ('passioné, mais noble et timide') is the character with which his imagination endows her ('comme celui qu'il prête à l'objet aimé'). The programme says almost nothing about the second movement, but in the 1855 version the beloved is present at the ball, no doubt dancing with someone else. Otherwise, and especially at the witches' sabbath, her presence is imaginary. The *idée fixe* represented longing for an absent beloved in *Herminie*, and in both works the adored person has paid no attention to a timid lover. If he had already invented the melody, and took it with him into the examination, we might guess that its original context was the Florian opera rather than the oratorio, or *Richard en Palestine*: but the trail is cold. This example may seem merely to demonstrate the appropriateness of a melody which few have felt to be inappropriate. The more curious derivation of 'Scène aux champs' from the 'Gratias' is considered in Chapter 9.

WORDS AND MUSIC

' "A faulty stress destroys the meaning and flavour of a word, and distorts the quality of a line of verse. Without a just appreciation of the stresses in a line of verse, you cannot sing it—for singing is first, last and all the time a form of human eloquence, speech raised to the highest degree." '[20] Word-setting is not only a matter of prosodic mechanics, but also of rhetoric—the mutual compatibility, or emotional fitness, of the two systems. Compatibility does

---

[19] NBE 6. 240.

[20] The fictional composer Giles Revelstoke, in Robertson Davies: *A Mixture of Frailties* (1958; Penguin edn., 157).

not imply identity: music is not so precise. When the boast of lustful Sardanapalus ('Le roi des rois impose l'esclavage') becomes the main theme of *L'Impériale* ('Du peuple entier les âmes triomphantes'), Berlioz was not subverting the new cantata's proclamation of a radiant new age; the texts share an element of defiance, of the preservation of something valued against an external threat. In 1855 nobody was in a position to 'read' *L'Impériale* through the long-forgotten prize cantata. The later text was clearly modelled on the earlier, following selection of the melody from Berlioz's store; the prosody matches exactly for three verses and although the fourth, in

Ex. 4.4*a* Statements of the *idée fixe*

L'Impériale, is an alexandrine, against ten syllables in *Sardanapale*, Berlioz readily adapted the music by note-repetition.[21]

In borrowings from *Cléopâtre* and *Sardanapale* (Ex. 4.1), the relevant characters are no less dramatically distinct. The ideas of happiness lost (Cleopatra) or at risk (Cellini) are further apart than the emotional archetype, lost or impossible happiness, which connects Sardanapalus to Cassandra; the musical differences in Ex. 4.1*a* are correspondingly more substantial than those in Ex. 4.1*b*, which in any case involves a subordinate phrase. In Ex. 4.1*c*, where a borrowed phrase is used as the principal material, the connection is the expression of love and dependence. Orpheus sings to his lute, 'seul bien

---

[21] *Sardanapale*: 'Le Roi des Rois impose l'esclavage;|Son front brillant ne l'acceptera pas.| Non, du soleil il restera l'image|Jusqu'à la nuit qu'apporte le trépas.' (The King of Kings imposes slavery; His radiant brow rejects it for himself. No, he will remain the image of the sun, Until the night which brings his death.); see NBE 6, p. xv. *L'Impériale*: 'Du peuple entier les âmes triom- phantes|Ont tressailli comme au cri du destin.|Quand des canons les voix retentissantes|Ont annoncé le jour qui vient de luire enfin.' (The triumphant spirit of a whole people Shuddered at the voice of destiny, When the resounding cannons Announced the day which comes to shine at last.) See also Ch. 3, n. 28.

Ex. 4.4*b* Comparison of developments of the *idée fixe*

qui me reste', while 'the imaginary voice [of Lélio]' fantasizes about a perfectly loving and dependent female, as ready for his caress as the lute for the
musician. The later version is transparently orchestrated. Divided strings play
the introduction, then leave the accompaniment to a group of woodwind and
the harp. The *Lélio* 'Chant [or Hymne] de bonheur', where the composer's
text is fitted to an existing melody, is superior in prosody. The original text is
as follows:

> Ô seul bien qui me reste! ô ma céleste lyre!
> Retentis dans ces bois, viens embellir mes vers,
> Ranime mes accents, seconde mon délire;
> Que tes brillants accords étonnent l'univers.

Berlioz ran through these long lines in measured music which might just have
passed for the recitative the examiners expected, closing with a strong cadence
in the mediant, C sharp minor (bar 82: the aria starts in bar 55). Confirming
that this is indeed an aria, he repeats the lines to similar music, with a rhyming
cadence in the dominant (bar 100). Only then does the melody first heard in
the orchestral introduction reappear. The first six bars are given in the dominant, then the whole melody is sung in the tonic, as in Ex. 4.1*c* (a similar exposition procedure appears in other places, for instance the *Benvenuto Cellini*
overture, from bar 35). The melody in full forms the climax and conclusion to
a freely organized aria, and simultaneously closes the first section of the

87

cantata by its reprise of the orchestral introduction. Even if it did not exist before Berlioz went *en loge* to compose his cantata, the melody may have been conceived instrumentally, and the word-setting juggles the middle lines of the quatrain to end the number half-way through the second line. The breakdown of the rehearsal pianist was surely not the only reason the judges took exception to *Orphée*.

Reicha's general rules of French prosody were not published until 1833; nevertheless they provide a reference point for understanding contemporary practice.[22] Reicha points out that where in other languages the prosody is *grammatical*, so that long syllables remain long regardless of the position of a word in a sentence, French prosody is 'logical' (*logique*), operating on the basis of syllable emphasis rather than poetic feet. The general rule, when a word is taken in isolation, is that the last syllable is long, unless it is a mute E, in which case the penultimate syllable is long. But in a line of verse, logical prosody allows length also to depend on *sense*. To obtain a shift of accent to what Reicha calls 'la syllabe logique', he says the line should flow more rapidly ('il faut glisser rapidement') than is implied by a stop-go policy of lengthening all final syllables; the goal is the 'logical syllable', which will be the emphasized syllable of the most important word. Hence, the general rule notwithstanding, the last syllable of some other words may be short. There may, of course, depending on sense, be more than one 'logical syllable' in a verse.

Using Reicha's methods on Ex. 4.1*c*, we obtain the following poetic emphasis (capitals implying 'logical syllables'): in *Orphée*, 'RaNIME mes accENTS, seCONDE mon déLIRE; VIENS, ô ma céleste LYRE, RetenTIS dans ces BOIS'. But Berlioz's setting clumsily lengthens MES and MON, on plain minims, whereas more significant syllables, while long, are subjected to ornamentation. The second half is better: the almost equal emphasis within 'céleste' is acceptable as we flow towards the object of Orpheus's apostrophe, the lyre. The long final syllable of 'retentis' is less strongly accented in pitch and metrical position than the first (earlier, bars 91–2, Berlioz used this musical motive for 'DANS ces BOIS' as well as 'retentis'). However, the lengthening of apparently insignificant words—'my', 'in', 'the'—is common in French word-setting and not necessarily offensive to French ears. In *Lélio*, Berlioz's own words to this melody begin: 'RePOSE DANS mes BRAS, rePOSE cette TÊte charMANte'. The removal of ornamentation has the effect of evening out the prosody and allowing the intelligent singer (nominally, within the mono-drama, the composer himself) to convey the importance of 'pose' and 'bras' relative to 'dans'; while in bar 5 'tête' replaces the insignificant 'mon'. The next line causes no problems; rests in the final line are expressive of 'éperdu', overcoming the marginal error of prosody, while the equal significance of the last two syllables is conveyed by the fermata on 'beaux'.

---

[22] Antoine Reicha , *L'Art du compositeur dramatique* (Paris, 1833), 2–5.

There were apparently different views as to whether Latin should obey the prosodic rules of French. Eugène Prévost, 1831 winner of the Prix de Rome, composed a *Messe solennelle* as his first *envoi* (1833); this treats Latin prosody as identical to French. Lesueur, and Berlioz in his Mass, treated Latin as a dead language whose syllables had lost their prosodic rights and could be treated either way. Thus in successive settings of 'propter magnam gloriam tuam' in the 'Gratias' (Ex. 4.5), Berlioz accents the first syllables in bars 33–6, but the final syllables of the same words in bars 46–9. The intrusion of rests upon certain words later in the extract suggests a musical idea preordained to follow a certain course, with the words fitted in willy-nilly. Another example of reaccentuation of the text occurs at the end of the Mass, when the soloists deliver the prayer for the king as 'DO-mi-NE, SAL-vum fac RE-gem' from bar 10, whereas the chorus from bar 33 prefers 'DO-mi-NE, sal-VUM fac RE-gem'. In his maturity, Berlioz decided against French prosody for Latin. In the 'Rex tremendae' of his Requiem, he first set the final plea as 'salVA me'; revision to 'SALva me' produces an eloquent syncopation.[23] In 'La course à l'abîme' (*La Damnation de Faust*), the peasant women's chant from rural Dauphiné ran 'SANC-ta Ma-ri-A, O-RA pro NO-bis'. Eventually he decided satire was misplaced at this critical point of Faust's fortunes, and 'corrected' it for publication to 'SANC-ta Ma-RI-a, O-ra pro NO-bis', quoting the original in his memoirs as 'the bad Latin prosody customary in France'.[24]

Prosody is most exposed in recitative, where there is no question of forcing the words into a pre-existent vocal line. Berlioz's first surviving solo recitative (Ex. 4.6) begins *Scène héroïque*. It is unremarkable; indeed it demonstrates how easily the conventional came to him. The declamation mainly conforms to Reicha's precept: chord changes should not be implied without confirmation from the accompaniment (as in bars 23 and 25 where the voice defines the harmony). But the first accidentals, which underline the shame of the Greeks ('de mépris et de honte'), are confined to the voice. More highly coloured recitatives in later works are foreshadowed by the addition of cymbals (the chains which bind the Greeks), the woodwind dissonance (bar 21), and horn crescendo (bar 22), the latter a traditional sign for a voice from beyond the grave: the voice joins with this, then drops an octave as a metaphor of the sleep of vengeance. These imaginative responses are coupled with string gestures which, except for their grammatical crudity (octave outer parts), are depressingly ordinary. It was probably shortly before writing this, however, that Berlioz first made use of choral recitative. In the opening C minor chorus of *Les Francs-juges*, the defiance of the people, demanding the return of the rightful ruler to end their oppression, changes to terror at the entry of the tyrant Olmerick (Ex. 4.7), accompanied by a solemn arpeggio in D flat minor, the first entry of the trombones since the overture, a tremolo, a death-like

---

[23] The original is in NBE 9. 170; *Memoirs*, ch. 43.
[24] 'la mauvaise prosodie Latine adoptée en France', *Memoirs*, ch. 43; NBE 8b. 455, 551.

Ex. 4.5 'Gratias' from *Messe solennelle*, from bar 29

Ex. 4.6 *Scène héroïque,* first recitative

Ex. 4.7 Choral recitative in *Les Francs-juges*

shudder in the strings, and a strikingly imaginative timpani part ('Timballes voilées').

Berlioz's response to words led him to mix genres, as when Herminia ends an aria with a fragment of recitative (and this in a cantata where he was trying to behave: Ex. 1.2). But in recitative he normally maintained stylistic contact with his Gluckian heritage, and with the expectations of his time, at least if his Prix de Rome rivals are a guide. His recitatives are among the most conventional aspects of his rhetoric, perhaps because he perceived them as the domain of words, rather than of an expressively liberated music. But if Berlioz's recitatives, from *Orphée* to *Béatrice et Bénédict*, are not his most loved passages, fine actors make a tremendous impact in the recitatives for Faust, Cassandra, Dido, and Aeneas; and many Berlioz recitatives, not least those he devised for *Der Freischütz*, contain, within the restrictions of the genre, musical invention of the highest calibre. As Faust decides to take poison (Ex. 4.8), Berlioz finds life in conventional orchestral gestures, thanks to a harmonic interest conspicuously absent in Ex. 4.5, to support the progressive intensification of the voice part. The interruption of the fortissimo B by a low, quiet, C♮ is the musical analogue of Faust's hesitation, further implied by the fermatas. There is no immediate and literal response to 'Je tremble', but when the shuddering figure does appear it is used four times, the first marking further harmonic reorientation (C to A flat), although the whole passage proves essentially to be a prolongation of C, ready for the F major of the Easter Hymn. A second progression by a major third (C sharp to A) exploits the identity of an augmented sixth (in C sharp) with a dominant seventh (in D), initiating a plainer progression: D minor, A minor (which nevertheless contradicts the implications of the voice's B♭), and E7, resolved backwards onto G♮. Faust's line contains many variants of the descending shapes characteristic of him throughout.[25] After two wider falling intervals comes a scale over a sixth (bar 43). The two forceful ascending semitones are succeeded by falling shapes. The first ('O coupe . . .') falls a fourth, then completes a sixth (D♭–F), with a curving shape reaching the sensuous ninth above the bass for 'désirs'; the second ('Viens, viens') disposes of the epithet 'noble cristal' with its falling fourth, but gains top F before another falling scale over a sixth. The final figures are conventional but effectively point the climax, gaining top G for the third time.

Spinning a vocal line upon an instrumental continuum is particularly characteristic of Faust, whose utterances grow in coherence as damnation closes in. The sketches of his 'Invocation to Nature' ('Nature immense') in Part IV show that it was composed from the declamation downwards, with harmonic changes resulting from the forceful vocal setting of Berlioz's own freshly minted words. But his first two solos are each built upon an orchestral fugato. In Part I (scene 1), he sings a kind of fugal answer, but leaves the whole melodic shape to the woodwind. His second couplet (bars 18–28) is draped over the accumulating orchestral texture; great gaps appear in defiance of grammatical sense (bracketed figures represent quavers' rest): 'Des cieux [7] la coupole infinie [10] Laisse pleuvoir [1] mille feux éclatants.' While the line rises finely and inspires the first orchestral climax, and each utterance is itself

Ex. 4.8 *La Damnation de Faust*, Part II

finely chiselled, as a discourse this lacks the cogency either of true recitative or aria. Later, the grammar is more cohesive, but partly because Faust adopts measured recitative, declaiming on repeated notes (bars 55–62) before attaining an independent lyricism (from bar 64), to cadence in a key remote from the tonic (B flat from D). In the opening of Part II, the instrumental fugue reaches its third entry before the singer enters, again partially doubling the instrumental line (Ex. 4.9). This time the grammatical fit is satisfactory, despite a couple of quaver rests which compel Faust to begin his phrase in the middle of an orchestral slur. Tiny details enhance his world-weary speech: the sterile curve of the first six notes (contrasting with the upward thrust of the fugue subject it essentially doubles), the echo of laughter when 'riantes' is set to a dotted melisma, the loss of contact with the fugue subject (third bar of Ex. 4.9), the sad back-fall onto C♯. In the sequel, a literal-minded composer might have insisted on sending the voice upwards to represent 'haughty mountains'; instead, Berlioz drops down to signify Faust's lack of pleasure at the sight. This section doubles the fugal entry more loosely still, at the octave.

Ex. 4.9 *La Damnation de Faust,* Part II (scene 4)

Faust's solos in Parts III and IV remain more declamatory than lyrical, even the 'Air de Faust'. The verbal underlay, especially in the invocation 'Nature immense', is a model of correct but vital prosody in which each line is directed towards Reicha's 'syllabe logique'.[26] But the same care for declamation is apparent in Mephistopheles' only new solo in the 1846 score, a good example of a lyrical declamation composed to words by Gandonnière.[27] 'Voici des roses' is the more remarkable in that its melodic substance is

[26] For detailed analyses, see *MLB* 234, 243.
[27] On the authorship of the libretto of *La Damnation de Faust*, see NBE 8b. 501, and Ch. 10.

adapted from music composed in 1829, the 'Chœur de gnomes et de sylphes', a revised version of which immediately follows in *La Damnation*. In the verse layout, which imitates that of the 1846 libretto, lines marked * end in a mute E, which when sung increases the number of syllables by one; thus an Alexandrine ending in mute E may require thirteen musical notes:

Voici des roses	4*	rhyme	A
De cette nuit écloses.	6*		A
Sur ce lit embaumé,	6		B
Ô mon Faust bien-aimé,	6		B
Repose!	2*		A
Dans un voluptueux sommeil,	8		C
Où glissera sur toi plus d'un baiser vermeil,	Alexandrine		C
Où des fleurs pour ta couche ouvriront leurs corolles,	Alexandrine*		D
Ton oreille entendra de divines paroles.	Alexandrine*		D
Écoute! les esprits de la terre et de l'air	Alexandrine		E
Commencent, pour ton rêve, un suave concert.	Alexandrine		E

The rhyming couplets are broken by the intervention of line 5; line 6 is longer and the last five verses are Alexandrines. Aspects of this growing poetic severity are reflected in the music, but Berlioz imposes his own methods of development (Ex. 4.10). The first four line-endings form a steady descent—A F♯ E D—before a kind of rebound to the opening pitch on 'repose!' The octave range d–d′ is not expanded until the last three verses, and then only by one step each way, a restraint unusual though not unique, and appropriate for an invocation to slumber. The initial two-bar units aim for the 'syllabes logiques', 'ro[ses]' and '[é-]clo[ses]', the mute endings set naturally to falling intervals, varied as an open fourth and a filled-in third. Starting the second unit on a strong beat (bar 3) does not preclude another relatively strong beat for the noun 'nuit'. The third and fourth units each present a noun ('lit . . . Faust') as a 'syllabe logique', on the strong beat. If the rising and expanded shape is more questionably used for the trivial words 'Sur' and 'Ô', any impropriety is overcome by the expressiveness of the sequence which, sincerely or not (this is after all Mephistopheles singing), seems to establish the principal affect of the aria; the syllable 'sur' is peculiarly suited, in French, to erotic invitation, while the 'Ô' covers, rhetorically, the possibly ironic musical rhyme—for Faust, surely, is not the demon's 'bien-aimé'.

In the next line Berlioz picks 'sleep' ('sommeil') rather than the qualifying adjective 'voluptueux'. This, the sixth two-bar unit, adds two new rhythmic characters: a full crotchet upbeat, and the dotted rhythm which adds innuendo to 'voluptueux'. The result is an extended line of verse fitted into another two-bar unit without expressive loss. The first Alexandrine (from bar 13) continues the sense of the previous eight-syllable line. It picks up the final G♯ and, by selecting 'toi' as the principal 'syllabe logique', allows the rhyme to complete an imperfect cadence in the dominant—again, sliding sweetly over 'baiser'; the bass, however, makes this a first inversion. Then the music opens

Ex. 4.10 'Voici des roses'

out into four-bar units for the remaining verses. 'Couche' is the main syllable. The expansion of 'leurs' may seem strange—what else but a flower has a corolla?—but it once again offers a *vocal* opportunity: ostensibly not a beautiful syllable, it conveys, like 'sur', a certain *volupté*. The voice must float the octave to the highest note, as of course the ironic 'divines' contains the main syllable. The line then becomes stuck on C♯, although the singer who takes the lower octave has another wonderful opportunity to seduce the listener, and, within the dramatic fiction, Faust. For Berlioz, judging from the following chorus and the featherweight 'Ballet de Sylphes', the spirits who matter are from the air. Having imparted this sinister but alluring message, the demon's voice resumes its lyricism by way of a sexy chromatic slide; and what is only his second clear sequence brings him to his cadence. Both the prosodic and emotionally sensitive aspects of the word-setting fully match what is usually remarked upon in this aria, and is no less marvellous: the brass accompaniment, with which the demon appropriates instrumental sonorities more usually associated with the Church. Examples of this kind, intended to demonstrate Berlioz's acute sensitivity to words, his own and others', in places where he really cared about the rhetorical effect, could be multiplied from *L'Enfance du Christ* and *Les Troyens*.

5 Techniques of Composition

MUSICAL LANGUAGE

In view of my frequent references to *The Musical Language of Berlioz* (*MLB*), and a return in this chapter to its main topic, the nuts and bolts of Berlioz's music, a summary of its contents and some updating of its conclusions may be useful; specific examples in these paragraphs add to those in *MLB*, to which page-references in parentheses refer. Discussion of Berlioz's education (Chapters 1 and 5) can be amplified by lessons from the *Messe solennelle* (see below and Chapter 8). Several chapters in *MLB* adopt the approach of earlier studies by tackling elements of technique and style separately.[1] Two chapters on pitch assume that Berlioz's development of the expressive and structural resources of rhythm, colour, and space did not entirely separate him from his contemporaries; melody, harmony, and counterpoint retain priority in defining the uniqueness of his music. In view of, for instance, *Les Nuits d'été*, 'it cannot even be said that Berlioz needed spatial and colouristic polyphony to compose his best music' (p. 25).[2] It may have surprised his contemporaries to learn that Berlioz's music is mainly consonant, but bold dissonances are used for expressive reasons (pp. 26–30); like Schubert he expanded tonality through 'mixture of major and minor . . . Neapolitan relationships, frequent use of mediants, often borrowed from the opposite mode' (pp. 30–7).[3] This point is epitomized by the 'pun' triads, or keys: one is major and one minor, they are rooted a semitone apart, but the third is the same (e.g. B flat major and B minor: D♮ is the third in both). This extreme key-relation may be connected to high emotions or the supernatural, as in the last recitative Berlioz composed for *Der Freischütz*, but also to comedy, as in the brilliant G major trio in *Béatrice et Bénédict*.

---

[1] Robert Collet, 'Berlioz: Various Angles of Approach to his Work' (1954); the 1956 special issue of *La Revue musicale*; Friedheim, 'Radical Harmonic Procedures in Berlioz' (1960), and 'Berlioz and Rhythm' (1976); Edward T. Cone, 'Inside the Saint's Head', in *Music: A View from Delft*; Primmer, *The Berlioz Style*.

[2] The argument here refers to Rudolf Bockholdt's thoughtful *Berlioz-Studien* (1979).

[3] The words of M. J. E. Brown on Schubert, *Grove's Dictionary of Music and Musicians*, 5th edn. (1954), vii. 560.

Other pitch characteristics include unexpected resolutions or contradiction of grammatical requirements (pp. 38–41), something Berlioz noted in Lesueur's offertory 'In media nocte'.[4] Berlioz followed his teacher in being attracted to chords on the mediant and submediant degrees (pp. 41–5), and to expressive oscillation (pp. 45–7), but Berlioz may owe his greater boldness to the example of Weber.[5] For instance, in *Der Freischütz*, the climax of Kaspar's aria twice pauses ('gelingt') on the mediant, F sharp minor, where a tonic chord is expected, an effect both strange and sinister. In *Les Troyens* Iopas's song modulates from E minor to A minor, beginning with the chord succession E minor–D minor, emphasizing the F♮ (bars 38–42); this might be modelled on Max's phrase in the Trio ('O! diese Sonne!'), No. 2 of *Der Freischütz*, from bar 93, although the Weber is in C major and the Berlioz in F. Berlioz commented that Lesueur's oscillation between D flat major and B flat minor chords evokes isolation, a *void* of feeling, which may be paralleled by his own use of this technique in situations of dramatic uncertainty. Berlioz's use of diatonic 'church' modes is more expressive than structural, since they co-habit with major or (usually) minor (pp. 47–50). His use of a whole-tone scale is probably accidental (pp. 50–1). In *MLB* I identified no interest in the octatonic mode of alternating tones and semitones. Allen Forte, tracing Debussy's octatonic antecedents, refers to passages in *Symphonie fantastique* and *La Damnation de Faust*, although special pleading is required for them to seem more than incipiently octatonic.[6] In Faust's 'Invocation à la nature', the first two bars take six pitches from an octatonic set; the third bar introduces one new pitch (A♭) foreign to that set, while bars 5–6 contain the equally foreign F♯ throughout. The weirdness of the F minor chord (bar 7) results not from one pitch (C♮) being foreign to a prevailing referential octatonic sonority, but from the remoteness of F minor from the tonality implied by the previous harmony, F sharp minor, which Forte rightly identifies as a local harmonic goal.[7] Such limited intersection with the octatonic mode does not constitute a compositional process. Romeo's first 'speech' (*Roméo*, 'Scène d'amour', from bar 144) is *nearly* octatonic, and the harmony is sufficiently odd for Berlioz to write 'there are no errors here, this chord is indeed C♯ minor'.[8] The only complete octatonic set I have discovered

---

[4] Berlioz, 'Troisième Messe solennelle de Lesueur', *Revue et Gazette Musicale* (10 June 1838) (HC 318). In the approach to the cadences resolution of the $^6_4$ chord on the dominant is twice delayed by a semitonal move in the bass. See Kohrs, '*La Veillée de David*. Hector Berlioz über Jean-François Le Seuer'.

[5] Mongrédien, *Le Sueur*, 999, includes within Lesueur's influence on Berlioz use of modality and the modal degrees III and VI.

[6] Allen Forte, 'Debussy and the Octatonic', *Music Analysis*, 10 (1991), 154–6 (note the extraordinary assertion that Berlioz composed *Symphonie fantastique* at the age of 18). Forte only finds a complete octatonic set by the dubious expedient of counting a chromatic scale (*Symphonie fantastique* V, bar 4) as an octatonic mode with passing notes.

[7] See *MLB* 243–53.

[8] NBE 18. 149. The scale in question (c♯ d♮ e♮ f♮ g♮ g♯ a♯ b♮) covers every note except the a♮ of bars 147 and 149, including the grace-note g♮; but the passage contains no a♯.

in Berlioz, which although not uncorrupted could explain an entire passage, occurs in the Te Deum ('Judex crederis'; see Ex. 8.8).

Comments in *MLB* on 'authenticity' in performance (pp. 89–91) are outdated thanks to period-instrument recordings of selected works from 1825 (*Messe solennelle*) to 1854 (*L'Enfance du Christ*). Instrumentation may, exceptionally, create formal patterns, rather than merely underlining them (pp. 73–82), while instrumental layering offers alternative readings of polyphony, when different orchestral families have a different bass (pp. 82–9): a precedent is in Beethoven's *Missa Solemnis*.[9] Berlioz's bass-lines have often been cited when critics and fellow composers question his aural competence. Some peculiarities arise from unusual deployment of common triads (pp. 92–8); chord inversion may be induced not by linear progression, but as pure colour (p. 97), a point challenged from a Schenkerian perspective in a searching review by James Ellis.[10] Berlioz also liked to use different harmonies (and basses) to repetitions of the same melody (pp. 98–107). This is part and parcel of his individual approach to counterpoint (pp. 108–26), and its formal application in fugue. Rhythmic aspects include occasional use of irrational metres and metrical combinations (128–32); superimposition of different tempi (slow melodies in fast movements, pp. 132–4); freedom in phrase lengths, illustrated by pieces with one beat to the bar (pp. 134–7); combined but independent rhythms; and rhythmic modulation (pp. 138–43). The rhythmic originality of Berlioz is also reflected in his melodies with their bold implied tonal progressions and tendency to asymmetrical phrasing (pp. 144–67). Melodic structures are the foundation of Berlioz's larger musical forms, and are viewed through the prism of Schenker's theories (pp. 169–80). Berlioz's individual sense of proportion and approach to tonal forms (pp. 181–201) are too often approached from the standpoint of 'what Stravinsky called "the great suspension-bridge forms of classical music"; [but] Berlioz's bridges are not less attractive for being supported by many piers'; his forms are like a painting on a curved surface: 'the eye is led from point to point. . . . it cannot comprehend the whole synoptically' (pp. 200–1). These points are summarized in chapters devoted to detailed analyses of the *Benvenuto Cellini* overture and of tonal and melodic integration in *La Damnation*, and characterization of the role of Faust. The following selective studies bring this picture up to date, rather than revising it substantially.

---

[9] Sanctus, bar 31. William Drabkin, *Beethoven: Missa Solemnis* (Cambridge: Cambridge University Press, 1991), 75. The dominant minor ninth appears over C♯ bass (organ, string basses, bassoons, third trombone, choral basses); but second horn and cellos sustain a low A, doubled by timpani, offering the residue of a root position.

[10] James Ellis, review of *MLB*, *Music Analysis*, 5 (1986), 270–80.

COMPOSITIONAL PROCESS[11]

The sketchbook of *c*.1832–6 (H.62), published too late for discussion in *MLB*, adds significantly to the documentation of Berlioz's working methods. Some of the ideas jotted down and never developed have no Berliozian character, resembling *aides-mémoire* rather than a complete notation of a thought.[12] A little phrase like Ex. 5.1*a* (fo. 1[r]) might eventually have found its way into a composition; it is notated above an empty bass staff. Ex. 5.1*b* (also fo. 1[r]) appears instrumental in character, but corrections (not transcribed) suggest musical notation by ear; I suspect this was music heard in the street which Berlioz found no use for. Folio 5[r] contains an Italian song of farewell, similarly corrected as from 'aural dictation'. Ex. 5.1*c* (fo. 1[v]), however, may be an original idea. The soughing syncopated shift between F♮ and an unresolved F♯ faintly adumbrates the slow melody of *Le Corsaire*; harmonization would surely require diminished sevenths. The later sketches for 'Je crois en vous'

Ex. 5.1 Three sketchbook notations

a.. fo. 1[r], crossed out; empty bass staff beneath

b. fo.1[r], corrections not included

c. fo. 1[v], beneath Hugo, 'Dans l'alcôve sombre'

[11] On sketches, see Holoman, 'Sketchbook'; id., 'Reconstructing a Berlioz Sketch', *Journal of the American Musicological Society*, 28 (1975), 125–30; id., 'Orchestral Material from the Library of the Société des Concerts', *19th-Century Music*, 7 (1983), 106–18; id., *Berlioz*, 213–27. See also Rushton, 'The Genesis of Berlioz's "La Damnation de Faust"'; Macdonald, *A Critical Edition of Berlioz's* Les Troyens; *MLB* 11–14.

[12] For a diplomatic transcription, see Holoman, 'Sketchbook', with which a facsimile was published. My debt to this work is not diminished by occasional differences in my transcriptions.

(H. 70) show that Berlioz did not always pick the right metre at his first attempt. Ex. 5.1*c* is written beneath Hugo's poem 'Dans l'alcôve sombre'; it would need some manipulation to fit words to music (the first four bars would need to be repeated), but the mood is appropriate; Holoman, however, is probably right to consider Ex. 5.1*c* to be of later date than the half-finished Hugo setting, which is in triple metre (fo. 2^r).[13]

The sketchbook also qualifies Berlioz's excuse, a month after 'Je crois en vous' appeared, for not setting another poem by Guérin: 'Things like this ought so to speak to be improvised, and when one does not get it right first time, it is better to give up, in my opinion.'[14] Certainly Berlioz did not follow this precept in 'Je crois en vous', for which the first two improvisations on paper led nowhere. Berlioz may have adjudged them too feeble to refine, but analysis suggests that he was working with definite objectives. Holoman deduces that the first version is the one entirely crossed out (Ex. 5.2*b*); my Ex. 5.2*a* is regarded by Holoman as the second sketch.[15] In favour of Holoman's order is that one sketch is in C and two sketches are in E. However, Berlioz might have determined the keys in the light of the tessitura; Ex. 5.2*b* would be far too high in E. The ink sketch (Ex. 5.2*a*, fo. 32^r) begins on the left-hand side of an opening in the sketchbook, with neater first clef and key-signature, as if Berlioz did not foresee any difficulty, and with near-complete underlay (in the transcriptions, editorial underlay is in brackets). The pencil sketch in C (Ex. 5.2*b*, fo. 31^v) was roughed out more quickly, and could be Berlioz's first response to unsatisfactory aspects of the (I suggest) earlier sketch. Knowing the poem better by this time, the composer only wrote in the catch-phrase at the end which gave the song its title.

The main reason for considering Ex. 5.2*a* to be the first sketch is its internal uncertainty. A blank staff intervenes before the roughly notated eleven bars in triple metre, the previous bar being incomplete. Unlike other versions, this setting begins with a rising interval, and the first idea is ornate in a neo-*galant* style. The chromatic bars 4–5 might be tricky to harmonize; the rest in bar 8 breaks up the sense ('N'ose . . . comprendre'); the rising scale is a fine vocal challenge, but the fall to the cadence (bar 18) begins with a weak sequence (if a falling shape for 'cieux', heavens, seems inappropriate, it was also Berlioz's final thought: Ex. 5.2*d*). This section ends, strangely, on the major supertonic, which might connect to the dominant of the first 3/4 bar. At the final cadence the alternatives, a moaning Neapolitan F♮ or an octave rise preparing an ornate downward sweep, seem barely compatible within a single conception.

---

[13] Holoman, 'Sketchbook', 284–5 and 288.

[14] 'Ces choses-là doivent être pour ainsi dire improvisées, et quand on ne réussit pas de prime abord, mon avis est qu'il faut y renoncer' (*CG* ii. 203).

[15] Sketchbook of 1832–6 (H.62), fos. 32^r to 30^v (the book was used upside down, hence the pages are read in reverse order); Holoman, 'Sketchbook', 307–9. Holoman also discusses these sketches in *Berlioz*, 218–20.

Ex. 5.2*a* First sketch for 'Je crois en vous'

Quand mon â - me ra - [vi - e N'ose en rê - vant de
vous] com - pren - dre le tré - pas, Ne me de-man-dez
pas [Si je crois dans les cieux et dans une au - tre vi - e!]
Je suis à vos ge-noux, Je pri - e, je
crois en vous,——— je crois, je crois, je crois en vous.

Ex. 5.2*b* ?Second (crossed out) sketch for 'Je crois en vous'

[Quand mon â - me ra - vi e N'ose—— en rê - vant de
vous com - pren - dre le tré - pas, Ne me de-man-dez pas—— Si je
[?#]
crois dans les cieux—— et dans une au - tre vi - e! Je suis à
vos ge - noux,—— Je pri - e je crois en
vous, je] crois—————— en—— vous.

Ex. 5.2c Third sketch for 'Je crois en vous'

Ex. 5.2d The three finished melodies

Ex. 5.2*b* opens by falling through a third from the tonic, has a central sequence, and approaches the climax with a rising sixth at 'Je prie', rather than the octave of Ex. 5.1*a*: these features, and triple metre, remain in the next sketch and the final version. The opening presents a prosodic poser, given that Berlioz carefully beamed the notes which appear slurred in my transcription.[16] Otherwise this melody is promising; characteristic features include the early drive to the mediant, E minor, the bold ascent which follows, the curling shape (bars 7–9), and a line-end on f♮ which would have to be harmonically incomplete.[17] Then a milder form of the exacerbated sequences of 'Élégie en prose' drives back to E minor (if F♯ is intended in bar 15). The third top G (bar 16) brings a transposed version of the opening; the recovery of the tonic, implicit in this chromatic descent to e″, is delayed by the curiously prolonged C♯. The implied supertonic of 'Je prie' is (I deduce) resolved by the first, chromatic setting of the title, developed from the end of Ex. 5.2*a*; tensions are released in the broader final phrase, to which Berlioz underlaid the last three words.

The third sketch (Ex. 5.2*c*, fo. 30ᵛ) *is* the eventual melody, with the falling third from the dominant, a new sequence, and the rising sixth (now major) for 'Je prie'. The rising scale over a sixth originates in Ex. 5.2*a*, but is now major, but Ex. 5.2*b* has a rising shape for the same words ('en rêvant de vous'). Bars 2 and 11 are adjusted to reach their final form (revisions appear in small notes in Ex. 5.2*c*; the dotted rhythm (tails up) in bar 5 appears to be the final reading but makes no sense of the underlay). A figure '3' overlies the first three bars, as if to point out the unusual phrase length, established in Ex. 5.1*b*. This page also includes sketched chords for the marked sequence, interlocking thirds and fifths ('Je suis à vos genoux'), probably made when Berlioz recognized this as the melody he wanted. Yet this sequence went through further melodic sketches (two on fo. 31ʳ) before Berlioz reverted to his simpler first thought. The chord sketch also sorts out details of underlay in which Ex. 5.2*c* differs from the final version. On paper now lost, Berlioz transposed the complete stanza to D flat and added the piano accompaniment. The refined expressive markings of the published version were further developed in the version for cor anglais in *Benvenuto Cellini*. One might read the publication in *Le Protée* as a sketch for the opera; in fact, however, there are three 'finished' versions, the romance, the instrumental 'aria', and the overture, the last two differently harmonized.[18] Indeed, the melody itself is changed when the three-bar phrase is expanded to four. In the overture, eloquent ornamental detail binds the second and third phrases, and develops the third by applying syncopation (Ex. 5.2*d*).

[16] Ex. 5.2*b* mis-accentuates 'âme'; alternatively, by slurring two notes in bar 1, 'âme' would appear in bar 2 without its mute E, for which the other sketches provide; the slurs in my transcription correspond to Berlioz's beaming, implying three syllables in bar 1 and two in bar 4.

[17] Walter Schenkman finds this kind of shape archetypal for Berlioz: 'Fixed Ideas and Recurring Patterns in Berlioz's Melody', *Music Review*, 40 (1979), 25–48.

[18] See *MLB* 103–7.

Another recently surfaced sketch, for 'Marche pour la présentation des drapeaux' (Te Deum), also shows uncertainties in the initial conception, although the main melodic ideas are in place from the start.[19] Berlioz tried various combinations of a rhythmically defined scalar motive with the grand descending theme taken from the first movement ('Te Deum laudamus'), and worked out the martial version of the fugue subject from the same movement. Nevertheless, a major rhetorical reconfiguration took place during the sketching process. The main theme in the first sketch is extended over forty bars, but the second sketch shifts it metrically by half a bar. As a result, it loses the emphatic sense of a first beat; in the introduction, which is not sketched, Berlioz took care to preserve this ambiguity by avoiding the establishment of a clear metric pattern. He seems to have made this metrical adjustment when working on staves 14–15 of this sketch, ironically on a section which he eventually cut. As much as 'Je crois en vous', this much later sketch shows Berlioz arriving with difficulty at an apparently simple inspiration. One wonders what the sketches can have been like for the 'Judex crederis'; but the care and hard work Berlioz devoted to a simple Romance and an occasional March, the first of which he cannibalized in an opera, and the second of which he was prepared to displace within the Te Deum, are eloquent testimony to his professionalism and, dare it be said, of his taste.

THE *MESSE SOLENNELLE* AND COUNTERPOINT

Berlioz began formal instruction in counterpoint only after his dismal failure in the preliminary round of the 1826 Prix de Rome. He had previously studied Catel's harmony treatise, which aimed to teach harmony by means of counterpoint; however, it does not tell you how to write a fugue (Reicha's and Cherubini's published counterpoint treatises post-date the Mass).[20] When Berlioz first visited Lesueur, he produced a three-part canon, and soon afterwards published 'Canon libre à la quinte': these (H.13, 14) may be the same piece, since 'Canon libre' is in three essential parts—two in free canon above a supporting bass, with piano right hand filling—and Berlioz could have misremembered the details in his memoirs. It is usually assumed, from what Berlioz said, that Gerono only taught Berlioz harmony according to post-Rameau principles.[21] It remains possible that Berlioz learned the rudiments of strict counterpoint with Gerono but did not report the fact. However, Cherubini's 1823 comments on composition pupils include: 'Gerono, 25 and a half, needs to work at counterpoint, to learn how to compose better.'[22] Berlioz accepted Reicha's teaching once the reasons for the rules were explained; an inexperienced student-teacher like Gerono might have failed to identify a problem, never mind resolve it. The 1826 fugue shows that Berlioz

---

[19] The sketches are in a manuscript vocal score, F-Pc- ms 17998. Holoman, 'The Present State of Berlioz Research' (1975), 40; id., *Creative Process*, 159–60; id., *Berlioz*, 219–25.

[20] Catel's treatise is discussed in *MLB* 52–5. [21] *Memoirs*, ch. 6.

[22] Holoman, 'Conservatoire', 292.

knew what such an exercise should *look* like; but his work is incompetent according to the prescriptions of contrapuntal practice as taught, approximately, from Zarlino through Fux and Albrechtsberger, to Reicha and Cherubini.[23] Worse, it would sound poor; it frankly looks as if he had mugged up the subject the night before.

   This cynical conclusion cannot survive knowledge of the *Messe solennelle*, from which it is clear that Berlioz already knew enough about counterpoint as early as 1824 to write two fugues, both with invertible countersubjects. In January 1827, Cherubini noted that 'he has only just enrolled . . . we must wait', and a year later that his fugue was 'passable'; by that time Berlioz had indeed passed the counterpoint and fugue exercise for the Prix de Rome (July 1827), only to bring disgrace upon himself, in the eyes of the jurors and his family, with the precocious *Orphée*. Cherubini, informed that Berlioz admired Beethoven's great Mass in D except for the fugue which ends the Gloria ('In Gloria Dei Patris, Amen'), riposted 'because the fugue does not like him'.[24] Thanks to this feeble *mot* Berlioz is still sometimes believed to have been hostile to fugue; for Jean Mongrédien, 'Berlioz's diatribes about fugue follow the example of Lesueur, who on this particular issue incontestably bequeathed Berlioz his ideas.'[25] In fact, fugato was one Berlioz's favourite textures; he objected only to rule-based composition and routine. In this respect he did indeed follow Lesueur, who, unlike Reicha, avoided placing fugues in such conventional positions as the end of the Gloria and Credo.[26] Berlioz's later discrimination in this respect is nicely anticipated by the two contrasting fugues in his Mass. The 'Quoniam' is fugal throughout (Ex. 5.3 gives the exposition). It was presumably after the second (1827) performance that Berlioz wrote in the autograph: 'I must re-write this abominable fugue. We should yield nothing to convention when it is absurd. I shall strive to treat this finale [*sic*] *en style foudroyant*. I swear that I shall never write another fugue, unless the situation in an opera requires something like a chorus of drunkards or a battle of incarnate demons.'[27] The reasons for this denunciation may not have been purely aesthetic. There was no convention of setting 'Quoniam tu solus' fugally, but Berlioz uses fugue to get through the rest of the Gloria text, including 'Cum sancto spiritu', words often treated fugally, which here function as a reprise of the exposition (bar 56). Berlioz's

---

[23] The fugue is in NBE 6. 3–5; on its defects, see *MLB* 117–19.

[24] 'Parce que *la fugue* ne l'aime pas.' Obituary for Cherubini, 1843 (Condé, 143). Holoman identifies another source; *Berlioz*, 42.

[25] 'les diatribes de Berlioz à l'endroit de la fugue; à l'exemple de son maître Le Sueur, qui sur ce point précis lui a incontestablement légué ses idées.' *La Musique en France des Lumières au Romantisme*, 172; see also Mongrédien, *Le Sueur*, 912, where Berlioz is 'comme son maître, un contempteur de cette forme musicale'.

[26] *Memoirs*, ch. 13.

[27] 'Il faut refaire cet exécrable fugue. N'accordons rien à l'usage quand il est absurde. Je tâcherai de traiter ce final [*sic*] en style foudroyant. Je jure que jamais je ne ferai du fugue à moins que dans un opéra la situation ne demande un morceau de ce genre, un choeur de gens ivres par exemple, ou une bataille de diables incarnés.' NBE 23, p. xv.

Ex. 5.3 *Messe solennelle, 'Quoniam'* (exposition)

Bracketed: false relations

term 'refaire' is ambiguous (revise or replace?), but he probably meant to substitute something homophonic in the 'style foudroyant' which the 'Quoniam', if performed fast enough, already possesses. So perhaps, in 1827, he rejected the 'Quoniam' mainly because he perceived it as technically unworthy.

The first bars introduce three-part invertible counterpoint. By bringing in all three parts together, in Italian style, and resting his fourth voice during the answer and later entries, Berlioz deprives the exposition of textural growth. The invertibility is almost acceptable, although there are indirect consecutive fifths when idea B is in the bass; idea C, consisting of two notes, is melodically inept. And fugue, even in an academic style, needs to work harmonically. Berlioz's false relations cut like a blunt knife: the bass, in bars 3–4, covers a diminished octave; worse, the bass d' almost touches the middle-voice d♯'; and the implied chord succession from bar 4 to 5 is a dominant seventh on E moving not to A, but to B (with no seventh). The equivalent progression works charmingly in the 'O salutaris hostia', but in a homophonic context, without direct false relations; a D major chord returns to C, so the f♯–g'' in the melody has the scent of the Lydian mode (Berlioz also uses the supertonic major chord at cadence points, but with a dominant before the tonic, at the end of the 'Quoniam' and bar 16 of 'O salutaris'). The poor effect in the 'Quoniam' results from the relation of the progression to the polyphonic context, at a speed too fast to assimilate. The fugue continues with a brief episode which at least has the benefit of colouristic variety (a touch of minor). In the stretto (bar 22) an air of desperation pervades the additional voices, as Berlioz struggles to avoid six-four chords (e.g. bar 23): in the fugal voices, too many downbeats attack only two separate pitches, the full chords being supplied by violent wind punctuation, while the harmony leaps grotesquely between tonic and dominant. A sequence of $\frac{6}{4}$ chords animated by syncopation (from bar 28) works better. The reprise ('Cum sancto spiritu') sinks with relief onto a tonic pedal (bar 65) which at least controls the next factitious stretto.

On the other hand, the fugal Kyrie, which eventually formed the basis of one of Berlioz's greatest movements, the Offertoire of the *Grande messe des morts*, is one of the most successful in the Mass. It helps that Berlioz does not write fugally throughout. The design of this fugue is directly indebted to Lesueur's *Oratorio de Noël*, but the departures from his model are a telling indication of what he could already achieve, and would achieve in the future.[28]

Unlike the 'Quoniam', the Kyrie has a texturally progressive exposition (Table 5.1; Ex. 5.4 shows the full four-voiced combination). The fourteen-bar string prelude gives the main theme (A) and one counterpoint (B). The subject remains within the tonic, ending b♭–a', ready for the vocal entry in D minor. With the vocal exposition, however, the basses end the subject b♮–a (unlike the tailles, Ex. 5.4), ready for the answer in the dominant. The vocal entry has a new countersubject (C, dessus), which introduces an angular false relation; no teacher would fail to blue-pencil the lightly filled-in augmented octave (e″–e♭') and the whole-tone segment. The answer brings yet another countersubject (D, hautes-contre), and the third vocal entry (bar 40) restores the original viola counterpoint (A) to make the four-part texture. With prophetic ambiguity, Berlioz doubles the tailles with violas and double-basses, so that A forms the acoustic bass. All the counterpoint is again roughly invertible (but D never appears in the bass). When composing the Offertoire, Berlioz still rejected this counterpoint, while retaining the subject. Compared to the 'Quoniam', its expression is appropriate, and it is technically less dubious, for chromatic angularities can be assimilated at this tempo. Nevertheless, the texture hardly ever uses four simultaneous voices. The rests might reasonably be condemned in an untexted fugue like the 1826 exercise, but they contribute to the strange melancholy of the Kyrie, especially when counterpoint (D) soars above the texture on violins, an octave above the sopranos.

Although there was no question of academic assessment of the Mass, Berlioz apparently wanted to show his capabilities in counterpoint as in other aspects of his art. From one point of view, both fugues are immature and

---

[28] *Oratorio de Noël*, the first piece in Lesueur's collected works (1826), is a short Mass consisting of Kyrie, Gloria, and seasonal motets. See Rushton, 'Ecstasy of emulation: Berlioz's *Messe solennelle* and his debt to Lesueur'.

TABLE 5.1 Invertible counterpoint in the Kyrie

Bar nos.	1	14	27	40
Instruments	Vns. A	Dessus C	Dessus A	Dessus D
and voices	Vas. B	Basses A	H.-c. D	H.-c. C
			Basses C	Tailles A (includes lowest pitches)
				Basses B
Key	Tonic	Tonic	Dominant	Tonic

Ex. 5.4 *Messe solennelle*, Kyrie from bar 40

incompetent; but in context the Kyrie strikes gold. After sequential homophony and a nearly pastoral 'Christe eleison', Berlioz reaches a reprise, accelerates, engages in a crescendo, amplifies the instrumentation with timpani, and breaks through into glorious D major. Contrapuntal duties are forgotten in a sublime surge which predicts, if anything, the symphonic Berlioz. Berlioz's major works are filled with fugal elements; not only sacred works, but some of the most expressive passages in *Roméo et Juliette* and *La Damnation de Faust*. But he did not wish to be restricted by the rules he learned from Reicha, later embodied in Cherubini's treatise, nor by the convention that certain texts, such as 'Amen', or 'Quam olim Abrahae' in the Requiem Offertoire, should be treated fugally (see Chapter 8). Berlioz pointedly ended the fugal Offertoire with a homophonic setting of 'Quam olim Abrahae', but he wrote, and repeated, a 'Hosanna' fugue in the Requiem, a rare concession to Cherubini's aesthetics.

HARMONY REVISITED

Analysing music by an inexperienced composer with little early training, it is easy to take for granted that certain combinations and progressions are 'better' than others; that consecutive fifths and octaves should be avoided, and so forth. Behind my strictures on 'Le Dépit de la bergère' in *MLB*, there lies a long tradition of centuries of composition teaching through the study of counterpoint, harmony, and ear-training.[29] The differences within this pedagogical tradition are legion, but they share the view that, at least in European tonal music, there are criteria of right and wrong. It is possible that no such consensus exists today. With Berlioz, questions of competence could be associated with his clear rejection of the integral relationship of melody and harmony, exemplified by his habit, mentioned above, of presenting a melody with alternative basses.

It will never be known whether the young Berlioz presented the same melody with different harmony from oversight, fantasy, or some aesthetic principle: in his mature works the second option seems probable. To reharmonize a melody in this way, often without intensifying its expression and apparently for love of variety, runs counter to the Rameau theory that melody is the surface of the harmony and thus integrally related to it. Reharmonization was part of Berlioz's method before he was inducted into Rameau's principles by Gerono, and there are examples in his first publications under the banner 'Pupil of Lesueur'. When he set a poem to music, he

---

[29] See *MLB* 60–3. These pedagogical traditions still exist, and were very much alive in Cambridge in the 1960s where I was 'trained'; the continuity from the way Berlioz's generation was taught is clear. It would be wrong to associate this tradition with the organ loft. Following revered theorists such as Zarlino and Fux in counterpoint, Rameau in harmony, strict part-writing and training in chord progression formed the basis of Mozart's teaching of Attwood, and the pedagogy of Cherubini and Reicha; it was a standard aspect of conservatoire training for opera composers in Italy and France, and entered the 20th century, despite their numerous local differences, with Riemann, Tovey, Schoenberg, and Schenker.

probably added the instrumental introduction later. In four of the early romances the introduction is based on the opening of the vocal line, and in every case, the accompanying bass and harmony are different (see Ex. 5.5). Mature examples include Lawrence's E flat aria in *Roméo* ('Pauvres enfants'), and in *L'Enfance* the introductory melody of Herod's aria, repeated at the end with a different bass-line. But Berlioz did not relinquish this practice in the period of his greatest devotion to Lesueur; it occurs in the second bar of the orchestral and vocal statements of the melody of the Agnus in the Mass, and in *Orphée* the instrumental epilogue reharmonizes the melody from the aria (both reharmonizations were carried over when the material was recycled in the Te Deum and *Lélio*). Berlioz turned reharmonization into a principle with the *idée fixe* in the *Symphonie fantastique*; but already in *Herminie* this melody received some harmonic alteration in its two appearances.[30]

Ex. 5.5 'Le Maure [L'Arabe] jaloux'

[30] See *MLB* 99–102.

With the rediscovery of the Mass, we can no longer say that 'Berlioz probably learned most from Lesueur. . . in a period (1823–6) from which nearly all his compositions are lost'.[31] A further look at the early romances may help assess the impact on Berlioz of the teaching of Gerono and Lesueur. Unfortunately the order of publication is not a sure guide to the order of composition. After 'Le Dépit de la bergère', two songs were published by Mme Cuchet ('Pleure, pauvre Colette' and 'Le Maure jaloux') before Berlioz claimed to be Lesueur's pupil. The former (H.11) is a clumsy piece, with a fidgety bass-line. Two songs with texts by Florian, 'Le Maure jaloux' (H.9) and

[31] *MLB* 56.

'Amitié, reprends ton empire' (H.10), were composed at La Côte, where auto-graphs survive, the former entitled 'L'Arabe jaloux' and the latter in A major rather than F.[32] Both were revised prior to publication, but 'Amitié' was pub-lished later, in 1823, by the self-proclaimed 'élève de M. Lesueur'. We cannot be sure whether the revisions were affected by his studies with Gerono or even Lesueur; internal and external evidence coincide with 'Le Maure' to suggest that the revisions were made on Berlioz's own initiative.

Berlioz said, in effect, that Gerono taught him good Rameau manners, conveying to the more mature, and perhaps by now more patient, genius what he had previously failed to grasp from d'Alembert's digest of Rameau, and persuading him to accept them, if only out of diplomacy. Given that all rea-sonable pedagogy would include a grey area between right and wrong, in which criteria of correctness might vary according to context, the individual teacher may take a different decision from the model. Rameau regarded the tonic six-four as consonant in principle: 'The first three chords [C major in root position ($\frac{5}{3}$), first inversion ($\frac{6}{3}$), and second inversion ($\frac{6}{4}$)] are all consid-ered to be consonant since they are products of the tonic triad.'[33] Other the-orists, basing their principles on counterpoint, regard the $\frac{6}{4}$ as dissonant. A fourth above the bass, even if it does not always require preparation to form a suspension, must be resolved downward by step, as in the normal cadential $\frac{6}{4}$. From this point of view, the $\frac{6}{4}$ chords in the early manuscripts of 'L'Arabe jaloux' and 'Amitié, reprends ton empire', perhaps legitimized by an unguided reading of Rameau, appear undiscriminating; some remain in the published form of 'Le Maure jaloux' (Ex. 5.5), while the revised 'Amitié' gets rid of them wholesale (Ex. 5.6). Contrary to Rameau's prescription, many of the chords are incomplete, lacking a fifth. And contrary to Berlioz's later practice, most of the dominant chords include the seventh, not only unpre-pared, but sometimes unresolved.

In Ex. 5.5, the unprepared seventh of the MS version (bar 4) is replaced by contrary motion. That some nonsense is removed from bar 5 suggests a composer trying to conform to pedagogical advice. But the consecutive fifths and a gross $\frac{6}{4}$ remain (bars 7–8); the helpless consecutive octaves of bar 9 are replaced by another $\frac{6}{4}$, where a schooled composer would use bass E throughout the bar and the mature Berlioz might have written A–E. Bars 12–13 repeat the melody of bars 4–5, but reharmonized in both versions; the $\frac{6}{4}$ in the revised version is hardly more 'correct' than the original. It would be easy to 'improve' this into something orthodox (for instance by the tail-less pitches added to the vocal staff in 4–5). Berlioz continued to tinker with details throughout, but the rest of the song contains fewer puz-zles, thanks to extended pedals and the fail-safe alternation of tonic and

---

[32] I am grateful to Ian Rumbold of the NBE for supplying copies of the early versions.

[33] Thomas Christensen, *Rameau and Musical Thought in the Enlightenment* (Cambridge: Cambridge University Press, 1993), 52–3; but Rameau also lists the $\frac{6}{4}$ among 'chords of suspen-sion' which are otherwise clearly dissonant (ibid. 126).

dominant; in the later stages, the published version hardly differs from the autograph.

In 'Amitié' (Ex. 5.6) the MS version is transposed to F for ease of comparison (in the three-voiced Invocation, the top parts cross, but Ex. 5.6 ignores this except in the eleventh bar where their rhythm differs; the third voice doubles the instrumental bass). Here Berlioz again eliminates an unprepared seventh (bar 6), though the octave between treble and bass is less than ideal, and approaches the dominant in the bass through a pleasant chromatic passing-note (B♮); the seventh in the voice (bar 7, last beat) is led into by the piano right hand. In bar 10 an attempt at a melodic bass is emended by a more orthodox choice of bass note (B♭ making a complete triad with the voice's outer pitches). At the cadence (bars 14–15) neither version seems adequate. But in the invocation, a lengthy tonic pedal is broken in the published version with further simple but appealing chromatic elements; and the clearly inept ⁶₄

Ex. 5.6 'Amitié, reprends ton empire': comparison of two versions

chords in the manuscript (from bar 28) are firmly eliminated (the second and third voice parts, the latter originally tenor, were rewritten). These changes could be seen as the fruit of experience, and possibly of instruction.[34]

---

[34] From the perspective of piano accompaniments to the Romance, some of these crudities may be the result of Berlioz's playing the guitar. Guitar and other fretted strings playing continuo frequently choose different inversions in realizing a thoroughbass (ibid. 67–8). On the influence of the guitar on Berlioz's musical thinking, see *MLB* 56–60.

117

Rameau's theory of chord inversion, by which the root is distinguished from the bass, influences teaching to this day. For him, harmony is progression, not just the succession of verticals, and counterpoint and melody are the animation of harmony.[35] Progressions, following the acoustic laws that produce the perfect triad, are best by root movement of a fourth or fifth; may be acceptable by a third; and should seldom be by step. Rameau explains away commonplace progressions by step (I–ii–V or I–IV–V) by asserting the functional identity of ii and IV, so that both progressions are 'really' I–IV–ii–V (a third framed by two progressions of a fourth); the circle can be completed by another fourth, returning to I. This ingenious sophistry (conceivably a stumbling-block for the teenage Berlioz) affects a progression in the multisectional romance 'Le Montagnard exilé'. The 6/8 stanza begins with a sequence. The movement by a second (E flat to F minor) comes between phrases, and is unpicked within six bars by a sequence of ascending fourths. In bars 7–12 the sequence is repeated and unwound the same way, but with a modulation to the dominant. For this Berlioz uses ii7 as a pivot (bar 11, second beat); read in B flat, this sonority contains both supertonic and subdominant, and consequently may be deemed a fourth above B flat, and also a fourth below F.

By contrast Exx. 5.5 and 5.6 contain elements characteristic of the later Berlioz, particularly a tendency not to change the harmony in accordance with the metre, where a thoroughly schooled composer would do so (see the tied notes in the fundamental bass line, Ex. 5.6). In 'Le Maure' (Ex. 5.5), bars 4–5, the chord changes position, but the chord itself does not change. In 'Amitié' (Ex. 5.6), bars 7–9, the bass clings anxiously to C; since the proximate goals (bars 11 and 15) are imperfect cadences, the quantity of C in the bass is, on the kindest reading, of minimal interest. The quantity of approved root-movement by fourths in the earlier versions suggests that Berlioz had worked out for himself that this was a normal progression. The fundamental bass added to Ex. 5.6 applies to the revised version only, and it shows the increased incidence of root-movement by a second. In bars 6 and 10, however this root-progression may be justified theoretically, it certainly enhances the poise of the music, while in bar 17 the ⁶₄ chord on the second crotchet is a small price to pay for a suspension on the accented beat; what it replaces is a seventh in the bass left unresolved. Removal of the pedal in the Invocation adds some root-movement by a third; the aesthetic of variety, rather than theoretical correctness, justifies the alteration.

HARMONY AND EXPRESSION

In 'Le Maure' (Ex. 5.5), the range of emotion is striking. The smooth harmony of the opening section underlines the poetic emphasis on the pure

---

[35] Christensen, *Rameau and Musical Thought*; Carl Dahlhaus, 'Harmony', in Stanley Sadie (ed.), *The New Grove Dictionary of Music and Musicians* (London: Macmillan, 1980), viii. 176; Albert Cohen, part 7 of Rameau, Jean-Philippe, in ibid. xv. 569.

pleasure of seeing the beloved; the change to minor (bar 21) reflects anxiety (his heart, 'in its intoxication, knows fury'); the renewed dominant pedal (bars 29–32) suggests the impotence of jealousy, and the oxymoron 'tendres feux' brings a bold cadence using an augmented sixth. The last lines move back to the major with Schubertian pathos. The only mystery is why the singer has to be a Moor (or an Arab). The sober 'Amitié' reflects the nature of the poem, which elevates friendship above the unstable passion of love; the music catches this to perfection, more through melodic than harmonic means. With 'Amitié', the musical problem is the weakness of the *middle*, which fails to take flight, pootling around the tonic and dominant with a token chromatic slide (bars 14–15, less impressive than the chromatic passing notes in bar 9). The question that this raises, as with the 'primitive' counterpoint of the Kyrie, is whether the 'mistakes' are musically ineffectual, as mistakes ought to be; or whether they contribute to the development of musical language in a century which would, eventually, come to relax so many of the hallowed, though in reality not very ancient, 'rules' of musical grammar.

In these early songs, it is not usually possible to detect technical or expressive reasons for Berlioz's unorthodox procedures. I shall not dig up again all the idiotic things people, including fine musicians, have said about Berlioz's alleged lack of competence, but merely reiterate my belief that Boulez's diagnosis, that Berlioz had a poor ear, is the opposite of the truth.[36] If Berlioz in his mature works lacked the routine smoothness of his contemporaries (Schumann and Wagner as well as Mendelssohn) in conceiving melody and accompaniment as a unit, and in writing linear basses, it was precisely because the accuracy of his musical hearing ran ahead of his training. He cannot be accused of writing orchestral music on the basis of working out chords on a guitar; we know he did not do that. He conceptualized in his inner ear and wrote down what he wanted to hear. This often resulted in chord inversions which routine would not prescribe but which possess an expressive impact that routine harmonization would lack.[37] The incidence of such choices tends to increase during his career. Berlioz preferred not to saturate his music with conventional linear basses; there are enough examples to show that he could write them if he wanted (for instance, *Harold en Italie*, I, bars 85–9; *Symphonie funèbre*, I, second theme).[38]

The two songs to words by his fellow Dauphinois Albert Du Boys have fewer of the expressively blank harmonic crudities which affect 'Le Maure' and 'Amitié'. 'Le Montagnard exilé' does more than illustrate Rameau's theory of double function. This lament for the Isère, balancing contrasted sections of music, prepares the way for the sectionalized solo and choral movements in *Irlande*; the major-minor mixture in E flat is developed with a more sustained line than in 'Le Maure'. This is still more apparent in the second Du

[36] Pierre Boulez, *Conversations with Célestin Deliège* (London: Eulenburg, 1976), 20; see *MLB* 52, and *passim*, particularly the epigraphs, on other criticisms of Berlioz's competence.
[37] See *MLB* 92–8. [38] On the latter, see *MLB* 164.

Boys song, 'Toi qui l'aimas, verse des pleurs' (see Ex. 7.2). The Mass, while one can hardly deny its immaturity, shows increasing confidence in the textural relationships generally discussed under the rubric of 'harmony'. The Romance-like 'Gratias' (Ex. 4.5) shows that Berlioz could already go beyond routine V/I progressions, and that he was possibly affected by Lesueur's attraction to mediant harmonies. In Ex. 4.5 the acoustic bass doubles the fundamental bass for six bars, but after the sudden scale (bar 35), the cellos and bass instruments drop out and the lowest part (violas and second violins) follows the melodic sequence in parallel sixths; in bar 40 there is no independent bass. The 'Gratias' continues to an orthodox cadence (bar 42) and a pedal. This texture is further refreshed when the bass twice takes up the principal melody. Another gentle movement, 'Et incarnatus', delicately treads the line between falling back onto pedals, and exploiting them rhetorically. The rocking figure in the voice eventually infects the cello pedal (bar 9), which flowers into an unexpected solo. The second vocal phrase (from bar 19) is still more static harmonically, outlining a triad, but the accompaniment is at least animated. The subsequent presentation of material on the dominant (one can hardly call it modulation), then a few bars in A minor ended by backward resolution of G♯ onto G♮ (bars 43–4), complete a tonal scheme which would not have stretched Berlioz's imagination some years before, but which acts as a perfect foil to the vigorous exploitation of the minor mode in the adjacent movements, Credo and 'Crucifixus'. In context, the very simplicity of the setting of 'Et incarnatus' is expressive as an analogue of the mystery of the incarnation.

Berlioz professed to have abandoned Lesueur's 'system' by the date of *Irlande*, but his rebellion did not lead him to abandon the main precepts of chord progression. 'La Belle Voyageuse' is an example of how harmonies do not always change in accordance with the metre, but this surface irregularity becomes part of a higher-level symmetry. Berlioz said he wrote this song like a counterpoint exercise, so no apology is needed for making it look like one (Ex. 5.7). Nevertheless, harmonic processes are also to the fore. The strange modulations of this song are controlled by roots descending by perfect fifths, extending beyond the diatonic scale (I, IV, ♭VII, ♭III). Movement down a third returns to the tonic minor, which is changed to major; the instrumental coda reverses this movement, going to the minor mediant (iii) with a considerable sense of release. Movement by a step down (V–IV, then iii–ii) is contrapuntally controlled, by contrary motion, and needs no further justification; the final cadence is a diatonic segment of the circle of fifths. In Ex. 5.7, one minim represents a whole bar, but I have halved the number of barlines to clarify the syncopation.[39]

---

[39] See also *MLB* 63–6.

Ex. 5.7 'La Belle Voyageuse'

THE *OUTRÉ*: 'LE BALLET DES OMBRES'

Berlioz rarely lacked the courage of his convictions, but he withdrew the first two works published since 1823: *Huit scènes de Faust*, Op. 1 and 'Le Ballet des ombres', Op. 2. The latter he never mentioned, but having recycled the former into *La Damnation* he remarked that it had been 'very badly written'.[40] Probably he felt the same about the 'Ballet', which, printed with an epigraph from *Hamlet* beginning ''Tis now the very witching time of night', is filled with musical signifiers for the supernatural: the opening appoggiatura, scrunched against C minor by the piano; the ostinato minor third, filled by the

---

[40] 'fort mal écrite': *Memoirs*, ch. 26.

vocal line; the spooky vocal glissando, one-upmanship on 'Uhui', in *Der Freischütz*, which uses the same device of a diminished seventh melting back to the tonic (there, however, F sharp minor).[41]

Berlioz matches the imagery of the text by a strategy of cadential evasion, using simple linear side-slips to produce decidedly *outré* harmonies, illustrated in my reduction (Ex. 5.8), which also suggests how varied are the phrase-lengths implied by the groupings of bars (this Allegro scherzando is beaten one in a bar). A simple F♯, neighbour to the dominant, finds itself supported by a sharp VII (B major, with seventh): three of the pitches are shared with the diminished seventh. The next phrase re-establishes the persistent marching pattern on the salient notes C, D, E♭, which fit within the same diminished seventh, but Berlioz lowers the E♭ to D (bar 62 in Ex. 5.8). Simple movement by fifths could cadence back in C minor, but instead of the likely dominant, G, Berlioz substitutes root-position B minor; and resolution of this outlandish sound takes the simple and radical form of pushing the entire triad up a semitone.

The following passage makes the semitonal 'pun' relationship by moving from C minor to A flat (with seventh), then A minor.[42] The opening semitone motive is now applied to full §️ chords of A minor and G sharp minor, resolving back again; eerily, Berlioz reduces the chord to a single, semiquaver a♮'. There follow two more identical stanzas; for each, the return to C minor is again unmediated. In the coda, a♮' is resolved to b♭', but a possible move to E♭ is quickly suppressed; despite the B♮ in the piano, however, Berlioz studiously avoids the dominant chord. In conclusion, the chorus develops the opening semitone further by failing to resolve an entire D flat triad above the pedal C; restoration of order is left to the piano, but only by assertion of C minor as it slips away, with a last couple of minor thirds. Curiously enough, therefore, Berlioz anticipates by ten years Schumann's practice in Lieder of leaving the voice part unresolved. In the Requiem, the Introit also ends with the voices on a dissonance and a fade-out, chromatically inflected, in the lower regions of the orchestra. The semantic connection is obvious, although the 'Ballet' is an example of the grotesque, and the Requiem, at least in this wonderful first movement, shows high seriousness in its metaphors of death and the beyond. Harmonically, the most remarkable aspects of the 'Ballet des ombres' are that Berlioz gets near to prolonging the diminished seventh as a referential sonority; and that the semitonal side-slips defy Rameau's (hence Lesueur's) austere system of progression. It was after Lesueur's failure to appreciate Beethoven that Berlioz decided he that must free himself, despite his still admired teacher's 'persistent and systematic opposition': 'I turned

---

[41] Perhaps the glissando was a performing tradition in *Freischütz*. The diminished seventh in question is the leitmotiv of Samiel, later much exploited by Berlioz in his *Freischütz* recitatives.

[42] In this form it appears again in 'La Reine Mab' in *Roméo*; the version of this melody cut from *Benvenuto* does not include this 'pun' relationship. NBE 1b. 607–9.

Ex. 5.8 'Le Ballet des ombres':
  reduction: one crotchet or dotted crotchet per bar
  small notes: piano only

sharply off the old highway to pick my way by hill and valley, across woods and fields.'[43] This passage occurs before Berlioz's memories of the Prix de Rome in 1828. There may be some chronological disorder, but the incident recounted in chapter 20 of Berlioz's memoirs, concerning Lesueur, his hat, and Beethoven's Fifth Symphony, must have taken place before composition of 'Le Ballet des ombres'. This work foreshadows many characteristic passages, for example the transitions and the coda of the first movement of *Symphonie fantastique* (see Chapter 9). It may have been the recognition that this particular gesture of defiance went a little over the top that led Berlioz to withdraw his Op. 2; but his quest to extend the limitations of expressive music was bound to lead him back to such wild terrain.

---

[43] *Memoirs*, ch. 20: 'persistance de Lesueur dans son opposition systematique' (heading); 'je quittais brusquement la vieille grande route pour prendre ma course par monts et par vaux à travers les bois et les champs.'

6 Signs and Evocations

INTRODUCTION

Arguments over the possibility, or desirability, of 'absolute' or 'autonomous' musical thought may never end. The validity of music—just music—as a cultured form of entertainment free of ideology and, in the view of E. T. A. Hoffmann or Hanslick, of connections with anything outside itself, has taken a beating from recent musicology, and there is no reason to exempt Berlioz from contextual treatment. Some of the concerns of contextual musicology will be touched on in this chapter, but I do not wish to disguise my own ideology, which is that the survival of artistic works is not brought about by their usefulness as a key to unlocking past ideologies or further understanding cultural history. To achieve those aims, the quality of the work is barely relevant: Meyerbeer, indeed, will do better than Berlioz because he was more successful. Works of art in any tradition, I believe, are open to different, sometimes contradictory, interpretations; and while I am not so relativistic as to believe that any interpretation is as good as any other, I would not go so far as to suggest that one interpretation need necessarily rule out another one which appears to contradict it, because each will arise from a different set of circumstances embodied, for convenience, in the mentality which produces the interpretation.

This chapter is not a contribution to debates on musical autonomy, nor does it try to explain Berlioz's work through his social ambience. My concern is with what Berlioz did as a producer of music; how he communicated through music, and how he related musical ideas to the extra-musical ideas expressed in titles, sung texts, and programmes. What follows is therefore a selection of looks at Berlioz's output from the viewpoint of signification, and it is intended, at least, to contain no particular bias other than what is occasioned by my strong predilection for his music.

Berlioz believed in musical freedom; but his belief did not imply the rejection of external associations desired by Hoffmann and Hanslick.[1] Yet his

---

[1] E. T. A. Hoffmann, essay on Beethoven's Fifth Symphony, *Allgemeine Musikalische Zeitung* (July 1810); see David Charlton (ed.), *E. T. A. Hoffmann's Musical Writings* (Cambridge: Cambridge University Press, 1989), 234–55, and E. Forbes, *Beethoven: Fifth Symphony* (New

aesthetic cannot be reduced to the post-Enlightenment philosophy of Lesueur, in which music was texted or at least imitative, and in which instrumental music was secondary.[2] Berlioz found that literary and pictorial elements contributed to, rather than restricted, his freedom, because they provided a justification for the extension of musical means—melodic, harmonic, formal, instrumental, and in the exploitation of space, noise, colour, and silence. The trajectory of Berlioz's output is from vocal to instrumental music and back again, but the composer of *Roméo et Juliette* did not regard these categories as radically distinct; the interpenetration of music with and without words has already been mentioned in considering self-borrowings.

Many aspects of Berlioz's musical language were conservative, but I see little point in perpetuating the argument about 'classic' and 'romantic' as if there were necessarily a complete break between them. These terms conveniently identify tendencies in Berlioz which are complementary, not contradictory. Certainly the student of Lesueur, a composer who came to maturity in the 1780s and composed important operas in the 1790s, is not without connections to the past. In the 1820s, admiration for Gluck and Spontini was as regressive as admiration for Beethoven was advanced, and Berlioz's oddity emerges as strongly from his refusal to conform to ancient contrapuntal and harmonic precepts as from his refusal to fall in with the contemporary fashion for Italian music. From a post-Wagnerian perspective such an attitude appears politically correct, but Berlioz is no more comfortable in a Trinity with Liszt and Wagner as a 'musician of the future' than with Mendelssohn and Chopin as a musician of the present. Contemporaries naturally took note of his cultivation of the grotesque and outlandish, and his autobiographical pose. When *Les Troyens* appeared it was assumed to be equally noisome, not to say tiresome; it has taken many years for its classicizing austerity and human truthfulness to be appreciated and for these qualities to be read back into earlier works such as *Harold en Italie*. Berlioz's artistic character is complex, even eclectic, but the last quality, which usually serves to relate musical communications to each other, is generally forgotten in the face of his evident oddity. Tracing his continuity with past forms of musical communication serves both to justify his work, as rhetorically effective through using contemporary codes, and to mark it as original where it appears to be developing means of musical communication.

TOPICS AND RHETORIC

Musical topics, classified for the late eighteenth century by Leonard G. Ratner, were recently defined by Vera Micznik as 'musical signs [which] sig-

York: Norton Critical Scores, 1971), 150–63; Eduard Hanslick, *Vom Musikalisch-Schönen* (Leipzig, 1854), trans. and ed. Geoffrey Payzant as *On the Musically Beautiful* (Indianapolis: Hackett, 1986).

[2] See the influential formulation of this view by J.-J. Rousseau, in Peter le Huray and James Day, *Music and Aesthetics in the Eighteenth and Early-Nineteenth Centuries* (Cambridge: Cambridge University Press, 1981), 109.

nify meanings whose general sense is understood regardless of whether it is stated in a programme or not'.[3] Romantic individualism and a consequent weakening of genre may have eroded, but did not eliminate, such sign systems. Frits Noske demonstrated the development of an exogenous 'death topos' from Gluck to Berlioz (curiously failing to consider *Les Troyens*), Verdi, and Wagner.[4] Imitation of natural phenomena and the sounds, including musical sounds, of human society, also represent continuity within musical signification.

Berlioz's storms originate in Gluck, belonging more to the theatre than the symphony (despite Beethoven's 'Pastoral'). Thunder is imitated literally by timpani (end of 'Scène aux champs'), wind and rain less literally; lightning can only be represented by a sound-analogue (usually the piccolo). The resulting musical complex, connected with the formally insecure fantasia tradition, is not only unmistakably a storm, but may be a metaphor for its destructive consequences: the wreck in *La Tempête*, the danger to Carthage of the union of Dido and Aeneas. Other surviving eighteenth-century topics include ritual, pastoral, hunting and battle, and signifiers for the exotic. Berlioz's admiration for the sacred marches of Gluck, Mozart, and Cherubini is reflected by the signification of the sacred in *Les Troyens*, in Andromache's pantomime (No. 6), and the scene of Dido's death (No. 49); one relevant sign is a series of quiet parallel § chords.[5] 'Pastoral' implies not the life of peasants but a metaphor of ideal serenity. Eighteenth-century pastoral music is often in 6/8, perhaps Berlioz's favourite metre; its exceptional prevalence in the courtly Act IV of *Les Troyens* marks the entire act as metaphorically pastoral. Musical signs for hunting, war, and the last judgement naturally bring out the brass. Berlioz took full advantage of mechanical developments which gave all brass instruments chromatic capability, particularly the cornets, which he deploys in *Les Troyens* with athletic brilliance (No. 5 'Combat de ceste') and ritual gloom (No. 49, 'Cérémonie funèbre'). But chromatic brass did not completely undermine connotations traditionally based on the natural harmonic series. Berlioz used diatonic fanfares which composers of the previous century would have recognized as signifying hunting or warfare. The 'Marche troyenne' reaches its ninth bar before the diatonic scale of the cornets exceeds the capabilities of the natural trumpet (Ex. 6.1*a*). But, just as in *Der Ring,* a distorted fanfare has sinister import; before the curtain rises on Act II, a diminished triad fanfare signifies the fall of Troy (Ex. 6.1*b*). The first hunting-call in *Les Troyens* (Ex. 6.1*c*) could not be played by natural brass, and is even vocal in idiom, but conveys no sense of distortion. The formal march is a

---

[3] Vera Micznik, 'The Absolute Limitations of Programme Music: The Case of Liszt's "Die Ideale"', *Music and Letters*, 80 (1999), 207–40, cited 216. Leonard G. Ratner, *Classic Music: Expression, Form, Style* (New York: Schirmer, 1980).

[4] Frits Noske, *The Signifier and the Signified* (repr. Oxford: Oxford University Press, 1990), on Berlioz, 183–4; Noske, 'Das exogene Todesmotiv in Musikdramen Richard Wagners', *Die Musikforschung*, 30–1 (1977–8), 285–302; see also 'Overture'.

[5] On the use of § chords in storms and sacred marches, see *MLB* 109.

Ex. 6.1 Three fanfares from *Les Troyens*

a. 'Marche troyenne'

b. Battle in the streets of Troy

Trumpet and cornet

c. 'Chasse royale' (Act IV)

frequently invoked topic throughout the nineteenth century, and Berlioz's 'speculative treatment' in symphonies lies on the road between Beethoven and Mahler.[6] Other signifiers, often in the introduction, distinguish marches as martial, funereal, triumphal, nocturnal, intimate, or grotesque (Ex. 6.2; it is only with the tune that we can be sure that Ex. 6.2*d* is in triple time).

Marches are commonplace in opera, but may be tied into a variety of dramatic functions. The 'Marche troyenne' meets the complicated and repetitive needs of a stage procession, but comes to no proper end; for concert perfor-

---

[6] 'Speculative treatment . . . refers to the use of dance rhythms as subjects for discourse in sonatas, symphonies, and concertos, as well as in church and theater music.' Ratner, *Classic Music*, 17. See also Wye J. Allanbrook, *Rhythmic Gesture in Mozart* (Chicago: University of Chicago Press, 1983).

mance Berlioz cut it decisively and tacked on a coda from Act V (No. 43). There, however, and in the finale, where the March reaches a second decisive conclusion, it is a musical symbol; there is no procession and in the finale, there are no Trojans left on stage. The 'Marche au supplice', originating in an opera, conforms to the grotesque requirements of *Symphonie fantastique*, but it remains a genre piece, motion-music divided into binary phrases which are far from typical of the symphony as a whole (see Chapter 9). The symbolism of marches goes beyond the obvious military and nationalistic allusions. 'Marche au supplice' represents justice, and the rabble gathered to watch the

Ex. 6.2 March incipits

a. Symphonie funèbre et tromphale, I

b. Symphonie funèbre et triomphale, III

c. '*Marche nocturne*' (*L'Enfance du Christ, I*)

d. Entrance of Dido (*Les Troyens*, Act IV)

e. '*Marche au supplice*' (*Symphonie fantastique*, IV)

execution; the finale of *Symphonie funèbre* is the apotheosis of a free people. March-like material is freely appropriated to represent the majestic: Sardanapalus's grandeur ('Le roi des rois impose l'esclavage') passes naturally into *L'Impériale*. In the Te Deum, for which Berlioz would have accepted the epithet 'grandiose' as a compliment, 'Tu Christe rex gloriae' incorporates a motive from the Resurrexit which fits its new musical context, already filled with dotted rhythms, more naturally than the old. The permeability of topics should be recognized, indeed savoured. Sketchbook material apparently designed for the triumphant return of Napoleon's army from Italy was eventually realized as the second theme in the 'Orgy of Brigands' in *Harold*.[7] With Berlioz, as with other composers, topical references usually get tangled in the outer movements of symphonies. An orgy might seem a simple finale topic, but the movement opens with allusions to the previous movements, one of which (the pilgrims' march) returns near the end.

As in the eighteenth-century symphonic works discussed by Ratner, topics like the march share space with material similar in tempo but of agitated rather than march-like character. In Part III of *La Damnation* the abrupt entry of Mephistopheles initiates a dramatic trio, in which vocal declamation is superimposed on the development of a crisp middle-register melody which is certainly not a march (see Ex. 10.4). The similarly abrupt entry of Narbal, bringing news of invasion, opens the finale to Act III of *Les Troyens*, enhanced by syncopations. When the Trojan and Carthaginian forces merge, and the tonal goal, B, is established, the same tempo is invigorated with a new march theme led by Aeneas (bar 162: 'Sur cette horde immonde d'Africains, marchons . . .'); this is reminiscent of the final, futile co-ordination of Trojan forces in Act II (No. 13, from bar 79).

Post-Napoleonic flattening of social hierarchies is reflected in a flattening of topical precision in the speculative deployment of dances in nineteenth-century music. The minuet, the most flexible of eighteenth-century dance types, was by now antique, and a mysterious irony imbues its use for the will-o'-the wisps ('follets') in *La Damnation*. The waltz, sprung from bucolic German dances, defined an increasingly urban culture in which aristocratic 'difference' declined in importance relative to the numbers, and purchasing power, of the bourgeoisie.[8] The waltz second movement seems to have been Berlioz's last addition to *Symphonie fantastique*. Beethoven's Ninth is a precedent for the Minuet or Scherzo preceding the slow movement, but in substituting a waltz Berlioz anticipated Tchaikovsky and Mahler. The dance evokes a crowded ballroom, and is only lightly subverted by intrusion of the *idée fixe*, which reflects the alienation of the protagonist; at first introduced by a disorientating modulation, it eventually comes to agree with the main key. In the second movement of *Roméo et Juliette*, as already noted, Berlioz

---

[7] Holoman, 'Sketchbook', 293–6.

[8] See Andrew Lamb, 'Waltz', in Stanley Sadie (ed.), *The New Grove Dictionary of Music and Musicians* (London: Macmillan, 1980), xx, 200.

avoids any obvious topical or dance allusion. At this point in Gounod's opera, Juliet sings a waltz-aria ('Je veux vivre dans ce rêve'), creating a character totally different from Shakespeare's Juliet, or from the Juliet implied by Berlioz's eloquent oboe solo (Ex. 4.3). Viewing 'Grand fête chez Capulet' in terms of 'multiple perspectives' conveys its impact as absolute music, as well as suggesting programmatic interpretations. The alienation of the main characters is conveyed ironically by the 'réunion des thèmes' which from a musical perspective looks like a gesture towards unity.[9]

A similar distinction might be made between the bells in the finale of *Symphonie fantastique*, which are real, and those in the second movement of *Harold,* imitated by harp and wind instruments.[10] The real bells make the fantasy of the witches' sabbath more naturalistic; the simulated bells evoke a realistic scene, from which the protagonist is alienated by theme (*idée fixe*) and instrumentation (solo viola). The steady plod of the pilgrims contains a residue of a march; pizzicato double-basses connect it to Dido's 'Cérémonie funèbre'. Berlioz reintroduced this essentially vocal idea into dramatic works. The off-stage monks in *Benvenuto Cellini* (first scene of Act II) are forced to chime in with some ingenious enharmonic modulations and the triple metre of the on-stage prayers of Teresa and Ascanio. In *Roméo*, Berlioz evokes a funeral bell by chiming violin octaves ('Convoi funèbre de Juliette'). The march topic is again eliminated in favour of counterpoint and lyricism, and the muttered prayer ('Requiem aeternam') was eventually cut.

Topics are signs of universal potential within a stylistic domain (such as nineteenth-century music). A defect of Michel Guiomar's often heroic attempt to classify and elucidate elements of Berlioz's musical language is its isolation from convention, so that simple rhetorical ploys, known to all composers, such as hitting a high note towards the end of a dramatic recitative, take on the semiotic significance of uniqueness.[11] But signs may be peculiar to one composer, or to a restricted circle; 'signs resulting from a relationship between a signified in the verbal or another extra-musical medium and music, are not naturally, conventionally, or socially established.'[12] Artificial signifiers, articulated by words, retain significance only within one composition (except in cases of intertextual quotation); the operatic Leitmotiv is the obvious example, and Berlioz's *idée fixe* is one of its begetters. Nevertheless, when something is clearly signified in one work through verbal, visible, or dramatic associations, the possibility may arise of transferring that signification to another work; hence operatic signifiers when they appear in instrumental music may blaze a hermeneutic trail. In Berlioz, certain areas of experience may be connected through the use in more than one work of definite idioms,

---

[9] On this see *MLB* 74–6, 194–6; Edward T. Cone, review of a recording of *Roméo et Juliette*, *Musical Quarterly*, 39 (1953), 475–8.

[10] The *Symphonie fantastique* bells are usually played an octave higher than the *highest* pitch Berlioz specified, which is middle C (c'): NBE 16, p. xv.

[11] Guiomar, *Le Masque et le fantasme*, 165. [12] Micznik, 'Absolute Limitations', 216.

amounting to a personal language, even if these are not necessarily exclusive to him, but could be paralleled in the work of his contemporaries. Some illustrations of broad topics more peculiar to nineteenth-century music follow.

THE GROTESQUE, THE SUPERNATURAL, THE SUBLIME

The grotesque and its connection with the sublime, articulated by Hugo in the Preface to *Cromwell* (1827), were integral to that part of French culture which abandoned its classics, rediscovered Shakespeare and Gothic architecture, and consumed romantic literature. The grotesque is the terrible beauty of the distorted and ugly, and reveals emotions which adhere to experience of the sublime. Hugo himself adapted *Notre-Dame de Paris* for Louise Bertin's *Esmerelda*, which Berlioz assisted in rehearsal.[13] Berlioz connects the far ends of the spectrum from the Gothick drama (*Faust*) to the eschatological visions of his sacred works. Much of the literature called Gothick derived from a distorted British view—long before Bram Stoker—of Europe as a dark continent; in Matthew Lewis's *The Monk*, the basis for *La Nonne sanglante*, two girls are drugged, so that they appear to be dead, and are left to wake up in an underground tomb, a motive which figures in *Cléopâtre* and *Romeo and Juliet*.

In the year of *Cromwell*, Ferrand took a willing Berlioz down the Gothick road in *Les Francs-juges*, so that the first musical results of Berlioz's fashionable preoccupation with the grotesque produced the villain Olmerick. The striding brass theme in D flat major (overture, bars 20–45) is always identified with him; it is alarming through power rather than distortion, but it crushes the overture's first attempt at lyricism, and its own third phrase breaks the four-by-four symmetry by repeating an oppressive semitone motive. From bar 45 a woodwind cry pares down lyricism to a residue of three chromatic notes, battered by fortissimo chords; the threefold suspension leading to an augmented sixth (bars 49–51) seems to ritualize despair. The reprise of the Olmerick theme nearly shatters the increasingly lively coda, temporarily splintered (bar 620) into atonality. But Olmerick's rhetoric is not far from that of the noble Prince of Verona, who quells the fighting in the first movement of *Roméo et Juliette*. Berlioz's best early Gothick evocation is 'Le Ballet des ombres', a piece fit for a churchyard thriller (Ex. 5.8). In the later 1830s, he veered away from these preoccupations, unless the Requiem text is considered in that light. Indeed, both the symphonies and both the operas set in Italy, which he had visited, are free of supernatural elements, whereas all his other non-liturgical works (if we discount *Les Francs-juges*) contain witches, ghosts, devils, or angels. In *Symphonie fantastique*, the supernatural is part of a dream, and the satanic thrills of the finale forget their psychological purpose

---

[13] Anselm Gerhard ends a chapter on *Esmerelda* by observing 'Perhaps it was all for the best that the illustrious poet never worked in the opera house again': *Die Verstädterung der Oper*, trans. Mary Whittall as *The Urbanization of Opera* (Chicago: University of Chicago Press, 1998), 246.

and become enjoyable for their own sake; the artist-hero fades into the background, like Harold in the 'Orgie des brigands'. The ballad of *La Nonne sanglante* (Ex. 6.3) gives us an idea of how the mature Berlioz might have tackled a Gothick subject; but *La Damnation*, in the more limited sense of evoking the demonic, is his finest work for which the supernatural is a central issue.[14] In *La Nonne*, all we have is the opening of the ballad, for which Berlioz's language intersects with a style he termed 'Chanson gothique' (see Chapter 7). Ballads are customarily in compound metre, as in the serene 'La Belle Voyageuse' and the stormy 'La Belle Isabeau', but here Berlioz used common time, detaching his idea from traditional expectations and heightening its gravity, just as he detached the ball in *Roméo* from direct reference to any dance-type. What this piece shares with a 'Chanson gothique' is a folkloric premiss contradicted by unexpected and twisting modulations: note particularly the sequential thirds in the bass-line, without rhythmic interest yet deeply expressive. The first verse is plainly accompanied, the second, which is reduced in Ex. 6.3, throbs with plucked double-basses disposed at opposite sides of the pit and alternating beats of bass drum and timpani; the horn chords are devised so that every note is hand-stopped (the instruments are written in A flat, E flat, G flat, and D flat), and the high croak of the bassoon anticipates early twentieth-century expressionism. Even in 'Invocation to nature' Berlioz did not seek so far for an orchestral effect of which Méhul or Meyerbeer would equally have been proud.

J. H. Elliot called the soothsayers in *L'Enfance* 'grotesque in the extreme . . . It was characteristic of Berlioz, who was attracted by the dramatic aspects

Ex. 6.3 The ballad of *La Nonne sanglante* (second stanza)

---

[14] Berlioz's preoccupation with *La Nonne* began before, and ended after, composition of *La Damnation*. Lewis's Lucifer mocks the desperate monk with an offer of remission of punishment, raises him onto a crag, then dashes him down. Mephistopheles similarly promises to rescue Marguerite, but flings Faust into Pandemonium. The devil's failure to keep his word, a departure from Goethe's conception, offended one critic in Dresden (*Memoirs*, ch. 55).

of his subject, that he should overshoot its mysticism and introduce the crudest of black magic.'[15] But in that case, Berlioz's misjudgement was literary; the music of the incantation and cabalistic dance should be grotesque, for these characters lack any urge towards the sublime. But when the soothsayers trigger Herod's furious breach of the psychological barriers, leading to the massacre of innocents, this gory birth of the Christian message, contrasted with the gentle scene in Bethlehem, raises human events towards the numinous; this form of sublimity results from the mixing of elements, not least the grotesque. Berlioz marks the climax of Herod's madness with baying brass

[15] J. H. Elliot, *Berlioz*, The Master Musicians (London: Dent, 1935), 192.

fanfares, which threaten tonal coherence (with hints of octatonicism); tonality is restored by the expedient of silence, and the creation of a new mood by the A flat duet of Mary and Joseph (Ex. 6.4).

Berlioz himself used the word 'sublime' in various contexts. In his first important article, he begins by announcing that religion should inspire masterpieces 'through the sublimity of its subject, the severe majesty of the ideas to which it is attached and the antiquity of its origin'.[16] In 1829 he called Cherubini's Communion March of 1825 'sublime', and repeated this view

[16] 'Considerations sur la musique religieuse', *Le Correspondant*, 21 Apr. 1829; *Critique musicale*, i. 13.

Ex. 6.4 *L'Enfance du Christ*, I (bridge-passage to Scene 2)

years later; comparing Cherubini to Gluck (than which he knew no higher praise), he distinguished Gluck's evocation of the 'poetic yet sensual' religion of antiquity with Cherubini's Christian serenity.[17] But he calls the passage in Euripides's *Alkestis*, where Admetus's father refuses to give up the little remainder of his life to save the young queen, 'an appalling scene according to our ideas and customs, but no less obviously sublime . . . One cannot read this without trembling; even Shakespeare never went further.'[18] This scene achieves sublimity through the grotesque, and reflects an earlier and broader view of sublimity which embraced the hostile aspects of nature. Writing in 1805, Michaelis applied the terms of Burke and Kant to music, among other arts, claiming that 'music can objectively be called *sublime*, like untamed nature, which arouses sublime emotions'; he escapes from this potentially circular argument by saying that a composer can communicate these emotions

by the use of unconventional, surprising, powerfully startling, or striking harmonic progressions or rhythmic patterns. Supposing, let us say, the established tonality suddenly veers in an unexpected direction, supposing a chord is resolved in a quite unconventional manner, supposing the longed-for calm is delayed by a series of stormy passages, then astonishment and awe result and in this mood the spirit is profoundly moved and sublime ideas are stimulated or sustained.[19]

In his specification of signs of the sublime Michaelis might have had Haydn's *Die Schöpfung* or Mozart's Requiem in mind, but he seems to be foretelling Berlioz's self-assessment: 'the predominant qualities of my music are passionate expression, inward intensity, rhythmic impetus, and unexpectedness.'[20] When passionate expression, inward ardour, and startling modulations cohere in a single utterance, Berlioz attains this sublimity, most wonderfully in Faust's 'Invocation à la nature' and in 'Judex crederis' from the Te Deum.

DEATH AND LIFE, HEAVEN AND HELL

Berlioz's first exploitation of harmonic unpredictability is the chain of diminished sevenths in the 'Crucifixus' of the *Messe solennelle* (some of these can be seen in Ex. 8.3). But this harmonic device has other possibilities (see below), and this evocation of Christ's torment and death involves more signs: the woodwind sigh, used again in *Les Francs-juges* and 'Scène aux champs', and the underlying tremolo from bar 12, the first of many such *frissons*. The music of death is usually subtler than this. Berlioz's first wholly successful supernatural invocation is the Meditation in *Cléopâtre*. The music alludes to the 'ombra' topic, of which the archetype for Berlioz's generation was the statue scene in *Don Giovanni*: both employ syncopation, grandly unpredictable progressions, and the minor mode. None of these features seem surprising for the

[17] *Critique musicale*, i. 15; *Journal des Débats*, 20 Mar. 1842 (Condé, 142).

[18] *A travers chants*, 157–9.

[19] Le Huray and Day, *Music and Aesthetics*, 289–90; Edmund Burke on the sublime, ibid., 69–74.

[20] *Memoirs*, Postscript.

death-devoted Cleopatra, and the musical symbols function equally well for the ghostly chorus in *Lélio*. Syncopation betrays the underlying beat; it produces animation, but also uncertainty; and it proliferates in *Cléopâtre* before the Meditation. But what elevates Berlioz's scene above mere harmonic groping (which may be how it appeared to his examiners) is the predominance of the melody, thanks to which the harmonic progressions are fundamentally secure; despite some wide leaps, the abundance of smaller intervals (semitones and minor thirds) assists melodic, and hence overall, coherence.[21] More usually singled out in the Meditation is its disturbing rhythmic pattern, which is not the traditional death-topos. The rhythm (crotchet, two quavers, crotchet) acquires signification by association with similar patterns. In Marguerite's romance, composed shortly before *Cléopâtre*, lyricism is undercut by throbbing pizzicato semiquavers, and the same iambic rhythm is used for Cleopatra's last death-rattle. Marguerite's 9/8 episode uses a crotchet-quaver rhythm in the conventional long-short pattern (later coloured, in *La Damnation*, by accenting the quavers). As conceived in 1829, the Romance precedes Faust's desertion of Gretchen; whereas Cleopatra, whose rhythm is less conventional, is beyond hope. The delay of resolution through an enharmonic excursion (bar 24) and suspensions (bars 42–4) is secondary to the linear drives of the voice part, as can be seen in an outline linear analysis which shows how clear are the main melodic progressions and the bass arpeggiation (Ex. 6.5).

Berlioz's noblest evocation of death comes at the end of *Les Troyens* (No. 49, 'Cérémonie funèbre'), where the dactylic rhythm is related to the 'fate' motive which appears in the orchestral coda of No. 48, Dido's aria.[22] The dactylic ostinato has an affective power comparable to Cleopatra's iambic pulse, but the interval distribution of the melody is less extreme, as befits a ritual. After an arpeggio opening, the melody moves predominantly by step, with a preponderance of whole tones until the final stages, when it falls through minor thirds to form a diminished seventh; but Dido sings mainly semitones. Other deaths in Berlioz occur in fast music (Orpheus, Romeo, Cassandra), but more memorable musically are scenes anticipating death, which are conventionally slow, and intersect with music of mourning. Death is ritualized, as in *Les Troyens*, by marching topics; otherwise melancholy chromaticism or tonal disruption, but with a strong diatonic basis, link movements as diverse as Cleopatra's meditation and the tomb scene in *Roméo*.

Berlioz's musical response to exceptional vitality is equally varied, but again inter-work connections can be made. The vital spark of certain characters is limned by fast triplet figuration. The obvious example begins the

---

[21] The voice part has sixty intervals, ignoring unison and octaves. Twenty-five are semitones, twelve are minor thirds, and two are tritones. Major thirds (part of minor arpeggios) and ascending minor sixths, representing the same interval-class, number seven. There are eight whole tones and six fourths or fifths.

[22] See 'Overture', 128, 141.

Ex. 6.5 *Cléopâtre*: linear reduction of the 'Méditation', omitting introduction and coda

Benvenuto Cellini overture, suggesting that the main theme portrays the hero (and the second theme Teresa). These triplets recur, in association with the hero, particularly in the original layer of the score (Paris 1 in NBE). That *life*, or liveliness, is a signified is suggested when just such sprightly triplets introduce Mephistopheles' claim 'Je suis l'esprit de vie'. This replaces the more plausible claim of Goethe's Mephistopheles, to be (in Nerval's translation) 'l'esprit qui toujours nie': the spirit of denial. The musical character brings to mind the diabolical mirth with which Liszt's Mephistopheles mocks Faust's most pretentious motive, and also Verdi's Iago ('Credo').[23] Laughing triplets

---

[23] Liszt, *Eine Faust-Sinfonie*, III, the E major signature (Eulenburg score, bar 201); Verdi, *Otello*, Act II, scene ii. Compare Liszt's first *Mephisto-Walzer*, where the strikingly similar semi-quaver groupings, however, are not triplets.

infect the principal motive of the overture and life-affirming Scherzino-finale of *Béatrice et Bénédict*. Such signs of vitality enhance dramatic irony in *Les Troyens*, in the Act I ballet (No. 5, 'Combat de ceste', the section in 5/8) and the Act IV 'Danse des esclaves' (Ex. 6.7); in symphonies, with less exact verbal analogues, this liveliness is reflected in the brigands' orgy and parts of the ball scene in *Roméo*, both movements in common time fired up by brilliant triplet figuration.

Berlioz's interest in the Last Things affects not only his liturgical works, but *La Damnation de Faust*, which ends with scenes in hell and heaven, perhaps recalling their simultaneous presentation on stage in an 1820s melodrama.[24] In the Requiem, oppositions of high and low, minor and major, work out the same metaphor more subtly, while death and damnation are potent fears in the Te Deum (see Chapter 8). The music of hell appears mostly in human responses, sometimes of an identifiable protagonist, like Cleopatra or Dido, sometimes of the notional persona or intelligence behind a work such as the Requiem. Besides these subjective hells, the objective representation in *La Damnation* is a valiant effort at the impossible. After the magnificently static oscillation of tritone-related chords in the first hellish uproar, which also resolve the kinetic intensity of 'La Course à l'abîme', Berlioz's devils resemble naughty schoolboys, playing at nonsense languages—an idea which is not even consistently applied, as their dialogue with Mephistopheles is in French.[25] The movement lacks impetus; small wonder that Berlioz reduced it by nearly 50 per cent after the first performances.[26]

Berlioz had had more practice at evoking heaven. The Easter Hymn is the first number of *Huit scènes de Faust*, opening with a carillon (pizzicato) and symbolizing upward aspiration by moving from male voices to mixed chorus, including a wordless section for a (soprano) chorus of angels. In Goethe, and in *La Damnation*, the same music is understood to come from an adjacent church. Berlioz fundamentally revised the music, deciding that the sopranos were no longer angels and depriving them of glossolalia because he required textural space for Faust to sing words of his own; a full heavenly vision is withheld for Marguerite's apotheosis. Thus the Hymn is ruthlessly stripped of its two harp parts, passing the accompanimental arpeggios to woodwind, and as if to remind us that the choir is of earth, not heaven, Berlioz grounds much of the second stanza in a pedal.[27] Heaven itself is D flat major, with harps, gently swooning violins, and high voices (the basses sing only the last tonic harmony). It is perhaps appropriate that this imagery hovers on the cusp of

---

[24] See NBE 8b. 455.

[25] The recitative was originally also nonsense: see NBE 8b. 491, 531. On the 'Course à l'abîme' and the tritone harmonies, see *MLB* 80–3, 254–5.

[26] For the cut music, see NBE 8b. 532–45.

[27] On this addition of a pedal to an already completed texture, see Rushton, 'Berlioz through the Looking-Glass', 65.

banality, but the tonality may be significant in relation to the nineteenth-century rhetoric of keys.[28]

EXOTICISM, EROTICISM, AND LOVE

From a recent anthology on musical exoticism, one might infer that Berlioz's contribution was nugatory, in a period in which exoticism flourished; it has been estimated that over 15 per cent of Opéra-Comique librettos made use of it.[29] While neighbouring Spain and Britain provided 'exotic' locations for numerous French theatrical works, erotic fantasy is usually directed farther afield. Félicien David, whose 'Symphonic Ode' *Le Désert* (1844) Berlioz reviewed sympathetically, and later Delibes and Saint-Saëns, attempted to reconcile the musical languages of Europe and the Orient.[30] For Berlioz, remoteness implies classical treatment, without recourse to realistic local colour. *Scène héroïque* is no more Greek than 'Le Maure jaloux' is Moorish or *Les Francs-juges* German. Since Berlioz never left France until 1831, it is a tribute to Scott that the fresh air of *Waverley* is markedly different from anything he had written up to that time. In *Rob Roy*, the gruff modal theme (bar 85) and lively piping tune (bar 170) sound no less Scottish than the borrowed 'Scots wha'hae', yet the piping tune migrates to *Harold en Italie*, showing the permeability even of local colour. Berlioz's direct interest in Scotland died there, although the second theme of the *Hamlet* march (from bar 37), perhaps intended as generically northern, sounds more Celtic than Norse. Berlioz never visited Spain, and his Spanish genre piece, the bolero 'Zaide', like the section in the last version of 'La Captive' in the same rhythm, is as charming and authentic as an armchair travelogue.[31] Berlioz had not reached Hungary when he arranged *Marche de Rákóczy*, whose character shines through his brilliant but occidental orchestration; and when Faust and Mephistopheles ride to the abyss, the peasant women they terrify sing a psalmody from Berlioz's native Dauphiné.

Berlioz came to know parts of Italy well. The droning violas and piccolo doubled with oboe lend credible local colour as a good imitation of *pifferari* of the Abruzzi in *Harold* (third movement), while the disgruntled workmen in *Benvenuto Cellini* develop a notation made in or remembered from Italy, the

---

[28] See the 'Judex crederis', in which D flat is important (see Ch. 8), and such heavenly evocations as the end of *Das Rheingold* and the slow movement of Bruckner's Eighth symphony.

[29] Jonathan Bellman (ed.), *The Exotic in Western Music* (Boston: Northeastern University Press, 1998). Hervé Lacombe examined 265 Opéra-Comique librettos, of which forty-five were 'exotic'; 'The Writing of Exoticism in the Libretti of the Opéra-Comique, 1825–1862', *Cambridge Opera Journal*, 11 (1999), 135–58.

[30] Berlioz reviewed *Le Désert* in *Le Journal des Débats*, 15 Dec. 1844 (HC 587). For a fine synoptic account of exoticism see Ralph P. Locke, 'Cutthroats and Casbah Dancers, Muezzins and Timeless Sands: Musical Images of the Middle East', *19th-Century Music*, 22 (1998), 20–53, reprinted in Bellman, *The Exotic*.

[31] James Parakilas places 'Zaide' within a well-established tradition; Bellman, *The Exotic*, 150.

'Buon giorno' of a friendly ruffian, Corsino.[32] The shepherds who visit Christ in the manger (*La Fuite en Egypte*) also play *pifferari* ('Adieu des bergers'), yet in Saïs the young Ishmaelites play a languid salon piece; although its allegro uses modal cadences, these scarcely amount to exoticism within the style of *L'Enfance*. Unlike Lesueur, Berlioz was not very interested in musical archaeology; he was attracted to modes for the expressive potential of departures from a tonal norm, usually a leading-note, rather than as a musical sign of otherness. The Trojan women use the Locrian mode to exploit European connotations of its fifth degree, the tritone. Cassandra's compatriots are not thereby distinguished from any other group, still less should this searing lament imply any *otherness* in relation to the perspectives of audience sympathy.[33] Berlioz showed relatively little interest in the augmented second that infects so much music which attempts to evoke the world of the Gipsy, or the orient, confining it to its classical position in the 'harmonic minor' scale (as in the *Marche de Rákóczy*). The signifiers of Jewish music which would have been understood in Paris if only thanks to Halévy's *La Juive* are missing from *L'Enfance*; neither the diatonic music of Mary and Joseph, nor Herod's Phrygian mode, has any connection with them.[34] Berlioz related the sharpened fourth of 'Le Roi de Thulé' to something he had heard in Swiss music, but when combined with the major-minor mixture so alien to folk-music it becomes wholly personal (neither Marguerite nor Thulé have any connection with Switzerland).

Berlioz knew the Janissary music of Gluck, Mozart, and Beethoven, but by his time cymbals, triangle, and drum had lost their Turkish affiliation and the 'pavillon chinois' in the 'Apothéose' of *Symphonie funèbre*—an instrument also known as 'Turkish crescent'—was already assimilated into French military bands (there was even one at La Côte). The Middle East was still an area for actual or potential French imperial expansion, a mind-cast triggered by Napoleon's Egyptian campaign and represented in Berlioz's lifetime by the annexation of Algeria (1830); yet only two of Berlioz's works are set across the Mediterranean. Besides *L'Enfance du Christ* (Palestine and Egypt), *Les Troyens* is set in Asia Minor (Troy, in modern Turkey) and North Africa (Carthage, in modern Tunisia). But the legends of Troy precede Greek and Roman domination of these regions, never mind the present-day populations and their predominant religion, Islam.[35] The soothsayers are supposedly of one race with Herod; their exotic dance, a seven-beat measure with woodwind whistles, connects with *Der Freischütz* as much as any oriental style, although

---

[32] *Memoirs*, ch. 38.   [33] On modes, see also *MLB* 47–51.

[34] The most famous aria of *La Juive*, 'Rachel, quand du Seigneur', contains several augmented seconds; it was first sung by Adolphe Nourrit, whom Berlioz knew, but he does not mention this aria in his review (*Le Rénovateur*, 1 Mar. 1835; *Critique musicale*, ii. 73–8).

[35] This did not prevent Saint-Saëns from using modern 'oriental' styles for the Philistines in *Samson et Dalila*. See Ralph Locke, 'Constructing the Oriental "Other"', *Cambridge Opera Journal*, 3 (1991), 261–302.

Ralph Locke may be right to suggest inspiration from tales of whirling dervishes.[36]

More traditionally, Berlioz did exploit exoticism to represent a subjugated race. The grand opera ballet was often the locus for experimental colours, including the allegedly Mediterranean.[37] Since Trojans and Carthaginians (both refugees from the Levant) sing essentially the same music, and unite to overcome Dido's Nubian enemy, their eventual clash is political rather than racial. The first Act IV ballet, 'Pas d'almées' (Ex. 6.6), embodies the dangerous seductiveness with which the West endowed the East, although possibly it was a case of art imitating art (European exoticism is often imitated from earlier European imitations).[38] Rather than oriental authenticity, Berlioz is concerned here to represent voluptuousness, most strikingly by a device well within the signifying parameters of European music, a chromatic slide over a static bass. The music further beguiles by coyly evading the expected four-bar symmetry, as the violins soar above the staff amid glittering woodwind figures. The first climax, a rapturous expansion of supertonic harmony (bars 12–13), goes further by threatening foreground metric stability. The coquettish second strain (bar 17) restores the normal metre, but twists the accents within the bar by dotted figures placed on the first and third quavers; the accompaniment now suggests a plucked instrument, and a surprising trombone intervention adds a sinister undertone (bar 21). After the reprise, a closing strain in the cellos (bar 46) epitomizes a view of Eastern allure, inviting comparison with the traditionally seductive low female voice (but Berlioz had used cellos for Romeo and for an evocation of Cellini before he enters).

The second ballet ('Danse des esclaves') is for athletic males, presumably Nubian, and is strikingly different despite also being in 6/8 and G major. The principal material is hardly exotic at all, although the movement is replete with rhythmic interest. It gains vitality from ornamental triplet figuration and unexpected passion from an imploring melody (Ex. 6.7a). The B minor (mediant) makes a punning relationship to earlier emphasis on B flat major (bars 37–9). There is a marked affinity to the broad melody which intervenes, also at a late stage, in 'Menuet des follets' (Ex. 6.7b), where the seductive aim of the imagined dancers is explicit. Since the music was intended to be danced, the Carthaginian ballet is more symmetrical, but its octave doubling (cellos rather than second violins) is still more seductive, the chromatic slides are equally suggestive, and the strange diminished fourth interval comes six

[36] Locke, 'Cutthroats and Casbah Dancers', 37 (see Bellman, *The Exotic*, 119).

[37] See Benjamin Perl, 'Berlioz, orchestrateur d'Opéras', *L'Avant-scène opéra*, 128–9 (*Les Troyens*), 143–8.

[38] Berlioz insisted the presence of Indian dancers in Carthage was no anachronism. In 1857 he said that he had witnessed a 'pas des Bayadères' 'sixteen or seventeen years ago', possibly danced by real Indian dancers, possibly only at the Opéra (*CG* v. 433). In 1851 he encountered Eastern musicians at the London Great Exhibition. A likely source for the title is David's 'Danse des almées' (Egyptian dancing women), in *Le Désert*, but Berlioz does not fall back on David's bolero-like rhythm.

Ex. 6.6 *Les Troyens*, Act IV, the first ballet ('Pas d'almées')

times, not once. The mixture of D minor and F sharp minor in the Minuet, incidentally, shows a still closer affinity to the Trio of 'La Reine Mab', which also represents an erotic dream.

If these male slaves could be low-caste whites, the female Nubian slaves in the third dance are accompanied by a regular untuned drumbeat, a genuinely oriental touch amplified by thrumming violas and cellos, and punctuated by flickering violin trills and brilliant passage-work in the manner of Weber's

Abu Hassan. The woodwind melody in double octaves (piccolo, flute, cor anglais) imitates a 'primitive' pipe, while four slaves sing in one of Berlioz's invented languages, concentrating on the minor third of the purest mode Berlioz ever used (Phrygian). No ethnomusicologist would accept this delectable piece of Eurovision Orientalism as North African; yet such is the working of musical semantics that no listener can doubt what is signified. Although these exotic elements are confined to the hors d'œuvre, the fact that these

Ex. 6.7*a* 'Danse des esclaves' (*Les Troyens*, Act IV), from bar 63

Ex. 6.7*b* 'Menuet des follets' (*La Damnation de Faust*, Part III), from bar 77

three ballets form an entertainment at Dido's court develops the political framework of the opera; Dido was a colonialist, Aeneas intends to become one, and the finale of Act III, which refers to 'exterminating the black army', suggests shared belief in the chimera of racial superiority.

Within the European context of most of his works, Berlioz's music is certainly no stranger to the erotic. His range is wide, embracing not only 'Scènes d'amour' but the oriental erotic, the naughty erotic, and, by far the most important category, erotic meditation. It should not be assumed that all such music reflects something in his own life; compared to contemporaries like Hugo or Liszt, he lived a life of artisan simplicity, with few serious love-affairs, and compared to Wagner's, his love music may appear restrained, even chaste. But the automatic association of love music with the erotic is too simple; eroticism is only a part of love, and should therefore be only a part of love music.

The oriental and naughty erotic reflect the ambience of contemporary Paris; in Delacroix, for example, interest in the world beyond the Mediterranean is frankly lubricious. In the Prix de Rome competition of 1830, Berlioz handled some chilly poetry on a subject made famous by Byron and Delacroix; the eroticism of the Sardanapalus story is intensified by its fatal outcome. Soon afterwards, Berlioz selected two poems from Hugo's *Les Orientales*, both tinged with meditative eroticism, by which I mean an art suggesting wistfully erotic sensation, rather than being burdened with erotic candour. In 'La Captive', touches of local colour refer to the singer's homeland (Spain) rather than her place of captivity. 'Sara la baigneuse', which has no exotic musical references, represents the naughty erotic: 'for nineteen stanzas, a girl wearing no clothes, blushing like a pomegranate, swung in a hammock for no apparent reason other than laziness'.[39] Berlioz's music is a metaphor for Sara's extravagant imagination; rather than work on the harvest, she dreams of luxury beyond her class until her companions come and mock her. Originally scored for a quartet of male voyeurs, the revised version with mixed voices complicates interpretation, and the final version for three choral groups presents Sara as the focus of a multiple gaze of persons of all sexes. Until the end, however, the compositional persona shares her delicious reverie; in the end, the wordless mockery is almost lewd. The naughtiness of 'Le Trébuchet' ('The Trap') is of incipient rather than actual erotic fantasy, because the trap is not sprung. This piece Berlioz never orchestrated, whereas teasingly transparent orchestral colour is an essential feature of 'Sara'. We should not be surprised at finding a touch of naughtiness in the output of a friend of Théophile Gautier. The preface to *Mademoiselle de Maupin* (1835) proclaims Art for Art's Sake, but the novel climaxes in scenes of brazen eroticism, the last one Lesbian. Berlioz also relished the frank bawdry of Mephistopheles' Serenade, whose melodic charm might too easily conceal the sharpness of its message (before you allow liberties, get married).

The literary element in all this should not be over-emphasized: Berlioz's eroticism is essentially musical. Musical rhythms can convey sexual energy, but without external (literary) evidence, music cannot ensure that we understand what kind of energy is signified. Given a clue, however, a good deal of typical nineteenth-century music might be considered to signify eroticism, not least the characteristic intensification through repetition, varied repetition, or sequence, and the suspension of resolution (climax) manifested throughout Wagner's *Tristan*. Repetition and suspension control our sense of time, and an erotic state of mind is one alienated from the merely temporal (the 'Nacht' of *Tristan*). The passage from *Roméo et Juliette* which best illustrates this is

---

[39] Graham Robb, *Victor Hugo* (London: Picador, 1997), 139.

not the 'Scène d'amour', but the scene before the ball, which Berlioz essentially invented (it is not part of the play, even in Garrick's version), and which he called 'Roméo seul—Tristesse'. An atmosphere of reverie is created by the mysterious opening violin monody.[40] Wagner, present at one of the 1839 performances, must have been impressed by the four-note motive (from bar 22), repeated with developing texture and harmony (Ex. 6.8), which contains the seed of the 'Liebestod'. Berlioz glossed this passage when he revised the Prologue; the chorus sings the four-note motive to 'Hélas, Roméo soupire, car il aime d'amour Juliette . . .'. Harmonic resolution is postponed and time suspended. The passage is based on appoggiaturas, or rearticulated suspensions, and describes a curve of intensification, ending in release. Bar 31 shows a relatively weak resolution (plagal) in the tonic. This self-indulgent relaxation, however, prefaces a further accumulation of energy which leads to two inventive distortions of the cadential drive. First, with a characteristic flat sixth (D♭, bar 36) in the middle, contrary motion of the outer parts returns to the original pitch, A♮, and within the A chord, D♭ becomes C♯. Secondly, a climactic surge to top F in the melody on a diminished seventh (bar 38) unwinds in a chromatic slide which may be derived from the opening of the movement, and leads to a temporary resolution in A flat. This is the finest kind of meditative eroticism. It grasps at an image which continually eludes the dreamer; he tries other musical images—a silky melody passed among the woodwind—then returns to the four-note motive in the dominant (bar 49), before another cadence figure which again combines the major third and the flat sixth (from bar 56). These elements coalesce twice more, in the oboe solo (bars 103–6) and in Romeo's declaration of love, in the following movement.

In *Roméo et Juliette*, the symphonic persona, the mental apprehension of words, music, feeling, has entered the mind of Romeo. Perhaps the impossibility of an equivalent division of empathy prevents the love scene from having as much erotic charge as 'Roméo seul'. The declarations of Romeo and Juliet are certainly passionate, but Berlioz had in mind the balcony scene, which is filled with practical and moral discussion: 'If they do see thee, they will murder thee . . . If that thy bent of love be honourable, thy purpose marriage, send me word tomorrow.' The dialogue concerns love and fidelity, ruled by other gods than Eros. The lovers who acquiesce in the Friar's insistence on marriage before sex are not concerned at this point solely with eroticism, but with a complete relationship between equals—which was certainly how Berlioz considered them: 'Romeo reaches up to the love of Juliet; she is his equal, they are equal, they are sublime; it is the love of Titans.'[41] Berlioz did not include the scene following the lovers' night together, and its lines about the lark and nightingale; nowhere did he attempt a love scene like Act II of *Tristan*, or Act I of *Madama Butterfly*. The 'Scène d'amour' sharpens the

---

[40] See *Roméo*, 27–8 for other comments on this scene.

[41] 'Roméo s'élève jusqu'à l'amour de Juliette, elle est son égale, ils sont égaux, ils sont sublimes, c'est l'amour des Titans.' Letter to Adolphe Samuel (22 Dec. 1855), *CG* v. 222.

Ex. 6.8 *Roméo et Juliette*, II: 'Roméo seul'

distinction between the fullness of love, where two people meet on equal terms, and eroticism, which is either mental rather than physical, as in Ex. 6.8, or is likely to imply one individual in a position of dominance. The scene, in which the lovers cannot touch each other, has erotic potential; consider the wealth of fantastic modulations on the basis of intensified repetition which occupies much of this mysteriously formed movement. 'Roméo seul' does not have greater depth than the love scene; on the contrary, a complete love relationship is 'deeper' than erotic meditation. But in the love scene, programmatic considerations (knowledge of the play) impart something chaste, certainly in comparison to its most obvious symphonic descendant, the love scene in César Franck's *Psyché*; the 'Scène d'amour' does not *ache* like 'Roméo seul'.

A preference for idealized rather than erotic lovers' meetings is confirmed by *Les Troyens*. At their first meeting, Dido's admiring aside on the nobility of Aeneas's bearing (No. 28, bar 148) is an immediate reaction, and her recitative hardly suggests that she sees its significance; certainly there is nothing in this busy movement (the Act III finale) as erotically suggestive as the duet with her sister (No. 24), in which her desires have no known object. During 'Chasse royale—Orage', the love of Dido and Aeneas is consummated, a proceeding decidedly at odds with operatic decorum (see Chapter 3); the musical climax superimposes storm music, fanfares in different metres, and the wailing mockery of fantastic creatures of the forest, their only intelligible utterance being 'Italie'—the fatal idea which quickly brings this love to an end.[42] The music is a cataclysmic upheaval, and cares nothing, or even actually mocks, the sexual congress in the cave. To find the musical climax itself erotic is either wishfully to project programmatic knowledge on to it, or to recognize a metaphor ironic to the point of violence—an interpretation I would prefer, as it underlines the epic nature of the opera. The lovers are decidedly not present in the music, just as they are scarcely visible when the scene is staged.[43]

The Act IV love duet shares features with its equivalent in *Roméo*. The 6/8 metre predominates in Berlioz's love scenes, though not necessarily in his most erotically charged music: the enchanting 6/8 duo-nocturne in *Béatrice et Bénédict* is love music, but not sung by lovers. The duet in *Les Troyens* is certainly more intense. The fact that, among the immediately preceding numbers, two ballets, Iopas's song, and the septet are also in 6/8, makes the continuation of that metre almost hypnotic: saturated with beauty, the operatic persona is absorbed into the scenery. The suspension of clock time is achieved by reaching and quitting G flat major by arbitrary modulations,

---

[42] On the rhythmic superimposition, see *MLB* 131–2.

[43] Robinson calls this 'the musical evocation of sexual bliss' and 'the Gallic counterpart of Wagner's *Tristan* Prelude' (*Opera and Ideas: From Mozart to Strauss*, 137), and Kemp also projects erotic content personal to the royal lovers onto the entire movement: *Les Troyens*, 150–7. I am sorry so totally to disagree with these excellent writers.

from F and to D. Unlike Romeo and Juliet, Dido and Aeneas are already lovers; they combat embarrassment or foreboding by idealizing their situation. Berlioz's poetry, which significantly he called a 'litany of love' and adapted from *The Merchant of Venice* ('In such a night as this . . .'), eschews raw passion.[44] If the love duet lacks the highest erotic voltage, that is because it is an aftermath of the first physical consummation of passion. Berlioz strikes a note of transcendence, perhaps awe, suggested by the key of G flat, and perhaps more difficult to attain than mere rapture.[45] To paraphrase Paul Robinson, Dido and Aeneas are trying to halt the progress of history; hence the poem's mythical reference, which leads them (following Shakespeare) to name themselves.[46] The duet exploits a vertiginous tenor tessitura, symbolically intertwined with Dido's mezzo-soprano (for a few moments, bars 95–8 and 111, he rises above her). But Berlioz probably expected the tenor to sing in head voice, which modern tenors might consider *infra dig*. Infiniteness, rather than erotic charge, seems to me the 'subject' of the music. Its most luxuriant passage is the characteristically delayed expression of the dominant (D flat, from bar 95), comparable to late expressions of the dominant in 'Le Spectre de la rose' and the *Roméo* love scene.[47] This lasts only a few seconds but the sudden warmth, following a passage in which the lovers nearly quarrel, floods the stage thanks to the string trills and an efflorescence in the horns. The refrain (bar 99) restores a sense of unreality; in the harsh world of epic, mutual erotic contemplation cannot endure. Of course, in making these observations, I mean to praise Berlioz. The triadic purity of this love music is exactly right for these people; the sultry chromaticism of Wagner, Franck, or Saint-Saëns would never do.

Berlioz's world-view was inevitably that of a man. The idealization and caricature of the *Symphonie fantastique* are male images of woman rather than representations, as are the erotic day-dreams of 'Scène aux champs' and 'Roméo seul' (both, incidentally, in F major, key of the *Troyens* septet). We never get the beloved's view of the besotted composer, nor Juliet's of Romeo, an imbalance which persists to their deaths (see Chapter 9). But the dramatist is not confined to an objectifying viewpoint; there is enough in Juliet, Fiordiligi, or Dido to suggests that Shakespeare, Mozart, and Berlioz, as dramatists, could partly transcend their maleness. *Symphonie fantastique* is a brilliant work of adolescent outlook. *Harold* is limited through its virtual exclusion of the erotic; even in the third movement we are inside the alienated mind of Harold rather than that of the serenading lover. The experience of marriage and fatherhood, and witnessing motherhood, no doubt developed Berlioz's understanding of femininity, but it took time to sink into his art.

---

[44] See Rushton, 'Misreading Shakespeare: Two Operatic Scenes of Berlioz', 217–25.

[45] See Hugh Macdonald, 'G♭ 9/8', *Nineteenth-Century Music*, 11 (Spring, 1988), 221–37, esp. 228; see also Rushton, 'Misreading Shakespeare'.

[46] Robinson, *Opera and Ideas*, esp. 143–51.

[47] Rushton, '*Les Nuits d'été*: Cycle or Collection?', in Bloom, *Studies*, 117.

The exact contemporary of Mlle de Maupin, *Benvenuto Cellini* is conventional from this point of view, except for the tender anxiety in the duet movement in F sharp minor ('Ah, le ciel, cher époux') which Berlioz omitted from the Weimar version. But in *La Damnation*, Marguerite has two monologues, musically interrelated, of erotic anticipation and bitter recollection. Under the first impact of Goethe, Berlioz had composed 'Le Roi de Thulé' and the Romance in 1829, but the passages in which he reveals most psychological insight date from 1846. In the operatic scenes of Part III, Faust's air relishes the purity of Marguerite's environment, but he is there to make her unchaste, to spoil, in fact, his own dream, and thus do the devil's work. In Marguerite's entrance scene, Berlioz pre-quotes the music of the Romance to reflect her nocturnal vision of the ideal lover; the (male) composer draws a dream image filled with erotic promise, communicated to her by the devil. Wandering music in C minor opens the scene, a nebulous, syncopated theme heard from what is perhaps Berlioz's favourite combination of timbres, flutes and clarinets, over viola tremblings; this musical idea never reaches a point of repose, but is invaded by the dream, represented by fragments of the so-far-unheard 'Romance'. But the most erotic moment in all Berlioz is the end of the love duet, which goes beyond mutual fascination to a point approaching sexual union; the lovers are interrupted by the precipitate entrance of Mephistopheles, whose aim is not to preserve the decencies of the (concert) stage, but to frustrate Faust's appetite and thereby increase it. The short-lived erotic tremor is created by music which does more than merely support the words (Ex. 6.9). At 'quelle langueur', the faint C major triad interrupts a subdominant move to A. Berlioz represents Marguerite's arousal—which she is sufficiently inexperienced to mistake for fainting—by a chromatic dissolve, mainly in diminished sevenths. A series of new bass figures, the urgent crescendo of Faust's libido, outlines mostly tritones: the higher instruments decline by semitones, 'perdendo'. With the conflict of dynamics, the music loses tonal orientation until an arbitrary braking process (a segment of the circle of fifths) restores E major. Preventing the banality of a reprise, the tremolo boils up towards F minor to bring on the devil.

This chromatic dissolve is perhaps the clearest signifier of eroticism. In *Les Troyens*, Aeneas sings of Diana letting fall her veil before Endymion, to a short chromatic dissolve in parallel triads (bars 72–82). 'La pudique Diane' recalls virginal Marguerite, but without her loss of self-control (Diana is after all a goddess). In 'Le Spectre de la rose' the young girl's dream substitutes the ghost of the rose she wore at the ball the previous night for a visit from her lover; when the rose tells her not to fear, as he only wants to die on her bosom, eroticism becomes manifest, in another chromatic dissolve (bars 37–40) where exclusion from directed, and thus temporal, tonal processes signifies the dream's suspension of time. The rose attains its paradise; while we may interpret Goethe's, and thus Schubert's, hedge-rose (*Heidenröslein*) as a girl subjected to the violence of rape, Gautier's rose is male, and a seducer.

PROGRAMMES

Fontenelle famously asked 'Sonate, que me veux-tu?' Berlioz's instrumental music certainly belongs among musical works which, to interpret that celebrated and cryptic question, want something from us, or try to tell us something. Most of his instrumental works have titles; few have programmes, and where these exist, they are differently related to the music (the relationship also fluctuates within each work: see Chapter 10). *Symphonie fantastique* has a programme and *Roméo et Juliette* a sung prologue and libretto, documents which offer literary narratives parallel to the music. But do programmes help

Ex. 6.9 Love duet in *La Damnation de Faust*, Part III, from bar 102

us understand the music? Or does the music help us understand the programme? Do we listen to music through the prism of a literary or pictorial source, or do we hear in it the composer's response to such a source? With *Roméo*, music and programme were inspired by the same source, but the story is incomplete; even before suppressing the second prologue, Berlioz ignored the lovers' marriage and night of love, and in the final scene, the families are reconciled by the Church, rather than the secular authority of the Prince. The concluding 'Serment de Réconciliation' offers an uplift wholly absent from the ending of the play, even when the final scene is given uncut.

Roger Fiske remarks that '[Berlioz's] "King Lear" is a splendid overture, though not, I think, wholly successful as a translation of Shakespeare into music'.[48] This echoes the views of very different musicians about *Le Roi Lear*, notably Hugo Wolf and Donald Tovey: 'we shall only misunderstand Berlioz's *King Lear* Overture so long as we try to connect it with Shakespeare's Lear at all.'[49] They imply that Shakespeare's play was meant to function as the overture's programme, and use the play to account for perceived shortcomings in the music. Strictly, Berlioz provided no programme for *Lear*, but his overture is still part of the reception history of the play. Perhaps we should ask what the overture can tell us about *King Lear*, surely a work more in need of explanation than Berlioz's overture. It is no more proper to criticize Berlioz's piece for not affecting us as the play does, than to criticize Verdi's *Otello* because its characters are not identical to those in *Othello*. Each work merits appreciation on its own. And if this applies to an opera, which is also a dramatic form, it must hold still more for a concert overture.

Hence in considering programme music, we should not confuse the meaning of the music with the meaning of the programme. The programme is part of the history of the composition, but it does not convey the meaning of the music. It may guide us in the direction of that meaning which, however, remains musical, and cannot all be translated into words or images. With *Symphonie fantastique* Berlioz's most elaborate programme is particularly in need of illumination from the music. He himself explained it in terms of a popular theatrical genre: 'The following programme is equivalent to the spoken text of an opera [*opéra comique*], which leads one from one piece of music to the next, motivating their character and expression.'[50] The same applies, *mutatis mutandis*, to the *Roméo* prologue, but a better analogy might have been opera sung throughout, including recitative and other scenes such as 'pantomime', where music accompanies an action without words. Roger

[48] Roger Fiske, 'Shakespeare in the Concert Hall', in Phyllis Hartnoll (ed.), *Shakespeare in Music* (London: Macmillan, 1964), 185.

[49] Henry Pleasants (ed.), *The Music Criticism of Hugo Wolf* (New York: Holmes & Meier, 1978), 29–31; Donald F. Tovey, *Essays in Musical Analysis*, iv: *Illustrative Music* (Oxford: Oxford University Press, 1936), 82–6.

[50] NBE 16. 3.

Parker suggests that study of contemporary *livrets*, detailed stage directions interwoven with the libretto, may help us 'move music out of the realm of the ineffable and begin to see it . . . as richly endowed with potential communicative codes, both through the formal shapes it assumes . . . and through the myriad of meanings it can accrue in association with a dramatic text'.[51]

A paradigmatic example is Auber's *La Muette de Portici* (1828), of which F.-J. Fétis observed: 'The blend of melodrama and singing will only annoy those who fail to understand the language of instrumental music.'[52] Paradoxically Fenella, the character with most to 'say', is mute; her inarticulate gestures are paralleled by what Berlioz was to call, in connection with Beethoven, the 'expressive instrumental genre'.[53] Auber's music for Fenella's mime is like an orchestral recitative deprived of its declamation, so that stages in the narration and even gestures are accompanied by their musical analogue; Berlioz, inspired by Beethoven, took comparable gestures into the musical texture so that, on one level, they become 'abstract'.[54] Fétis was offended by the programme of Berlioz's symphony; so, more interestingly, was Schumann, who refuted Fétis on musical grounds.[55] Yet the aesthetic position of Berlioz and Fétis rested on a similar understanding of the powers and limitations of music. For Fétis 'the full power of this art to affect our feelings is due to its essential vagueness and indeterminacy'.[56] Berlioz, justifying programmatic instrumental music in the preface to *Roméo*, described the 'instrumental language' as 'richer, more varied, less restricted, and thanks to its very indefiniteness, incomparably more powerful' than that of vocal music.[57]

Boileau's truism 'La musique ne sait pas narrer' was intended to deny the validity of opera, but if music *could* tell stories, opera and programme music would be redundant; it is the wish to *associate* music with narratives that leads to these lively, generically tangled forms. Moreover, music itself may be experienced as possessing a narrative voice; and a good deal of excellent recent

---

[51] Roger Parker, *Leonora's Last Act* (Princeton: Princeton University Press, 1997), 132.

[52] 'Le mélange du mélodrame au chant ne peut déplaire qu'à ceux qui ne comprennent pas le langage de la musique instrumentale.' Fétis, *La Revue musicale*, 3/3 (Mar. 1828), 179. See John Warrack, 'The Influence of French Grand Opera on Wagner', in Bloom, *Music in Paris in the Eighteen-Thirties*, 575–7; Sarah Hibberd, 'Magnetism, Muteness, Magic: Spectacle *and the Parisian Stage c.1830*', Ph.D. (Southampton University, 1999), 134.

[53] 'genre *instrumental expressif*', see 'Aperçu sur la musique classique et la musique romantique', *Le Correspondant*, 22 Oct. 1830; *Critique musicale*, i. 63–8 (extracts Condé, 97–8; *Roméo*, 90). Berlioz had already published a series of articles devoted to Beethoven (*Critique musicale*, i. 47–61).

[54] These remarks owe something to Mary Ann Smart, 'Wagner's cancan, Fenella's Leap', a paper read at the International Musicological Society Congress, London, 1997.

[55] Schumann, 'Symphonie von H. Berlioz', *Neue Zeitschrift für Musik* (July and Aug. 1835); see his *Gesammelte Schriften* (Leipzig: Georg Wigands Verlag, 1854), 118–51. References are to the translation in Cone, *Fantastic Symphony*, 220–48.

[56] François-Joseph Fétis, in *La Revue musicale*, 1 Feb. 1835, in Cone, *Fantastic Symphony*, 215–20 (cited, 219).

[57] NBE 18. 2; complete trans., *Roméo*, 87–8.

criticism is concerned to unpick the meanings of instrumental music, with or without benefit of programme.[58] The contemptuous dismissal of narrative and expressive interpretations by modernists, such as Stravinsky in *The Poetics of Music* and Hindemith in *A Composer's World*, is testimony to their ubiquity. Music shares with narrative such rhetorical foundations as introductions, developments (or thickening plots), climax, and dénouement. The 'problem' with programmatic instrumental music is that narrative specifics, names and places, cannot form part of the performed work, as they can with opera. The composer can either attempt to control the listener's responses, at least partially, through a title or programme, or allow the music to speak for itself, and thus permit alternative listening in terms of absolute, even autonomous, musicality, or, of course, as an imagined narrative. Schumann claimed, in his ethnically skewed (but possibly ironic) rejection of the *Symphonie fantastique* programme, that '[the German listener] was already offended that Beethoven should not trust him to divine the sense of the *Pastoral* Symphony without assistance'.[59] Beethoven's Sixth is pastoral not because of its title, but because it contains figures which conventionally signified 'bucolic' (the opening drone), as well as frank imitations of nature (birdsong, storm). For Schumann, autobiographically significant comments like the first movement's 'Erwachen heiterer Empfindungen bei der Ankunft auf dem Lande' (Awakening of happy feelings on arrival in the countryside) were superfluous, because the tempo, harmony (a virtual absence of minor chords), and diatonic melodies convey as much, or more.[60]

Beethoven's 'Pastoral' may be the formal model for *Symphonie fantastique* (see Chapter 9), but Berlioz's programme represents a psychological progression for which the music is a metaphor no less potent, and no less revealing, for being fictitious. Berlioz never saw Harriet at a ball; he imagined that in such a situation, she would ignore him. If he dreamed of her in the countryside, with cowherds and thunder in the offing, the third movement is inwardly concerned with a deeply ingrained sense of rejection going back to adolescence when, having few to share his interests and confidence, he had suffered Virgil- or Estelle-inspired spleen in the countryside near La Côte. The 'truth' of the symphony does not depend on fact, nor on the real experience of dreams which may themselves have been imaginary. What Berlioz experienced through his ingestion of medicinal opium is unknown, but nothing in his voluminous correspondence suggests that his mental balance was affected

[58] See for instance Carolyn Abbate, *Unsung Voices* (Princeton: Princeton University Press, 1991); Edward T. Cone, 'A Lesson from Berlioz', in *The Composer's Voice*, 81–114; Anthony Newcomb, 'Once More "Between Absolute and Program Music": Schumann's Second Symphony', *19th-Century Music*, 7 (1983–4), 233–50, id., 'Schumann and Late Eighteenth-Century Narrative Strategies', *19th-Century Music*, 11 (1987–8), 164–74; Timothy Jackson, *Tchaikovsky: Symphony No.6 ('Pathétique')* (Cambridge: Cambridge University Press, 1999).

[59] Cone, *Fantastic Symphony*, 246.

[60] David Wyn Jones, *Beethoven: Pastoral Symphony* (Cambridge: Cambridge University Press, 1995); on the first movement, 54–61.

by narcotics. The programme's status as fiction is confirmed by the major change made *c.*1855, when he decided that performance with *Lélio* would make better sense if the whole symphony, rather than only the last two movements, was read as a dream.[61] Edward T. Cone remarks à propos the *Symphonie fantastique* that 'the persona is always to be distinguished from the composer . . . In choosing as his persona a figure *identifiable as* Berlioz, but not *identical with* Berlioz, the composer was symbolizing—no doubt unconsciously, but nonetheless appropriately—the relationship of every composer to his musical voice.'[62] The *persona* of instrumental music, the experiencing subject, rises to the surface, whereas in, say, Beethoven's Fifth or Schumann's Second, the persona, though no less real, is not identifiable. It is Berlioz's symphony, rather than the 'Pastoral', which is 'more the expression of feeling than painting'.

Typically, Berlioz did not repeat the formula. For *Harold* he provided only movement titles and an allusion to Byron, equivalent to calling overtures *Waverley* or *Le Corsaire*: Wolfgang Dömling declares roundly that *Harold* 'does not set literature to music'.[63] Long after it entered the repertoire, Berlioz provided clues to his thinking in *Lear*; but while the opening can be mapped onto Shakespeare's first scene, at least until Cordelia becomes unexpectedly eloquent, Berlioz himself referred the potent drumbeat to court ceremonial under Charles X. He did locate the place in the music where the King goes mad (bars 340–1), but such isolated points do not control the overall design.[64] With other concert overtures, he offered nothing, and although *Le Carnaval romain*, like an opera overture, may be 'interpreted' through *Benvenuto Cellini*, little of either formal or hermeneutic value is revealed. The determination to rid Berlioz of his wild romantic image led Barzun to misconstrue the evidence and assert that Berlioz did not want the programme of *Symphonie fantastique* distributed to the audience, unless it was followed by *Lélio*. This argument has been sufficiently refuted: Berlioz sanctioned withholding the programme 'à la rigueur' (if absolutely necessary), drolly adding that he hopes there is 'enough musical interest in itself'.[65] This I take to mean that unless it was too expensive; his preference was for having it available for the listener who may have chosen to read it or not.

---

[61] NBE 16. 170.

[62] Cone, *The Composer's Voice*, 84–5; he contrasts *Symphonie fantastique* with *Harold*, 91–3.

[63] Dömling, *Zeit*, 122 ('ist . . . kein Literaturvertonung'). A good case for a consistent interpretation based on Byron's *Childe Harold* has been made by Janet L. Johnson, 'Byron and the Poetics of Berlioz's *Harold* Symphony', read at the Congress of the International Musicological Society, London, 1997 (publication forthcoming), and in an unpublished paper by Paul Banks; my thanks to both these authors.

[64] *CG* v. 601; *MLB* 192.

[65] See NBE 16, p. x; in French, p. xix; Barzun, *Berlioz and the Romantic Century*, i. 158, reproduced on a reissue of Charles Munch's fine 1954 recording (RCA Victor 09026 68979 2), and no doubt the excuse for routine omission of the programme on CD inserts. See also Nicholas Temperley, 'The *Symphonie fantastique* and its Program', *Musical Quarterly*, 57 (1971), 593–60; see also NBE 16, p. x.

As Cone observes, Berlioz progressed from possible identification of himself with the protagonist, through the distancing of *Harold*, towards *Roméo et Juliette*, which 'eschews autobiography entirely, devoting itself instead to the exposition of a well-known literary theme, in part by frankly dramatic methods'.[66] 'Entirely' is too strong; in 1839, the Prologue's summons to remember the playwright ('Cette poésie elle-même, Dont Shakespeare lui seul eut le secret suprême') surely recalled 1827 and Harriet to knowing members of the audience. Generally, however, Cone is right: *Roméo*, as I have suggested elsewhere, is a covert opera.[67] In the following year, 1840, Berlioz finally objectified symphony into patriotic ritual; thereafter he wrote mainly vocal music. Thus despite his present-day reputation, programme music played a relatively minor part in his output. But in those works which do have a programme, he posed acutely the question of what we actually listen to, and for, in music. Even in dramatic music, can we pay full and simultaneous attention to the 'programmatic' elements of character and plot—even though they are made visible to the eye and articulated by words—*and* to the music? If we focus on the feelings of a character, does the music recede, or does it become, like film music, the insidious progenitor of our involuntary empathy? Is this situation changed by *La Damnation*, where there is, or should be, no staging, only a musically shaped scene, in the 'theatre of the mind'?[68] In *Roméo et Juliette*, still further removed from the theatre, do we, or the virtual persona of the symphony, merge with the feelings of the characters, or do we contemplate them from a suitably alienated standpoint, as the prologue rather suggests? With *Symphonie fantastique* again, since the programme cautiously names no names, do we experience thoughts or feelings about Harriet, balls, cowherds, guillotines, and witches, *during a performance*? The answer may vary between individuals: I can only say with certainty that despite my own belief that the programme is part of the work's essence, I do not think or feel these things while listening, for then I am riveted by the sounds—textures, melodies, instrumental combinations—and primarily by elements of pitch and rhythm, elements so denuded of interest in mediocre music, so intensely gratifying in music we love.

---

[66] Cone, *The Composer's Voice*, 93.   [67] *Roméo*, 80–6.

[68] John Warrack, 'Berlioz and the Theatre of the Mind', *The Listener*, 72 (1964), 738, reprinted in Felix Aprahamian (ed.), *Essays on Music* (London: Cassell, 1967), 49–52. See also Langford, 'The "Dramatic Symphonies" of Berlioz'; Dömling, *Zeit*, 77–80.

Part III

The Works

7 The Lyric Berlioz

ROMANCE, BALLAD, AND 'GOTHIC SONG'
The central place of the romance in Berlioz's musical culture is disguised by
his avowed ambition towards 'higher'—less domesticated, larger—genres.
But he was preoccupied with simple song forms up to the drinking song in
Béatrice et Bénédict, and a retrospective collection of 'Mélodies' with piano
accompaniment was published in 1863, although this collection includes
choruses and two cantatas, *Chant des chemins de fer* and *Le cinq mai*, printed
like vocal scores convenient for rehearsal, since their impact is heavily dependent on the orchestra (see Chapter 3). The justification for the title 'Mélodies'
lies in the predominance of solo song, including forms descended from the
strophic romance. But the anthology only partially represents Berlioz's devotion to lyric forms. No attempt was made to recover the earliest songs, and
nothing was extracted from larger, canonical works—not even the easily
detachable 'Chanson du pêcheur' (*Lélio*), or 'Strophes' (*Roméo et Juliette*),
which had twice been published separately.[1] Today we need not take Berlioz's
choice of lyrical works as canonical, and besides reviving early songs and
choruses such as 'Le Ballet des ombres', performers sometimes choose
extracts from longer works in preference to independent short works, a proceeding very much in the spirit of nineteenth-century anthologies.[2] Of the
cycles and collections, the greatest, *Les Nuits d'été*, is often heard in full,
although seldom in its original keys. In performances with orchestra, sopranos transpose the songs Berlioz set for low voices ('Le Spectre de la rose' and
'Sur les lagunes') up to their original pitches, restoring the key scheme of the

---

[1] In Paris in 1839, and in London in 1846. Holoman, *Catalogue*, 201.

[2] Austin B. Caswell draws attention to numerous anthologies of romances, including those
originating in opera ('Loïsa Puget and the French *Romance*', in Bloom, *Music in Paris in
the Eighteen-Thirties*, 99). A recorded choral anthology (HMP 3901293) includes the *Mab*
Scherzetto, a section from *La Tempête*, and Somarone's drinking song, with choruses from
Lélio and *Irlande*, 'Adieu des bergers', etc. A song anthology 'Hector Berlioz: Mélodies' (DGG
435 860–2) contains several early songs, and threatens the integrity of *Benvenuto Cellini* by
including the de Wailly 'Chansonette', and working gallantly through six stanzas of 'Je crois en
vous'.

piano version, which Berlioz designed in 1840 for mezzo-soprano or tenor.[3] Contraltos, including those styled 'mezzo-soprano', retain Berlioz's low pitches for these two songs but transpose others down by as much as a major third, a procedure particularly deleterious to 'Villanelle' and 'Absence'. At least *Les Nuits d'été* is recognized as a coherent group, whereas *Irlande* is almost always splintered into choruses and isolated songs on the assumption, widely shared but challenged by Annegret Fauser, that it is a mere anthology and not a coherent collection, never mind a cycle.[4]

Any attempt to reconstruct the *mentalité* of early nineteenth-century France must assign the romance a considerably more important place than it would occupy, were one's choice based on survival in the repertoire. Just as critics once failed to read *Les Troyens* other than through Wagnerian spectacles, and thus, at best, as a dignified failure, we can all too easily view the romance through the distorting prism of the Austro-German Lied, or through the songs of Fauré and Duparc which are its legitimate descendants. Yet even a teleological view of musical history should not cold-shoulder a masterpiece of the romance repertoire such as Martini's *Plaisir d'amour*, which Berlioz himself orchestrated (H.134). We need not look austerely at songs merely because they first appeared in vanity publications, paid for by the authors, like Berlioz's early songs, *Irlande*, for which Berlioz and Gounet shared costs, and *Huit scènes de Faust*; nor because they were offered to the public in a fashionable periodical or an anthology of mixed origin.

Romances were not confined to domestic spaces. They also belonged in the theatre, and they were not all, in any sense, sentimental, being quite often works of political and social engagement: 'Such promiscuity of genre is a characteristic trait of the *romance* as Berlioz surely understood.'[5] The natural theatrical space for a romance was *opéra comique*, where it had long played a role considerably more complex than an engagingly simple musical surface might suggest.[6] By the 1830s the romance had also established itself at the Opéra. If Cellini's romance 'La gloire était ma seule idole' is problematic, it is not because of its strophic form; *couplets* had inhabited this august stage since *Robert le diable* (1831). The spirit of the romance is expressed in directness of communication, clarity of form, eloquence of melody, and simplicity of accompaniment; any two or three such elements can bring to mind the most popular of vocal genres. Hence the romance may be implicated in serious

---

[3] See Peter Bloom, 'In the Shadows of *Les Nuits d'été*', and Rushton, '*Les Nuits d'été*: Cycle or Collection?', in Bloom, *Studies*; Annegret Fauser, 'The Songs', in Bloom (ed.), *The Cambridge Companion to Berlioz*.

[4] Both OBE and NBE split up *Irlande* into solo and choral numbers. Fauser, 'The Songs', makes a case that *Irlande* is a cycle and the *32/33 Mélodies* is a carefully ordered anthology.

[5] Fauser, 'The Songs', 111.

[6] David Charlton, 'The *Romance* and its Cognates: Narrative, Irony and *vraisemblance* in Early Opéra Comique', in Herbert Schneider and Nicole Wild (eds.), *Die Opéra Comique und ihr Einfluss auf das europäische Musiktheater im 19. Jahrhundert* (Hildesheim: Georg Ohms Verlag, 1997) 3, 43–92.

arias, even those not in strophic form. The loose-limbed 6/8 of Cellini's rondo 'Sur les monts les plus sauvages', in which the hero reflects on the charms of country life ('sans labeur inutile') intersects with the romance as pastoral; romance texture surfaces near the end in a flowing quaver accompaniment (bars 120–4), only to disappear in the expansive cadential period which equates heroism with a high, ringing tessitura.[7] The pastoral connection is explicit in Iopas's song in *Les Troyens*, set within the Act IV *divertissement*, also in F and in rondo form, and also reflecting, to harp accompaniment, on the imagined delights of rural life.

Berlioz's contributions to the romance may appear the most conventional area of his output. Nevertheless, departures from routine are as prominent here as in other genres, such as symphony and opera; and the lyric genres remain fundamental to his thinking, even in such complex works as *Roméo et Juliette* or *Les Troyens*. It is easy to locate these departures by vague gestures towards genius, unique melodic impulse, and so forth; Berlioz's tendency, at least from 1829 (*Huit scènes de Faust*), to fill romance-like pieces with asymmetrical phrasing and cadential evasion certainly provides some excuse for such judgements within a musical culture which has long rated complexity a virtue (*Irlande* has too often been underrated in this respect). But the source of Berlioz's tendency to complexity lies mainly in the words, and less in their metrical qualities than in their meaning (see Chapter 4). This is not to say that other composers of romances were not stimulated by words; but Berlioz was gripped from the very first by the need to bring out what Reicha called the 'syllabe logique', not only as an effect of prosody, but in order to create from each song a unique poetic and musical persona.

That this tendency was evident from the first is suggested by what may be, in a sense, his first surviving 'mélodie'. Berlioz's setting of Florian's romance 'Je vais donc quitter pour jamais' is strictly speaking lost; if he is to be believed, the melody survives, but without stylistic indicators of romance accompaniment, and of course without text underlay, in the Largo of *Symphonie fantastique*. But for Berlioz's avowal, we might not suspect that it was composed earlier than 1830, particularly as there is little other early Berlioz in a minor key with which to compare it. Berlioz's claim has been doubted, but although he was young to conceive such a haunting idea, 'Le Dépit de la bergère' makes clear that he could already conceive characteristic shapes.[8] The early stages of the melody fit the words well; it may follow that the melody itself, and not just its mood, was generated by the rhythms of the

---

[7] The c″ before the romance allusion may be intended as a glided head voice, whereas the b♭s supported by an orchestral fortissimo (bar 136) and in the cadenza could be sung in chest voice. A draft cadenza extends to the 'Ut de poitrine'. See Joël-Marie Fauquet, 'La Voix de Persée', *Avant-scène opéra*, 142 (*Benvenuto Cellini*), 84–93.

[8] Noske, for instance, says 'the young Berlioz of 1820 would hardly have been capable of creating such an accomplished melodic contour'; *French Song from Berlioz to Duparc*, 96.

text (Ex. 7.1).[9] The underlay becomes less convincing as the melody develops; but other instances for which the original is known show that Berlioz habitually developed the later stages of a melody when turning a vocal original into something idiomatically instrumental. The predominance of one-syllable words licenses the composer to place emphasis on the ego ('Je'), on 'donc' (therefore: the cause for departure), sweetness ('doux, douce'), and the homeland ('pays'), while implying that the greater wrench is parting from the beloved ('douce amie'). The second phrase is unsatisfactory because of the rows of quavers, and consequent under-emphasis on 'trainer' and 'pleurs' relative to 'vie'; 'regrets', however, is the 'parole logique' of this thought. Despite the regular series of minims every two bars, implicitly appoggiaturas descending by step, the four-by-four phrasing is not at all square, in the pejorative sense. Within phrase 1 (bars 1–4) the second unit unbalances the first by premature entry as an upbeat ('Mon doux pays'), and the construction of bar 3 is totally unlike that of bar 1. In phrase 2 (bars 5–8) the third minim appoggiatura ('vie') is overcome when its resolution initiates the quaver figure, a feature which connects bars 5 and 6; the second phrase, therefore, has a less marked caesura and not only sweeps over the ascending octave, but nostalgically decelerates towards 'regrets'.

Ex. 7.1 Reconstruction of 'Je vais donc quitter pour jamais'

In default of Berlioz's original underlay, these comments may seem over-interpretative. But the tune is easily imagined with a gentle guitar accompaniment, securely based on tonic and dominant harmonies; there is no compulsion to use chord VI, as in the symphony, bar 7, where the intricate chromaticism of the orchestral texture is generically remote from the romance. That fact in itself, however, has expressive weight when we hear the melody part-supported, part-subverted, by its accompaniment, particularly on the repeat when the harmonization implies, at first, another key (bars 28–32; E flat rather than C minor). 'Le Maure jaloux', which we can be rea-

---

[9] Julien Tiersot (*La Musique aux temps romantiques* (Paris, 1930), 81) underlaid the melody in G minor, a more likely vocal tessitura than the symphony's C minor, adopted by Temperley (NBE 16. 194).

sonably sure was composed no later than *c*.1821 (see Ex. 5.5), provides a useful comparison, in that it includes minor-mode music. Despite the regularity of the two-bar units, the phrasing is again flexible; the words produce different upbeats (quaver, two quavers, three crotchets, etc.) as well as suggesting affective detail in analogues to 'murmure' (minor, oscillation), 'ivresse' (a sharper dotted rhythm), and 'transports jaloux', where the line is broken by a 'soupir', the quaver rest, like the hypothetical final phrase of the Florian song (*Symphonie fantastique*, Largo, bar 15). The composer of 'Le Maure', probably no older than 18, could certainly have written the Florian song not long before. 'Le Montagnard exilé', 'Toi qui l'aimas', and 'Canon libre à la quinte' were probably composed in Paris. Except for the canon, their lesser immaturity is shown in a more confident handling of the lyrical and rhetorical prototype common to most short forms, and in their sense of formal adventure.

The prototype I have in mind is a feature of the musical landscape, no more than the successful disposition of beginnings, middles, and ends.[10] In its lyric manifestation it can be observed in romances and arias by Berlioz's contemporaries, such as Louise Bertin, to whom the first version of *Les Nuits d'été* is dedicated, or his rivals for the Prix de Rome. In the first phase of the prototype, songs and arias begin with a period founded in the tonic, and often on a tonic pedal, above which simple harmonies and even an occasional chromatic chord can appear without threatening the tonal ambience. In a common variant, this first section ends in a key other than the tonic. 'Pleure, pauvre Colette' (*c*.1820) has a pedal, 'Le Montagnard exilé' a mobile bass which appears in five out of the first six bars of the vocal section. That the former seems the feebler piece is nothing to do with its static bass, and the mature Berlioz frequently made use of a pedal in the opening stages of a lyric. The same principles apply to the second section of 'Le Montagnard', although it starts in C minor and ends back in E flat. The second (middle) phase in the prototype involves sequence, and with it modulation or other application of harmonic colour; this phase may be expected to end in or on the dominant. The third phase is normally in the tonic; even if not a reprise of the opening, it restores order and achieves closure. Each phase will usually consist of one or two units, and the phases may be unequal in length. In the marvellously piquant 'Hélène', from *Irlande*, for example, the first phase equals in length the second and third combined.

The early romance which gives the strongest foretaste of *Irlande* is 'Toi qui l'aimas, verse des pleurs' (Ex. 7.2), despite its square phrasing and the near-absence of prescribed dynamic nuances. The first phase (2 + 2 + 4 bars) prolongs tonic harmony (this is not affected by the guitar-like figuration which produces unaccented dominants as the lowest pitch). The melody twice gropes its way from the third to the fifth (B to D), before reaching the high

---

[10] See V. Kofi Agawu, *Playing with Signs* (Cambridge, Mass.: Harvard University Press, 1991).

tonic that this motion implicitly predicts (bar 21). This high G is lightly subverted by the harmony, which is not tonic; the melody rolls back as far as the
dominant. The middle phase establishes that the sleeping shepherdess is dead;
this accounts for the finality of a tonic cadence (bar 20), albeit in the minor.
Rhetorically typical features of a middle, however, are the use of the minor
mode and of sequence, taking the melody to a point (bars 13–14) where the
relative major, B flat, seems about to be confirmed. The seventh at this point
(bars 13 and 17) may seem the product of inexperience, at least in harmonic
theory, but it is contrapuntally prepared and—most importantly—expressive: the word 's'élève' tells us that the flower at least ('fleur chérie') is not dead
(this melody incidentally anticipates the motive in *Sardanapale* which Berlioz
used in *Roméo*: Ex. 2.1). The closing phase re-establishes the tonic major,
moving by agonizingly small steps before a noble arpeggio for 'l'arbre sacré'.
The close in the minor, with a weeping piano figure and bass imitation, anticipates much in the mature Berlioz, but the real importance of this song is that
his guitar-trained ear is at last producing something personal which still
works when transferred to piano. It is more characteristic than usually realized that Berlioz should thus find himself in a piece at once plaintive and
restrained.

Ex. 7.2 'Toi qui l'aimas, verse des pleurs'

lè - ve au - près___ de son___ tom - beau, S'é -

lè - ve au - près___ de son___ tom - beau.

Vo - ya - geur qui, cher - chant___ l'om - bra - ge,

T'ar - rê - tes sous___ le vert feuil - la - ge De

l'ar - bre sa - cré des dou-leurs,___ Laisse un ins -

tant cou - ler tes pleurs!

As far as we know, Berlioz wrote no songs between 1823 and 1828. One surviving number of *Les Francs-juges*, the pastoral trio, intersects with the romance style apparent in earlier works like 'Le Dépit de la bergère' or 'Le Montagnard exilé', but the genre had already penetrated his sacred music, in the 'Gratias' of the Mass (see Ex. 4.5). In the dramatic cantatas, a flavour of the romance may be found in Orpheus's aria, partly through the harp accompaniment, but it is not strophic like the later invocation to the instrument in *Irlande*, 'L'Origine de la harpe'. His return to this form was part of his excited response to Gérard de Nerval's translation of Goethe's *Faust: Der Tragödie erster Theil*. Faust offers many opportunities for musical set pieces even in an operatic version—witness Gounod's *Faust*, although he avoided the scintillating Rat and Flea songs, perhaps because Berlioz's versions appeared definitive (but no such inhibition affected Gounod with 'Le Roi de Thulé'). Only four of Berlioz's eight 'scenes' are strophic songs; of these Mephistopheles' Serenade, with guitar accompaniment, could be used on stage as it stands. Curiously, however, the 'scene' headed 'Romance' is not strophic, and in essence is not a romance but an aria of considerable formal sophistication (see below).

The most romance-like movement is the ballad, 'Le Roi de Thulé'. Around 1828–30 Berlioz included in his scores quotations (like the Shakespeare and Moore added to *Huit scènes de Faust*) and indications of context, many of them suppressed when he revised the pieces concerned. But for 'Le Roi de Thulé' he retained, in *La Damnation*, the cryptic subheading 'Chanson gothique', apparently intended in the sense 'folkloric' and thus (as is suggested by the *Oxford English Dictionary*) uncouth, unpolished, rather than medieval.[11] Holoman attributes the term to the modality of a scale with altered fourth and sixth degrees, and Macdonald draws these meanings together: '"gothic" by reason of its melancholy viola solo and the sharpened fourth in the melody, close to a flattened sixth, creating a mode of imagined antiquity'.[12] Yet while Marguerite is a simple soul, she is apparently a *bourgeoise*. Berlioz locates her home near a barracks, but in *La Damnation* her room has silk curtains, unless the devil supplied them, as he supplies jewels in Goethe (and Gounod). 'Le Roi de Thulé' was composed at the end of 1828 for voice and piano, the version represented in Ex. 7.3.[13] Pedals hint at a pastoral ambience without quite constituting a drone; the bass swings into action for the modulations, which as with the slightly later 'La Belle Voyageuse' tend to be flatward. Apart from bar 5, every chord of phase 1 (bars 1–10) is in root position, as are the first chords of phase 2 (bars 11–14), if we construe appoggiaturas (bars 11–12) by their notes of resolution. Yet phase 1 modulates, unusually, to the subdominant. Phase 2, more radically, proceeds to flat III (B flat) with-

---

[11] OBE nevertheless offers the translation 'Mediaeval song'.

[12] Holoman, *Berlioz*, 97; Macdonald, *Berlioz*, 85.

[13] The autograph, a fair copy and probably the earliest notation of any of Berlioz's Faust music, was traced only after publication of NBE 5.

Ex. 7.3 'Le Roi de Thulé', Chanson gothique (1828 version)

out closure, and curves back to an imperfect cadence in the tonic minor (bar 17). Contrapuntally considered, the opening fifth above the bass represents a relatively stable *point de départ*; octaves mark temporary points of repose, permanent only at the end; thirds (tenths above the bass), and occasional chord inversions, are used in modulating. Thus the elements of counterpoint and harmony work together, supporting the exceptional rhythmic fluidity of the melody.

Such modulations are far from rustic, and the phrase-lengths mutate the romance towards art-song. Nerval's metric and rhyme scheme (rhymes ABBACDCD, octosyllabic, with additional mute E for the B and C verses) invites the mid-bar endings. But the opening four-plus-four is extended to four-plus-five by sustaining the last syllable of 'ciselé', and the harmony seems to dispute the position of the barline; 'd'or', signifying expensiveness, arrives on a weak beat but receives agogic emphasis by syncopation, an inspired piece of word-setting. Metric order is restored in phase 2, with a four-bar phrase ending on a first-beat fermata, but the next unit lasts three bars, and phase 3 again cadences in mid-bar. Barring according to harmonic rhythm would require bars 8–10 and 19–21 to be represented as two bars of 9/8. Of course such quickly cancelled discrepancies, which become a feature of Berlioz's mature style, do not need rebarring to be heard. In 'L'Origine de la harpe', he went further, breaking the 4/4 metre into 3/4 for a cadence which, despite this unusual expedient, sounds natural and spontaneous.[14] Berlioz rethought the metrical scheme of 'Le Roi de Thulé' for *La Damnation de Faust*, where the voice starts half-way through the bar. The phase 1 cadence ('ciselé') falls on a first beat, two empty beats precede 'Reçut à la mort', and the syncopated 'd'or' consequently falls in the middle of a bar. But the rest before the next line ('Comme elle ne le quittait') is extended, restoring its original metrical position, and phase 3 therefore cadences as in Ex. 7.3. Clearly Berlioz's alterations were not motivated solely by a desire to rationalize the metre. And in either version, it would be hard to maintain that merely because it is strophic, the 'Chanson gothique' is any less an art-song than the lament, 'D'une amoureuse flamme', which Berlioz entitled 'Romance'.

'Le Roi de Thulé' broke new ground, and not only as his first *Faust* setting and possibly his first solo song for five years. It established a topic, 'gothic song', by which he inflected the gracious simplicities of the romance into something at once artless and artful. Its immediate successor, the epitome of 'chanson gothique', is 'La Belle Voyageuse', the song Berlioz said he wrote like a counterpoint exercise, a couple of bars at a time, and whose rhythmic and harmonic evasions I have discussed elsewhere.[15] For inclusion in *Huit scènes*, 'Le Roi de Thulé' was provided with an obbligato viola. This anticipates the elaboration of 'La Captive' and 'Le Jeune Pâtre breton', but in these the cello and horn solos are used to vary the strophes, which remain identical

---

[14] See Rushton, 'Berlioz and *Irlande*', 230.   [15] See Ex. 5.7; *MLB* 63–6.

in 'Le Roi de Thulé'. A later example of the artless vein of 'Gothic' song is the charmingly mournful 'Petit Oiseau', which Berlioz set beside his overtly artful setting of the same words ('Le Matin'). More importantly, the 'Gothic' topic turns up within larger works, sometimes disguised by the rejection of strophic form; Iopas's song in Act IV of *Les Troyens* was sketched as a strophic song and elaborated into a rondo.[16] The ambience of *L'Enfance du Christ* is partly pastoral, in the tradition of Christmas pieces, and this is musically reflected by an exceptionally high incidence, even for Berlioz, of compound metres. The strophic 'Adieu des bergers' can be mapped onto the scheme of Marguerite's ballad: phase 1 (bars 5–20), two units divided by an imperfect cadence which close in a related key (here the mediant); phase 2 (21–36), with the sweeping sequential descent, involving the farthest modulation as well as the widest vocal range (sopranos, b–g″) and ending on a minor-mode half-close; a short phase 3 by way of closure. In Part I of *L'Enfance*, Mary begins the duet alone; the mobile bass and accompaniment have shed all vestiges of the romance, but the carefully wrought phrases are each two bars long, and the modulation is again to the flat side—indeed, as in 'La Belle Voyageuse', it is to an unrelated key a whole tone below the tonic (here A flat to G flat).

The central position of the romance within Berlioz's dramatic thinking emerges from the way in which 'Le Roi de Thulé' was presented. On the autograph of the piano version, he took the trouble to write not only 'Chanson Gothique', but also that Marguerite 'sings while getting undressed'. The fragmented coda, its words reverting to the first stanza, already appears in this first version; it suggests that her thoughts have left the song entirely (in Goethe, this is when she finds Faust's box of jewels). Berlioz elaborates this idea in *Huit scènes de Faust*, prefacing the song with 'Elle se met à chanter en se déshabillant' (Goethe's stage direction in full), and adding a footnote:

In performing this ballad, the performer should not seek to respond to the various nuances of the stanzas by expressive singing; on the contrary, she should try to make them as undifferentiated as possible; for it is clear that Marguerite is thinking of anything but the problems of the King of Thulé; it is an old story she learned in childhood, which she sings absent-mindedly.[17]

In *La Damnation*, the footnote is removed and the context changed. Faust is lurking behind the silk curtains, so rather than undressing, Marguerite sings 'en tressant ses cheveux'. It need not follow that Berlioz wanted the singer to reintroduce expressiveness. In the piano autograph the voice part includes two diminuendo signs on long notes ('d'or' and 'joyeux'), and in *Huit scènes* three ('ciselé', 'joyeux', 'yeux'); in *La Damnation* these are reduced to one ('joyeux'), although another covers the 'deep sigh' in the coda. In *Huit scènes* the viola solo already has more nuances than the voice; in *La Damnation*, it is elaborated with two more variants of the opening motive, several additional

---

[16] See *MLB* 171–2; the sketches are reproduced in NBE 2c. 784.   [17] NBE 5. 78.

marks of expression, and a raised dynamic level to enhance its pale, nasal tone (a governing *p* is raised to *mf*, with *f* and *sf* at crescendo peaks). Thus Berlioz increasingly transferred the 'expressive' nuances to the instrumental commentary; rather than wanting the singer to add expression, he may have decided, in 1846, that his caution against doing so was no longer necessary.

The archetypal Gothic song may indeed be a legend, like 'La Belle Voyageuse', which Berlioz 'framed', in the 1830 publication, by subtitling it 'Ballade' and identifying the (female) singer as 'jeune paysan'.[18] Within this publication, 'Le Coucher du soleil', 'Adieu Bessy', and 'Élégie en prose' are for tenor, but the other legendary narrative, 'L'Origine de la harpe', also subtitled 'Ballade', is for soprano or tenor. The latter, and 'Hélène', show that ballads need not always be in compound time; moreover, as already suggested above (Chapter 6), 6/8 is Berlioz's usual key for love music. In 'Le Coucher du soleil' and 'Adieu, Bessy' Berlioz adopts compound time for material which is not at all 'gothique'. Yet while both exploit the metrical subtleties to which compound metres lend themselves, they are not necessarily more sophisticated in this respect than the ballads, and other qualities draw them back into the sphere of what Noske, in a happy pleonasm, called 'the Romantic romance'.[19] Nevertheless, they reach out, with 'Élégie en prose', towards the pure art-song which came to be called, partly as a result of Berlioz's Thomas Moore-inspired title, the 'mélodie'.

This generic stretching is present both in accompanimental figuration and the harmony. In 'Le Coucher du soleil' the melody floats on the surface of the chords, rather than being, as in 'La Belle Voyageuse', the agent of harmonic change. The piano begins neither with a 'till ready' figuration nor a fragment of the melody, the introduction types Berlioz normally used, even as late as *Les Nuits d'été* (both appear in 'L'Origine de la harpe'). Instead, the call to order (appropriate in the first song of a cycle) is a strident octave A♭ (Ex. 7.4 is a reduction, not the complete texture). The sighing chromatic $^6_3$ chords threaten tonal stability before any has been achieved, reaching a fermata on the mediant major: given the immediately preceding A♮, this chord of C is not simply approached as the dominant of the relative F minor, although it is resolved that way. Even when a romance accompaniment prepares the vocal entry (bar 8), a deliberate insecurity of tone is not eliminated, and when the first cadence comes on G, the leading-note, this shock breaks off the accompanimental pattern; the piano is left to grope chromatically back towards F (bars 16–17). According to the three-phase prototype, the next passage, with its sequences, is the middle, but the composing-out of the introduction, already responsible for the move through G to F, extends as far as bar 20,

---

[18] Evidently a (mezzo-)soprano is intended for 'La Belle Voyageuse'. Holoman suggests 'Tén.', and changes the treble G clef to tenor (octave) G clef (*Catalogue*, 77). But a tenor represents an adult voice. The orchestrated versions are for one or two female voices.

[19] Noske, *French Song from Berlioz to Duparc*, 12 ff. On 'Le Coucher du soleil', 'L'Origine de la harpe', and 'Adieu Bessy', see Rushton, 'Berlioz and *Irlande*'.

where the romance accompaniment resumes, and the introduction reappears in diminution in the bass (bar 24). The doubling of the bass in tenths (22–3) resembles the equivalent place in 'Le Roi de Thulé' (Ex. 7.3, bars 12–13). The horizon expands when the music touches the dominant of the dominant (B flat, bar 25). The third harmonic phase, 'Alors dans mon âme ravie' (not included in Ex. 7.4), begins unusually early, less than half-way through the vocal section (discounting the introduction, the stanza covers forty bars; phase 3 begins in the nineteenth). The piano accompaniment evokes an orchestra, striding in the bass, tremolo in the right hand, then dissolves into *soupirs* (bars 34–6); in the prolonged falling cadences, the piano imitates a harp. This brew of instrumental styles goes with a harmonic simplification appropriate to a prototypical phase 3, and the resulting semiotic tangle

Ex. 7.4 'Le Coucher du soleil' (reduced, to bar 26)

underlies the suicidal drive of the poet. The tremolo on 'mon âme ravie' (in the second stanza, 'régions radieuses'); the *soupirs* aspiring 'vers l'astre' ('des îles heureuses'); the harp, associated with 'soupirs' in stanza one, but with 'voiles d'or' in stanza 2, suggests that the distant islands veiled in a golden sunset are the isles of the dead.

A similar generic claim could be made for 'Adieu Bessy', which is excluded from the domain of the simple romance by tremolos and the particularly feverish figure which accompanies the entry of the voice. The voice part opens, with more despair than decorum, on a diminished seventh. The major-minor antithesis of the introduction frames the stanzas neatly by reappearing when the poem reaches the title-words, and provides a frame to control the emotion, now tinged with irony, within the romance category.[20] But pent-up feelings break loose again in the last number of *Irlande*. In the declamatory 'Élégie en prose', the two balanced strophes are disguised, coinciding musically only in phase 3 of the prototype, to form a true through-composed 'mélodie'. Rhythmic tensions operate on several levels. Phase 1 begins by placing the characteristic dotted rhythm on both third and first beats, and ends in mid-air (bar 11), without either harmonic or rhythmic closure. The unstable phase 2 is the longest (bars 12–24) and its sequential ascent, *en route* like 'Le Coucher du soleil' to chords on the leading-note (D sharp minor and E flat major), sets the voice in 4/4 metre, whereas the harmonic changes still define 3/4 (bars 12–15). The second stanza adapts the dotted rhythm to a melodic echo of 'Chant guerrier', a chorus from earlier in *Irlande*, and this idea is presented boldly in sequence before coming to rest in C major (flat VI, bar 47). Phase 2 presents a new sequence with the pun-related keys of F major and F sharp minor, and replaces the cadence in the dominant of stanza 1 (bars 23–4) by a boldly plunging V7 (bars 55–6). Thus only phase 3, an insidious chromatic departure from a dominant pedal only slightly altered from stanza 1, provides formal stability.[21]

AFTER *IRLANDE*: ROMANCE TO *MÉLODIE*

It is typical of Berlioz that having made a breakthrough in the conception of song, combining the familiar with the adventurous in such a way as to make *Irlande* one of his more readily accepted compositions, that he should stow *Huit scènes* away for later reference and move on to something completely different. The year of *Irlande* was also the year of *Symphonie fantastique*. He revised and orchestrated several songs, but for ten years new ones appeared only sporadically. The later songs continue to develop the prototype, while sometimes covering its traces. Taking a cue from the second stanza of the 'Élégie', 'La Captive' employs sequence at the beginning as well as the cadential phase; the chromatically insecure middle (bars 11–14 of the vocal part)

---

[20] The gentle mockery of the return to major corresponds to that in Wilbye's madrigal 'Adieu, sweet Amaryllis', a correspondence of musical signification which is undoubtedly coincidental.

[21] On the third phase, see *MLB* 95–7.

consists of a single plunging descent. 'Le Jeune Pâtre breton' adopts a binary (A A′) pattern, reflecting the requirement that it be sung 'naïvement'. With 'Je crois en vous' (Ex. 5.2) the boundary between phases 1 and 2 is blurred, although phase 2 ends with a sequence and phase 3 ('Je prie') is clearly marked; with 'La Belle Isabeau' the stanza, which also opens with a sequence, is interrupted by the real-life storm, and phases 2 and 3 are inextricably linked. Another fine sequence marks the variation in the final stanza at 'Venez, venez, avant l'aurore'.[22]

'Les Champs' also has a long phase 1, with its own binary pattern, returning to the opening at bar 13 (Ex. 7.5 is taken from the revised version). A is open, and A′ closes in the mediant, G minor (bar 19). Phase 2 represents the uncertain search for happiness by using all three diminished sevenths, rather than any sequence. Phase 3 could be identified by the final words (bar 27, 'Viens aux champs'), but closure only begins after the fermata, so that phases 2 and 3 cohere as a larger unit (the last phrase is repeated with an authentic cadence). 'Les Champs' is not the only one of Berlioz's songs to strike a note of ironic detachment; it is not a pastoral, but a summons to the reluctant beloved to escape from Paris where (Béranger's poem continues) 'les beaux-arts font des miracles . . . la tendresse n'en fait plus'. The bustling opening thus evokes the busy futility of urban life, in complex figuration that scarcely escapes its original pitches; other accompanimental ideas are required when the music moves, including scales in thirds (bars 10, 17) and an unquestionably pastoral drone (bars 17–18). The continuum is also subverted by the registral dislocation of the bass (bars 11–12), and the hollow octaves of bar 20. There are reminiscences of *Irlande* in the semiquaver figure of bars 9 and 12 (compare 'Adieu Bessy') and the pulsing climax ('bonheur') whose chromaticism and register recall 'Le Coucher du soleil'. When Berlioz elaborated 'Les Champs' for publication in *Fleurs des landes*, stanza 3 strikes a note of late-Berliozian nostalgia (bars 77–88), and the final plea to the beloved gains amplitude from his favourite backward resolution of dominant onto subdominant (bars 122–3).[23]

THE MATURE *MÉLODIE*

Songs like 'Les Champs' show how Berlioz was never afraid to make an original gesture, even within the context of a commercial romance. He was also prepared to unbend far enough to publish songs in periodicals, at least until 1850. This possibility explains the existence of 'La Belle Isabeau' and 'Le Chasseur danois'.[24] 'Prière du matin' and 'La Mort d'Ophélie' were also published in periodicals, but in 1848, some time after their composition. Only 'Le

---

[22] See *MLB* 148.   [23] See *MLB* 42–5.

[24] *Album de Chant du monde musical* published 'La Belle Isabeau' (Dec. 1843) and 'Le Chasseur danois' (Dec. 1844), but not 'Zaide', written in time for December 1845; Fauser, suggests it was too difficult to sing ('The Songs', 112).

Matin' and 'Petit Oiseau' followed, in 1850. Yet ten years earlier Berlioz had composed what are often considered the first masterpieces of the *mélodie*.

What most obviously differentiates *Les Nuits d'été* from the conventions of the romance is the expansiveness of its through-composed forms.[25] It is tempting to see this as a deliberate progression. Berlioz experimented with the form of the romance as early as 'Le Dépit de la bergère', with its fragmented coda, an idea which recurs in 'Le Roi de Thulé' (with elements of the melody

Ex. 7.5 'Les Champs'

[25] See Noske, *French Song from Berlioz to Duparc*, 107–12; *MLB* from p. 171; Rushton, 'Les Nuits d'été: Cycle or Collection?'; Bloom, 'In the Shadows'; Fauser, 'The Songs'; Laurenz Lütteken, '"erfordert eine ziemlich grosse Sensibilität bei der Ausführung": Anmerkungen zum Liederzyklus *Les Nuits d'Eté* von Hector Berlioz', *Musicologia Austriaca*, 8 (1988), 41–64.

in the 'wrong' part of the bar) and many later pieces; the classic examples are 'Sur les lagunes' and 'L'Île inconnue', followed by the last (orchestral) version of 'La Captive' (all songs in 6/8). The early fragmented codas are additions to strophic forms, even one with variations or multiple strophes like 'Le Montagnard exilé', in which thirteen stanzas are varied by three musical sections, each repeated as required to cover the long poem; the final reprise of the opening stanza constitutes Berlioz's first fully characteristic fragmentation coda. The main exception in the early songs is 'Canon libre à la quinte', which besides its unusual contrapuntal texture, is not strophic, and, to excellent effect, abandons canon for a new homophonic idea for a concluding section headed 'Invocation'.

The next important non-strophic vocal pieces are Marguerite's 'Romance' and 'Élégie en prose' (see above). The Romance (in *Huit scènes*, 'Une amoureuse flamme'; in *La Damnation*, 'D'amour l'ardente flamme') is a broad ternary form, if we only consider the disposition of the text; if we include the instrumental interludes, which repeat the opening melody on the principal orchestral voice, a haunting solo cor anglais, the form becomes a rondo (Table 7.1).[26] At least four versions of the lyric prototype are imbricated within the structure, as every restatement of the opening melody can function as a first or a third phase. Table 7.1 represents the music as it appeared in 1829. In *La Damnation*, the rondo interpretation is fortified because the throbbing accompaniment no longer continues through 'Son départ, son absence', and after the fragmented reprise of the songs of the soldiers and students, the cor anglais and voice join in a further, fragmented coda on the A theme.

Les Nuits d'été opens with a strophic form, 'Villanelle', but the vocal part, as well as the accompaniment, is subtly varied in each stanza. The vagrant modulations, varied codas with bassoon solo rising systematically in pitch, and formal asymmetry resulting from the interlude before the final stanza act together as a metaphor for the progress of spring, single-minded in the burgeoning of new life but delectably disordered in details. This metaphor is reinforced by the counterpoint. In stanza 1, a single fragment (bars 28–9) shadows the voice by melodic inversion (starting an illicit fourth below); in stanza 2 (from bar 43), a mock canon at the octave dies back, picks up, doubling the voice in thirds (bar 48), breaks into athematic staccato (bars 50–3), then resumes canonic imitation at varied intervals for nearly seven bars. The interlude starts in D minor, so that stanza 3 begins with the voice answering at the upper fifth, in A. Every ten bars (88, 98, 108) the cellos try another canon, at varied intervals and eventually two bars rather than one behind the voice. The first breaks into more staccato quavers, slithering and chromatic; the second only works with further chromatic twists which compress, then expand, the ambit of the voice part; the third occurs where no imitation has been before, but manages a strict canon at the fifth for four bars.

'Villanelle' gently mocks the strict 'topic' of imitation which elsewhere Berlioz used with the utmost seriousness, and this lightness of touch, as much as the texture and form, distinguishes this song from its companions. The equally simple form of 'Absence' contributes to its haunting expression of longing for the absent beloved; and the difference of the two episodes is a wonderful example of intensification by varied repetition. While the bass begins these sections respectively on D♮ and D♯, the latter section places the voice a third higher (from bar 42). In the first episode the tonality slides almost imperceptibly to the dominant of D sharp; the second time the section begins and ends in that key. Despite tonal rationalization, however, the second episode reaches a harrowing climax over a chord of B with a grinding neighbour C♮ in the bass; resolution to B is followed by further resolution to A sharp, the local dominant. The climax, implying the remote key of E, is a metaphor of imaginative distance, past cruel valleys and mountains ('A lasser le pied des chevaux!').

---

[26] See also M. Lensky, 'Characterization in the Dramatic Works of Hector Berlioz', 169.

TABLE 7.1 Design of 'Une amoureuse flamme' (*Huit scènes de Faust*)

Key, text incipits	Rondo interpretation	Ternary interpretation	Rhetorical prototype (phases)	
F 'Une amoureuse flamme'	A Introduction A First stanza	A Introduction A First stanza	A1	B1
F, f, A♭, f 'Son départ, son absence'	B, new violin motive, new melody	A', same bass figure	A2	
F	A (instrumental)	A (instrumental)	A3, also C1	B2
F, to C, a, d 'Sa marche que j'admire'	C, 9/8, new accompaniment and melody	B, 9/8, new accompaniment and melody	C2	
F 'D'une amoureuse flamme'	A (vocal)	A (vocal)	C3, also D1	B3
F, f, A♭, D♭, b♭, F 'Je suis à ma fenêtre'	D	A", same bass figure	D2	
F 'O caresses de flamme'	D continued	Coda	D3	
F	A (instrumental)	A (instrumental)		

'Au Cimetière' is hardly more complex in feeling and form; but it has been perceived as peculiarly difficult to 'take', just as 'Villanelle' has been criticized for quirky modulations.[27] Such views, quaint in view of the cycle's modern reputation, are based on resistance to perceived originality. In 'Au Cimetière', the atmosphere of hopelessness is conveyed by a sense of drift between sections.[28] The poem may take some credit for this melancholy lack of definition. The six-line stanzas are divided into twice three, lines 3 and 6 having four syllables instead of eight. The rhyme scheme is A B B A C C, but the metric repetition within each stanza, marked by the short line, affects the musical setting, tending to emphasize shorter (three-line) units. Berlioz only repeats words ('passe dans un rayon tremblant') near the end of the middle stanza, and only rarely is the 'syllabe logique' not in the last word of the line (bars 44–6, emphasizing 'soupir', are an exception; the first statement of 'rayon tremblant' favours 'rayon', but the second 'tremblant'). Nearly all these final syllables involve a change of harmony, often one which fails to predict any particular continuation; alternatively, as in bar 31, they hover on a harmony which seems inexplicable (A♭ with an appoggiatura from the sharpened fourth, although the song is in D). The governing ternary plan links two stanzas as a large phase 1 in the tonic (to bar 49), then a new vocal style, declaiming on a single note, marks the beginning of the middle ('On dirait que l'âme éveillée'). The downward enharmonic drift pursues similar tonal strategies to the first section, and when sustained melody resumes ('Sur les ailes de la musique') it is in an alien tonality, C major, with a suddenly lush texture. But at the key-word 'souvenir', in this section rich in irony, Berlioz reaches A major, the dominant, which in other pieces provides a last burgeoning of erotic passion.[29] Here he risks a platitude—A major surmounted (bars 76–9) by a flute melody resembling a slow waltz—which in context can prove agonizing.

'Le Spectre de la rose' is a vocal appendix to the love scene from *Roméo*, for all the latter's vastly greater scale.[30] More appropriate, perhaps, would be comparison with Marguerite's Romance (compare Table 7.1), but without the formal ambiguity given by purely instrumental reprises. Rondo form is additive, and so here is the rhetorical prototype. Phase A1 (to bar 17) deals with facts: 'I am the ghost of the rose you wore at yesterday's ball.' Phase B, a rondo episode, represents the rose's triumph, subverted by its resolution in the key a semitone below the tonic (B flat, bar 28; compare 'Élégie en prose'). Thus the critical text 'O toi qui de ma mort fut cause' (bar 30) bridges episode and reprise (B1 and A2). The reprise is abbreviated, and the start of episode

---

[27] See for instance W. H. Hadow, *Studies in Modern Music* (London: Selley, Service, 1926), 138; J. H. Elliot, *Berlioz* (London: Dent, 1938), 150–3.

[28] The fundamental line for this song is disputed between voice and accompaniment, but it must be admitted that they do not work expressively against each other as this might imply. *MLB* 179; Rushton, '*Les Nuits d'été*: Cycle or Collection?', 123–4.

[29] Compare the love duet in *Les Troyens* (see Ch. 6); 'Le Spectre de la rose' (below); *Roméo*, 'Scène d'amour'.

[30] Rushton, '*Les Nuits d'été*: Cycle or Collection?', 117.

C is undefined; the new poetic stanza begins in tonal uncertainty at bar 38, but a new extension of the A music begins at the end of bar 34. Thus the song is directed to the rose's destination: 'J'arrive du paradis'; the glorious, delayed flowering of the dominant, expanded by word-repetition. Phase A3 is the ghostly reprise from bar 50. This piece has been called operatic, but such formal intricacy is unlikely in an operatic narrative. Where such dramatic situations can be conveyed by words and music alone, a responsive listener will not need a theatre. The same might be said of the very different feelings evoked in the orchestral version of 'La Captive', and in the other songs of the cycle, 'Sur les lagunes' and 'L'Île inconnue'.

SMALL CHORAL WORKS

The domestic vocal ensemble, or small chorus, with or without accompaniment, is among the most neglected areas of nineteenth-century music. Berlioz's relatively slender output hardly matches Schubert's, but it spanned his entire career, from 'Amitié, reprends ton empire' to what may be his last composition, 'Tantum ergo'. While 'Le Ballet des ombres' (Ex. 5.8) takes fantasy to extremes, the choruses in *Irlande* are robustly appealing. 'Chant guerrier' ('N'oublions pas les champs') begins challengingly, with the progression I–iii–vi, the latter (A minor) weirdly inflected by a B♭, and the haughty refrain has a sprung rhythm with many syncopations. Few composers would have dared the jump from C to D flat for the tenor *couplets* ('Ils sont tombés'): its eventual goal is A flat, but progress is wonderfully oblique (C: D flat, A flat, G major implying C minor, then E flat, with an added seventh leading back to A flat). Gradually the tenor adopts rhythmic features of the refrain ('Monde nouveau', bar 26). The bass solo is not on the same level, but its dignified melodic language anticipates *Le cinq mai* and other patriotic works. Berlioz's gift for the vividly rambunctious also enlivens the refrain of 'Chanson à boire', first cousin to the orchestrated 'Chanson de brigands' (*Lélio*), but less extreme in harmony and more varied in mood. The Italianate wistfulness and roaming harmonies of the tenor *couplets*, marked 'malinconico', call up the tears of one whom drink has led to introspection and self-pity: we gaze through the liquor down to the lees. The remaining choruses are 'Chant sacré', whose beauties are more fully revealed in orchestral guise, and 'Hélène', also delectably orchestrated, whose unaccented syncopation and insinuating modulations are among the most ingenious things in *Irlande*, and the most haunting.

The main interest in 'Le Chant des Bretons' lies in the revision.[31] Berlioz broke the original accompanimental continuum by rests, depriving the voices of unison support, and making the harmonies more ambiguous: in bar 8, for instance, voice and piano in the first version present a frank tonic chord (E

---

[31] NBE 16, version I, 31, version II, 34. An orchestrated version of 'Le Chant des Bretons' has not survived.

major), whereas in the revision the voices' unison B invites dominant harmony; this the piano rejects with its brusque entry (between two bars of rest) on E. There are other subtleties, but the main effect of the revision is to lighten something too solid and to freshen its lines; a little interlude before the third stanza (as in 'Villanelle'), and an elaborated conclusion, leave the first version well behind aesthetically, and are typical of Berlioz's compositional thinking around 1850, when he was revising a number of pieces for republication. Perhaps the most interesting point here, since nothing will make this a major achievement, is why Berlioz did not get it right first time, as he already had with the choruses in *Irlande*, and later did with the exquisite 'Prière du matin'.[32]

The rondo design of refrain and *couplets* remains standard in several later choruses, including the patriotic repertoire. But gems like 'Sara la baigneuse' create their own formal designs, or resist formal analysis through consistency of motive and absence of structural modulation. Of course there is a refrain which returns from time to time. The tonal trajectory involves feinting at, rather than establishing, the mediant in the early stages, a lucid subdominant later on (bar 163), and a melody in B minor recapitulated up a fifth (bars 134, 178). Perhaps the most remarkable feature, however, is that the chromaticism is nearly all foreground, even when it controls the progression from the bass up (bars 81–95). In a piece in A major which underlines a melodic peak with C sharp minor (bars 17, 205), once replaced by G sharp major (bar 59), Berlioz would normally supply a balancing C♮ and G♮. Although the dominant is not emphasized, the sharpened pitches have a tonal function, whereas any flattened pitches are immediately resolved; and this harmonic tendency is part of the unique coloration of the piece, the pitch analogue of its pellucid vocal and instrumental texture and its innocent-sounding note-against-note counterpoint. It is not surprising that a piece so strangely scored—three choral groups, eight woodwind, three horns, timpani, and strings—should not be often programmed, but those who know it, love it.

The later choruses light few flames. The pan-European sentiments of 'Le Temple universel' are matched by some tidy canonic writing and imaginative textures, but there is hardly enough invention to overcome the hollowness of its quasi-millennial rhetoric. Of the two versions, it may be best to be bold, and take the unaccompanied one. Of the two late Latin choruses, 'Tantum ergo' for high voices and organ is the more elaborate, perhaps the more Berliozian, but the simplicity of the unaccompanied 'Veni Creator' allows greater effect to its occasional touches of colour, including a characteristic cadence in flat III. It is a pity, however, that Berlioz found no occasion to explore this vein of composition with larger forces in emulation of Bortnyansky, two of whose Russian choruses he adapted with Latin words. Berlioz's feeling for the beauty of religious sentiment remained after faith

---

[32] For a partial analysis of 'Prière du matin', see *MLB* 92–4.

deserted him, and in a culture which still believed in the efficacy of aesthetic beauty as an aid to worship, he might have made a substantial contribution. The evidence for this, however, is more to be found within his larger works, sacred and secular.

ARIAS IN DRAMATIC WORKS

His dramatic works show Berlioz's lyrical gifts fertilized by his wish to communicate the emotions he found in Shakespeare, Virgil, and Goethe. Before establishing a reputation as a symphonist, he showed in his prize cantatas and *Les Francs-juges* that he could shape lyrical texts into original musical forms, and in *Benvenuto Cellini*, perhaps mistakenly, he turned on the full heat of invention in an attempt to impress an audience by then conditioned to expect Berlioz to write symphonies. In the arias, Berlioz selected particular forms as a means of characterization. Perhaps it was the thought that neither Balducci nor the Pope (Cardinal) were the type to sing arias which led to the repression of the former's 'Ne regardez jamais la lune', in which the treasurer's obsessive paternal control emerges not only from the text but from the music: the form of three strophes, each with two statements of the main melodic figure (the second inverted), hammers home the moral by the rhythmic and rhetorical over-emphasis of a crass preacher.[33] Teresa, by contrast, treats the opportunity for an aria as the first breath of freedom in her repressed existence. The *Rêverie et caprice* version (Ex. 4.2), mingling fast music with slow, might make one describe the character as *nerveuse*. The more expansive replacement aria treats its two tempos separately, and thus more conventionally. Berlioz returned to this kind of aria only for Hero in *Béatrice et Bénédict*. He may have associated it with higher sopranos than those he preferred in principal roles (Marguerite, Marie, Cassandra, Dido, and Beatrice are all mezzo-sopranos). Like Teresa, Hero is awaiting her lover who, according to the perception of marriage as the ideal female goal, will liberate her from the paternal roof. But Hero's wedding is approved and creates no dramatic tension. The Andante is in 3/4 like Teresa's, and both feature oboe on the melody, but Hero's is divided in half by a reprise (bar 44), and having cadenced in A moves stiffly to the subdominant, rather than to an indirectly related key (in Teresa's case, D after B major). Yet the Allegro contains surprising hints of introspection, even doubt, in the cadences on the text 'My hand will be the prize' (of Claudio's constancy and heroism). This prepares the way for the more detailed exploration of a female dilemma in Beatrice's aria.[34]

The tenor Cellini is a man of action with two reflective arias, complicating the interpretation of his personality (see Chapter 10). The arias for Fieramosca and Ascanio show how a solo utterance can make us laugh both

---

[33] This aria is published for the first time in NBE 1a. 127.
[34] See Rushton, 'Berlioz's Swan-Song'.

at and with a character: Fieramosca's fencing aria includes a metrical experiment which suggests the hit-or-miss quality of his swordsmanship, while Ascanio ('Tra la la . . . mais qu'ai-je donc?') parodies everyone else in the popular rondo form, where part of the joke is how you find the refrain again; particularly apt is the way the 'Tra la la' is replaced for the last reprise by the closing words of the couplet. Arias are not usually included in symphonies, but the subject-matter of *Roméo et Juliette* is reflected upon in the contralto's 'Strophes' ('Premiers transports') which stands not only outside the dramatic framework, but outside that of the surrounding Prologue itself. Lawrence's aria ('Pauvres enfants que je pleure'), on the other hand, is purely operatic, and its Larghetto is designed in a way which Berlioz increasingly favoured, as continual evolution, virtually without seams.[35] This type is developed in *La Damnation de Faust*, in the music composed in 1845–6; all the strophic forms originated in the *Huit scènes*. Faust himself, therefore, avoids the strophic forms adopted by all the other characters and sometimes the chorus. With *L'Enfance du Christ*, Berlioz might have made use of traditional melodies, like Lesueur in his *Oratorio de Noël*. Instead, however, he continues, without going beyond, the point reached in *La Damnation*, where dramatic circumstances prescribe the musical forms. The shepherds sing a strophic chorus with the lightest (orchestral and dynamic) variation in the third stanza. The second duet for Mary and Joseph ('Dans cette ville immense') has repeated elements ('O par pitié, secourez-nous'), but only because they must make the same desperate plea wherever they knock. Herod's melancholic aria is surprisingly solid in its ternary structure, a form of musical archaism to match its modal colouring. On the other hand, the first duet for Mary and Joseph, while it uses internal repetition of material like the imitative passage which finally brings in Joseph ('Répands encor ces fleurs'), never reverts to its opening idea, instead re-establishing the main key with a new melodic shape, and a touch of canon ('Oh! sois béni').

An exception to this progressive tendency is *La Nonne sanglante* where, perhaps mindful of the suspicions of the Opéra management, the surviving arias, at least, have clear points of reprise, the bass aria being binary, the tenor aria ternary. But with *Les Troyens* Berlioz returned to his practice of engaging with lyrical forms tailored to each situation. Cassandra is steadfast in character, but suffers unique mental torments; when she gathers herself for an aria in the second scene ('Malheureux roi'), she begins in E flat minor, and when the opening strain returns in the major, the effect is of a terrible resignation. Her second aria ('Non, je ne verrai pas') develops so freely that the end is thematically and tonally far away from its point of departure, until the arrival of the procession and Trojan March absolve her from the responsibility of attaining closure. Choroebus, on the other hand, is a simple soul; he uses the

---

[35] On strophes, see *Roméo*, 24–5; on Lawrence's aria, Rushton, 'Misreading Shakespeare', 214–17.

short melodic stanzas of Rameau and Gluck, and after Cassandra's appalling vision of his death, he can only repeat himself. To vary the repetition, Berlioz the musical craftsman adds something to the texture, but because he was also a dramatist, it is Cassandra's despair that we hear in the oboe, as well as her muttered prophecies (see Ex. 10.6). Like Cassandra, Dido finds her truest voice when reconciling herself to disaster. Her lyrical utterances are as varied as any of Berlioz's characters, and nothing else in Berlioz's output explores a psychological state with such penetration as her monologue and aria after Aeneas has departed.[36] Her first aria ('Chers Tyriens') begins in one key and ends in another, but the keys are related as relative minor and major, and the relationship is prepared already before she begins. Berlioz used these linked keys several times in this opera. As is fitting in a public scene she repeats the entire stanza, as if ritualistically, with choral commentary; this and the repetitions of the Carthaginian anthem ('Gloire à Didon') make a thematic complex in the manner of Gluck.

Dido's second air ('Errante sur les mers', Ex. 7.6) corresponds to Cassandra's 'Non, je ne verrais pas' in its freedom of melodic design and incorporation of a definitive change of topic. Both these arias precede numbers based on the Trojan March, while a processional entry is prepared, but unlike Cassandra, Dido is oblivious to the future, nor is her nervous eagerness yet tinged with expectation of love: she is more than curious, but hardly knows why. Accordingly Berlioz lets her retain her tonality (F), but no thematic profile. Yet 'Errante sur les mers' conforms to the lyrical prototype, freely interpreted with respect to reprise, in which it may be compared with 'Voici des roses' (Ex. 4.10). Phase 1 consists of five two-bar units of varied rhythmic physiognomy (although the first two are the same). The middle phase picks up the imperfect cadence to prolong the dominant of F minor by a sequence ('Hélas, des coups du sort'), but then treats C as a tonal centre in a passage which evokes the capricious elements through sharp gusting orchestral motives, immediately adopted by the voice. These words are then repeated as Berlioz prepares to stabilize a tonic which has never been far away; this phrase (the repeat of 'Au malheur') is the first to recover the f″ heard near the beginning. The tendency of the line to descend is complemented by the generally narrow tessitura of the last phrases: one attempt at a wider spacing (the ritenuto, 'souffrance ne pourrait') is reined in by the interrupted cadence, and the repetition of the last words is tightly controlled by movements almost entirely by step. Her final aria, 'Adieu, fière cité', is a culminating point in Berlioz's achievement of developing, non-repeating forms in a single tempo; the equivalent in multi-tempo arias is Aeneas's 'Ah! quand viendra l'instant', headed 'Air' although the previous recitative is measured, having some of the character of an aria. The increasing use of pliable, coherent, but essentially free musical designs allows Berlioz to distinguish personal

---

[36] See 'Dido's Monologue and Air', in Kemp, *Les Troyens*, 161–80.

utterance from ritual, a crucial component throughout this opera, but one missing from *Béatrice et Bénédict* in which the musical forms, befitting an *opéra comique*, tend towards familiar archetypes, notably the rondo.

Ex. 7.6 *Les Troyens*, Act III, No. 25, Dido: 'Errante sur les mers'

ci - le pour nous___ Qui con - nut la souf - fran - ce,

qui con - nut la souf - fran - ce ne pour - rait voir en vain souf - frir,___

Qui con - nut la souf - fran - ce ne pour - rait voir en vain souf - frir.

8 Architecture, Patriotism, and the End of the World

The Mass and Berlioz's developing aesthetic

Berlioz sought employment in the theatre and the Conservatoire, but never in the Church, and his pronouncements about religious music are the aesthetic views of an increasingly unbelieving outsider. The *Messe solennelle* is one of three large-scale liturgical works in Latin, completed at twelve-year intervals. It shows signs that his taste was already developing in directions he later maintained. But his attitudes were not yet fully formed, although they were hardly novel and had a direct source; for Jean Mongrédien, Berlioz's first article on religious music (1829) 'seems almost to have been dictated by Lesueur'.[1] Just as Hugo, in the preface to *Cromwell*, associated modern literature with the drama, so both composers perceived the essence of modern music to be dramatic. A year later, Berlioz had parted from Lesueur in that he also canonized modern expressive instrumental music (Beethoven).[2] But he continued to agree with Lesueur that music with a religious purpose need not be deprived of any modern musical resource, albeit of secular origin, so long as triviality was kept at bay. In this they were unwittingly in agreement with modern perceptions of earlier composers such as Bach, Haydn, or Mozart.

On a spectrum ranging from the frankly operatic to the liturgically functional, Berlioz's Latin sacred works are nearer the 'dramatic' end than the ritualistic. His aesthetic is epitomized in scribbled notes in the 1832–6 sketchbook, apparently intended for a review, never published, of an unidentified mass. Salient phrases, excluding more general comments, notes about musical technique, and remarks about the performance, include: '[Kyrie] of true

---

[1] 'semble presque avoir été dicté . . . par Le Sueur'; Mongrédien, *Le Sueur*, 982; Berlioz, 'Considérations sur la musique religieuse', *Le Correspondant*, 21 Apr. 1829; *Critique musicale*, i. 13–16.

[2] 'Aperçu sur la musique classique et la musique romantique', *Le Correspondant*, 22 Oct. 1830; *Critique musicale*, i. 63–8.

and expressive character [. . .] a great outcry on eleison excellent [. . .] fugue
. . . like all fugues on amen [. . .] resounding trumpets at Deum de Deo—I don't
see the point [. . .] Passus containing fine woodwind lament strikes a serious
note [. . .] the prosody is excellent throughout [. . .] pleni sunt in E minor rather
ordinary [. . .].'[3] Approval of the 'great outcry' and 'fine lament' reflects the
appropriateness of such musical expression at 'have mercy' and 'He suffered'.
His questioning of the trumpets at 'Deum de Deo' is puzzling, since this clause
('God of God, Light of Light') is a glorification of Christ, though Berlioz may
have been worried about an outburst so early in the Creed rather than withholding it for places where he had exploited brass himself ('Et iterum venturus
est'). Berlioz's comment on 'Pleni sunt coeli' rejects the commonplace as
unworthy, and the dry remark about Amen fugues recalls his execration of his
own 'Quoniam' (see Chapter 5), and his words of 1829:

Let people who have never heard anything like it, imagine what kind of devout expression arises when fifty voices, howling with fury in a lively tempo, repeat *Amen* four or
five hundred times, or vocalise on the syllable *a*, so as to sound like raucous laughter
. . . I defy anyone with the slightest musical feeling . . . not to interpret such a chorus
as an army of incarnate devils, making fun of the sacrament, rather than a gathering
of the faithful praising God.[4]

Berlioz proclaimed Cherubini's C minor Requiem a masterpiece of truthful
expression, except for the fugue in the Offertoire, on 'Quam olim Abrahae',
where the offence is compounded, since it is performed Da Capo after the
Hostias.[5] Berlioz may seem unreasonably annoyed by 'Amen' fugues, as he
was by vocal coloratura and Bellini's appoggiaturas.[6] In *La Damnation de
Faust*, the 'Amen' fugue sung by students in Auerbach's cellar wins the caus-
tic praise of Mephistopheles: 'The style is learned and truly religious; one
could hardly put across better that devotion which the Church, at the end of
its prayers, summarizes in a single word.'[7] It is a palpable hit; nevertheless,
one wonders what piqued Berlioz into adding the fugue to an already complete score, when performance was imminent.[8] The fugue is ingeniously based

---

[3] '[Kyrie] d'un caractère expressif et vrai [. . .] un grand cri sur eleison excellent [. . .] fugue . . .
comme toutes les fugues sur amen [. . .] Sonneries de trompette sur le Deum de Deo dont on ne
voit pas le but [. . .] Passus contient de beaux gémissements d'instruments à vent d'air très grave
[. . .] la prosodie est toujours excellente [. . .] *pleni sunt* en mi mineur un peu commun [. . .].'
Sketchbook of 1832–6, fos. 22ʳ–27ʳ; pages used in reverse order. A full diplomatic transcription
is in Holoman, 'Sketchbook', 312–13. My selections silently complete Berlioz's abbreviations
and ignore line breaks.

[4] 'Considérations sur la musique religieuse' (see n. 1), *Critique musicale*, i. 14.

[5] *Journal des Débats*, 20 Mar. 1842, HC 480; Condé, 142. Reviewing an 1835 performance
(*Journal des Débats*, 9 Aug. 1835), Berlioz gives Cherubini the advantage over Mozart's
Requiem, but he calls the 'Quam olim' fugue an 'orgy'; *Critique musicale*, ii. 247–53.

[6] See his views on Donna Anna's 'Non mi dir' (*Memoirs*, ch. 17); his second obituary of
Bellini, *Critique musicale*, ii. 501.

[7] 'Le style en est savant, vraiment religieux; on ne saurait exprimer mieux les sentiments pieux
qu'en terminant ses prières, l'église en un seul mot résume.'

[8] Performance material had already been copied before Berlioz inserted the 'Amen' fugue and
associated recitative, and these lines are not in the printed libretto of 1846. NBE 8b. 457.

on the tune of Brander's immoral song, but the real joke is that however tipsily it is sung, its tonal answer, pedal, and stretto remain mindlessly correct.

In the Mass, Berlioz set the first 'Amen' emphatically, but homophonically, at the end of the fugal 'Quoniam'; at the end of the Resurrexit, 'Amen' is extended melismatically, but not fugally, to the 'Cujus regni' melody. In the Requiem, 'Amen' forms a series of numinous, and homophonic, final cadences. Berlioz was not opposed to fugues in the right place; in an article on the Mozart Requiem, Berlioz claimed that Lesueur's fugues were 'always motivated and in perfect accordance with the sense of the words'.[9] Berlioz selected fugal texture for the same reason, and its incidence in his work is higher than for most of his contemporaries, at least those writing dramatic music.

The Mass is the most orthodox of Berlioz's liturgical works, and its large-scale organization owes little to Lesueur, who had produced no complete and unified setting to this date.[10] Lesueur may have advised orthodoxy in a beginner; the authorities at St Roch may have required a complete setting; or Berlioz may have wanted his Mass to be widely acceptable, and perhaps more nearly in line with the other contemporary master of the form, Cherubini, to whom the general style of the work nevertheless owes little. The sectional divisions (Table 8.1) are presumably Berlioz's own. As was normal in France, he included an Offertory motet, an 'O salutaris' for the elevation of the Host, and 'Domine salvum' (God save the King); Lesueur set the latter pair of texts many times. In Table 8.1, 'choral' implies a standard full chorus of Dessus (treble: D.) and three adult male voice-types: Haute-contre (high tenor, H.-c.), Tailles (tenor), Basses-tailles (or Basses). Berlioz varies the vocal scoring considerably, sometimes omitting hautes-contre and tailles, and asking for a small group rather than a tutti.[11] This kind of variety reflects Lesueur's practice.

Lesueur's Masses are dramatic only in so far as they evoke ritual scenes in opera, themselves imitated from the Church. His illustrative tendencies also affected Berlioz, but there is nothing to match the explanations of musical topics, instrumentation, and vocal combinations, that fill Lesueur's published scores. In his first *Messe solennelle*, intended for Christmas, Lesueur heads the Gloria 'Duo pastoral', an angel (soprano) singing the first clause after which

[9] Mongrédien notes that Berlioz admired the fugue in Lesueur's Offertory 'Quis enarrabit' (*Journal des Débats*, 9 Aug. 1835; *Critique musicale*, ii. 253; see n. 5). In 1850 he included it in a programme of his Société Philharmonique. Mongrédien, *Le Sueur*, 912–13.

[10] The Tuileries chapel, a 'royal peculiar', owed no allegiance to a bishop and possessed greater freedom than the cathedrals, but services were severely restricted in length and could not accommodate complete settings of the Ordinary (Mongrédien, *La Musique en France des Lumières au Romantisme*, 164–83). Mongrédien says that Lesueur assembled his *Messes solennelles* for publication with an eye to clerical approval (*Le Sueur*, 863 ff.).

[11] Modern performances tend to ignore these dispositions in French choral music, as did OBE (Resurrexit); but altos (male or female) on the haute-contre line radically alter the sound.

TABLE 8.1 *Messe solennelle*: list of movements

Introduction	Orchestra	D major
Kyrie eleison	Chorus (fugue)	D minor
Gloria		
1. 'Gloria in excelsis Deo'	Chorus (D. divided; 4 H.-c.; 3 B.-t.)	G major
2. 'Gratias agimus'	Chorus (as Gloria)	E major
3. 'Quoniam tu solus sanctus'	Chorus (fugue)	A major
Credo		
1. 'Credo in unum Deum'	Bass solo, 4 D., 4 B.	C minor
2. 'Et incarnatus est'	Duet (soprano, bass)	C major
3. 'Crucifixus'	Chorus (D., B., tutti)	C minor
4. 'Et resurrexit tertia die'	Chorus (and B.-t. solo)	G minor–E flat major
Motet pour l'offertoire ('Quis similis tui')	Solo B.-t., chorus	G major
Sanctus ('Pleni sunt coeli', 'Benedictus')	Chorus	E minor, E major
'O salutaris hostia'	Chorus (at opening, 3 D., then tutti)	C major
Agnus Dei	Solo tenor, chorus (D. only, div. A 3)	G minor, ending G major
'Domine salvum'	Solo tenor and bass, chorus	D minor–D major

a shepherd (tenor) sings 'Laudamus te'. But there is no musical contrast between glory and peace, heaven and earth, such as Berlioz achieved by pitting dynamic energy and a dotted rhythm ('Gloria in excelsis Deo') against a steady stepwise descent ('et in terra pax hominibus'). Where Berlioz, like Cherubini and Beethoven, happily made a long movement out of a short text, Lesueur swells it with interpolations: the Kyrie of his *Troisième Messe solennelle*, an agreeable symphonic movement in moderate tempo, is built of cantus firmus, pedals, percussive choral writing, and other devices, and includes a large proportion of the Gloria text. Berlioz commented that this avoided excessive word-repetition and helped Lesueur introduce 'all sorts of rhythmic shapes, while varying the character of the prayer to develop the principal idea to best advantage'.[12] Putting together an Agnus to complete his *Troisième Messe solennelle*, Lesueur ignored the musical implication of its threefold text, and inserted other words to produce this idiosyncratic prayer: 'Agnus Dei, qui tollis peccata mundi, miserere! Tollis, Jesu, peccata mundi! Miserere nobis! Dona nobis pacem! Miserere nobis. Jesu, da pacem! Qui tollis peccata mundi, suscipe deprecationem nostram. Miserere nobis [etc.].' The 'suscipe' clause is from the Gloria; 'Jesu' is Lesueur's insertion, imitated by Berlioz in

---

[12] *Revue et Gazette Musicale*, 10 June 1838 (HC 318).

the Requiem ('Rex tremendae', see below). Even when keeping closer to the liturgical text, Lesueur builds massive musical structures by returning to words which have already been given ample space, for instance the threefold 'Laudamus te' in the Gloria of *Oratorio de Noël*.

Berlioz uses 'Laudamus te' to start a distinct section without changing tempo (Gloria, bar 61), after which he returns to the opening and repeats the text as a whole (from bar 103). He ends, however, with 'adoramus te' rather than the usual 'glorificamus te'. In the Sanctus, 'Pleni sunt coeli' resurfaces after the first 'Hosanna' (bar 65, the change to E major), and again after the Benedictus (bar 87). But his grandest plan is the Resurrexit, where 'Et iterum venturus est' is proclaimed by the solo bass (six basses in the revised version), and repeated by the chorus to a different motive, followed by 'cujus regni non erit finis' (bar 158/168).[13] The clauses in the Creed relating to God the Son end, and 'Et in spiritum' (bar 184/195) proclaims the doctrine of the Holy Spirit. Berlioz is not the only composer to struggle for musical analogues in this section of the Creed; he sets up a bumpy measured recitative, with dynamic explosions—of which 'I don't see the point'; the music risks becoming formless. A symphonic mass composer, like Haydn, would deal with the problem by declaiming the text over an orchestral development. This was beyond Berlioz's capabilities in the 1820s, but, more to the point, such a procedure would fall outside the aesthetic of the Lesueur school, so that to produce a *musical* design, Berlioz has to repeat the striding 'Cujus regni' (bar 210/221). He then treats Church, baptism, and death much as he treated the Holy Spirit, but spiced with woodwind syncopation; then he returns to 'Et iterum' (bar 268/289). Admittedly the text itself returns to eschatological matters (resurrection of the dead) at this point, but not to the same words. This brief reprise, followed by adaptation of the 'Cujus regni' theme for 'Et exspecto' and 'Amen', feels like a musical device.

The Mass reviewed

The instrumental introduction may have seemed jejune to the composer of *Les Francs-juges* at the second performance (22 November 1827). Nevertheless its soughing syncopations have a raw energy characteristic of much of the Mass. The sudden lurch from diatonicism into a diminished seventh (bar 17) prepares for the D minor Kyrie, while memory of D major might prepare the ending of the Kyrie and the minor to major pattern in 'Domine salvum', imparting to the whole Mass a tonal connectivity generally irrelevant to Lesueur. In the Kyrie, the fugal exposition (modelled on Lesueur) is followed by a grandiose diatonic progression of fifths from A major to A minor (bars 53–70), also perhaps inspired by the teacher.[14] Freed from fugal

---

[13] Bar numbers in the Resurrexit represent the two principal versions: 1825 (NBE 23)/1828 (NBE 12a).

[14] For instance, Lesueur's *Troisième Oratorio du sacre* contains the progression e–a–d–G7–C7–B flat 7 (first inversion)–E7 (p. 61 in the published score). If Mongrédien is right

constraints, the 'Christe eleison' feels fresh, despite being derived from elements already heard. An acceleration in phrase-lengths, successive groups of eight, seven, and six bars (71, 79, 86), foreshadows many later passages, as does the thickening of the texture by a kind of factitious canon (arpeggio themes which fit easily together without contrapuntal tension).[15] The larger structural shifts are systematic, like some movements in the Te Deum (see below); the 'Christe' begins with a drop of a third, from A to F, and ends with another, from F to D. In the middle, however, Berlioz dramatizes the 'Christe' text with massive diminished sevenths, faintly echoed by the bassoons and disrupting the flutes' attempts to relaunch the theme, before a stable episode in D major (bar 121), over a pastoral drone. The counter-exposition of the Kyrie fugue (bar 164) leads through a massive crescendo and accelerando to the D major breakthrough which is the finest compositional achievement of the Mass.

Lesueur lacked interest in instrumental music, but did not deprive his sacred music of colour; nevertheless, much of his instrumentation consists of doubling the voices, with or without ornamental figuration. Berlioz faithfully imitates this technique, and learned from Lesueur's variety in handling choral textures. The voices are required to imitate instrumental styles, as at bar 77 of the Gloria ('Glorificamus te'), where the Dessus semiquavers would be better suited to flutes. Lesueur liked to repeat words on a single note, usually a bass pedal resembling a drumbeat. Berlioz adapted this texture to varied ends in later works (like the whispering sylphes in *Huit scènes de Faust*, but also satirically in the 'Amen' fugue of *La Damnation*). In the Gloria, he sets up a sprightly keyboard-style accompaniment beneath the merry 'Laudamus te' tune (bar 61, and with additional bass, bar 150). Its reappearance in *Le Carnaval romain* fulfils the natural comic potential of this tune, in a vocal style whose probable source is *opéra comique*. Yet when the repeated crotchets invest all the voices (bar 172) and suddenly change to semibreves on 'Adoramus te' (bar 184), a sense of awe is palpable, besides providing an emotional bridge to the 'Gratias'. Similar, but rather less grateful, vocal writing appears in 'O salutaris', to characterize 'Bella premunt hostilia, Da robur, fer auxilium' ('Give strength in the face of the enemy', from bars 38 and 56). Berlioz uses declamatory rhythmic unison for 'Qui tollis' ('Gratias', bar 73) and 'Et in unum sanctum' (Resurrexit, see above). Such ideas extend, rather than merely copy, Lesueur's practice.

The unique borrowing of the 'Gratias' for the third movement of *Symphonie fantastique* will be considered in Chapter 9. The contrasting material (bar 50) is of the simplest, a swaying figure colouring the intrusion of

---

and it was not written until the 1825 coronation of Charles X (*Le Sueur*, 863), Berlioz probably had no knowledge of it when he wrote his Mass—although Le Sueur may have seen Berlioz's score before composing his 'oratorio'. But Lesueur said he had used this music already for the coronation of Napoleon. On the fugal modelling see Rushton, 'Ecstasy of Emulation'.

[15] On later canons of this kind, see *MLB* 116.

the relative minor (see Ex. 4.5). Serenity is barely threatened and is fully restored when the basses take up the melody in the dominant (bar 58). When its ninth bar is passed to the treble, the full texture produces an early example of Berlioz's use of non-functional scale-degrees (from bar 66, B7, E, C♯7, f♯, d♯ diminished, g♯, E). An attractive sequence prepares a move to the sub-dominant, but scarcely ruffles the atmosphere (bar 72); the *ff* markings (bars 70, 72) perhaps try to express more than the notes—a sequential lead-in to the 'Qui tollis'—themselves imply. Berlioz neglected the common practice of starting a new movement for this threefold supplication 'Qui tollis . . . Qui tollis . . . Qui sedes'. Instead, he set the first clause (bar 73) as a subsection, only a little distinguished from its surroundings by a declamatory style and a slightly slower tempo; and with unexpected indifference to what is often a harrowing plea for mercy, and in an unusual departure from liturgical decorum, he omitted the second and third clauses. Calm is restored in the instrumental coda, which repeats the introduction from bar 14 an octave lower, before a last original touch, the lightly scored but widely spaced cadence. The 'Gratias' is certainly one of the most unusual and appealing movements of the Mass. The 'Quoniam', while it can never escape its composer's obloquy, contains an ostinato belted out nine times by horns and hautes-contres (bars 32 ff.) against elementary imitation at the octave, a procedure which foreshadows many more effective passages, the most mesmerizing being in the Te Deum ('Judex crederis', see below).[16]

Following these exercises in pastoral eloquence and severe counterpoint, Berlioz took much of the Creed as a text best presented in a declamatory style. In over sixty bars of the Credo, the solo bass (perhaps the voice of a priest) moves towards a more aria-like style, with grandiose arpeggios for 'omnipotentem', and modulates to the relative major, E flat, for the clauses about the Son (bar 54). The presence of something like bird-song at 'visibilium et invisibilium omnium' (bars 41–9) may be an elaborate metaphor (sound standing for sight), but is more likely a simple piece of musical decoration. The repetition of 'et invisibilium' is set to securely composed suspensions, further evidence that Berlioz learned the rules before defying them (bars 49–53). Four chorus basses take up the theme of 'et in unum Dominum', returning to the word 'Credo', another device learned from Lesueur. The priest's counterpoint 'Deum de Deo' is taken up by four chorus Dessus in augmentation (bar 84, 'Consubstantialem Patri'). As with the surprising augmented seconds at 'Genitum non factum' (bars 76–9), where the music presents a complete 'Gipsy scale', there seems no textual clue for this procedure; whereas the metaphor is clear when slower harmonic rhythms find release in the conventional falling scales of 'descendit de coelis'.

For Berlioz 'Et incarnatus est' becomes a lyrical interlude, like a duet for Mary and Joseph. The swaying theme over a pedal, and flute and violin trills,

---

[16] Macdonald makes this point, '*Messe solennelle*', 280.

hint at a pastoral representation of the Christmas story, but Berlioz eschews Lesueur's literalism, and the pain of incarnation is hinted at in a stylistically prophetic cello line, in which a chromatic figure is exposed, unaccompanied, and which turns into a measured trill at the reprise (bar 64) over sixteen bars of tonic pedal. This harmonious vision sets into relief the shock tactics of the 'Crucifixus', where the priest's declamation is illustrated by a 'fine woodwind lament'. Another prophetic passage is the chromatic movement of diminished sevenths, in which the chorus joins, crude on paper but effective in performance, particularly as preparation for the tragic setting of 'passus', over a 'fate' rhythm in the strings which anticipates the death of Cleopatra (Ex. 8.1).

Ex. 8.1 *Messe solennelle*, end of 'Crucifixus'

No.8, 'Resurrexit'

Berlioz conceived the Credo as a unit, joining movements with the words 'de suite'. The beginning of the Resurrexit gains from being heard against the mixture of ferocity and tenderness in the preceding dominant preparation (end of Ex. 8.1). The Resurrexit crowns the edifice by its length and energy, and also because it reaches E flat, relative major of the Credo's C minor, for the fanfare of the last judgement, and restores the full chorus—hautes-contres and tenors have been silent since the 'Quoniam'—and adds full brass and percussion, silent since the Kyrie. Although Berlioz found four ideas worth recycling, the Resurrexit stands out from the Mass less for the quality of its invention than for its effective large-scale planning of periods of shock and stasis, and control of climax; no doubt this was why it had a short independent life in performance.

The finest movement of the Mass may be the Agnus, as Berlioz implied when he took it as a whole into the Te Deum, while greatly enriching its detail. With due deference to the brute energy of 'Domine salvum', the other later movements do not reach the level of the best of the Credo, or the Kyrie. The pure-minded 'O salutaris', with its touch of Lydian mode and late entry of a heavenly harp, gained Berlioz a memorably coarse compliment.[17] In 'Domine salvum', the rhythm of the splendid choral entry in bar 33 is nearly identical to one of Lesueur's numerous settings of this text.

Borrowings identified from the *Messe solennelle* are summarized in Table 8.2. They include only one solo section (the Agnus), perhaps because the other solos are declamatory and the best tunes came in choral sections. Passages governed by striking harmonies and declamation (like the first three sections of the Credo) are difficult to reconceive with another text, and these were not transferred. A dramatic coup in the Resurrexit is the interruption of material just acquiring a comfortable pace (at 'Et ascendit') by the brass entry for 'Et iterum'. One of the best features of the Mass is its disposition of contrasts between drama and tenderness—between 'Et incarnatus' and

TABLE 8.2 Use of the *Messe solennelle* in later works of Berlioz

Messe solennelle (numbers as in NBE 23)	Reuse of material
KYRIE	
1. [1] 'Kyrie eleison', bar 1	[1] *Grande messe des morts*: Offertoire (1837)
[2] 'Christe eleison', bar 71	[2] *La Damnation de Faust*, 'Valse des sylphes' (1846, theme of 1829)
GLORIA	
2. 'Gloria in excelsis' [3] 'Laudamus te', bar 63	[3] *Benvenuto Cellini*, Carnival scene (1838); overture, *Le Carnaval romain* (1844)
3. [4] 'Gratias agimus'	[4] *Symphonie fantastique*, III: 'Scène aux champs' (1830)
CREDO	
8. Resurrexit	
[5] 'Et ascendit', bar 32	[5] Te Deum: 'Tu Christe rex gloriae', bar 95: 'Tu ad dexteram Dei' (1849)
[6] 'Et iterum venturus est', bar 76	[6] *Grande messe des morts*: 'Tuba mirum' (1837)
[7] 'Et iterum', bar 101/108	[7] *Benvenuto Cellini*: Finale to Act I: 'Assassiner un capucin! Oui, c'est infâme!'
[8] 'Cujus regni', bar 158/168	[8] 'Ah! quelle nuit, noire et profonde' (1838)
AGNUS DEI (tenor solo, chorus)	
11. [9] 'Agnus Dei, qui tollis'	[9] Te Deum: 'Te ergo quaesumus' (1849)

---

[17] The compliment from the singer Mme Lebrun is reported in *Grotesques*, 215–16; Cairns, *Making of an Artist*, 170/176–7. The Lydian f♯″ in C major is matched by a part of the Requiem 'Lacrimosa' (bar 82) where, however, the shift from C to E minor assimilates the sharpened fourth into the tonal system.

TABLE 8.3 Evolution of the Resurrexit: changes in the version of *c*.1828

Bar nos.	Revisions in the version of *c*.1829
76–90	expansion of the fanfare instrumentally by an extra pair of timpani, serpent, and ophicleide; sharpened rhythm in the fanfare: ♫ ♩. revised to ♫ ♩. . Increased forces affect all later tutti passages
91–8	'Et iterum' for six basses, not solo; removal of trombone and clarinet harmony (bar 92), leaving voices and timpani only; removal of harmony on first beats (bars 95–8), strengthened second beats
98–9	melodic alteration, reaching V of C minor instead of E♭ Additional seven bars before the Allegro, setting 'Tuba mirum spargens sonum, coget omnes ante thronum'
99/106[a]	Allegro, new 'Et iterum' motive
104/111 and 119/125	removal of doubling in thirds and sixths
111/118 and 125/132	removal of contrary motion
127/134 *et seq.*	removal of piccolo
134/141	sharper phrasing, slurs over paired quavers not the whole bar (not applied consistently)
149–51/156–61	three bars expanded to six, syncopation provides a more solid cadence to the section
158/168	'Cujus regni' motive: all voices in unison
164/174 and 177/187	theme rises to f″ instead of d″ (but returns to original pitches after six beats)
183/193	bar inserted to separate text clauses
183/193 *et seq.*	'Et in spiritum.' Stabilizing bass notes instead of string unison
193/204 and 205/216	scale added in upper strings and cellos; elimination of top c″ in first (alto) trombone
210/221	'Cujus regni' altered as before but harmony retained from 218/229 and 231/242
235/246	bar inserted to separate text clauses
236–61/248–82	'Et in unum.' Substantially rewritten. From 270 (revised version) dramatization by means of rests ('Et resurrectionem'). Textural changes and cadential scales as in 'Et in spiritum'
249–55/261–75	expanded by nine bars, to accommodate slower declamation and restoration of Latin prosodic accents rather than French
253/264	harmonic changes resulting from the expansion. 1825: C♯ (diminished 7th), enharmonic from D♭ D7, G minor in 255. 1828: D♭ pedal, D♭7 leads to G♭; enharmonic shift to D7 (but G♭ bass = F♯), G minor in 275
255/275	one additional bar, so 256 = 277; some revision of declamation to 282
304/325	quaver slurs as 134/141
353, 367/374, 388	theme rises to dominant as before, this time a climactic b♭″

[a] Where bar nos. diverge, they are presented in the form 1825/1828.

'Crucifixus', Agnus and 'Domine salvum'. Berlioz's efforts to salvage the Resurrexit included its partial transformation into *Le Jugement dernier*, although the surviving manuscript from *c*.1828 represents this more as an idea than a finished conception; its ludicrous signing-off in a brief flurry of celestial harps can never have been intended for performance.[18] But there are many more careful revisions, which extend the movement by twenty-one bars while leaving its form unchanged. The vision of judgement is charged up by lines from the 'Dies irae' ('Tuba mirum'); some bars, inserted to enhance the declamation, also result in a more dramatic enharmonic recovery of G minor (bar 255/275). The orchestral parts are overhauled in several details (see Table 8.3). With his *Messe solennelle*, the aspiring Berlioz made his first real impact. Although he may have gone against his natural inclinations, in making an orthodox setting of the central text of the Catholic liturgy, he did not do it only to please his teacher (or his pious mother), but to impress the capital; as Henri IV put it, 'Paris vaut une Messe'.

A SECOND VISION OF JUDGEMENT: *GRANDE MESSE DES MORTS*

There must have been some people at the Invalides on 5 December 1837 who remembered the uproar of the Resurrexit, last performed on 1 November 1829 as *Le Jugement dernier*. In the *Grande messe des morts* (Requiem), the vision of judgement provides an obvious motive for reuse of this music. The fanfare is expanded and enhanced in harmonic and rhythmic substance (as well as by extra brass), but the vocal entry (now for all the basses) was unchanged, and Berlioz accidentally wrote the 'Et iterum' text in his autograph.[19] It is as if he flaunted the act of self-borrowing, saying: 'I did not do this idea justice; now I have a government commission, this is how it should be.'

The brass groups have diverted critical comment on the Requiem towards loudness, space, and orchestral 'experiments', overlooking the delicacy and subtlety of much of the score. The full brass appear in only three movements, all within the Sequence (Dies irae); trombones reappear in the 'Hostias' and Agnus, mainly piano. The first and last movements reach grand climaxes but end pianissimo, or below. Most of the Requiem is at the quieter end of an enlarged dynamic spectrum which is itself more remarkable than mere volume; if the 'Tuba mirum' and the climax of 'Lacrimosa' are among the loudest things in Berlioz, the attenuated 'Quid sum miser' and unaccompanied 'Quaerens me' which abut these movements are among the quietest. Nowadays the Requiem is sometimes performed with the brass groups disposed around the performing area. Wonderfully exciting though that can be, it was not what Berlioz intended; his requirement that they are seated at the corners of the orchestra is still stereophonic, but the Te Deum's intended spatial opposition of organ and orchestra more radically embraces the whole performing space.

[18] NBE 12a. 404.   [19] NBE 9. 174.

A revolutionary commemoration is not a liturgy.[20] Berlioz, a true pupil of Lesueur, could choose which parts of the text to set. Edward T. Cone has made a comprehensive analysis of Berlioz's selections, mapped against the liturgical text, but much of Berlioz's oddity consists in returning to texts already set, and ending movements with the first line of a stanza rather than the last.[21] He omitted whole lines of text and, as in the Mass, some repetitive incantations; further changes resulted from musical revisions undertaken after first performance and publication.[22] The principal alterations, however, are the result of choice; they include reordering the stanzas of the Sequence, and the intrusion into its central movement, 'Rex tremendae', of lines from the Offertoire (see below).

The overall musical form of the Requiem, as defined by the traditional parameters of theme and tonality, is critical ground almost as heavily trodden as that of *Symphonie fantastique*. In summary, the movements run as in Table 8.4. The Sequence includes Nos. 2–6. Keys in parentheses represent points of tonal focus within a movement, or at the beginning, when the first chords do not imply the eventual tonic; hyphens mark a change of key or mode at the end. The principal tonality is G, as in *Harold en Italie* with which the Requiem shares a minor-major trajectory, and *Benvenuto Cellini*. The directional force of the change of mode is made clear when the last movement returns to material of the first.

Such large tonal progressions can hardly be perceived on their own, but Berlioz establishes a background structure through elements in the musical

TABLE 8.4 Design of *Grande messe des morts*

Movement	Key
1. Introit ('Requiem aeternam'); 'Te decet hymnus', 'Kyrie eleison'	g (B♭) g
2. 'Dies irae: Tuba mirum'	a (b♭, d)–E♭
3. 'Quid sum miser'	g♯
4. 'Rex tremendae'	E
5. 'Quaerens me'	A
6. 'Lacrimosa'	a–A
7. Offertoire ('Domine Jesu Christe')	d–D
8. 'Hostias'	(G) b♭
9. Sanctus, 'Hosanna'	D♭
10. Agnus Dei, 'Te decet hymnus', 'Requiem aeternam', 'Amen'	(A, G), b♭–B♭–g–G

[20] The changed circumstances of the first performance, which was part of the funeral ceremony of General Damrémont, meant that it was after all sung liturgically (Cairns, *Servitude*, 146).

[21] Cone, 'Berlioz's Divine Comedy', in *Music: A View from Delft*, 139–57; see 141–4.

[22] On the cuts see NBE 9, pp. ix–x and 170–1. The cut in 'Quaerens me' remained in the vocal score edited by Leopold Damrosch and published by Schirmer and Chappell, and is sometimes performed.

foreground, using a triple recapitulation and double tonal resolution.[23] No listener is likely to miss the infamous chords for flutes and trombones in the 'Hostias' (see below). The Agnus Dei begins with an A major chord only tenuously connected (as flat VI) with the end of the Sanctus, but after a series of chords designed to emphasize, if anything, tonal distance, it recapitulates the 'Hostias' exactly, except for a metrical change dictated by the words, until the final cadence flowers into B flat major instead of minor. This allows a smooth shift into a (non-liturgical) reprise of 'Te decet hymnus'. The music follows the same course as in the first movement, and thus reaches G minor. In the Introit, the glowing climax represents eternal light by G major (bars 160–73), and this key covers the first muttered 'Kyrie eleison'; but the lamenting figure used to such tremendous effect as an ostinato returns for 'Christe eleison', snuffing out the light in a desperate appeal for mercy (Ex. 8.2*a*). Bar 161 of the Agnus corresponds to bar 160 of the Introit, but the music remains in G major, and 'Quia pius es' (light eternal will shine upon the believer) takes music from the 'Rex tremendae', at 'fons pietatis' (the divine fountain of mercy), transposed to G major (Ex. 8.2*b*).[24] The crucial changes to the major mode both make use of the relative minor, which is peculiarly alien to the preceding tonic minor mode. In the Agnus the change to B flat major is effected when, as the tenors reach their top b♭′, G minor is substituted for the G flat major of the equivalent passage in the 'Hostias'. G minor powerfully contradicts B flat minor by its D♮ as much as its G♮.[25] The 'cum sanctis' (Agnus, from bar 172), like the corresponding 'Kyrie eleison' at the end of the Introit, is muttered over a chromatic slide which this time reaches D♯. The implied relative minor (E minor) is resolved, typically, by reinterpretation of D♯ as E♭, returning to D as dominant of G. The first movement's pizzicato chords are replaced by timpani, whose gently rhythmicized chords of G, spread over eight instruments, punctuate the six ethereal 'Amen' cadences, as if to relate earth to heaven.

Berlioz was setting 'Kyrie eleison' for the second time, but not as a fugue; yet fugue is the principal texture of the Introit. Here and in the Te Deum, he resolutely kept at bay any deplorable 'caractère de légèreté', while preserving a marked difference of style from dramatic music. David Rosen argues that Verdi's Requiem is not operatic, as criticism traditionally has it; neither it nor Berlioz's Requiem is 'dramatic' except in the debased sense, equivalent to 'exciting', or filled with 'contrast and expressiveness'.[26] Verdi's extensive use

---

[23] Referring to Wagner and Strauss rather than Berlioz, Edward T. Cone doubts whether 'even if one could combine Schenker and Lorenz, and prove that each Wagnerian act could be analyzed as a structural unity . . . that would not prove that each act could be so *heard*'. Much the same applies to Berlioz's multi-movement works. Cone, *Musical Form and Musical Performance* (New York: Norton, 1968), 96.

[24] On the thematic links between these ideas, see Cone, *Music: A View from Delft*, 153.

[25] See *MLB* 33–5.

[26] David Rosen, *Verdi: Requiem* (Cambridge: Cambridge University Press, 1995), 92–7; for a mild abuse of 'dramatic' in this sense, see Schacher, *Idee und Erscheinungsform des Dramatischen bei Hector Berlioz*, 98.

of solo voices brings him rhetorically closer to opera than Berlioz, and his theatrical temperament would have precluded repetition of the fanfare for the last judgement ('Tuba mirum'). That Berlioz's rhetoric is primarily that of ritual is confirmed when the fanfare comes again, its texture added to rather than developed, for the 'Liber scriptus' (No. 2, bar 203), a text which brings a new melody from Mozart and a new movement from Verdi. If stylistic elements intersect with those of theatre music, Berlioz's presentation is not even metaphorically dramatic (in the sense of imitating an action): there cannot be two last judgements. The whispered 'Kyrie eleison' and 'Cum sanctis tuis' in the first and last movements recall the prayers in *Harold* and *Benvenuto Cellini*, but the model is spoken, rather than sung, prayer; even in the opera, this mode of expression is not inherently dramatic. The Dies irae poem (also referred to as the Sequence) is in the first person, suggesting an individual sensibility, but Berlioz uses the chorus throughout, confining the solo voice to the ritualistic evocation of the numinous in the Sanctus.

Ex, 8.2a *Grande messe des morts*, No. 1 (Introit)

Ex. 8.2*b Grande messe des morts*, Agnus

The 'polyphony of cries' which forms Berlioz's Requiem is no drama, but a series of tableaux.[27] Heinrich Heine noted Berlioz's affinity with the furiously imaginative biblical landscapes of his English contemporary John Martin.[28] Spontini supposed that he had been inspired by the last judgement

[27] The Requiem as the climactic polyphony of Berlioz's 'esthétique du cri et de la plainte' becomes convincing, in Guiomar's interpretation, through sheer accumulation of detail. Guiomar, *Le Masque et le fantasme*, from 165; on the Requiem, mainly 223–46.

[28] *Memoirs*, Postscript.

frescoes in the Sistine Chapel; Berlioz thought otherwise: 'I see there scenes of hellish torment, but of the complete and ultimate gathering of humankind I see nothing. But then I am ignorant of painting and have little feeling for conventional beauties.' This staggering take on Michelangelo, which ends chapter 50 of Berlioz's memoirs, reminds us how creative originality feeds on its own limitations in appreciating others. What follows is not a complete, synoptic account of the Requiem such as Cone provides, but commentary on selected aspects, a procedure which will be followed for much of the rest of this book.

Introit

The strange orchestral exordium is an aspiring, partly chromatic figure topped by potentially threatening extensions—swelling sound and dotted rhythms—to the final notes. The four-note fugue subject is set against strange, detached countersubjects. The tenors (bar 28) and basses ('Dona eis', bar 59, a two-crotchet unit within the 3/4 metre) show Berlioz developing Lesueur's quasi-instrumental vocal writing, already tried out in the Mass; this taxing vocal style reaches an extreme point in the tenor part of the 'Dies irae'. The long melisma in the sopranos from bar 44 is the first intimation of serenity and of B flat major.[29] The first section closes (bar 78) with a prayer for eternal light, still within the penumbra of G minor. 'Te decet hymnus' follows in B flat. Its lyricism is partially subverted by a chromatic rising line (bar 105, tenors, bassoons, violas), which resembles the instrumental exordium; rising mightily to top A, it brings in the reprise explosively, in a tremendous stretto (the soprano answer follows after only two bars instead of four). The inner drama intensifies when Berlioz halts this powerful impulse in its tracks after only six bars. The overall form is partly defined by the ending of attempts to establish B flat major. The later stages contain both disintegration and reintegration, with an increase in surface chromaticism. The signs of uncertainty and terror (bar 116, 'defunctis Domine') are tremulous pitch-repetitions, harmonic indeterminacy (a move to A minor and back), and a measured woodwind trill. Earlier in the movement, descending chromatic and diatonic fragments, including the original countersubject and the treble-register figure in bars 49–52, led to the plangent ostinato heard four times from bars 57 to 68. At the climax, bar 128, this returns six times (one entry (bars 140–1) is incomplete), and generates the cramped ostinato (flutes, violins) from bar 144. With admirable ingenuity, Berlioz places the first note of this figure (E♭) over the successive bass notes C, F, G, B♭, and F♯; its last gasp, at 'Christe eleison' (Ex. 8.2*a*), definitively returns the movement to the minor after the glowing 'Et lux perpetua'. Confidence has drained away.

---

[29] This vocalise resembles an Agnus Dei fragment published in *Grand Traité*, which Macdonald speculated (before 1991) might come from the then-lost Mass: *Berlioz*, 79.

The Sequence

The outline plan of the Sequence in five movements disguises a more complex scheme in which the first movement changes tonal orientation three times and ends in a totally unrelated key; the 'Dies Irae—Tuba mirum' is indeed experienced as two movements. The A major of 'Quaerens me' can be interpreted on paper as a logical return to the tonic, but is unlikely to be experienced that way; there is no supporting thematic or instrumental evidence, as there is for the tonal connections of the Introit, 'Hostias', and Agnus. Both the 'Dies irae' and 'Lacrimosa' achieve a mighty crescendo towards the brass intervention. After the apocalyptic 'Tuba mirum', 'Quid sum miser' is a reprise of the 'Dies irae' in the form of a ruin—not the ruin as a plaything of early-romantic Gothic revivalism, but ruin as a metaphor of abject penitence. The material is taken from bar 53 of the 'Dies irae', which is itself the culminating point of a most original process. Berlioz's composed 'Dies irae' plainchant is presented in a pure Aeolian mode, on string basses. At bar 13, high voices enter with a different melody. In a progressive synthesis, the 'plainchant' acquires words only at bar 25, where for the first time two melodies are combined; the counterpoint, however, is new. Berlioz skips the third line of the first stanza, to begin the next ('Quantus tremor'), exposed similarly and reaching three parts by bar 49. At bar 53 he returns to the first stanza and displays the combination of three melodies implied by the music to bar 36.

In a highly original process of intensification, Berlioz refrains from extending the movement by invertible counterpoint, like that of the Kyrie and 'Quoniam' of the Mass. The music up to 'Tuba mirum' is a skilfully controlled three-stage crescendo (periods in A minor, B flat minor, and D minor) and a progression towards madness marked by the arbitrary orchestral transitions between these unrelated keys. From bar 68, in B flat minor, the plainchant is set to the second stanza while the new and particularly instrumental counterpoint (tenors) finally completes the first stanza with 'Teste David cum Sibilla'. From bar 88 the instruments acquire textural independence, though only through a pedal B♭. After a second volcanic eruption, reaching D minor, the orchestra adds tremolo articulation, maintained to the point where the brass enters in E flat. From this music founded in contrapuntal discipline, the 'Tuba mirum' emerges as a new world of sheer, overwhelming sound, subduing any rebellious feeling that the musical invention is otherwise undistinguished. Yet this movement, turning back and, like several others, not ending with the last line of a stanza, concludes in near-silence with 'Mors stupebit'.

Once past the 'Tuba mirum', the brass is deprived of its surreal impact, and Berlioz used it sparingly. In 'Rex tremendae' it enters at bar 70 and plays in fourteen of the next forty bars. The 'Lacrimosa' is a vast five-section design, the main idea being fugal, although fugue is not usually employed at this

point in the Requiem.[30] The brass enters in the third section, adding a gigantic, unbalancing colouristic element to an already complicated ostinato. An
occasional snarl from the ophicleide and a doom-laden bass drum punctuate
the reprise of the second, lyrical, idea.[31] The final brass entry crunches home
the dominant, E, against the choral and orchestral F. The bounding 9/8, stylistically akin to a waltz, is metamorphosed when the chorus yields and the
brass responds by taking over the main melody (bar 164). The singers, far
from sounding defeated, exult: not even the 'Tuba mirum' is as enthralling.
Rather than end the text 'correctly' ('pie Jesu, Domine, dona eis requiem,
Amen'), Berlioz reiterates 'Lacrimosa dies illa' to the last, the tears of the
damned becoming the triumph of the righteous. The 'Lacrimosa' is the best
justification for Heine's metaphor, to which the composer took exception, of
Berlioz as a 'colossal nightingale, a lark the size of an eagle'.[32]

The Offertoire

In adapting his precocious Kyrie for the Offertoire, Berlioz adopted a new
metre and a new contrapuntal fabric; all that remains is the outline of the
fugue subject. The new movement is essentially instrumental, punctuated by
the choral monotone, an 'upper pedal' or 'intermittent sound', as described
by Berlioz in an article published shortly before the Requiem's first performance as evidence of the independence of rhythm as a musical parameter.[33]
The conceptual difference of the Kyrie and the Offertoire has its basis in differences within the subject (Ex. 8.3), affecting melodic tension between the
opening tonic and the eventual goal, the dominant. This goal (a') is immediately touched upon (as the third note), so that interest is tactically sustained
by inflecting the successive, and increasingly decisive, returns. In the Offertoire Berlioz refreshes the rhythm with a characteristic ornament (neighbour-note) and a rest. The interruption to the sound means that, while the
first two-bar units both reach the dominant, the ascent d'–e'–f' moves to the
foreground in the Offertoire. Phrase 2, the sequence on the Neapolitan flat II,
not only supports the upper neighbour b♭' but begins the out-of-order
chromatic ascent (f' precedes e♭'; g♮' is already accented in bar 3). In the
Offertoire, although Berlioz might have brought the voices in almost any-
where, he waits until the tonality is questioned by the subject's F♯. That the
voices continually articulate the dominant tends to weaken its melodic impact

---

[30] The movement has elements of sonata form. Its overall configuration has been compared
by Vivian S. Ramalingan to the second movement of Beethoven's Seventh Symphony ('Berlioz,
Beethoven, and "One fatal remembrance"', in Bryan Gillingham and Paul Merkley (eds.),
Beyond the Moon: Festschrift Luther Dittmer (Ottawa: Institute of Mediaeval Music, 1990)).

[31] Before the second episode, bar 124, many conductors change Berlioz's A major chord to A
minor. In Berlioz's bolder concept, A major is overlaid upon the residual echo of the minor, an
excellent effect in the right acoustic; although Berlioz often leaps across modes, the substitution
underlines a potential banality.

[32] *Memoirs*, Postscript.

[33] 'Strauss, son orchestre, ses valses—De l'avenir du rhythme', *Journal des débats*, 10 Nov.
1837.

Ex. 8.3 Kyrie (*Messe solennelle*) and Offertoire (Requiem): fugue subjects

within the subject (bars 10 and 11); we hear bars 10 and 12 as an augmentation of the vocal motive (bar 10 is also its diminution). The outcome seems increasingly uncertain when Berlioz finally resolves the subject onto the dominant, but drives the line on through b♮' to c" for the fugal answer, a marked improvement on the Kyrie's fall-back to a' (compare Ex. 5.5).

The Offertoire is the still centre of the Requiem, a 'chorus of souls in Purgatory' (the title Berlioz used when performing it by itself), following the ferocious triumph of judgement. But it is not yet the 'profound calm' Berlioz achieved in the Sanctus. The slow movement of *Harold*, also ritualistic, punctuates equal-length phrases with a bell-imitation, whereas in the Offertoire, the constant pitches of the vocal part scarcely compensate for the mental disturbance resulting from their unpredictable entries. Until the coda, and the turn to D major, the movement would feel more coherent without the chorus, particularly as Berlioz made a cut which 'brings the proportions perfectly into focus'.[34]

[34] See *MLB* 121–6, 138, and 270, n. 58 (but to say 'the choral entries . . . control the musical flow' (p. 123) is misguided: 'disrupt' would be better).

The problem of the 'Rex tremendae'

The ruins of 'Quid sum miser' are assaulted by 'Rex tremendae' (Sequence, stanza 8), in which Berlioz, like Mozart, relished the contrast between awesome majesty and humble prayer: '[forte] Rex tremendae majestatis|[piano] Qui salvandos salvas gratis|Salva me fons pietatis.' But Berlioz's setting is not so simple, even in dynamics. Strident antiphonal chords and dotted rhythms epitomize the majestic; a mid-bar harmonic change (E to F sharp 7, bar 16) is accommodated by the smoother melody for the second line. The first 'salva me' is a desperate plea, accelerating, crescendo, breaking into silence (bar 29). The whole stanza, and stanza 9 ('Recordare', already heard during 'Quid sum miser') is delivered in another accelerating crescendo. At double the original speed Berlioz leaps to stanza 16 (bar 42, 'Confutatis maledictis'), twice interrupted by his own parenthetical 'Jesu!' The music sticks on a furious dissonance ('flammis acribus addictis', Ex. 8.4), then breaks off ('Voca me. . . .'); the following text is the middle of a line from the Offertoire. The text as Berlioz set it runs 'Confutatis maledictis (Jesu!)|Flammis acribus addictis,| Voca me . . .|Et de profundo lacu.|Libera me de ore leonis,|Ne cadam in obscurum,|Ne absorbeat me Tartarus.' ('When the evil are damned (Jesu!)| And doomed to burn|Call me . . .|And from the deep lake.|Free me from the lion's mouth,|Let me not fall into darkness,|Nor let Tartarus swallow me.')

The last three lines are duly omitted from the Offertoire, which at this point uses the third person plural: 'eas', not 'me' and 'ne cadant in obscuram': free *them*, let *them* not fall, nor let Tartarus swallow *them*. The 'persona' of Berlioz's Requiem, whom Wolfgang Dömling associates with the 'I' of *Symphonie fantastique*,[35] in panic at the impending apocalypse, babbles dimly remembered lines, oblivious to differences of rhyme, rhythm, and authorship. The music underlines this interpretation: 'Voca me' breaks free of the acrid dissonance, to find itself poised on the edge of a silent void. The music halts in terror, then resumes as a hectic crescendo in imitative stretto, here (as in the introduction of *Roméo et Juliette*) a metaphor of conflict, and halts again for awed contemplation. Music analysis can comfortably reduce this passage to a parenthesis, within a prolongation of the dominant, in preparation for a reprise. But the skeleton of harmonic coherence has to fight silence, broken rhythms, and emphasis on alien pitches (notably C♮); while the reprise never comes. Instead a desperate struggle ensues between evocations of the mighty King (here the brass intervenes), and the plea 'salva me', pianissimo, syncopated, and almost completely lacking in hope. The eventual cadence fails to banish chaos and it requires its extended reprise, in the Agnus, to attain peace (Ex. 8.2b).

This passage has naturally aroused controversy. Alec Robertson chastised Berlioz's indecorum as a 'complete disregard for grammar and sense . . . This

---

[35] Dömling, *Zeit*, 41.

Ex. 8.4 *Grande messe des morts*, No. 4, 'Rex tremendae'

juggling and mangling of the texts . . . should not . . . be excused even in an obviously non-liturgical work'; Robertson considers it a blunder caused by 'frenzied hurry to get the music on paper'.[36] Berlioz's careful alterations to the Latin suggest otherwise. Thomas Schacher says the fermata after 'voca me' 'must be understood as the negation of these words . . . theologically speaking, the bridge which links mankind to God is broken'.[37] Kurt von Fischer

[36] The stanza should end 'Voca me cum benedictis' (number me among thy saints). Alec Robertson, *Requiem: Music of Mourning and Consolation* (London: Cassell, 1967), 91–2. He remarks that Berlioz's biographers have not tried to find any purpose in Berlioz's 'mangling' a text he knew intimately; Robertson was perhaps unaware of Lesueur's example.

[37] Schacher, *Idee und Erscheinungsform des Dramatischen bei Hector Berlioz*, 108.

asks 'Is such a procedure to be described as dramatic?' The obvious answer ('yes') still leaves a passage difficult to account for in traditional terms, and its fractured continuity suggests less dramatic action than interior monologue.[38] Cone carefully analyses the harmonic implications.[39] The sense of isolation, the spleen which Berlioz so vividly described, here gains a new dimension.

Space and time: trombones and flutes

Isolation and its cognates, distance and space, colour the entire Requiem, and contribute much to the coherence which survives its diversity of scale, forms, and tonality. The spatial element has little to do with the disposition of the brass; at the representation of the last trump, Verdi's smaller forces contrive a more potent use of actual space. Space is defined more by silence, by pitch-span, and by alienation between music which moves, and music in which what Dömling calls Berlioz's 'discovery of slowness' causes the suspension of a sense of passing time.[40] The Introit initially defines a middle range, g–d', and gradually expands it to the first forte; typically, however, Berlioz develops this musical dimension when *away* from the tonic sonority. At bar 45 the flute soars to f'''; this vision is quickly veiled, but at bar 81, before 'Te decet hymnus', f''' returns as a pedal and a gaping chasm opens between flute and cellos, gradually filled by the voices. As Cone observes, the same f''' is poised as the dominant of B flat at 'Pleni sunt coeli' (Sanctus, bar 24), and is reinterpreted as the third of D flat (bar 30), an event which coincides with the introduction of new words, and contributes to the musical form of the Sanctus.

The timpani chords of the Requiem were anticipated in 'Scène aux champs', to evoke distant thunder; the spatial implication remains. The three pairs of cymbals struck pianissimo in the Sanctus likewise seem to intervene from afar. The most controversial passage of the Requiem, and the climax of Berlioz's concern for space, is the chordal punctuation to the hieratic declamation of the 'Hostias', scored for flutes and trombones (Ex. 8.5). Macdonald suggests that this passage should have been confined to the pages of the *Grand Traité*.[41] His reasoning is based on the strength of the overtones from eight unison trombones in their deepest register.[42] Usually instruments in middle registers would cover these, but there are none; the gap between trombones and flutes is over three octaves. When the flutes play a major triad and the

---

[38] Kurt von Fischer, 'Das Dramatische in der geistlichen Musik', *Archiv für Musikwissenschaft*, 34 (1977), 38–55 (see 54–5): he continues: 'From the viewpoint of the Viennese classics it is in any case scarcely comprehensible. Its character is more like what R. Szondi, using an example by Friedrich Hebbel, called "interior monologue".'

[39] *Music: A View from Delft*, 150–1.   [40] Dömling, *Zeit*, 86.

[41] Macdonald, 'Berlioz's Orchestration: Human or Divine?', 256. Earlier criticisms included Cecil Forsyth's 'it probably sounds very nasty' (not surprisingly, given the date, he had not heard it): *Orchestration* (London: Macmillan and Stainer & Bell, 1914), 135–6. But Norman Del Mar, having conducted it in an appropriate acoustic, said the passage could be 'wholly convincing': *Conducting Berlioz*, 202.

[42] The notes B♭ and below are pedal-notes; Berlioz assures us that some players had not previously known of their existence.

Ex. 8.5 *Grande messe des morts*, 'Hostias' and Agnus Dei

a. No. 8. 'Hostias'

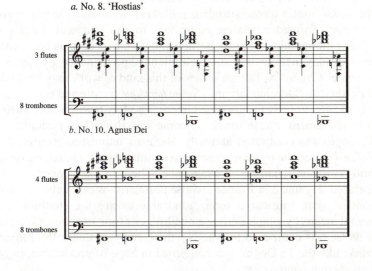

b. No. 10. Agnus Dei

trombones its root, the flutes double the strongest overtones one octave higher (Ex. 8.5 shows the overtones up to the seventh harmonic in small notes). In the second-inversion minor (bar 10) and first-inversion major chords (bar 26) the overtones clash with the flutes, each with two semitonal dissonances; even B flat minor in root position (bars 19, 45) conflicts with the overtone's major third.

Rather than an error, as Macdonald suggests, this could be careful calculation of dissonance levels to achieve a sense of harmonic resolution. Berlioz heard these chords, and chose not to revise them, as he might easily have done. Each choral phrase ends on a cadence, open or closed. The flute and trombone chords enter as if from another world, and form their own harmonic progression, leading to two perfect cadences. Conventionally the dominant (even without a seventh) is understood as dissonant relative to the tonic; here the tonic, being minor, is more dissonant than the dominant. Thus within the 'Hostias' there is no final resolution, and Berlioz omitted the lines 'fac eas, Domine, de morte transire ad vitam' ('may they, Lord, pass from death into life') which imply some kind of spiritual breakthrough. When he rearranged the same progression in the Agnus Dei, the final chord is major; the cadence achieves a sense of resolution at the tonal turning point (bar 82). The subsequent reprise of the 'Te decet hymnus' and much of the first movement, which allowed Berlioz to fill temporal space which close adherence to the liturgy might have denied him, is also a vital stage in the wave-like motion taken from the extreme flat keys of the 'Hostias' and Sanctus to the luminous G major of the close.

215

ARCHITECTURE AND PATRIOTIC FERVOUR

From the 1790s, music whose grandeur reflects socio-political ideals—revolution, empire—formed a secular equivalent to the liturgical dramas of Lesueur. The monarchical regimes Berlioz knew were as keen as the revolutionaries to display their virtues, and their intended permanence, by means of the arts. Under Charles X, Berlioz's view of this kind of work may be shown by his over-the-top 'Domine salvum'. *Scène héroïque* transferred the struggle for liberty to romantically fashionable Greece. The July revolution of 1830, a republican movement whose ironic outcome was the citizen-monarchy of Louis-Philippe, was celebrated annually. Berlioz's unfinished project, *Fête musicale funèbre*, fed the two commemorative commissions, *Grande messe des morts* and *Symphonie funèbre et triomphale*. The monster concerts of the 1840s featured 'Hymne à la France', whose popularity is explicable more by socio-political than musical criteria, admirable as are the rhythmic and instrumental means by which Berlioz embellishes its four strophes. *Chant des chemins de fer* was composed for the Northern railway; under the Empire, *L'Impériale*, like the Te Deum, was composed in hope of preferment, rather than to any actual commission.

Berlioz's preoccupation with the grand style was musical first, and occasional out of necessity. His later works sustain their exalted manner resourcefully, making the Requiem seem febrile in comparison. Berlioz described his architectural style in terms of a rhetoric of conviction rather than persuasion: 'either one understands nothing, or one is crushed by terrible emotions'; certain movements owe their imposing character to their 'breadth of style, and the formidable slowness of some progressions, whose outcome cannot be foreseen'.[43] This remark sums up Berlioz's rhetoric of the sublime, which found primitive expression in the Kyrie and in the descending progressions by thirds in the first chorus of *Scène héroïque*, the more effective coming after a pedal-point.[44] A sequential descent in the central 'Prière' of this cantata, developing the first phrase (from bar 22, G, E flat, C minor, A flat, D—the home dominant), is echoed twenty-two years on, at bars 33–6 of 'La Menace des Francs'. Such marmoreal progressions work differently to more overtly dramatic gestures, like the moment near the end of the finale of *Scène héroïque*, when after another extended pedal and a sudden silence, the expected C major is replaced by E flat. This procedure anticipates Berlioz's usual harmonic rhetoric of conclusion, most crisply expressed in the last chords of *Le Corsaire*, A flat, E flat, G, C, which hit us between the eyes even if we do not recognize that these chords imply the principal keys of the overture.

Another architectural idea adumbrated in *Scène héroïque* is the union of contrasting themes. In the finale (bar 168), the Dessus enter with the first

---

[43] *Memoirs*, Postscript.   [44] See also *MLB* 43.

theme, and male voices join them with the second theme. Both themes are in doubled note-values, but the tempo has also doubled, so the themes sound at their original tempo (a fanfare has already reappeared in doubled values; compare bars 58 and 102).[45] The mood is exultant, however, and Berlioz depends not so much on slowness, as on the absence of harmonic progression. The descendants of this idea are mainly instrumental, and in some cases bear programmatic significance. In *Les Francs-juges*, Berlioz combined the effect of slow and fast music, but the fast material is not the main theme of the Allegro.[46] In *Waverley*, motives from the first theme are combined with the reprise of the second; thereafter few of Berlioz's works lack a combination of some kind, the most excellent in rhetoric, and the most dramatically apposite, being the Pope's theme near the end of the *Benvenuto Cellini* overture, and the central climax of the Ball scene in *Roméo*.

There is nothing comparable in *Symphonie funèbre*, whose deliberate simplicity appealed to musicians as remote in temperament (and importance) as Wagner and Adam. The architecture of the first movement finds its expression in an expanded sense of time; the funereal pace allows surprising modulations even within its most lyrical theme.[47] One of music's sublimest evocations of ritual grief is the first-movement crescendo which substitutes for a tonal bridge-passage. A short motive is reiterated over the pulsating principal rhythm and a dominant pedal (from bar 70), before a concise modulation to the relative major. In the recapitulation (from bar 175) the passage is repeated rather than developed, but amplified by an inner-register melody (trombones). Like the oboe solo in the first movement of *Symphonie fantastique*, this additional melody actually gains in expressiveness from being so evidently constrained by the pre-composed chord sequence. In a pianissimo valley between two peaks, the cadence is prepared in A flat as in the exposition; the fortissimo cuts back in, to emerge into the tonic major. This granite music can only be compared to the mightiest passages of Bruckner.

Did such public music come from Berlioz's outer or inner needs? In this case, the music was probably conceived well before the commission, for *Fête musicale funèbre*, and is as much Berlioz's personal conception as the later Te Deum. A romantic composer might expect to function best under purely internal pressure; yet while some of the Requiem had earlier origins (the Mass, perhaps *Fête musicale*), most of it was new. Even so, the motivation to fulfil this commission was internal; something like this had been struggling to get out for a long time. Ironically, Berlioz's commissioned works were precisely those most indifferent to commercial practicality, for the contractual obligations of the government included the expenses of preparing material and of the first performance. In the market-place, the march-like *Apothéose*

---

[45] A recording of *Scène héroïque* (Denon, CO-72886) continues unaffected by Berlioz's written direction (bar 60: 'double plus vite'), with predictably leaden results. On the erroneous metronome mark and its misinterpretation in OBE, see Wotton, *Hector Berlioz*, 187–8.

[46] See *MLB* 132.   [47] See *MLB* 164–7.

took on a life of its own while the wonderful first movement of *Symphonie funèbre* languished. Berlioz's monster concerts required architectural works as much as the works required the events, and this combination served to gain the composer notoriety; but with no such events in prospect around 1849, completion of the Te Deum (and perhaps later of *L'Impériale*) suggests that he actually wanted to write grandiose pieces (naturally enough, since he did it well).

The cantata *Chant des chemins de fer* might have been the most attractive of these occasional works, but that the high speed of composition led to excessive repetition. It adopts a tonality, B major, important within the work it interrupted, *La Damnation*. From the Mass onward, Berlioz believed in introductory calls to order—a fact which makes the openings *in medias res* of several orchestral works, and *La Damnation*, the more remarkable (see Chapter 9). The opening gesture sets a tone of banal nobility, with a brass fanfare on the dominant (bars 3–4), but this introduction is all in B minor, as is the start of the tenor solo. At 'triomphe', however, the music arrives at the tonic major. The cantata consists of six massive strophes, each ending with a statement of the B major 'triomphe' cadence. New images begin each section (bar 58, 'Les cloches sonnent . . . le canon répond'; bar 126, 'Que de montagnes effacées! Que de rivières traversées'), but Berlioz refrains from imitation (neither bells nor bass drum are heard, but the river bridges a stunning modulation from B minor to B flat). The fourth section (bar 190) brings the first change of metre and tempo; the poet invites the old to celebrate the technological advances they will not themselves witness; Berlioz must have enjoyed writing this smooth minuet, ending with a two-octave descent into the tomb. The fifth section consists of proclamations to an admirably outrageous progression, each chord a whole-tone step down, descending eventually through a tritone, F♯ to C♮.[48] The sixth stanza is marked 'Andante religioso', and includes another way of moving a tritone, tonally and by enharmony, from D♮ to G♯ (reduction in Ex. 8.6). Possibly these harmonic experiments are Berlioz's reaction to a commission he might have preferred not to receive: since the piece was sure to be performed in a relatively uncritical ambience, why not try something on? As far as Berlioz was concerned, however, the first performance of this work was also the last.

L'Impériale fared little better, since its few performances were all in the year of its première, 1855. It contains few experiments; work without a commission has to be sold on its merits. It is the most sophisticated of this group of compositions, and the most grandiose, with double chorus and optional wind band on top of heavily doubled orchestral forces. The first chorus executes the more difficult passages, but is otherwise strengthened by a 'far more numerous' second chorus (in a small hall, Berlioz suggests solo voices instead of the first chorus). The music mingles public gestures which risk banality with ripe

---

[48] See *MLB* 44.

Ex. 8.6 *Chant des chemins de fer*, bars 300-10 (harmonic outline)

inventions in which, however, the harmonic progressions seldom lose touch with their immediate goal.

The form is certainly more complex and worthy of companionship to the Te Deum. Although broadly similar in tempo and metre throughout, *L'Impériale* begins in E flat and ends in A flat, a 'progressive' tonal plan defined by the reprise of the first theme in a different key. This theme from the second aria in *Sardanapale* is appropriately raw in style, as is its presentation over a rhythmically defined ostinato (continually changing pitch) in the basses, a technique which could be paralleled in several other works (for instance the finale of *Roméo*). The technique differs from the striking medium-register melodies deployed in *La Damnation* and *Les Troyens*; the latter control an orchestral discourse which counterpoints the dramatic action, and suggest a more complex interpretation, whereas rhythmic ostinatos, even those as complex as in the 'Lacrimosa', complement the prevailing topic. In *L'Impériale*, the opening crude 'till ready' bars and the *Sardanapale* melody occupy twenty-eight bars, followed by a development probably not taken from the earlier cantata. Wind instruments, and tenors, are added to the basses and strings; *L'Impériale* is a model of what Berlioz called the 'law of crescendo'. The melody is restated with accretions from the trombones, at bar 58, starting with a kind of measured glissando. A repeated section and amplified cadence conclude the material in E flat at bar 92. There follows the moment of harmonic mystery which joins E flat to the eventual tonic, A flat, but without bringing them into any audible juxtaposition to emphasize their tonic-dominant relationship (see Ex. 3.3). A flat is established by the refrain, in a tempo somewhat below the original (crotchet = 100 instead of 132), and making a fine entry for second chorus; but the instrumentation is still modest. The section up to bar 153 is framed by two statements of the refrain, closing with exuberant acclamations of 'Vive l'Empereur'.

The episode in D flat (bar 154) makes a contrast by scoring (contraltos and basses of chorus 1, woodwind and strings) and by sharply pointed imitation (from bar 172). It moves gradually to C minor, but attempts at closure are overwhelmed by the second chorus (bar 186) with the A flat refrain. Unlike the more literal 'Hymne à la France' or *Chant des chemins de fer*, this refrain is varied—'Veille sur son Empereur' is in awed augmentation—and truncated by a further episode which adopts the characteristic sequence of fourths from the *Sardanapale* theme. At bar 216 the refrain reappears in full; then the wind band is added, the tempo speeds up, and the choruses conclude the refrain material by reiterating its closing acclamation (bar 251). Further acceleration is required to gain the original tempo for the reprise, in A flat, of the *Sardanapale* theme, in the grandest of choral unisons. The coda includes rhetorical intensification through alien harmonies (from bar 277, A flat, E, A, F sharp minor, B, a diminished seventh, and so home in on a massive $\frac{6}{4}$ in bar 283), and the orchestra closes with the musical equivalent of applause.

TE DEUM

The text

The canticle 'Te Deum laudamus' is prose; for convenience, Table 8.5 arranges it into thirty 'lines'. It opens with praise of God, then invokes the other persons of the Trinity (lines 12–13), and Christ's second coming in glory (lines 14–20). The prayer for eternal life (21–5) precedes a final plea for mercy on a sinful world. Composers normally take the thundering of eternity (line 30) as an excuse for a peroration: 'In te Domine speravi' brings from Mozart (K. 141) an austere, from Haydn a thoroughly cheerful, and from Bruckner an imposing, double fugue. Only Verdi, with the honesty of extreme age, resisted temptation and ended his Te Deum on a note of fear.

Berlioz's Te Deum shows less direct formal influence from Lesueur than his Mass, except that Lesueur's third Te Deum sets 'Te ergo quæsumus' as a prayer for solo tenor.[49] In contrast to the Requiem, Berlioz set the whole text, until a cut in the 'Judex crederis' made, presumably, on musical grounds, as in the Requiem's 'Quaerens me', removed one line (23 in Table 8.5).[50] Two of Lesueur's settings are very far from complete, and none of them has a tonal plan of the conventional kind. One begins in B minor and two in B flat, but they all end in C; and nos. 1 in B minor and 3 in B flat share the same final chorus. In two of his settings, Lesueur omitted lines that Berlioz privileged by beginning a movement with them: 'Dignare Domine' and 'Judex crederis'. In Table 8.5, text [bracketed] is cut; text (enclosed) is Berlioz's own.

In a press release before the first performance, Berlioz wrote: 'A *Te Deum* is generally supposed to be no more than a ceremonial thanksgiving.

---

[49] Lesueur's *Trois Te Deum* appeared as the fourth volume ('Troisième Livraison') of his complete works, and survive also in the Tuileries manuscripts (nos. 30.1, 45, and 40 in Mongrédien's catalogue).

[50] The cut of forty-nine bars is between bars 72 and 73 (NBE 10. 181).

Ceremony is indeed its predominant character; but many of its lines are really prayers, in which humility and sorrow contrast with the majestic solemnity of the hymns: there is even a *Miserere* in the *Te Deum*.'[51] By rearranging many of its lines, he improved a somewhat straggling and repetitive text into movements headed 'Hymne' and 'Prière'. Within No. 2, minor differences from the canticle result from considerations of prosody: the principal motive sets only the first three words of line 3 (or four, since 'Tibi' is repeated); it is too short for the rest of the line, even with note-repetition, so Berlioz omitted 'universae'. In this movement, taking care that the Latin still makes sense, Berlioz devised a structure which required a return to the incantatory text 'Omnes tibi incessabili voce proclamant: Sanctus . . .' after line 9, and a variant of this after line 13, thus producing a threefold acclamation ('Holy, holy, holy') with the opportunity for rich colouristic variation.[52] Oddly enough, this is just the opportunity for musical expansion which the text invites, and Berlioz declines, in the 'Qui tollis' and Sanctus of the Mass, although the Agnus—borrowed here for No. 5—and the Requiem Sanctus, tenor solos with ritualistic responses from the chorus, are constructed in this way.

From No. 3, the alterations are more substantial. Praise of Christ is postponed to No. 4, avoiding a third successive hymn. For his first 'prayer', No. 3, Berlioz leapt nearly to the end of the canticle to retrieve perhaps its most beautiful line (26), then inserted an earlier line before line 27. He then went into reverse, making an arched text for an arched musical form; but like Lesueur, he mingles lines within the reprise. Since Latin grammar is not dependent on word order, the result is reasonably intelligible, but in such a hieratic musical setting it hardly matters:

(26) Dignare, Domine die isto sine peccato nos custodire.

(21) Aeterna fac cum sanctis tuis in gloria numerari.

(27) Miserere nostri, Domine, miserere nostri, (32–3) cum sanctis tuis fac numerari in aeterna gloria.

(26, 21, 27) Dignare, Domine, nos cum sanctis in gloria numerari. Miserere nostri.

(26) Dignare, Domine die isto sine peccato nos custodire.[53]

No. 4 is based on lines 20–7, with 22–3 and 24–5 reversed; the emphasis on 'thou' ('Tu') is remarkable, even given its repetition in the canticle. The second prayer, No. 5, takes a further plea for mercy (lines 28–9) as a choral response to the solo tenor's development of lines 19–20. This manipulation enabled Berlioz to improve the musical pattern borrowed from the Agnus, in

---

[51] NBE 10. 194.

[52] The repeated Sanctus is anticipated by Lesueur in the second Te Deum (M40 in Mongrédien's catalogue).

[53] 'Vouchsafe, O Lord, to keep us this day without sin. Make them to be numbered with thy saints in glory everlasting. Have mercy upon us, Lord, have mercy upon us; make them to be numbered with thy saints in glory everlasting. Vouchsafe O Lord to number us with thy saints in glory everlasting. Have mercy upon us. Vouchsafe, O Lord, to keep us this day without sin.'

TABLE 8.5 Text of the Te Deum

Canticle	Berlioz's textual alterations
1. Te Deum laudamus, te Dominum confitemur,	**No. 1** (1–2)
2. Te aeternum Patrem omnis terra veneratur.	
	No. 2 (3–13)
3. Tibi omnes angeli, tibi coeli et universae potestates,	3 Tibi omnes angeli, tibi coeli et potestates
4. Tibi cherubim et seraphim incessabili voce proclamant:	
5. Sanctus, sanctus, sanctus, Dominus Deus Sabaoth,	
6. Pleni sunt coeli et terra majestatis gloriae tuae.	Te gloriosus chorus apostolorum:
7. Te gloriosus apostolorum chorus,	
8. Te prophetarum laudabilis numerus,	Te martyrum laudat candidatus exercitus.
9. Te martyrum candidatus laudat exercitus.	Omnes tibi incessabili voce proclamant: Sanctus [etc.]
10. Te per orbem terrarum sancta confitetur ecclesia:	
11. Patrem immensae majestatis:	
12. Venerandum tuum verum et unicum Filium;	Omnes tibi proclamant: Sanctus [etc.]
13. Sanctum quoque Paraclitum Spiritum.	To No. 3 (line 26)
14. Tu rex gloriae, Christe, tu patris sempiternus es filius.	**No. 4** (14–17): Tu Christe, tu rex gloriae, patris sempiternus filius (on to 16)
15. Tu ad liberandum suscepturus hominem, non horruisti virginis uterum.	15 (follows 16; on to 17): Ad liberandum
16. Tu devicto mortis aculeo, aperuisti credentibus regna coelorum.	16 (follows 14; on to 15)
17. Tu ad dexteram Dei sedes, in gloria patris.	17 (follows 15; on to 14)
18. Judex crederis esse venturus.	**No. 6** (18 begins No. 6; on to 30)
19. Te ergo quaesumus, tuis famulis subveni,	**No. 5** (19 begins No. 5: on to 28):
20. Quos pretioso sanguine redemisti.	quæsumus, Domine, [humilibus] famulis tuis subveni, Quos pretioso
21. Aeterna fac cum sanctis tuis in gloria numerari.	21 (follows 26; on to 27)
22. Salvum fac populum tuum, Domine, et benedic hereditati tuae,	22 (follows 30) . . . tuum, et benedic hereditatae tuae, Domine.
23. Et rege eos, et extolle illos usque in aeternum.	[23 is cut in the final version]
24. Per singulos dies, benedicimus te, et laudamus nomen tuum	
25. In saeculum, et in saeculum saeculi.	
26. Dignare, Domine die isto sine peccato nos custodire.	**No. 3** (26 begins No. 3: on to 21)

Canticle	Berlioz's textual alterations
27. Miserere nostri Domine, miserere nostri.	
28. Fiat misericordia tua Domine super nos,	28 (follows 21)
29. Quemadmodum speravimus in te.	29 (follows 20) Fiat super nos misericordia tua, Domine, Quemadmodum . . .
30. In te Domine speravi; non confundar in aeternum.	30 (follows 18: on to 22–5)

which the choral responses merely repeat the soloist's text. He extended the original movement by a new coda, requiring more text-repetition and min-gling, or mangling, of lines. For No. 6, Berlioz combined hymn and prayer, although the 'hymn' is mainly fugal, its subject running together lines 18 and 30. Berlioz clearly decided to gather the lines concerned with the last judge-ment into a single movement, and with more poetic economy than the origi-nal author, he uses the prayer for salvation, lines 22–5, for contrast. Then, by returning to the 'hymn' text, he ends with the last line of the canticle.

TABLE 8.6 Overall form of the Te Deum

1	'Te Deum laudamus'	Hymne	F major; coda moves to B major
2	'Tibi omnes'	Hymne	B major
[2a	Prélude	Orchestral	Open: ends V of D]
3	'Dignare, Domine'	Prière	D major
4	'Tu Christe'	Hymne	D major
5	'Te ergo quaesumus'	Prière	G minor, ends G major
6	'Judex crederis' ('Salvum fac')	Hymne et Prière	Roving tonality: D♭, B♭ minor; ends B♭ major
7	Marche	Instrumental	B♭ major

Berlioz planned an orchestral movement to vary the pattern, at the point where he begins seriously to depart from the canticle (between Nos. 2 and 3). The March was composed after the choral movements, perhaps with the coronation of Napoleon III in mind; it was sketched in B major, fitting with the tonality of 'Tibi omnes' (No. 2), and was performed at that point in the first performance, although presumably in B flat, the key of the autograph score.[54] No. 3 follows in D major, an acceptable juxtaposition in nineteenth-century music, whether with B major or B flat major; in the former case, one might hear the setting of the word 'Dignare', although harmonized in D, as a B minor arpeggio (f♯–d–b); the same tonal connection occurs, of course, in performances which omit the instrumental movement. The March was then

[54] Holoman, *Berlioz*, 219; facsimiles of the sketches, 221–2.

transferred to the end, where it appears in the published score. More vexed is the question of the 'Prélude' between Nos. 2 and 3. It begins with the rhythm of the 'Te Deum laudamus' fugue subject rapped out on the military drum; this is developed in stark contrapuntal textures, while the music veers alarmingly back to F major, and then to its relative minor, ending on the dominant of D, ready for 'Dignare, Domine'. The Prélude 'which contains dubious modulations', as Berlioz explained to Liszt, was cut a fortnight before the first performance, whereas Berlioz did perform the March, and never withdrew it.[55] The fugue subject is also used in the March, together with the grand unison theme of the first movement. The suppression of these instrumental pieces (nowadays almost invariable) does not alter the tonal scheme of the Te Deum, but it removes a substantial element of coherence through the recall and apotheosis of these themes; the two entries of the organ during the March with the striding scalar theme fulfil an expectation frustrated when the grand tonic cadence of the first movement (to bar 123) is succeeded by quiet and thoroughly ambiguous harmonies, before the themes disappear and the music finds its way to the dominant of B.

The tonal fracture at the end of No. 1, between keys a tritone apart, gives place to more conventional key-relations. The move from B to D is not entirely stable, given the curious design of No. 3, which is based entirely on bass pedals a third apart; it needs No. 4 to affirm D major convincingly, although even so, 'Tu Christe' immediately cadences in the mediant, F sharp minor (bar 8). A descending fifth, the standard tonal connection throughout much of the Requiem, leads to No. 5, and from G minor to B flat for No. 6 is conventional. One might conclude that Berlioz designed a pattern of progression from unrelated keys (F to B) through an indirect relation (B to D) to the security of direct relations (D to G minor to B flat). But foreground elements militate against this interpretation: No. 5 ends in G major, and the organ prelude to No. 6 begins on the open fifth Eb/Bb and suggests (bar 3) still flatter keys (Ex. 8.7a). The voices enter in B flat minor, and the imposing fugue subject immediately introduces the Cb which is its proximate goal. Any broad tonal design such as an expanded perfect cadence from F, No. 1, to B flat, No. 6, is thoroughly factitious.

Systematic composition: Nos. 1 and 2

The long gestation of the Te Deum, and its eventual completion without a commission, suggest that Berlioz may have been stretching his muscles by setting himself compositional problems. This is the work most coloured by what may be termed systematic composition. Contemporary criticism of Berlioz was all too wont to refer to his 'system', without explaining what this was supposed to mean; Berlioz himself referred to Lesueur's 'system' without elucidation, as something from which, about 1828–9, he felt he should free

---

[55] 'où se trouvent les modulations *douteuses*'; *CG* 5. 53.

himself (he probably meant post-Rameau laws of harmonic progression). Except perhaps for No. 4, each number in the Te Deum revels in some compositional difficulty, and the tension between expression and technique only adds to the vitality and fascination of the result—rather, if the comparison is not presumptuous, as in certain works of J. S. Bach.

The first problem Berlioz set himself was a double fugue. By now he had composed many expressive fugatos, some, such as the Offertoire, of considerable extent, and a fugue for harmonium. But since we must discount the wretched 'Quoniam' and the satirical 'Amen' of *La Damnation*, his only true choral fugue was the Requiem's 'Hosanna', its least interesting movement and hardly even Berliozian, though rescued from his own strictures on choral fugues by the appropriate text, and his direction to sing it smoothly. 'Te Deum laudamus' is another act of emulation, possibly of Mendelssohn, not because of any musical resemblance but because, like Mendelssohn's best fugues, it contrives to be both characteristic and scholastic.[56] Berlioz first imposes his spatial conception of the Te Deum through alternate chords for full orchestra and organ. The challenge of 'Pope and Emperor' is symbolized harmonically: in the sequence F–d–B♭–a–C, major chords are for orchestra, minor for organ. The orchestra proposes F as a tonality, but the organ caps the cadence with an A, to begin a statement of the noble striding line already mentioned, which Berlioz treats as an intermittent cantus firmus: this at first implies the key of D minor, but ends with a rhythmic diminution, cadencing crisply in F.

Periodic re-entries of the cantus firmus may have been suggested by the ripieno chorale superimposed on the double chorus in Bach's *Matthäus Passion*, heard in Berlin in 1843. Although Berlioz's double fugue is in Italian style (the countersubject, tenors, enters against the subject rather than waiting for the answer), it is surely part of nineteenth-century Bach reception, and the Berlin chorus of three hundred modernized Bach's sound-world to that of Mendelssohn.[57] Berlioz uses a strict tonal answer—something he neglected in other expressive contexts.[58] The episode (from bar 38) does not develop, but holds fast to dominant harmony for a paean of close canonic imitation. There follows a brief development, two entries of the cantus firmus combined with the fugue subject, and two statements of the first four bars of the cantus firmus. Berlioz's strategy leads us to expect periodic cantus firmus entries by way of climax, but he also perceives 'Te omnis terra veneratur' as an awed contrast to 'Te Deum laudamus', like 'et in terra pax' after 'Gloria in excelsis Deo'. While developing the countersubject, the passage from bar 79 gradually

---

[56] Berlioz was impressed by *Elijah* in London in 1847 (Cairns, *Servitude*, 396), but may already have planned his 'Te Deum laudamus' fugue.

[57] The ripieno is not mentioned in his report (*Memoirs*, ch. 51, ninth letter). The Te Deum ripieno (children's) chorus, whose first entry (bar 50) is with the cantus firmus, was added after the composition was essentially complete.

[58] See *MLB* 122–3.

becomes homophonic, and sinks to psalmodic repetition (major changing to minor, bars 88–9). The significance of this incident is revealed later, after a tremendous fugal reprise with stretto, capped by the cantus firmus (bar 105), and resolution in the tonic of the canonic paean (bars 123–6: compare bars 38–40). The following bars liquidate the fugue subject; the cantus firmus is heard in a thickened unison; the declamation, now extended, marks the end of all thematic content; the harmony dissolves until the bass reaches up to F♯ as a dominant of B major, an unsurpassable moment of sublime awe.

The second movement adjusts our viewpoint to contemplation of the superior beings who proclaim God's holiness. Variation is the system. The invocations which begin each section are varied in harmony and contrapuntal detail. The first three (sopranos), and the next three (tenors), preserve the same pitch-level; when the basses require the motive to be transposed, they vary it sequentially, rising by steps (from bar 119: B, C♯, D♯). The threefold 'Sanctus' affects us by its sudden slowing of harmonic change (up to eight bars per chord against a previous norm of flowing quavers and crotchets).[59] When woodwind evoke celestial harps behind gently roving string lines, we hear in embryo Wagner's rainbow (*Das Rheingold*, however, was composed before publication or performance of the Te Deum); each glorious acclamation is orchestrally varied. The other element in this, the most beautiful movement, is the organ. Its introduction, with strict canon, intervenes within the movement and is transferred to strings at the end. In addition it closes each section with cadences whose disarming simplicity aroused the ire of Arthur Hutchings.[60] The organ modulates in readiness for the bass entries and varies the chord positions as if improvising (in the treble: bars 69 and 174, tonic; bar 117, mediant; at the end, dominant), and its appearances paradoxically signify the terrestrial; the organ is functionally of the church, as the 'Sanctus' is of heaven; these poles are mediated by the choral invocations, their intricate counterpoint resembling the organ's and their ritualistic grace preparing for the homophonic 'Sanctus'.

Nos. 3, 4, and 5

'Dignare, Domine', as Berlioz proudly told Liszt, is a prayer 'for two choral lines in canonic imitation on this singular series of pedal points'.[61] The 'canon' is not formally determining, and could be described as free imitation at the octave, but the movement is undeniably ingenious, a lucid set of interlocking lines spanning pedals on D (major), F♮ (major), A (minor: Berlioz incorrectly says 'minor and major') and C♮ (major then minor). The entrance of the second line overlaps with the last upward shift to E flat (major): 'en

[59] See *MLB* 45.

[60] Introducing the Te Deum for BBC Radio 3, a context in which advocacy rather than critical niggling is usually considered appropriate (Hutchings was otherwise enthusiastic).

[61] 'à deux voix (de chœur) en imitations canoniques, sur cette singulière série de pédales', *CG* iv. 258.

enharmonique', as Berlioz explained his next move, D sharp to E, marking the radiant climax ('in gloria numerari'). The descending ladder of thirds explores the sharp side: E♮, C♯, A, F♯, D. The shift to C♯, a sudden pianissimo, brings a shadow, the prayer for mercy: 'Miserere nostri'; Berlioz then reintroduces the previous line of text, reaching a gentle A major cadence. The return to the opening text coincides with the bass F♯, and blends into a final tonic pedal, subtly disturbed by minor and Neapolitan inflections (bars 102, 110).

'Dignare, Domine' is the most systematic movement, despite which its melodic charm is what lingers in the memory. 'Tu Christe' has no particular system, but an electric rhythm that recalls Berlioz's patriotic, military style. Following an interlude in slower tempo ('Ad liberandum'), a reprise might be expected; instead, a new theme, Berlioz's last borrowing from the Resurrexit, reanimates the music (bar 95). Pizzicato arpeggios are borrowed with the tune, but in context recall the second 'Sanctus' from 'Tibi omnes'. The layered choral entries from bar 117 are a triumphantly successful example of the energetic choral style Berlioz first developed in *Scène héroïque*, but the boldest stroke is not the vigorous reassertion of the opening (from bar 127) but the near-breakdown the music suffers thereafter: the bass C♮ (bar 134) initiates a semitone descent emphasizing the alien pitches (B♭ and A♭); temporary resolution on G leaves the chorus, suddenly unconvinced of its message, trying mantra-like repetition around F♮. But this is also a crescendo to fortissimo (bar 156), where confidence is restored. Or is it? Flat-side pitches like C♮ (against D♯), B♭ and F♮ continue to threaten the choral D major, and only a piece of sharp-side cadential rhetoric from the orchestra (from bar 189) banishes doubt.[62]

The Agnus of the Mass forms the basis for the complete fifth movement (Table 8.7); for nearly eighty bars, in rhetoric and construction, including the imitative bass, the pieces are the same, as is the general sense of the text. Throughout, the mature hand of the 45-year-old composer is everywhere apparent. The Agnus text, once rediscovered, sounds obviously right, but more words means less repetition, and the revised underlay is carefully done; the dotted rhythms of 'quæsumus', 'misericordia', and 'Domine', repeating pitches originally sustained, are characteristic, not forced, and the strained setting of 'sanguine' matches the agony implied in the shedding of Christ's precious blood. The syncopated accompaniment brings the conception into the nineteenth century, replacing fierce, Gluckian anapaests. The added woodwind phrase is handed to the voice in the extension; the cor anglais adds a sombre glow; and most tellingly, the monotone choral responses are transformed as well as lengthened into something beyond liturgical symmetry by a

---

[62] The oblique resolution of the earlier A♭ as G♯, and of this B♭ as A♯, recall the method Berlioz used in the Largo of *Symphonie fantastique*: *MLB* 32–3.

TABLE 8.7 Comparison of Agnus Dei with 'Te ergo quæsumus'

Agnus Dei (*Messe solennelle*)	'Te ergo quæsumus' (Te Deum)
1–12: Introduction: Orchestral melody, fully closed in G minor	1–19: Introduction: seven new bars at the beginning
13–24: Tenor solo: 'Agnus Dei, qui tollis peccata mundi, miserere nobis'	20–31: Tenor solo: 'Te ergo quæsumus Domine, famulis tuis subveni quos pretioso sanguine redemisti'
Fully closed in G minor	The same
25–42: 'Agnus Dei, qui tollis peccata mundi, miserere nobis'	32–49: 'Quos pretioso sanguine redemisti; Te ergo quæsumus, humilibus tuis famulis subveni'
Orchestral melody, fully closed in G minor; voice counterpointed	The same
42–5: Choral psalmody, unison (d″) 'Agnus Dei, qui tollis peccata mundi, miserere nobis'	50–4: Choral psalmody, octave d′–d″ 'Fiat super nos misericordia tua Domine' new brass melody
45–63: Solo: 'Agnus Dei, qui tollis peccata mundi, miserere nobis'	54–72: Solo: 'Fiat super nos, Domine, misericordia tua, quemadmodum speravimus in te. Fiat misericordia tua'
B♭ major	The same, with new woodwind figure
63–6: Choral psalmody, 'Agnus Dei, qui tollis peccata mundi, miserere nobis' B♭: in two parts (b♭′/d″)	72–6: Choral psalmody, 'Fiat super nos misericordia tua Domine' f′–f″ falling to d′–d″: brass melody modulates back to G minor
66–75: Solo, 'Agnus Dei, dona nobis pacem' Melody in bass, in G minor; plagal cadences	76–85: Tenor, 'Domine, quemadmodum speravimus in te' The same, with woodwind figure
75–8: Choral psalmody, 'Agnus Dei, qui tollis peccata mundi, dona nobis pacem' G major chord in three parts	85–92: Choral psalmody, 'Fiat super nos misericordia tua Domine' Unison d″ then in 2 parts, with brass melody, G major, V–I cadences
FINE	92–113: Solo with chorus, 'Speravimus in te Domine' Solo takes woodwind figure
	113–28: Choral coda *a cappella*, 'Fiat super nos misericordia tua, Domine, quemadmodum speravimus in te' Original melody in bass, G major

syncopated brass chorale. The G major coda magically transfers the melody to the bass, for strangely archaic four-part harmony.[63]

No. 6. Hymne et prière: 'Judex crederis'

In his finest evocation of the last judgement, Berlioz synthesized the tonal unpredictability of the Requiem 'Dies irae' with the fugal form of the 'Lacrimosa'. Berlioz wrote of one of Lesueur's Te Deum settings, heard in Notre-Dame in 1835, that 'the last line, *non confundar in aeternum*, has frightening energy . . . Lesueur's is essentially music for a cathedral'; its broad progressions would appear too simple in a drier acoustic.[64] Berlioz again determined to outdo his teacher, but he also reverted to convention by using fugue for the end of the canticle; composers usually begin the fugue with 'In te Domine speravi'. Berlioz's composite text combines a 'hymn' (A) and a 'prayer' (B):

A: Judex crederis esse venturus. In te Domine speravi; non confundar in aeternum.

B1: Salvum fac populum, et benedic haereditati tuae, Domine,
[Et rege eos, et extolle illos usque in aeternum.
Laudamus te, benedicimus nomen tuum, in saeculum, in saeculum saeculi.]

B2: Per singulos dies, benedicimus, laudamus te, Et laudamus nomen tuum. Salva haereditatem tuam, Domine.

A': Judex crederis esse venturus. In te Domine speravi; non confundar in aeternum.

Broadly, this implies a ternary structure, but words and music of the outer and middle sections join in a tense struggle towards the end, combining compound and simple metres (9/8 and 3/4). Berlioz considered this his finest apocalyptic movement, calling it 'Babylonian' and 'Ninevite'. It is an endless source of fascination from the point of view of tonality and hermeneutics. The movement serves to illustrate Cone's view of Berlioz's formal processes as 'a wave-like series of motions towards a succession of proximate goals, each of which in turn initiates a further motion'.[65] Its rhetorical action depends not only upon the massive slowness with which each goal is approached, and the unpredictability of the route, but on the frustration of goals at the moment when a breakthrough seems within the music's grasp.

The tonality, as Schacher observes, resembles 'chaos at the end of time'.[66] Following a pellucid G major cadence, the organ begins on the dyad E♭–B♭; equivalent moves to flat VI have portentous significance within *Les*

---

[63] On this harmony see Friedheim, 'Radical Harmonic Procedures in Berlioz', 284; *MLB* 94–5.

[64] 'Le dernier verset, *non confundar in aeternum*, est d'une terrible énergie. . . . Sa musique est essentiellement une musique de cathédrale.' *Critique musicale*, ii. 254.

[65] Cone, *Music: A View from Delft*, 223.

[66] 'endzeitlichen Chaos'; Thomas Schacher, *Idee und Erscheinungsform des Dramatischen bei Hector Berlioz*, 111.

Troyens.[67] Overall, the tonality can only be interpreted as B flat; but this, or at least B flat major, is a distant, not a proximate, goal, and to assist clarity of notation Berlioz refrained from using a key-signature for most of the movement. The head-motive of the fugue subject is presented by the organ (Ex. 8.7*a*); its repeated notes have a sinister urgency, and the following turn tends to cast doubt on the tonality by introducing the semitone above the note locally defined, at bar 8 and subsequently, as the tonic. In the organ prelude, moreover, the first harmonic change is to A flat, a move in the opposite direction from B flat.

The movement may be considered as a search, sometimes desperate, for clarification—some acknowledgement of praise, some answer to its prayer. When the fugue subject appears in full, C♭ proves to be its 'proximate goal', so that each successive entry is a semitone higher; this *visibly* fractures the tonality by compelling Berlioz, several times, to change his notation enharmonically. And although the introduction reaches B flat minor, the subject's C♭ implies the subdominant, confirmed by the harmony of bar 9 (Ex. 8.7*b*). Harmonically, the subject swings past the subdominant's relative major, G flat, down a fifth to C flat, duly confirmed by a blast of brass covering four octaves; the first enharmonic change treats C♭ as B♮, and the sopranos duly end the subject on C♮. The tenors follow, and although the long-term outcome of this kind of sequence is arbitrary, D flat is a predictable local goal; in a synoptic view we would understand this as the relative major. Clarification is assisted because the fugal entries come at regular intervals, and harmonic clarification underlines the soprano entry (bar 16) where, with more counterpoint and a linear bass, the progression is easier to hear. In bar 17, instead of a dominant seventh on B, the partly chromatic bass leads to E minor (bar 18, corresponding to E flat minor, bar 10). Where in bars 11–12 the key of G flat

Ex. 8.7*a* Te Deum, opening of 'Judex crederis'

---

[67] See 'Overture', esp. 137–9.

Ex. 8.7*b* Te Deum, 'Judex crederis', clarification of harmony within the exposition

is only hinted at by the largely unison texture, and then undermined by the diminished seventh in the brass, the equivalent bars (19–20) aim clearly for G major; subsequent inflections, although implying essentially the same harmonization, are again supported by a strong, contrary-motion bass. In the third entry, the subdominant (F minor) is omitted and the harmony reaches its relative major, A flat, in the third bar (26). This fall of a fifth to the goal, and the soprano counterpoint, which replicates much of the subject itself in a sort of canon, make this section still more confident. Constructive use of a favourite device, reharmonization, and the hint of canon, provide cross-references to Nos. 2 and 3 (see above), so that we can hear this fugal exposition as both progressively integrated with what came before, and teleologically, as progress towards eventual clarification. But the arrival on D flat major is typically frustrated by a *cadence rompue*: the subject, indeed, ends on D♮ (tenors, bar 32). With something of a struggle, menaced by an insistent string rhythm, the chorus completes the cadence four bars later.

In a fugal design, the material from bar 36 would constitute an episode, but it terminates in a tonic cadence, and fugue soon ceases to be a useful explanation of the rest of the movement. Bar 36 marks the next enharmonic change. The minor ninth attacked in bar 37 verticalizes the first, ambiguous interval of the subject; the desperate cry of 'non confundar' is repeated with changed harmony, then sequentially, like a traditional episode (bar 42). Berlioz continues to strive for tonal clarification by using the conventional way of establishing a key: arrival on a dominant bass to a (tonic) $^6_4$ chord, as when a classical composer provides the aural signal for a cadenza. His approach here is straightforward, using contrary motion in the outer parts and strengthening the arrival rhythmically by means of hemiola.[68] Thus approached, D major (bar 46), the only key previously used for two movements of the Te Deum, coincides with the first fortissimo, aided by a strengthened brass entry and a rap of the drum. As a harmonic goal, however, this moment of glory lacks foundation: the edifice collapses at once, in a radical sequence of descending fifths (D–G–C–F–B♭), all major until the last which cruelly applies the brake. Nothing in the previous passage has prepared for a tonic outcome, however; B flat minor is clung to for dear life, in repeated V–i chords which certainly provide clarification, but in a context of tonal rejection, matched by a fall in register when the head-motive of the subject is unambiguously harmonized in the tonic for the first time (bars 53–6).

This defeat is symbolized by the key-signature of five flats at bar 57. The battlefield is generic: hymn (a topic) and fugue (a texture associated particularly with sacred music) have failed to attain more than a glimpse of positive resolution. The second section tries prayer ('O Lord, save thy people, and bless thine inheritance'), and is simpler, with a ternary design. A smooth

---

[68] Hemiola: three duple accents spread over two triple-metre bars; thus bars 44–5 *sound* like three bars of 2/4 or 6/8, whereas the notation remains in 9/8.

melody, and gentle instrumentation without heavy brass, allow the straight-forward harmonic trajectory (B flat minor to D flat) to intensify the prayer enough to retain forward momentum, without breaking through to enlightenment. Berlioz starts with a lyrical period: eight bars in the tonic, the same eight bars a third higher (hence already in D flat), a sequential middle (bars 73–6), and an arrival, to new text, 'Per singulos dies'.[69] The new melody (from bar 77) is based on small intervals, and sounds like a hymn in the conventional (congregational) sense; but above it, like the beating wings of a great bird, the first bar of 'Salvum fac, Domine' is transformed into a mantra, prayer by repetition (it comes twenty-six times, the most stubborn of the ostinatos adumbrated, however remotely, in the 'Quoniam'). Rich string accompaniment and orchestration, drawing in most of the brass, mark bars 77–102 as the first stable tonal plateau within the movement.

Such stability cannot last in view of the implications of the principal text. From this point, words and their characteristic music become dangerously tangled. 'Per singulos' is sung to the music of 'Salvum fac . . .' (sopranos, violins, bars 103–14), but the bass-note (the local dominant, A♭) is given to basses singing 'Judex crederis' to the rhythm of the fugal head-motive. Thus the middle section never quite ends. Instead—to borrow otherwise inappropriate sonata-form terminology—it merges with a retransition. The six-bar phrase is repeated a tone higher, on B♭; and as if in recognition that we are returning to where we started, the vocal drum-beat is passed across from first to second chorus basses. The rest of the transition restores the tonal chaos of the opening. In pitch-organization, these are perhaps the most remarkable bars in the whole movement, since they are nearly octatonic (Ex. 8.8).[70] The head-motive climbs over a diminished seventh: B♭–D♭–F♭–G♮–b♭. Where B♭ lasts twelve bars, the next two steps each occupy four bars and the last two move twice as quickly. The potential stability of the B♭ at the beginning and end is not achieved when the systematic ascent of an octave is complete; instead the bass moves in succession to the neighbour-notes defined in the subject's turn. The first wave of this crescendo breaks in bar 134, to a bass C♭ perilously supporting an F♭—or E♮—$^6_4$ chord, fortissimo. Instead of resolving this by V–I in E major, the head-motive hammers out B♭ again, then slides down to A♭ (D♭, $^6_4$, bar 140), with the same outcome; then the bass boldly plunges down to F for a $^6_4$ chord which brings B♭ major—at last. This is the eventual goal, but is hardly recognizable as such here, where it is corrupted by an A♭, not least in the timpani. This pitch seizes the initiative, so that the energy of this third

---

[69] It is within this section, before the 'middle', that he made a substantial cut which develops the 'Salvum fac . . .' material for the omitted lines of text, and begins 'Per singulos dies' against a first re-entry of 'Judex crederis' in the bass. The loss is regrettable but removes a tautology; moreover, for the only time, Berlioz seems to be shaping the music with excessive dependence on the words.

[70] The notes c♮, g♭, and a♮ supplement the octatonic set b♭, c♭, d♭, d♮ (e♭♭), e♮ (f♭), f♮, g♮, a♭; c♮ is heard in passing, g♭ is a neighbour-note, but a♮ is the root for a whole bar (129).

Ex. 8.8 Te Deum, 'Judex crederis', from bar 118

great wave dissipates. But a cadence in A♭ is hardly conclusive, and it is immediately represented as G♯, the key-signature being withdrawn.

At least this *démarche* clears the textural air sufficiently for a counter-exposition of the fugue. Starting from G♯, the second and third entries are on A♮ and on the point of departure, B♭, and this last entry (bar 160) is in emphatic unison, as in the 'Lacrimosa'. It marks a climax, helped by an entry for the organ, silent since the introduction, on a steady descending scale which might be related to the cantus firmus of the first movement. Although B♭ is inevitably blocked when the unison duly reaches C♭ (bar 168), the episode material (bar 169, compare bar 36) means that a symmetrical thematic reprise is firmly in

234

place as a major element of clarification. While the remainder draws the theme of the middle section into the tonic ambience, at bar 171 the harmonic goal is still remote and the frantic declamation, in 3/4, of 'Salvum fac Domine' (bar 172, interrupting the previous text at 'confundar'), recalls the confusion at the height of the Requiem's 'Rex tremendae'. The orchestra heads for E minor, then the chorus, back to the opening line of text ('non confundar'), makes a second climactic assault on D major (177), which is still untenable. But rather than the total collapse which followed D major in bar 46, the pianissimo 'in aeternum' brings it into relation with the tonic clutch of keys, as Neapolitan (flat II) for D flat (notated C♯, and at first minor, a moment to catch the breath). The bass suspends action on A♮ at the whispered 'in aeternum', but after the silence it falls back to G♯, C sharp major becomes D flat, and the $^6_4$, for once, is properly resolved (bar 183). Another point of integration is that the 'Salvum fac' motive is sung to 'non confundar in aeternum'. This expansive Neapolitan complex recalls the two great invocations, at the same pitch (D to c♯), in *Roméo* and *La Damnation*; but this is the most involved, for those pieces are actually in C♯ minor, not B flat.[71]

The 'in aeternum' (bars 185–6) carries the music to B flat minor, and the final objective is near at last. From bar 188, the head-motive is reconciled to the tonic, the turn including C♮ and A♮, rather than flats; another organ scale covers only the tetrachord B♭–F, and the unblemished $^6_4$ at bar 194 produces the first really convincing cadence. The tonic is sustained over six bars, surmounted by the ostinato from the B section, and the remaining harmonic excursions, although they introduce new elements, are immediately resolved, being heard as characteristic rhetorical amplification of the functions of the tonic (dominant of G minor, bar 205; supertonic, bar 209; subdominant, bar 211). The descending tetrachord, now fully chromatic (bars 216–19), tames the wilder ambiguities of the fugue subject, although a last and Cassandra-like cry appears in the massive minor ninth (bar 221) at the last choral cadence. In the orchestral coda, the contrapuntal texture of the 'bless thine inheritance' melody (bars 227–8) and military dotted rhythms respectively recall 'Tibi omnes' and 'Tu, Christe'.

This synthesis makes a magnificent conclusion, for all that the blaze of trumpets and cornets appears entirely new. The outcome suggests an acknowledgement of the hymns, an answer to prayer: divine acceptance. Sober historical consideration tells us that Berlioz had in mind occasional use for his work, in which case the fanfares prepare for the 'Marche pour la présentation des drapeaux', though what imperial victories he could foresee in 1849 are hard to imagine. It is easier to believe that this blaze of glory represents his final tribute to the memory of the great men of France, and to the great Napoleon in particular, and that it is shot through with memories of his recently deceased father, a sceptic who took communion on his deathbed. For

[71] See Ex. 9.8 and *MLB* 243–8.

Cairns it derives from 'the call of the past'.[72] Certainly there is a retrospective element in manner and technique throughout the Te Deum, despite its radical exploration of space, harmony, and systematic composition. When Berlioz said 'at last the Requiem has a brother' he was surely thinking of the affinities of the two great fugal visions of judgement; of these, the 'Lacrimosa' is chronologically senior, but 'Judex crederis' is the older in experience, and wisdom.

[72] Cairns, *Servitude*, 428–31.

9 A Fantastic Symphonist

ORCHESTRAL RHETORIC: FIRST ESSAYS

By the time Berlioz published his thoughts on instrumental expressiveness, he had composed three titled overtures and a symphony, although *Symphonie fantastique* and *La Tempête* had not yet been performed. In his 1830 article, Berlioz mentions Weber in the same breath as Beethoven, presumably thinking of the overtures. *Les Francs-juges* and *Waverley*, his first two sharply contrasted pieces, had been performed without detailed programmatic exegesis, and in their original form were written without much knowledge of Beethoven. The former, however, may have been revised after Berlioz's exposure to Beethoven; the autograph is lost and the earliest complete sources are from well after 1830.[1]

Les Francs-juges is an opera overture, whose 'programme'—the opera—exists only in part. The surviving libretto is of later date, but cross-references to the opera can readily be inferred, and confirm the opening topic as a lament, for which there is ample dramatic justification; the opera is about the oppressed people of Freiburg-in-Breisgau. As far as we know, they do not sing this tune, and when the tyrant enters, the D flat minor unison (Ex. 4.7) is unrelated to the unison theme in D flat major which threatens the overture's tonic. Despite this relatively low intersection of signs, the unison theme must be associated with Olmerick.[2] It is harder to find a correlative in the libretto for the sprightly second theme (an acknowledged borrowing from an early quintet), or for the lengthy C minor interpolation in the development, although it is derived from the opening: it is a lament, but whose? But even if we could associate every theme with the personalities of the drama, that would not amount to a programme with power to explain lines of musical

---

[1] Macdonald, *Berlioz Orchestral Music*, 14; Holoman, *Catalogue*, 42. The earliest complete source, not quite the final version, is a German copy, presumably from *c*.1833 when orchestral parts were published by Richault.

[2] Thomas Schacher associates it with Olmerick's lines: 'Que l'inspiration descende en traits de flamme|Et vous brûle des feux allumés en mon âme', a 'récit. Mesuré' from the last scene (Holoman, *Creative Process*, 322). He may be right, but this is the end of the speech; if fitted to these words, the melody would be cut off at mid-point. Schacher, *Idee und Erscheinungsform des Dramatischen bei Hector Berlioz*, 7.

thought. This overture brings the world of Weber and Gothic romanticism into French music, striking a new note with such creative energy that its rawness can easily be forgiven; but, as Thomas Schacher observes, it is not an operatic précis.[3]

Waverley appears to be Berlioz's first orchestral music designed only for the concert-hall, and its composition before the Société des concerts inaugurated its public performances is remarkable. In the autograph, Berlioz inserted an extended patchwork of citations from Scott's novel (in French), which he decided not to publish, sidelining it with 'fatiguant, fatiguant, fatiguant'. He replaced this with the simple verse motto, also drawn from the novel: 'Dreams of love and Lady's charms|Give place to honour and to arms.' These lines connect straightforwardly with the standard overture plan of lyrical 'introduction' and vigorous allegro, and they perhaps explain why there is no thematic connection between them, as there is in most Berlioz overtures and several by Beethoven and Weber. Nevertheless the citations in the score enlarge perception of the implicit 'programme', in a manner both revealing and prophetic. They suggest four sections: (1) the adolescent Waverley, 'mélancolique et rêveuse', loving solitude and indulging his imagination with fantastic scenes—Berlioz will have recognized how such a vivid mental life can increase one's isolation; (2) the young officer's dreams of Flora MacIvor; (3) a Highlanders' prayer before a battle, which greatly agitates him ('ni la crainte ni l'ardeur du combat; c'était une mélange de ces deux sentimens qui l'étourdit d'abord et lui causait un essor de délire'); (4) a battle (there is nothing on Waverley's political problems in 1745). For Macdonald, the opening bars 'surely probe further than "Dreams of love"'; they represent Berlioz's first objectified recollection of his own adolescent spleen.[4] In the *Symphonie fantastique* programme, 'a young musician, affected by that mental illness which a celebrated writer [Chateaubriand] calls the FLUX OF PASSIONS . . . reflects on his isolation; he hopes soon to be alone no longer'; this is a variation on the theme of *Waverley*, more deeply probed in 'Scène aux champs'. The overture can also be connected to the text notated in the score. The slow section is divided into (1) unfocused rêverie (bars 1–30) and (2) an ardent male gaze (cello melody; compare the cello music of *Roméo et Juliette*). The sonata-form Allegro may appear to banish programmatic literalism, but following the reprise of its second theme, brilliantly enhanced by imitation and counterpoints derived from the first theme, the passage from bar 336 suggests (3) a sudden access of mingled fear and exhilaration. The headlong approach to a cadence, by way of an enhanced supertonic and relative minor,

---

[3] Schacher, *Idee und Erscheinungsform des Dramatischen bei Hector Berlioz*, 13 ('keine "opéra en raccourci"'). Schacher associates the central lament with Amélie (pp. 10–11), and criticizes my comments on this section (*MLB* 132, 191) for ignoring the dramatic context ('Handlung'); but comments on the overture's proportions would hardly be affected even by confirmed dramatic intentions unless the overture was indeed an 'opéra en raccourci'.

[4] Macdonald, *Berlioz Orchestral Music*, 12.

swerves off course when the F sharp 7 chord is replaced by the diminished seventh on A♯ and oblique resolution to B flat minor (rather than B minor); this is decidedly uncanny. Ex. 9.1 shows the progression in reduced form, with one crotchet equivalent to a whole bar revealing an asymmetrical macrorhythm. Motivic activity derived from the first theme, represented by bass notes on the lower staff, accelerates until the massive cadence allows the recapitulation to proceed.[5] Admittedly this leaves much of the Allegro (a generalized view of a young officer?) and the cheerful coda unaccounted for, and there does not appear to be any battle music.

Ex. 9.1 *Waverley,* from bar 336 (one crotchet stands for one bar)

Formularistic openings

The *Waverley* verse motto could be the narrative outline for almost any introspective introduction and active allegro, but Berlioz preferred some interrelationship between slow and fast sections, as in *Le Roi Lear,* or he preceded the slow section with a burst of allegro. Every composer's first rhetorical task is to engage the attention of the audience. Whereas nearly everything Berlioz composed ends loudly (exceptions after the Prix de Rome cantatas are the *Requiem, Les Nuits d'été,* the *Hamlet* march, and *La Damnation*), his varied openings repay careful inspection. James Hepokoski has demonstrated how many early Debussy pieces begin with a melodic line unencumbered by harmonic definition, a gesture normally laid out in three parallel, developing phases.[6] Berlioz anticipates Debussy in using unaccompanied or lightly

---

[5] This is not yet the coda. The cadence at bar 364, in view of what precedes it (shown in Ex. 9.1), could never be the end of the piece, and the next passage is transposed from the exposition, and is thus still recapitulation. The faster tempo from bar 401 marks the structural coda.

[6] James Hepokoski, 'Debussy's Formulaic Openings', *19th-Century Music,* 8 (Summer 1984), 44–59.

accompanied lines, which are sometimes fugue subjects (including the two works—*Roméo* and *La Damnation*—which, long before Mahler's Tenth Symphony, begin with the unaccompanied viola section). His slow movement before the main Allegro normally includes a lyrical period, such as the *idée fixe* in *Harold* or the cello melody in *Waverley*. Berlioz is not usually considered a formularistic composer, at least in the sense of employing conventions with any regularity; but an effective compositional rhetoric cannot only be based on personal quirks. Katherine Reeve points out that the foundation of the Société des concerts du Conservatoire in 1828, a landmark in French musical life and critical attitudes, meant that it was no longer only opera that mattered: an aesthetics of instrumental music was developing.[7] Elizabeth Bernard adds that 'the concerts of the Société were not an everyday or social event, but a ritual event'; Habeneck compelled the auditorium to silence by a rap of his conducting bow.[8]

Criticism developed modes of discourse which Reeve calls 'first person' (the purely subjective account of an experience); 'second person' (the reader is addressed, often by 'écoutez . . .' or 'entendez . . .' and exhorted to listen in a particular way); and 'third person', the classical mode, an apparently objective account of the music. These critical categories are conveniently transposable into consideration of musical discourse. The first and third, calling attention respectively to 'beauty' and 'structure', cohere in their implicit submission to the sonorous allure of music: both, though from different directions, anticipate the contemplative, transcendent aesthetic position of Hanslick. But within the second category, instrumental music may embody a metaphorical narrative, with or without literary allusion, and openings are calls to attention. The second-person mode says: 'Listen to this story.'

Deeply affected by Beethoven's symphonies, Berlioz nevertheless rejected his type of introductory exordium, such as the majestic *all'ouvertura francese*, which Berlioz admired in the Second Symphony; the Allegro with athematic *coup d'archet*, descendant of the noise-killer which Mozart found the French required, in the 'Eroica'; or an immediate plunge into the main theme, in the Eighth. Nor did Berlioz try harmonic mysteries of the kind which begin Beethoven's Fourth; perhaps in symphonic music for a French public it was better to risk harmonic mysteries only later, as in *Waverley*. Nevertheless, in his three earliest symphonic works Berlioz tried to compel attention with a whisper. He must have intended his openings to catch the ear, and reach the mind of his audience; yet in early works the opening often risks sounding tentative.

[7] Katherine Kolb Reeve, 'Rhetoric in French Music Criticism', in Bloom (ed.), *Music in Paris in the Eighteen-Thirties*, 537–51.
[8] 'Non pas une cérémonie mondaine ou sociale, un concert à la Société est une cérémonie rituelle.' Elizabeth Bernard, 'Les abonnés à la Société des Concerts en 1837', in Bloom (ed.), *Music in Paris in the Eighteen-Thirties*, 41–53 (cited, 44). See also James H. Johnson, *Listening in Paris: A Cultural History* (Berkeley and Los Angeles: University of California Press, 1995).

Table 9.1 classifies the openings of several major works, in chronological order, as monodic, fugal, brilliant, or other. These patterns can be combined, as in the Requiem, where the first movement is fugal, but the opening monody is not the subject. Lightly accompanied monodies are usually lyrical in character. Later overtures, after the folksy opening of *Rob Roy*, all begin with an explosion of brilliance (*alla Rossini*) before the slow section. Similarity of process does not exclude variety of affect. Of the works composed before Berlioz went to Rome, *Les Francs-juges* and *Waverley* have much in common with *Symphonie fantastique*, but *La Tempête* begins atmospherically, conforming neither to the monodic nor to the fugal type. Table 9.1 suggests that monody prevails in early works (other than cantatas), while fugal openings are characteristic of the middle period, and brilliant openings of the later works. Table 9.2 further classifies the melody-dominated openings. Apart from the use of violas in two contrasted fugal pieces, there appears little that is formularistic, except a marked preference for exposing a line before showing the full power of the instrumental forces, and in many cases before introducing much in the way of harmonic context.

In contrast to contemporaries such as Chopin and Schumann, Berlioz's openings (even the modal fugue of *La Fuite en Egypte*) are not often tonally ambiguous. A qualified exception is *Lear*, where the monody at first sounds like A minor, but soon clarifies the tonic, C (the organ cantus firmus in the Te Deum makes the same move, but only after opening chords). Some of the early openings, simple as is their material, nevertheless have a narrative flavour: 'once upon a time'. *Lear* is again an exception; the opening topic is measured recitative which, by analogy with Beethoven's Ninth and retrospectively with *Roméo et Juliette*, we associate with authoritative speech rather than narrative. Since Berlioz presumably aimed at rhetorical efficiency, one might assume that his later preference for energetic openings resulted from experience with audiences. Beethoven and Rossini hardly ever begin quietly; even *Leonora No.3* begins forte before the tonally ambiguous resolution of the downward scale.[9] But Berlioz's early works were not failures, and he had a model for quiet beginnings in Weber. Both *Der Freischütz* and *Oberon* begin monodically; Berlioz inverts the *Oberon* horn call in *Waverley*. A touch of uncertainty at the opening clearly appealed to Berlioz; he says of the 'Eroica' that 'at the start, contrary to custom, the composer only allows us to see part of his melodic idea', a perception published in 1837 which may have come to him in 1828.[10] From that year on, at least until the mid-1830s, Berlioz surely aimed at being understood by the kind of people who

---

[9] Berlioz in *Le Corsaire* followed a C major opening with a swift modulation and a lyrical period in A flat. But rhetorically this could hardly be less like Beethoven's overture, and the opening material (which is fast) is used several more times to punctuate the overture.

[10] *A travers chants*, 41, originally *Revue et Gazette musicale*, 9 Apr. 1837. Oddly enough, Berlioz says nothing about calls to attention in the obvious place, *Le chef d'orchestre: théorie de son art* (published in the second edition of *Traité*).

TABLE 9.1 Chronological list of beginnings

Year	Monodic or single note	Monodic, fugal	Brilliant	Other type of openings
1826	*Les Francs-juges**			
1827(?)	*Waverley*			*Orphée*: textural (accompaniment preceding melody)
1828				*Herminie*: textural
1829				*Cléopàtre*: gestural
1830	*Symphonie fantastique* (song)*			*La Tempête*: textural
1831	*Le Roi Lear*(*?)		*Rob Roy*	
1834		*Harold en Italie**		
1836–8		*Benvenuto Cellini*, Act I	*Benvenuto Cellini*, overture	
1837	*Grande messe des morts* (Introit)*			
1839		*Roméo et Juliette**		
1840				*Symphonie funèbre**
1844			*Le Corsaire*, *Le Carnaval romain*	*Hamlet**
1846		*La Damnation de Faust* (Parts I and II)		
1849	Te Deum, preceded by grandiose chords	fugue follows		
1850		*La Fuite en Egypte**		
1854		*L'Enfance du Christ*, Part I* (after recitative), Part III*		
1857	*Les Troyens*, Act IV ('Chasse royale')	*Les Troyens*, Act I		*Les Troyens*, Acts II*, III
1862			*Béatrice et Bénédict*	

* In minor mode.

TABLE 9.2 Varieties of monodic opening

Waverley	Solo oboe: then violin melody
Les Francs-juges	Violin line, lightly accompanied
Symphonie fantastique	Wind chord; then violin line, lightly accompanied
Le Roi Lear	'Speaking basses'
Harold en Italie	Fugato: basses, adagio
Grande messe des morts	Solo violin line which is not the fugue subject
Roméo et Juliette	Fugato: violas, allegro
La Damnation de Faust, Part I	Fugato: violas, andante
Part II	fugato, cellos, andante
Te Deum	Organ theme which becomes the fugue subject
La Fuite en Egypte	Fugato: violins, andante
L'Enfance du Christ, Part I	Recit, then fugal march

frequented the Société des concerts, despite its scandalous neglect of his music; its concerts included instrumental pieces with programmatic associations, such as dramatic overtures by Beethoven, and although Berlioz developed rather than merely adding to this repertoire, his works should have fitted well with the Society's aesthetic.

Les Francs-juges, used as a concert overture from 1828, enhances its tragic power with a highly original disposition of plangent brass; the interventions of a trumpet in E during the 'Olmerick' theme in D flat are peculiarly gruesome (bars 37–41). But the opening is reticent, even tentative, although written with the utmost precision; the accompanimental details are themselves expressive (Ex. 9.2), as is the strong subdominant emphasis. The emergence towards the light in bars 15–17 brings a virtual quotation from *Oberon* (which Berlioz can hardly have known when he composed *Les Francs-juges*). One feature of the orchestral layout particularly invites alert listening. The melody and harmonic support are all in the strings; the other sound is a sustained horn. This use of notes detached from the main melodic and harmonic argument recurs in other early works, and clearly signifies something; here the communicative force of the gesture lies in tone-colour, which can be assimilated thanks to the pitch being sustained without rhythmic disturbance. When in *Les Troyens* (Act II, No. 12, bar 40) Ascanius pauses to listen ('il écoute'), the scurrying music gives way to an isolated horn note.

Although *Waverley* includes a slow song-period, it begins strangely, with a single note from the humble second oboe.[11] This is repeated by both oboes, and developed, punctuating the first thirty bars (Ex. 9.3). Until bar 30, it is virtually impossible to distinguish the main voice from subsidiary pitches; the oboe notes are F♯, E♭, and C♮, while the solemn lower strings develop towards

---

[11] Did Berlioz imagine that second oboes, like second horns, were specialists in lower notes?

243

Ex. 9.2 Overture, *Les Francs-juges,* opening

a short climax. This unpredictable series describes a wide-spaced diminished seventh; the highest pitch level (c♮‴) corresponds to a growing coherence in the texture, but still avoids the tonic, preparing instead for the pre-cadential supertonic (bar 25: the whole passage thus expands the simple progression I–IV–ii–V–I). In relation to the 'programme', the sighing responses of the lower strings speak for themselves; the very brevity of the violins' assertion of a higher register, left exposed in bars 21 and 26, is also eloquent; and in the last bars before the texture settles into a Romance-like accompaniment, a solo horn gives an intimation of heroism. When Berlioz repeats the cello melody (bar 55) the tattoo of the timpani, for all its soft drumsticks, is another intimation of battle, particularly as it frequently strikes a tonic D against dominant harmony—most remarkably in bar 74 where the bass is a dominant pedal. Can Berlioz really have conceived this before hearing Beethoven's Fifth?[12]

In *Symphonie fantastique* only two bars precede the song-period. This opening combines rhetoric from the two overtures: the song-period, in *Waverley* a full-throated romance, begins the movement, but it is presented with the tentativeness of *Les Francs-juges.* Berlioz gave no hint to his first audience that they were hearing a piece originally conceived with text (Ex. 7.1). What they heard, therefore, was a new form of the sustained-note idea: a softly pulsating dominant resolved into a melancholy minor chord, then a melody whispered by violins, but blocked by fermatas and with minimal harmonic support. Indeed, the voice-leading implies still more uncertainty than the implied sequence of chords by itself.

A striking feature of these early monodic openings is that they all descend from the dominant. The goal of descent is rhetorically crucial. In *Les Francs-*

---

[12] Berlioz analysed the drum solo before the finale (*A travers chants*, 53), and imitated it again in the *Benvenuto Cellini* overture, bars 312–23 (*MLB* 221).

Ex. 9.3 Overture, *Waverley*, opening

juges (Ex. 9.2) a downward skip to the mediant is followed by a scalar fall over the pathetic interval of the diminished fourth, A♭ to E♮. In *Waverley* (Ex. 9.3) the initial fall, reinforced an octave lower by violas, covers a solid perfect fifth, and subsequent chromaticism questions, but does not subvert, the tonality (this hero's meditations are hardly the stuff of tragedy). The *Symphonie fantastique* melody falls only a fourth from the dominant, but its span is a tritone; like *Les Francs-juges*, it emphasizes the semitones, but muted lyricism suggests melancholy rather than tragedy. In his attempt to capture something of the essence of Shakespeare's *King Lear*, Berlioz's next monodic opening (Ex.

245

9.4) inevitably uses different sorts of gesture; but if read in A minor, the opening falls diatonically from the fifth degree. Tonal ambiguity, quickly resolved, nevertheless contains seeds of destruction, and is intriguingly nested with a version of the held-note idea. The recitative melody is played on all the lower strings, but sinks below the range of the violas. Rather than dropping out, they hold on to d, blurring the recitative topic and halting the phrase on a bare tritone against the bass G♯. The second phrase, an unexpected example of isorhythm, denies the leading-note, rather than resolving it: G♯ moves to G♮. The violas stick on their low C, and this eventual tonic is confirmed by the perfect fourth, dominant-tonic; the horns' repetitions modify the atmosphere to one of courtly chivalry, akin to *Waverley*.

Ex. 9.4 Overture, *Le Roi Lear*, opening

Berlioz presumably relied on the first of the gestural phases identified in Debussy's openings by Hepokoski: audience silence before the first sound. None of these openings begins with a 'coup d'archet'. Instead they require us to listen attentively, even to expressive detail. Each presents generically similar material, adapted to the narrative in question. For musical listening it matters little, as Berlioz recognized, whether the human feelings are those of Waverley or some other young man: the title and motto provide a broad framework for understanding a piece which also falls within other expected formal patterns. *Mutatis mutandis*, the same is true of *Lear*, where, however, there is an added dimension when the 'recitative' is quoted within the Allegro, and repeated there only to disintegrate. But the destruction of the opening recitative within the Allegro relates *Le Roi Lear* to the pre-Italian Berlioz, making with *La Tempête* a pair of Shakespeare overtures broadly concerned with a narrative parallel to the play. In *Lear* the opening suggests the King's disposition of his kingdom, the listening courtiers (horns), and the unctuous responses of his elder daughters, represented by muted violins repeating what the basses say. But whereas in the play Cordelia, unable to speak hypocritically, says little and loses her inheritance, Berlioz, more concerned with her character than with programmatic literalness, composed an eloquent lyrical melody for oboe, his usual instrumental choice for sympathetic females. When this is resonantly repeated on brass, in the opposite tonal field to the opening (E flat against the implied A minor), we may be hearing a portrait of the King of France who takes Cordelia without a dowry, or perhaps the expression of her noble spirit; who can tell?

Harold en Italie also begins with a monody, and the slow section of the first movement exposes a lyrical melody. But this monody is a fugue subject; the texture conveys qualities such as thoughtfulness, learning, complexity, and yearning, suited to the symphonic persona. Much the same may be said of the opening of *La Damnation*, where the viola theme uses the pitches of *Waverley*, but, as in *Harold*, questions the tonic through chromaticism.[13] The progress of the fugue also suggests something less than certainty; the cello counterpoint enters before the 'answer', which is vocal, and in the mediant. Thus the lessons of early concert works are applied to dramatic and texted music. Although Berlioz had already changed his rhetorical approach with overtures, and the dynamic start of *Roméo*, in *La Damnation* he again tried aural seduction as an opening tactic; and despite the work's initial failure, he saw no need to revise this opening. Perhaps, however, the first bars induced the generic confusion which led several people to consider *La Damnation*, successor to *Roméo et Juliette*, as a kind of symphony.

Thematic rhetoric

The main purpose of rhetorical analysis of music is to try to understand the work as a discourse, in which we know, for example, when we are coming to a climax or an ending, or when something significant is being said. Thus we may be persuaded, not of the truth of an argument, but of its musical truthfulness. If the music is not rhetorically conceived, a programme will not rescue it. Berlioz's well-known practice of linking separate movements by transferring themes among them may be read in the light of such rhetorical necessities as coherence, supporting cross-reference, and peroration; and in this area, his practice clearly extends across from symphonic works into those which are explicitly dramatic.

Harold en Italie has many complex facets, but rhetorically it is unproblematic compared to the autobiographical symphony, or the one based on a play. The scenes it develops are Berlioz's, not Byron's, and are not necessarily his own experiences: he makes no mention of an orgy of brigands, and if he came across a procession of pilgrims, it was as a witness, not a participant. The persona of *Symphonie fantastique* is the centre of attention; the persona of *Harold*, as Berlioz was the first to say, is an observer, signified by the isolation of the solo viola from the orchestra. Berlioz himself pointed out, not quite accurately, that *idée fixe* in *Symphonie fantastique* is transformed in each

---

[13] The successive employment in this subject of the flat and natural sixth degrees (as in the *Symphonie fantastique idée fixe*) is identified as a Berlioz fingerprint by Cone, *Fantastic Symphony*, 276–7.

movement, whereas in *Harold* it remains unaffected by its surroundings. In fact, while the *Symphonie fantastique* melody is lightly adapted for the ball and severely caricatured in the finale, it is almost unchanged in the slow movement, the complicated notation being devised so that it preserves its original rhythmic proportions and duple metre, stretched over the notated 6/8; only gaps between the phrases are lengthened to accommodate the biting commentary of the bass instruments.[14] This method recurs in the middle movements of *Harold*. From bar 64, long bars of 3/2 metre are spread over the 2/4 of the pilgrims' march, whose phrases tend to fall into patterns of four bars (4/2 metre).[15] The resulting metric dissonance is curiously restful, and some conformity with the march is achieved by adding a 'beat' (one empty bar) after the first two phrases of the melody (bars 76 and 89). But in the third movement the viola makes a false start, accommodating to the serenade by playing the melody in duple metre (bar 65). Only after trying the first phrase this way, in the dominant (G, main key of the symphony) does it revert to its proper triple metre, and the local tonic, C. Here again an empty bar (an extra 'beat') separates the phrases.

The involvement of observer and observed varies between the movements. The pilgrims establish a change of texture (bar 56) before the viola begins its tentative counterpoint, which then blossoms into its theme; we, observing the observer and the observed, witness their resistance to any connection until, as the viola reaches a potential reprise (bar 102), the pilgrims return to their original melody with renewed strength. Thereafter the viola is mainly confined to an accompanying role, not so much dismissed from the scene as assimilated. In the serenade, when the melody is 'corrected' to triple metre from bar 72, the viola is supported by most of the strings, while the serenade (Ex. 9.5) continually develops in order to retain harmonic and rhythmic connection to the *idée fixe*. In bars 79–80, three echoes add a bar to the serenade's normal grouping of two. Another pair of bars, and then the *idée fixe* adds its own rest bar (84); the serenade, however, from bars 83–91, can be read in three-bar units. Thus the two melodies reach some accommodation, before 'Harold' gives way and resumes his accompanying role from bar 96. In the enchanting coda, 'Harold' tries to recall the serenade, but, uncertain of the metre, continually stretches it by added rests or lengthened notes; his own melody is appropriated by flute and harp, who play it without modification.

Thus Harold is drawn into the heart of one scene, making more definitive his exclusion (by death or evasion) from the orgy. His theme disappears before he does; the viola's last intervention (finale, from bar 483) is connected to the distant reprise of the pilgrims' march. Perhaps a falling arpeggio (b″ g″ e″) at the top of his little phrase, and the off-beat sighs, although only one in eight covers a third, refer to his melody, but such a tenuous thematic link is

---

[14] See Dömling, *Zeit*, 93–7; Bockholdt, 'Die *idée fixe* der Phantastischen Symphonie'.
[15] See Dömling, *Zeit*, 97–100; id., 'En songeant au temps . . . à l'espace', 250–4.

Ex. 9.5 *Harold en Italie*, III: counterpoint

all the more potent as a symbol of the theme's disappearance than no late viola entry at all. This kind of suggestive connection does little to enhance the coherence of the movement itself; instead, and more valuably, it adds an expressive dimension, querying the autonomy of the musical discourse.

In a clearer programmatic context, recurring themes have a more obvious function; where their meaning might be open to doubt, in *Symphonie funèbre et triomphale*, Berlioz does not use them. His nearest approach to the Wagnerian method lies in the original layer of *Benvenuto Cellini* (which NBE calls 'Paris 1'), which never reached performance. His elimination of several leitmotiv-like allusions indicates a relatively low evaluation of this rhetorical method, which was far from new in French opera, and which is arguably tautological when it accompanies a visible action (the incidence of recurring motives is further reduced in the final revision, ironically made for Weimar, the spiritual home of the New German School of Liszt and Wagner). In his later works, the meaning of transferred themes may not always be transparent, but they are mostly laid out as melodies rather than motivic fragments, making manifest the existence of some compositional intention. Where they appear just below the surface, casting doubt on intentionality, a network of allusions may result whose imprecision is not necessarily less suggestive within the dramatic context, notably of a long opera like *Les Troyens*.

Characteristic of operatic, rather than symphonic, thinking are the three statements of the Trojan March. In Act I the March suggests Trojan triumph, but mistakenly; in Act III it appears 'dans le mode triste', B flat minor. This use of parallel minor may seem naïve, but it requires careful manipulation of the material, particularly effective when the major-minor mixture of the March resolves into the minor. A second theme passes into the low strings, merging the March with the orchestral commentary. The March is not used when the Trojans join forces with Carthage against the Numidians; in Act V it comes to symbolize the new Troy in Italy. In Acts II and IV the March is not heard because the Trojan destiny is derailed: in Act II, the city is sacked, in Act IV Aeneas is lured away from his destiny by his love for Dido. The symbolism is much less clear when Part III of *L'Enfance* opens with a harsh fugato based on the same theme as the opening fugue of Part II. The harshness is understandable—the holy family is facing the rigours of crossing the desert—but why connect it to the shepherds gathering peacefully in Bethlehem? Although the technique recalls the marvellous variation interludes in Part II of *La Damnation*, this may be considered a false economy, as it arouses more questions than it offers answers.

The richly evocative use of thematic *anticipation* in *La Damnation* is exceptional. The peasants' dance, the Hungarian March, the chorus and ballet of sylphes, all appear as fully-fledged versions of material adumbrated in a previous section; the first two are heard as it were in the distance as the sun rises at the end of the first scene, and the sylphes are anticipated by 'Voici des roses' (Ex. 4.10). But these anticipations are immediately complemented by hearing the piece in full, whereas in Part III (scene 10) Marguerite's return home is announced by an instrumental fragment of 'Le Roi de Thulé', and something akin to a magic guitar introduces the melody of Mephistopheles' serenade even before he announces its forthcoming performance. Both passages represent a thought in the demon's mind, music preceding words.[16] The serenade

[16] See Lensky, 'Characterization in the Dramatic Works of Hector Berlioz', 153–75, and 'Berlioz's Symbolic Use of Anticipation Technique in *La Damnation de Faust*', in Jeff Bernard and Gloria Withalm (eds.), *Signs, Music, Society—Proceedings of a Transdisciplinary Colloquium, Vienna, March 1999* (forthcoming).

is again anticipated in the coda which Berlioz added to the 'Menuet des follets'. Semantically the richest example of anticipation is the preparation for Marguerite's downfall. Before singing 'Le Roi de Thulé', she remembers her dream, anticipating material from the Romance, which is not heard until Part IV. Then, since the scene is understood to take place after her desertion by Faust, anticipation is replaced by reminiscence; the Romance itself is the full statement of material already heard, and the songs of the soldiers and students, which Marguerite says she heard on the day Faust first came to her, recall material from Part II, when Faust sets off on his conquest of the girl seen in *his* dream (see also Chapter 10).

I have already discussed at length some cross-references of the compositionally subliminal kind, in both *La Damnation* and *Les Troyens*; no doubt they could be traced in other works.[17] This kind of thematic analysis resembles analyses of *Symphonie fantastique* which show that melodies known to have existed before its conception (the Florian romance; the *idée fixe*; 'Marche au supplice') nevertheless belong together. It is therefore time to consider other aspects of this perhaps over-analysed composition, which is sometimes held to bring operatic techniques into the concert-hall.

SYMPHONIE FANTASTIQUE

Programme and form

For conductors, audiences, and even, unfortunately, some musicologists, *Symphonie fantastique* epitomizes Berlioz to the extent that it seems hardly necessary to know anything else. Intensive commentaries on it include several articles and even a number of books.[18] The symphony can be used to prove that Berlioz's music is tightly constructed by theme and tonality and conforms to once-canonical principles of artistic autonomy, but also to prove that it makes no sense without a programme.[19] The programme is silent about musical form; nevertheless arguments about form are better for acknowledging its existence. For comprehension of the work as a whole, the programme is no less necessary than the sung prologue of *Roméo*, and the dramatic dialogue of *La Damnation*.[20] Weirdly imaginative as it is, the programme does explain the sequence of ideas, and certain kinds of musical continuity, including deformations of normative procedures, without recourse to *Formenlehre*, in a 'deliberately discontinuous structure, which clearly prefigures Berlioz's treatment of narrative in the dramatic works'.[21]

[17] See *MLB* 228–34, and 'Overture'.

[18] The most thorough motivic and tonal breakdown is Berger, *Phantastik als Konstruktion*. See also Cone, *Fantastic Symphony*; Dömling, *Hector Berlioz: Symphonie fantastique*.

[19] See Bockholdt, 'Die *idée fixe* der Phantastischen Symphonie'; Dömling, 'Die Symphonie fantastique und Berlioz' Auffassung von Programmusik'; Rudolf Reti, 'Bloom and Dissolution of the Thematic Principle', in *The Thematic Process in Music* (New York: Macmillan, 1951), 280–94; Temperley, 'The Symphonie fantastique and its Program'.

[20] For a contrary view see Barzun, *Berlioz and the Romantic Century*, i. 152–67.

[21] Banks, 'Coherence and Diversity', 40.

Berlioz's comparison of the programme to operatic dialogue (see Chapter 6) is echoed by Leonard B. Meyer, for whom the programme provides 'the causal connection between the successive moods or connotations'.[22] Reicha considered the order of keys to be of less importance in *opéra comique* precisely because the music is not continuous, but in a symphony this licence would not apply.[23] Berlioz's symphony may also be measured against models, generic and specific; the standing of its first movement in relation to sonata form has exercised criticism ever since Schumann's analysis.[24] A symphony with no Scherzo, but with Waltz and March in lieu, clearly involves a rhetoric of genre. The relationship of programme to music is inconsistent; its first twenty-four lines explain the *idée fixe* and the idealized beloved before reaching the actual music.[25] For the first movement, the heading 'Rêveries, passions' matches the Largo-Allegro design, like the *Waverley* motto (see above), and the programme fills in some details (see below). Then the programme runs the second and third movements together, although Berlioz explains the 'Ranz des vaches' and its treatment, ending 'distant thunder . . . solitude . . . silence'. The March is an operatic procession, involving no dramatic development until the end, often criticized as literal-minded. The *idée fixe*, which otherwise plays no part in the movement, is heard and truncated; the nightmare ferocity of the March blots out memories of the beloved until a moment before the guillotine descends. As Paul Banks observes, 'it is precisely the March's relative lack of relationship to the earlier movements . . . which the composer exploits in his overall design'; the pattern of the whole is partly articulated by the diminishing importance of the germinal *idée fixe*.[26]

In 1829 and 1830 Berlioz published his first writings on Beethoven, including the Ninth (an analysis based on reading the score: it had not yet been performed in Paris), and his manifesto about expressive instrumental music.[27] Where so awesome a predecessor is concerned, one might invoke Harold Bloom's 'Anxiety of Influence', as Mark Evan Bonds does in connection with *Harold en Italie*.[28] But Berlioz appears not so much anxious as optimistic, blazing his own trail from a point unreachable without Beethoven as precedent. His five-movement design is modelled on the *Pastoral*, with explicit homage to 'Szene am Bach'; 'Scène aux champs' includes a quail and other bird-like sounds (from bars 67 and 158), and delicately evokes a Beethoven cadence (from bar 113). But Berlioz also traced a sequence of ideas *against* this model. Table 9.3 places Berlioz's slow movement before the waltz, in

---

[22] Leonard B. Meyer, *Emotion and Meaning in Music* (Chicago: Chicago University Press, 1956), 272.

[23] Reicha, *L'Art du compositeur dramatique* (Paris, 1833), 77.

[24] The argument continues at least to Nicholas Cook, *A Guide to Musical Analysis* (London: Dent, 1987), 279–93.

[25] See NBE 16. 4, which prints the programme with numbered lines.

[26] Banks, 'Berlioz's "Marche au supplice" ', 19.　　　　　　[27] *Critique musicale*, 47–68.

[28] Bonds, 'Sinfonia anti-eroica', in *After Beethoven*, 28–72.

accordance with the plan outlined only a month before the first rehearsal.[29] Despite Beethoven's disclaimer (see Chapter 6) he supplied a programme which can be matched to Berlioz's, suggesting the latter's deliberate perversion of the model. Berlioz introduces sublime menace earlier, as a metaphor (unlike Beethoven's peasants, Berlioz's protagonist is not in physical danger from the storm), and ends with religious alienation rather than pious thanksgiving. He also had other Beethoven symphonies in view. His climactic combination of a noble melody—the 'Dies irae'—with a fugue may have been learned from the finale of the Ninth, explaining why comparable means are not used in *Harold* and *Roméo*, which otherwise refer more obviously to the Ninth.[30] Berlioz also perverts the design of the Fifth Symphony (Table 9.4), with its breakthrough into triumph, prototype of the *per ardua ad astra* narrative beloved of nineteenth-century symphonists; Berlioz's narrative disintegrates into nightmare.

TABLE 9.3 Form of *Symphonie fantastique*: the 'Pastoral' perverted

Beethoven, 'Pastoral'	Berlioz, *Symphonie fantastique*
I. 'Happy feelings' . . .	I. 'Reverie, passions'—optimism, also fear; religious consolation
II. 'By the brook'—tranquillity, bird-song.	III. 'Scene in the country'—tranquillity, bird-song; sublime menace (distant thunder)
III. 'Merry gathering' (Scherzo): collective, bucolic, welcoming	II. 'A ball' (Waltz): collective merrymaking, urban, protagonist excluded
IV. 'Storm': sublime menace	IV. 'Execution': grotesque: menace of the collective
V. 'Thanksgiving': sublime tranquillity: religious sincerity	V. 'Dream of witches' sabbath': grotesque: anti-religious parody

TABLE 9.4 The *ad astra* narrative perverted

Beethoven: Fifth Symphony	Berlioz: *Symphonie fantastique*
I. Struggle, but severe, unified mood	I. Struggle with manic mood-changes II. Dance
II. Slow movement: serenity hard won	III. Slow movement: serenity threatened to the end
III. Grotesque dance	IV. Grotesque march
IV. Finale: return and banishment of grotesque	V. Finale: victory of grotesque

[29] Letter to Ferrand, 16 Apr. 1830, *CG* i. 319; NBE 16. 169. Paul Banks discusses the implication of the changed movement-order ('Coherence and Diversity in the *Symphonie Fantastique*').

[30] I owe this suggestion to David Mateer.

'Ronde du sabbat'

If the finale owes anything to a pre-Romantic formal archetype, it is one which defines little: fantasia and fugue. Calling it a 'hybrid', and invoking rondo and variations (the latter as process rather than form), Wolfgang Dömling suggests that its unity 'clearly does not derive from standard categories of formal and thematic integration', and that one needs to invoke a 'semantic dimension'.[31] The segmentation in Table 9.5 is conventionally dictated by tonality, theme, and texture, and aims to clarify to what extent Berlioz attempts integration on a musical level. Space is devoted to exposition, development, and recapitulation, but this is no sonata; the first 'Exposition space', some 20 per cent of the movement, lacks structural modulations and thematic contrast, unless we consider the funeral bells a theme. This does not mean that arguments are worth pursuing over formal archetypes, or which of the 'Dies irae' or the fugue subject is 'the main theme', without reference to the programme. Nevertheless, the semantic dimension is not fully elucidated by the programme, whose content is rapidly exhausted. Barzun remarks of one salient point, the combination of 'Dies Irae' and 'Ronde du sabbat', that there is 'no hint of programmatic significance'.[32] But only the programme can account for the presence of the plainchant in the first place. Given such alien importation, why seek musical coherence at all, if it conflicts with other objectives?

Tracing the music against the programme reveals musical patterns resulting from twofold statements of ideas, which the programme certainly does not require. This is particularly evident at the start, when the programme sets the scene—'une troupe affreuse d'ombres, de sorciers, de monstres de toute espèce'—before listing sounds clearly reflected in the music: 'Bruits étranges, gémissements [bars 1, 12], éclats de rire [bars 6, 16], cris lointains [woodwind, bars 7, 17] auxquels d'autres cris semblent répondre [horns]'. The arrival of the beloved, with the *idée fixe* transformed into 'un air de danse ignoble, trivial et grotesque', is also in two stages: foreshadowed on the C clarinet (bar 29), greeted by 'rugissement de joie à son arrivée', then heard entire, in close-up, on the E flat clarinet. But the striking, angular unison (from bar 78) and the foreshadowing of the 'Ronde du sabbat' (bar 84) are unmarked by the programme; musically, we recognize signs of transition (tonal uncertainty, thematic fragmentation). 'Glas funèbre [102], parodie burlesque du *Dies irae* [127]', almost reaches the mid-point of the movement, and the programme's 'Ronde du sabbat' (from 241) suffices for 173 bars. No signifieds are offered for the fugue, the distortion of the subject, the deformed fanfares, or the whole-tone and diminished seventh concatenations, but the grotesque is a

---

[31] 'die Einheit des Satzes offensichtlich nicht aus den Kategorien formaler und thematischer Integrations ableitbar [ist] . . . Der Sinn dieses Satzes—dies gilt ebenso für den 1. Satz—greift über das technisch-analystich Feststellbare hinaus'. 'Die Symphonie fantastique und Berlioz' Auffassung von Programmusik', 263; see also Berger, *Phantastik als Konstruktion*, 126.

[32] Barzun, *Berlioz and the Romantic Century*, i. 155.

TABLE 9.5 *Symphonie fantastique*, 'Songe d'une Nuit du Sabbat'[a]

Bar		Phrase-lengths[b]	Criteria for segmentation
1	Introduction space: *Larghetto*	11, 9	4/4: bar 12: transposed reprise of bar 1
21	*Allegro*	8	6/8: *Idée fixe* in C
29	*Allegro assai*	11	4/4 uproar in E flat
40	Exposition space (1): *Allegro* [Hauptzeitmass]	25	6/8: *Idée fixe* in E flat
65		7, 6, 24	First transition: 'Ronde' fragments
102	[Parallel systems: bells binary; **'Dies irae'** (bar 127) ternary]	8, 11, 13, 12, 11: 8, 13, 16, 12, 10, 8[c] [25], 36, 24, 35	Bells (C and G) 'Dies irae' (E flat / C minor)
222		19	Second transition: 'Ronde' fragments (E flat, E minor, V of C)
241	Exposition space (2): **'Ronde du Sabbat'**	7, 7, 7, 7	Fugal exposition in C [G][d]
269		10, 10	Episode A
291		7, 7	Middle entries in G C to E flat[e]
305	Development space	5, 5, 5, 11 [8+3][f]	Episode B
331		17	Distorted subject
348		7, 3, 6	'Dies irae' and chromatic subject fragments
364		4, 5, 6, 7	Chromatic fugal exposition
386		9, 8, 4	Stretto, syncopation, preparatory upbeats to:
407	Recapitulation space	7	Subject in C
414	**'Dies irae'** and **'Ronde du Sabbat'** ensemble	21[g]	Answer in G, but 'Dies irae' in C/A minor
435	Secondary development	5, 4, 4[h]	A minor episode
448		12[i]	Subject augmented in A minor
460	Closing period	7, 13	Woodwind cadenza; tutti leading to fractured cadence
480		5, 11	Tutti (diminution), 'Dies irae' with diminution, full cadence
496	Coda	16, 8, 4 + fermata	Reminiscence of *idée fixe*: implosion of E flat: cadences

[a] Bold and italic: Berlioz's own headings.

[b] Note the predominance of irrational phrase-lengths, often two-bar units with expansion by an uneven number at the end.

[c] The last two bars overlap with the second transition; hence this totals 122 not 120.

[d] Tonal answer: S, A, S, A.

[e] False entry in bar 289, G minor; A, S.

[f] In bar 327, the last of the 8, the accented second beat means that the 11 could be 7.5 bars plus 3.5: or 327–8 are metrically displaced, forming a 3/8 plus a 9/8 bar.

[g] Ends first beat of bar 436.

[h] Final bar includes upbeat to augmented fugue subject.

[i] Subject not completed, hence 12 rather than 14.

255

broader signified to which all such elements readily relate. 'La ronde du sabbat et le Dies irae ensemble' (bar 414) gratuitously draws attention to the combination of themes, but the programme ignores subsequent developments including the last reprise of parts of the *idée fixe* (bar 496).

The organization of the finale is deliberately opposed to the preceding March, with its binding isorhythm—Christian Berger's 'Rhythmus als Thema'[33]—and even-numbered phrases; both its themes are in units of eight bars and are repeated with variations (the second is preceded by expanded units amounting to thirteen and eleven bars respectively; the development-cum-reprise includes four nine-bar units). The phrase-lengths of the finale fall predominantly into irrational units (see Table 9.5), and during the 'Glas funèbre' and 'Dies irae', parallel but disassociated systems obtain.[34] Each bell statement lasts eight bars, but intervening rests make the entries irregular, forming expanding and contracting units. After twenty-five bars of bells and foreshadowing of the fugue, the 'Dies irae' has three phrases, each followed by two diminutions; against this, the bells sometimes sound syncopated (e.g. bars 134, 194).

The tonality begins by mixing E flat with C minor. In the nineteen bars before the fugue proper, Berlioz puns E flat and E minor, before establishing their common third, G, as the dominant. The breakthrough into C major is signalled by a fugue whose regularity exposes Berlioz's anti-academic agenda.[35] If the seven-bar units are validated by repetition, the displaced accents, the coarse trill in the countersubject, and the seventh-bar brass punctuation sounds ruder on repetition (yet this idea, descended from the Kyrie of the Mass, is an ancestor of Verdi's 'Libera me'). This second 'exposition space' includes an episode and two middle entries. Berlioz adds further burlesque to the 'development space', which consists mainly of fragmented material from both exposition spaces; the phrase-lengths are at their most erratic, once past the consistent quintuple phrasing from bar 305, but phrase expansion (4, 5, 6, 7, bars 364–85) is used for a snarling chromatic version of the fugue subject.

Synthesis by closer association of ideas takes the place of recapitulation. Although there is an emphatic reprise of the fugue (bar 407), the answer collides with the 'Dies irae' and the resulting bitonal combination quickly self-destructs. The answer is in G, the chant begins on C and obstinately resolves to A minor, the opposite pole to the E flat prominent earlier on (Berlioz juxtaposes these pitches with some violence in the coda, bars 507–8). The third fugal entry is a cackling augmentation in A minor, anticipated at the moment (bar 435) where the 'Dies irae' has triumphantly overcome the 'Round Dance', prepared by eight bars of dominant (from 440), and spiced by strings

---

[33] Berger, *Phantastik als Konstruktion*, 111.

[34] See also Dömling, 'En songeant au temps . . . à l'espace', 248–50.

[35] That the harmony of the *idée fixe* is most orthodox in the parody may be another hit at routine: *MLB* 99–102.

col legno. The augmented subject is truncated by the woodwind cadenza (bar 460). The first decisive cadence is approached by a screaming tremolo onto a V7 which the wind greet with a shriek (bars 473–9).[36] The tutti refuses to close, leaping away on a spree based on the fugue subject before collapsing into a compressed reprise of the 'Dies irae' and its burlesque, piled up in stretto. Since the coda refers to the *idée fixe*, the passage around the cadence at bar 496 synthesizes two fine themes into the vulgar jig; appropriately for a dance, the music is finally formed into four-bar units. Thus despite the continued fantasy of the development, which extends to the final bars, elements of integration can readily be perceived which make the music 'ride' to its conclusion: although certain conductors will never cease to misrepresent this symphony, the finale usually suffers less than earlier movements from their efforts.

Fantasy: the first movement

An array of feelings—ending 'ses mouvements de fureur, de jalousie, ses retours de tendresse, ses larmes'—is the programmatic metaphor for the first movement's unprecedented flux. It is not easy, in music, to distinguish fury or jealousy from an 'accès de joie sans sujet'. From bar 451 the *idée fixe* 'returns to tenderness'; the following crescendo and vehement dominant prolongation (from bar 473), and the acerbic cadence (recalling the opening of the Allegro), leave room for interpretative manœuvre. The movement originally ended at bar 491. Deciding to end less brusquely, Berlioz could have programmed the music to end with renewed tenderness and tears, led by the athematic oboe semibreves (bars 491–500), which not only echo this instrument's earlier development of the *idée fixe* through a turn to the minor and the Neapolitan D♭ (bars 456–8), but also foreshadow the death of Juliet. Banks suggests that the coda prepares for the subdued opening of the second movement, and that its recollection of the A♭–A♮ motive from the *idée fixe* contributes to the symphony's coherence.[37] But this would not explain the choice of plagal cadences, signifying 'Amen'; Berlioz cannot have written the music from bar 511 before deciding to add 'religious consolations' to the programme. The revised coda introduces the first topically marked musical analogue in the symphony.

The argument about classifying its form tends to direct attention away from the distinctive feature of the first movement, which is fantasy. Schumann tried to define the Largo as two variations on a theme, contriving to hear, in the mysterious A♭ pedal-point, a reference to the Florian Romance.[38] He was right to read the Largo as theme (bars 3 and 28) and episode ('plus vite', bar 17), but the sections are blended through the retransition (from bar 24), while the thematic section overlaps with the A♭ pedal

---

[36] See *MLB* 29–30.   [37] Banks, 'Coherence and Diversity', 42–3.
[38] See Cone, *Fantastic Symphony*, 229 and 250.

(from bar 46), as the strings complete a previous thought. Thematic shapes re-emerge only in bar 49, but the first theme does not recur; we are leading towards the Allegro, yet a flat 6 pedal is no dominant preparation. However, since the pedal resolves as G♯ onto A minor, the passage changes the mode of C to major, and joins the Allegro by metric modulation, one bar of Allegro 'equivalent' to a Largo crotchet. With the Allegro ♩ = 132 and Largo ♩ = 56, the arithmetic is inexact, but a skilled conductor, aided by Berlioz's chordal ricochets between strings and wind (bars 63–7), can introduce the *idée fixe* seamlessly at the point when we might have expected a third statement of the Romance.

The topic of fantasy is not unusual in the introduction to a symphony, although the term 'introduction' is clearly inadequate to the sheer length of Berlioz's slow sections. It is the extension of the 'fantastique' throughout much of a five-movement symphony which is remarkable; Dömling concludes that Berlioz might have echoed Beethoven by calling it 'Sinfonia quasi una fantasia'.[39] And the *idée fixe*, a fully cadenced melody, is hardly what an audience accustomed to Beethoven would expect. As a musical unit and representative of an idea, however, its fluidity and originality are beyond argument, and it provides motives susceptible of separate development. The first was already developed in *Herminie*, where its text, a cry to the indifferent beloved, is as pertinent as Florian's Romance or the 'Gratias' (see below). As musical rhetoric, its two complete statements represent, within the movement as a whole, the stability which even a fantasia requires. If Berlioz's first movement, read as a sonata form, appears inadequate, it could be the result of wrong reading rather than any flaw in music which possesses conviction even in its composed hesitations. Nicholas Cook, asking 'if it has so little connection with the music's underlying structure, why did Berlioz give his movement the superficial resemblance to sonata form . . . ?' appears to blame the composer for the rigidity of analysts, and his response, that 'in 1830 sonata form was something a composer took for granted when planning a symphony', would hardly apply in France.[40] Berlioz's expected audience may not have listened that way, and would have had no encouragement to do so from Berlioz's essays on Beethoven. And the resemblance to sonata form is hardly even superficial. *Waverley* shows that Berlioz knew this model well enough to know when he was flouting it. Yet he tempts analysis on these lines by repeating the 'exposition'—a late and possibly bad idea.

In this movement all well-sculpted musical shapes are offshoots of the *idée fixe*. With minimal thematic contrast, the Allegro is best understood as the alternation of stability and flux, the latter comprising both athematic and thematic, and tonally identifiable and unpredictable, passages. The almost exclusive adherence to tonic and dominant in stable areas, which Schumann noted

---

[39] Dömling, *Zeit*, 66; his discussion on fantasia as a topic, 56–66.

[40] Nicholas Cook, *A Guide to Musical Analysis* (London: Dent, 1987), 292–3.

without rebuke, is a necessary counterweight to this fantasia-like design.[41] About half the 549 bars of Allegro (including the repeat) are in flux, but of these 100-odd may be considered locally stable. Such proportions are antithetical to sonata norms, as is the complete restatement of the *idée fixe* in the dominant (bars 232–78) within what 'ought' to be development space. But this stable passage is welcome amid the brilliantly original musical images, and the passage remains fantastical in other ways—the melody floats perilously over a pulsating accompaniment, creating an erotic tension that finds no release in the frantic scrambling passage that follows.

The periods of maximum flux differ sharply from fugal episodes or sonata bridge-passages in which developing material directs a modulation. The passage which separates tonic and dominant in the first movement emerges classically on the dominant of G thanks to the unclassical process Chailley terms 'accrochement'.[42] Ex. 9.6 simplifies this passage of maximum instability, flooded with quaver figuration, to show the underlying progression.[43] Relatively solid ground before this leap into the dark is offered by bars 125–32, which repeat bars 111–18. Bar 128 treats the dominant seventh in C as a neighbour to a diminished seventh—rather than, conventionally, the other way about; there follows a torrent of descending thirds against rising bass fourths (bars 129–30), promptly reversed. Berlioz's goal is the dominant, but he begins with two steps in the opposite direction. Instead of F major (bar 119), bar 133 hits the dominant of F minor, resolved (bar 134), and repeated (bar 135), with its resolution evaded (bar 136). The progression disintegrates back to the original diminished seventh; bars 113–38 might be construed as prolongation of this dissonance, the bass shifting from G to E. But surface energy militates against hearing it that way; and the sequel does everything possible to render tonal connections imperceptible. Foreshadowing the collapse in 'Judex crederis' (see Chapter 8), the final circle of fifths (bars 142–6) extends beyond the reach of the diatonic scale. The music is equally manic in other parameters; dynamics range between *ff* and *pp*, the scoring between full ensemble and a single line, and the rate of harmonic change is equally inconsistent. When the dominant of G is resolved, the new key lacks space to establish itself; it is continually challenged by its relative minor, and the only connection between dominant and tonic is the perfunctory first-time bar.

Thanksgiving before the storm

Why did Berlioz base his slow movement on a song of thanksgiving—'Gratias agimus tibi, propter magnam gloriam tuam'? Why, indeed, does this—the only 6/8 movement in the three liturgical works—have the air of a pastoral Romance? In the 'Gratias', the pastoral topic is not comprehensively defined,

---

[41] Cone, *Fantastic Symphony*, 231 and 252.

[42] Jacques Chailley, 'Berlioz harmoniste', *La Revue musicale*, 233 (1956), 23–4.

[43] For Berger, the passage is 'ohne dem Bezug auf ein zweites Thema nicht zu beschreiben'; *Phantastik als Konstruktion*, 163.

Ex. 9.6 *Symphonie fantastique*, first movement, transition (simplified)

but the tempo, 6/8 metre, and stepwise, folklorie melody, clearly suggest the pastoral, and are features derived from Lesueur. All other borrowings from the Mass are retexted, even when the later work is secular; here the text sinks beneath the new 'language' of expressive instrumental music. Berlioz may have hoped that memories of the Mass would not intrude, any more than of the unperformed *Herminie* which supplied the *idée fixe*; yet this intertextual knowledge brings us nearer the heart of Berlioz's *mal d'isolement*, a condition subtly analysed in his writings and music by Susan Ironside: its 'most characteristic aspect . . . is the alternation of exaltation and dejection, felt as dissolution of the self in space, and congelation, or spleen'.[44]

The 'Gratias' has a long text; Berlioz's repetitions are in brackets: 'Gratias agimus tibi, propter magnam gloriam tuam. Domine Deus, Rex coelestis, Deus Pater omnipotens. [Gratias, etc.] Domine Fili unigenite Jesu Christe [Gratias, Deus Pater, Domine Fili]. Qui tollis peccata mundi, Miserere nobis.' The more declamatory 'Qui tollis' (from bar 73) leads from subdominant harmony to a dramatic pause; but the original mood is restored by an instrumental coda closely corresponding to its opening. This parabola, from serenity through slight disturbance to serenity restored, anticipates the arch-shape of 'Scène aux champs' at a lower emotional charge. Other topical signs point beyond the temporal aspect of pastoral, to the numinous. The 'Gratias' follows the sudden withdrawal of dynamic energy from the Gloria into slow plagal cadences ('adoramus te', Ex. 9.7). Berlioz marked 'De suite' (*segue*), but the tonalities, G and E, do not form an exhilarating juxtaposition, as they might at a higher dynamic level or with fuller harmony; the E major triad unfolds only gradually, within the unaccompanied melody. There is a large hiatus in the liturgical text, thanks to the long introduction. Remoteness and silence are gradually occupied by an unaccompanied line (first violins and clarinet), itself incorporating silences; and rather than the developmental energy of a fugal answer, bar 14 brings repetition, in the same instrumental grouping, with no counterpoint, but only doubling in thirds. After a more static section in C sharp minor, serenity is restored when the basses take the tune in the dominant (Ex. 4.5). After the brief 'Qui tollis', the coda restores the silences of the opening ritornello.

'Scène aux champs', one of Berlioz's finest symphonic movements, can accommodate a surprising range of tempos, but it is clearly meant to be slower than the Mass, Adagio rather than Andante, a significant difference.[45] In the symphony, the melody is separated from the brilliant conclusion to the waltz by the 'Ranz des vaches', a duet for cor anglais and oboe *lontano*. This has eleven quavers of silence and four fermatas within ten bars, but eventually the silence is plugged by tremolo violas, an ominous sound anticipating the distant thunder of the end of the movement. In this context, the 'Gratias' melody comes to mean something different, or at least, to mean differently. When it arrives, the pitch, higher by a semitone, is a lesser affective difference than the tempo and instrumentation; flutes replace clarinets, doubling violins and referring to the original scoring of the *idée fixe*. As with the latter, the

---

[44] Susan Ironside, 'Creative Developments in the "Mal d'Isolement" in Berlioz', *Music and Letters*, 59 (1978), 33–48 (cited 33).

[45] The Mass has no metronome markings; a later pastoral Andante in 6/8 is 'Chant d'Iopas', at ♪ = 132; the symphony Adagio is ♪ = 84. See Macdonald, 'Berlioz and the metronome', in Bloom, *Studies*, 17–36. Recorded performances of 'Scène aux champs' range from twelve to eighteen minutes; the metronome suggests just over fourteen, but with fermatas and tempo fluctuations about fifteen minutes is probably 'right'.

Ex. 9.7 *Messe solennelle*, transition from No. 2 Gloria (bar 184) into No. 3 ('Gratias')

No. 3. 'Gratias agimus'

accompaniment is fragmentary; whereas the 'Gratias' has ten quavers of silence in fourteen bars, the symphony has only four, the tune being gently grounded by soft pizzicato chords. Since 'Scène aux champs' has already opened with an unaccompanied melody, a second harmonically and metrically unsupported idea might have been hard for contemporary—or modern—ears to take. The spare textures of the Mass are undeniably effective in performance and arguably less conventional, whether through radicalism or inexperience, than the reworking of the same material in 'Scène aux champs', where punctuation defines both tonality and metre.[46]

---

[46] This point bears on a critical appreciation of the Mass itself, as it points to the fine line dividing radicalism and incompetence.

The repeat, doubled in thirds as before, is further filled by burgeoning clarinet and horn counterpoint, referring to the flat and sharp sixth degrees prominent in the *idée fixe*. Pizzicato cello semiquavers impart a new, purely instrumental, animation. Otherwise the borrowing is literal for twenty-six bars, and while the movements diverge markedly in their development, both are shaped by returns to this theme. The bass entry in the 'Gratias' establishes the dominant key relatively late in a movement of 101 bars. In 'Scène aux champs' the dominant entry comes relatively early (bar 69 out of 199), but functionally resembles the dominant re-exposition of the *idée fixe* in the first movement; it too highlights a violent mood-swing which then brings the *idée fixe* in the subdominant, cool amid the jealous turbulence of the basses. The resistance of the *idée fixe* to its metric surroundings is anticipated by many passages implying duple grouping of quavers, notably in the episode before the dominant-key statement of the theme, from bar 60. Despite its relative tonal security, however, this section is the most disruptive in texture (the orchestra from bar 87 splits into two hostile groups); tensions explode when the *idée fixe* fails to continue beyond the flat seventh to the tonic (a♭″ in bar 100 corresponding to b♭″ in the first movement). The rest of the orchestra, representing the artist, reacts with hostility; through D flat it drives to F minor, then to a passage of tonal indeterminacy, rising diminished sevenths implying frustrated eroticism. Calm is restored but without resolution, the cello D♭ in bar 112 nagging against the restoration of the home dominant. After the decorated reprise with woodwind counterpoint, the duple-metre motive becomes emotional from bar 164 (modulating to D minor); from bar 173 the motive finally agrees with the 6/8 metre, affecting a synthesis. But the thunder returns more vividly, on timpani. Macdonald hears this as an orchestration problem: the timpani play F, C, A♭, and B♭, but in performance even the F minor chord (bars 183, 192–4) is indistinct, its Mahlerian conflict with the melody's F major easier to read than to hear. The implied inversions of seventh chords involving B♭ (bars 178–83 and 188–9, where all four instruments play together) are indistinguishable by ear and lack harmonic meaning. Macdonald praises the general effect, the exact imitation, and the formal significance of a passage which is 'extraordinarily poetic, because it perfectly matches the design of the movement, and suggestively replaces the offstage oboe heard at the beginning'—enough, one may feel, to justify the orchestration.[47] Liszt conscientiously transcribed these chords for piano, but placed them an octave lower, similarly obscuring the pitch. No doubt he too understood that non-functional harmonies, if perceptible, would lose colouristic impact; Berlioz should perhaps have written more timpani 'dissonances' than he did.

---

[47] Macdonald, 'Berlioz's Orchestration: Human or Divine?', 255–6.

Song and dance: an interpretation

The revelation of earlier music in *Symphonie fantastique* poses no problems for its integrity. If integrity depended upon the associations of ideas when first conceived, we would have to question the integrity of *Messiah*, the Mass in B minor, the late operas of Gluck, operas of Rossini, Bellini, and Verdi; even *Fidelio*. With these, as with Berlioz, there remains room for speculation about the hermeneutic value of knowing the topic with which certain ideas were originally associated. Earlier ideas contained in *Symphonie fantastique*, known and hypothetical, are listed in Table 9.6. The only instrumental source, and the largest, 'Marche au supplice', is unchanged until the end; the other known sources were all vocal. No sources have been found for the principal material of the second and final movements, other than the 'Dies irae'. Berlioz might have conceived the fifth movement for one of his *Faust* projects of 1828–9 (see Chapter 2), and the waltz, conceivably, for *Romeo and Juliet*.[48] The absence in *La Damnation* of the musically tempting Cathedral scene, in which 'Dies irae' is sung, or of a Walpurgisnacht, is suggestive; he had written these into the symphony's finale. The ball theme and the main theme of the finale may well have been invented to fit the programme of the symphony; equally, their previous existence might have played a part in dictating the eventual programme. David Cairns challenged British critics who blamed Berlioz for patching up his symphony out of old material: 'in today's more enlightened climate that is no longer a fatal admission'.[49] There is of course no evidence that any Faust or Romeo projects, other than *Huit scènes*, reached the point at which musical ideas were associated with them, but the lack of evidence need not silence speculation. Where the ground is firmer, with *Herminie* and the 'Gratias', intertextual poietic information may feed aesthetic appreciation. So, of course, may analysis; but the most ingenious seekers after unity would have to agree that the *conception* of the symphony is hardly conducive to organicist interpretation, while evidence of pre-existing music might tip interpretation in other directions.

Table 9.6 offers a pattern which takes into account known and possible sources of the symphony. At the point of interpretation, the origin of the dance sections matters less than recognition that they *are* dance sections, and intertextual evidence is chiefly valuable for confirming the vocal origin of parts of the first, third, and fifth movements. The pattern shows an increasing incidence of dance; it becomes intricately bound with parody, whose incidence also increases. The waltz replaces a scherzo, but as a genre piece it is anti-symphonic (the minuet had long lost its dancing quality in symphonies). A genre piece is not a parody, but its inclusion is indicative of generic stretching, in this case towards opera. The March was written for an opera; in a symphony marching

---

[48] The latter suggestion I owe to Hugh Macdonald (personal communication).

[49] 'Reflections on the *Symphonie Fantastique* of 1830', in Bloom, *Music in Paris in the Eighteen-Thirties*, 81–96 (cited from 83).

TABLE 9.6 Sources of *Symphonie fantastique*

Movement/section	Known sources	Hypothetical sources	Notes	Genre
I. *Rêveries, passions:* Largo (bars 2, 28). C minor	Romance (Florian: 'Je vais donc quitter pour jamais')		Berlioz, *Memoirs*, ch. 4 Original key unknown	SONG
I. Allegro: *Idée fixe* (main theme), C major, G major	*Herminie* (Prix de Rome, 1828); No. 1, G major, No. 2, F major, recit. D major		No. 1 (Orchestral introduction), No. 2 (Aria, recitative)	SONG (Aria)
II. *Un bal:* Valse: main theme, A major	None	*Faust* or *Roméo et Juliette*	*CG* i. (12 Nov. 1828, 2 Feb. 1829)	DANCE
II. *Idée fixe*, F major	None			SONG
III. 'Scène aux champs' Adagio (Ranz des vaches)				Pastorale
III. Adagio: main theme, F major	*Messe solennelle* Gloria: 'Gratias agimus tibi', E major			SONG (sacred, thanksgiving)
III. *Idée fixe*, Bb major				SONG (with storm)
IV. 'Marche au supplice', G minor	*Les Francs-juges*, 'Marche des gardes', G minor		MS (*Symphonie fantastique*)	DANCE (March)
IV. *Idée fixe*, G major		*Faust*	Introduction	SONG
V. 'Songe d'une nuit de Sabbat'	None			
V. *Idée fixe*, C then Eb major				SONG used as DANCE— 'ignoble, trivial et grotesque'
V. 'Dies irae'	Gregorian		bar 123	SONG (parody)
V. 'Ronde du Sabbat' (Fugue, bar 241)	None	*Faust*	'Ronde du Sabbat'	DANCE
V. 'Réunion des thèmes', bar 414			'Dies irae' and 'Ronde du Sabbat'	SONG and DANCE combined

is more usually a topic within a complex movement, such as the finale of Beethoven's Fifth. But the first and third movements thrive on song rather than motivic and harmonic development (although these are present, particularly in the first). In the third movement, there is presumably a vocal origin for cattle-calls, but the piping of oboe and cor anglais is too chromatic for functional use, an escape from realism which keeps at bay the parody which might be suspected if Berlioz had composed something more like the 'Ranz des vaches' in *Guillaume Tell*. These instruments dialogue like operatic voices; in the framing coda, the absence of the oboe completes a little drama of desertion which parallels the plight of the programme's protagonist. The thanksgiving cantabile from the 'Gratias' signifies serenity, even confidence, particularly when exposed in the dominant; once back in the tonic (bar 117), it is ingeniously figured by pizzicato violins, serving to accompany another song on the clarinet, an instrument which reappears at the end of the March to play the *idée fixe* (this highlighting of the clarinet may have led to the decision to open with flutes rather than the clarinets of the 'Gratias').

I read in this pattern that song signifies grace, associated through the *idée fixe* with the ideal beloved. Dance represents a threat: the beloved is glimpsed at the waltz, presumably with another partner; the march leads to execution. The 6/8 metre of the round dance is introduced by a gross parody of a previously pure song, the *idée fixe*. Parody stands for debasement; the genre pieces, waltz and march, begin a process which the round dance confirms. Moreover the round dance is preceded by the blasphemous parody of the purest form of song, liturgical chant. Where all this stands in relation to Berlioz's programme should be obvious: it suggests a psychological, as much as a literal, narrative interpretation of the symphony. That, of course, is not a new observation, but it is one which new information gleaned from the *Messe solennelle* allows us to develop with more confidence than before.

BRIGANDS IN THE MOUNTAINS: *HAROLD EN ITALIE*

Mark Evan Bonds unlocks part of the significance of *Harold* as one of a series of symphonic works responding creatively (through 'anxiety of influence') to Beethoven's Ninth. For the title 'sinfonia anti-eroica' he suggests other sources: no more than with *Symphonie fantastique* can we confine the debt to a single model. The strongest Berliozian anticipation in Beethoven may be the slow movement of the 'Eroica'; from bar 168 the fluttering flute and violin and the heaving bass surely affected him strongly, as did the recitative-like fragmentation of the final bars, a death-topic present in *Cléopâtre* and the *Hamlet* march. But the first movement Allegro of *Harold* evokes the Seventh by its 6/8 impetus, mingling dotted with straight quaver patterns. Berlioz's version adds a dash of local colour, and a tendency to deformation and fragmentation: the second theme is not only 'Scottish' piping, but is peculiarly elusive in shape and tonal implication. Other strategies may be related to Beethoven's overtures, where the opening slow section is connected to the

Allegro; Berlioz had already worked this way in *La Tempête* and *Le Roi Lear*. Within the Allegro, 'Harold' is almost entirely uninterested in his own *idée fixe*; the solo viola dallies with the second theme, and responds to the orchestra with concerto-like flourishes, but is mainly devoted to the first Allegro theme. In the long accelerating peroration, the fugal treatment of the *idée fixe* (bar 323) is carried on without the viola until bar 352, when it modestly merges with the woodwind. Its last solo concerns the second theme, which it finally supplies with a proper melodic consequent (from bar 442).[50]

The fact that the woodwind are the first to play the 'thème de l'Adagio' or *idée fixe* is often overlooked; their lamenting exposition in G minor (from bar 14) is no mere foreshadowing, but a full, sixteen-bar period, superimposed on growling semiquaver figuration derived from the opening fugue. This sets up the first solo entry, playing the same tune in G major. The revised mode is obtained by the simple and thoroughly inorganic expedient of juxtaposition; Harold and the woodwind become light and dark sides of the same image. This instrumental connection is pursued throughout the movement, especially with the second theme, but also the first when it is recapitulated by a unison of viola and four bassoons. Also often overlooked is that these 'scenes of melancholy and joy' take place in the mountains, no doubt the Abruzzi, scene of recent Berliozian spleen and glee. For much of the movement Harold and his theme are lost in the caverns, torrents, dark clouds, and sudden brightness: transient images both natural and metaphorical. From such memories come the strange turns of the second theme, setting out in F major and never really making it to the 'proper' goal, the dominant (D); the startling harmonic change when the forte dominant of G of the first-time bar is replaced by triple-piano in the second-time bar (bar 192), and with so little pitch change (B♭, 191, slips to A) that the listener experiences something like a rash descent of a hillside, loose beneath one's feet;[51] subsequently, the threats directed at the soloist in the form of harsh modulations and brief stabbing motives, culminating in a fierce minor ninth (from bar 256); the sudden discoveries and further losses of safe paths through the main themes, constituting a thoroughly refreshed recapitulation.

On a poetic level this markedly eccentric first movement owes little to Beethoven, unless to the 'Pastoral'. The second movement is one of a series of nineteenth-century compositions related to the slow movement of the Seventh, including the slow movement of Mendelssohn's 'Italian' symphony (did the two composers discuss pilgrims' processions in Rome?).[52] This influence may be found in metre, tempo (Allegretto), a $\frac{6}{4}$ chord near the beginning (bar 7, the first triad), and a tendency in the main material to periodicity.[53]

---

[50] See *MLB* 198–9.

[51] Unlike that of *Symphonie fantastique*, this repeat seems absolutely obligatory.

[52] Another example is Schubert's 'Great' C major, unknown in 1830, which Mendelssohn later promoted and Berlioz came to admire (Cairns, *Servitude*, 453).

[53] Berlioz commented on Beethoven's minor $\frac{6}{4}$ chord beginning and ending of this movement with particular approval. *A travers chants*, 65.

But there is no question of consistent modelling; and if there is influence, it is without anxiety. It is in the central movements that Harold, the observer, is represented by the viola's concentration on his theme (see above). In the finale, the problems of balance presented by using a solo viola with a large orchestra no longer apply, because the performer stands in silence most of the time; but this, of course, creates a visible problem in live performance. The question of *why* Berlioz chose to begin this movement, otherwise so unlike Beethoven's Ninth, with reminiscences of earlier movements, may be unanswerable; what in Beethoven had some philosophical purpose, here appears a mere *jeu d'esprit*, although in detail it is brilliantly executed. Nevertheless, it is essential to an interpretation of the symphony as a deformation, or (as Thomas Mann's Adrian Leverkühn put it, a 'taking back') of the Ninth.[54] This finale, too easily performed with brash superficiality, has many passages of haunting beauty, and its built-in critique of orgies shows a sense of irony worthy of Shostakovich. The orgy proper, from bar 118, begins by stabilizing the rhythm that punctuated the five references back to previous movements. The crotchet octave-drop had been used to imply metric units of three crotchets instead of four. In the theme itself this figure still implies a unit of six; rhythmic adventurousness, through the expansion and contraction of implied bars, is part of the special character or 'tinta' of *Harold*, the outer movements especially.[55] The playful arpeggio figure (from bar 140) assimilates Mozart (the G minor symphony, K.550), and at bar 163 comes a wistful transformation of the principal motive, in B flat. This key is confirmed by the march theme (bar 177), derived from a sketch for *Le Retour de l'armée d'Italie*. The brigands show a military countenance; it is hard to see what difference in orchestration Berlioz might have intended, had the idea retained its original connotation. In this exposition, before the written-out repeat (from bar 280), there is a flood of textural and motivic ideas, oscillating between B flat major and G minor: athematic syncopation (bar 200); the harmonic trick of the D/E♭ pedal (bar 211) with the drunken trombone theme marked 'con gravità', and music of heartache, where energy is exhausted in pianissimo sighing (bar 231) and suppressed lyricism (bar 248).

Lyricism doubles as a retransition to the repeat, and at the corresponding point (bar 411) it is replaced by a dispute between the sighing theme and a crisp development of the march, notably its scuttering triplets; the march wins (fugato, bar 428), merges with the syncopation (bar 441), and brings the reprise (bar 450) in G major, its key in the sketchbook. But these brigands find it hard to keep their minds on their orgy, unless the music is intended to evoke their unhappy victims. The nearest we have to a programme is Lélio's evocation of the life of brigands: 'rich spoils piled up in the caves, women with dishevelled hair, quivering with terror, a concert of screams of horror backed

---

[54] See Bonds, 'Sinfonia anti-eroica', in *After Beethoven*, esp. 34–45.
[55] On 'tinta', see Ch. 10 below.

by an orchestra of rifles, swords and daggers . . .'.[56] But the brigands' song in *Lélio* is fantasy, in the wishful mode of 'Let's do this', ending 'Allons!' The finale of *Harold* is the real thing, but like the later 'Pandemonium', it represents a hollow existence, revealed for a moment when the veil is torn aside. In contrast to the immense solidity of the exposition-space repeat, and the clear and full, albeit reversed, recapitulations in the first movements of both symphonies, this recapitulation simply collapses after the second theme (the first theme is not recapitulated). At bar 464 the orgy is frozen into immobility, like Gounod's Mephistopheles at the sight of the Cross; the Pilgrims' song is heard, from a distance, on solo instruments, as chamber music (the solo viola makes it a full quartet). What happens next, on the dramatic plane, is not explicit. One interpretation is that Harold is dead; another, that he runs away. A more Byronic possibility is that Harold participates in the orgy, but his voice is too weak to be heard on its own; the viola's silence represents the loss of his individuality and his objective stance as an observer as he sinks into the collective. His nostalgic response to the distant pilgrims is a last hankering after something better, but the returning triplet figures (from bar 499) buoy him up to a cadential trill; the viola closes fortissimo and the orchestra emits a 'rugissement de joie', as for the arriving *idée fixe* in 'Songe d'une nuit de Sabbat'. There is no reason to suppose that the remaining uproar represents anything more than additional orgy, but the inability of the music to settle down, its continual harping on a chord rooted in the leading-note F♯, and the snarling plagal cadences with minor supertonic from bar 571, resume—with no little musical originality—the coarse brutality which is the real topic of the movement.[57]

ITALIAN LIEBESTOD: 'ROMÉO AU TOMBEAU'

Having recently published a book about *Roméo et Juliette*, I shall risk the disappointment, or the relief, of the reader by confining myself to a more developed account of its most controversial movement (on the finale, see Chapter 10). In No. VI, 'Roméo au tombeau' Berlioz's thoroughgoing programmatic approach lost him the sympathy of his original audience, despite the general acclaim for the 'dramatic symphony' in 1839.[58] The published programme takes the form of a long title:

Roméo au tombeau des Capulets. Invocation: Réveil de Juliette. Joie délirante, désespoir; dernières angoisses et mort des deux amants.[59]

---

[56] NBE 7. 23.

[57] The chord on the leading-note is often exploited in *Harold* and is another aspect of its peculiar 'tinta'; seven bars from the end of the first movement (F sharp minor): the first cadence of the Allegretto, bar 23 (D sharp minor), and finale bars 29–44, including the citation of the Allegretto, within the main theme (bars 128, 291), the build-up to the repeat (bars 270–7), and bars 564–7.

[58] See *Roméo*, 66, 77–8.

[59] In the 1839 libretto this appears as 'Roméo au tombeau des Capulets.|Invocation.—Réveil de Juliette. Elan de joie délirante, brisé par les premières atteintes du poison.—Dernières angoisses et mort des deux amants.' The variant does not represent any musical revision.

Romeo at the Capulets' tomb. Invocation: Juliet's awakening. Delirious joy, despair; last agony and death of the two lovers.

There are three sections, in a fast-slow-fast pattern (A B A'). In practice, however, one experiences six subsections, whose programmatic content is not much open to doubt.

(A1) Romeo breaks the tomb open; *Allegro agitato e disperato*.

(A2) Awed, Romeo enters the tomb; nominally the same tempo, this section is a timeless series of fermatas, on or around the dominant of C sharp minor.

(B3) An instrumental aria headed 'Invocation' ('O my love, my wife, Death, that hath sucked the honey of thy breath, Hath had no power yet upon thy beauty'); *Largo*, in C sharp minor (12/8). Romeo takes poison.

(B4) Juliet's awakening; fragments separated by fermatas which are gradually reduced, allowing a 6/8 metre to emerge, of uncertain tonal polarity but working towards A major, and quoting her material from the love scene.

(A'5) Delirious joy; *Allegro vivace ed appassionato assai* (tempo of A1 but mixing simple and compound metres), using Romeo's material from the love scene.

(A'6) Last agony and death; dislocated by silences, orchestral recitative; from bar 148, Romeo overcome by the poison and dying; violin recitative (from bar 191), stabbing chords (211) and decay into silence, Juliet's determination to die, her suicide, her death (solo oboe).

This is a lot of action for a few minutes' music, unfolding at something like the pace of a cut version of the scene.[60] The closest analogy is mime or ballet-pantomime, and Berlioz surely associated it with Harriet Smithson's acting in 1827 and later. In a review published in Paris and in Schumann's *Neue Zeitschrift* in 1839, Stephen Heller was reminded of the orchestral rehearsal of an opera, without the voices.[61] Berlioz soon came to question his own musical coherence, and inserted a peevish note in the printed score:

The public has no imagination; pieces which address themselves only to the imagination have no public. The instrumental scene which follows is such a piece, and I consider that it should be omitted on every occasion, except those on which this symphony is performed before an elect audience extremely familiar with the fifth act of Shakespeare's tragedy with Garrick's ending, and whose poetic feelings are of the highest: that is to say, it should be cut ninety-nine times out of a hundred.[62]

Despite the living example of Richard Strauss, early twentieth-century critics also found this programmatic explicitness hard to swallow. Elliot dismissed Berlioz's 'insolent manifesto' and this 'broken, disjointed number . . . there is

---

[60] Ian Kemp elaborates this programme, to my mind with excess detail: '*Romeo and Juliet* and *Roméo et Juliette*', in Bloom, *Studies*, 75–6; see also *Roméo*, 52–6.

[61] See *Roméo*, 66.   [62] NBE 18. 253.

an invocation with a rather artificial melody. I for one can make nothing of all the rest, apart from the vaguely hysterical references to previous material.'[63] More recent critics have at least tried to assimilate the programme: Cone commented that 'the obvious programmatic intention helps explain the formal peculiarities'.[64] But Barzun evades the issue: 'The music consists simply [*sic*] of four very brief contrasting sections . . . These twenty or thirty pages . . . are extraordinarily vivid and may induce visions in some listeners, but one can safely defy anyone to say what they imitate.'[65]

None of these views seems adequate to music which defies even the sorts of consistency found in the 'Songe d'une nuit du sabbat'. The problem relates to the genre of the whole work, in which Ernest Newman hazarded the view that Berlioz had 'on the whole failed to accommodate his symphonic intentions to his dramatic, or vice versa'.[66] Berlioz was firm that *Roméo* was a choral *symphony*, but his comment on the tomb scene makes clear that this piece is meant to be representational. In treating it for orchestra only, however, he was being consistent; so far he had used voices for explanation, from a standpoint outside the drama (Prologue), and operatically, within the drama (chorus of Capulets after the ball; Juliet's funeral procession). Action, including the fight and prince's intervention, Romeo's invasion of Capulet's ballroom, and the love scene, had all been instrumental. Berlioz suppressed programmatic details in the ball scene as well as the tomb scene when he compressed his two prologues into one.[67] The problem faced by criticism has been that the earlier instrumental movements are straightforwardly enjoyable without detailed programmatic exegesis. There seems no reason why the tomb scene should not be consistent with the rhetorical patterns of the work so far, and thus as open to musical enquiry, including enquiry into issues of coherence, as any other section.

Describing the music is not difficult. The principal tonalities are E minor, C sharp minor, and A major, whose triadic relationship offers a central role to the common pitch E, certainly a fundamental element—indeed, in Schenkerian terms, the initiating point of a fundamental line (in which octave is not so easily settled). In subsection A1 the first phrase, despite its wild harmony and rhythm, is a closed period in E minor; the second dives through d' to c♯', harmonized as the mediant of A major, then suggests C sharp minor as a tonal goal, with the violin pushing through c♯' to b♯' in an inner part, while the upper line falls to d♯'. Subsection A2 prolongs this G sharp major chord; and the local harmonic action is resolved by the 'Invocation' (B3), which despite its chromaticism never quite loses touch with its tonic. It peaks with a

---

[63] J. H. Elliot, *Berlioz*, The Master Musicians (London: Dent, 1938), 172.

[64] Edward T. Cone, record review in *Musical Quarterly*, 39 (1953), 477.

[65] Barzun, *Berlioz and the Romantic Century*, i. 334.

[66] Ernest Newman, *Berlioz Romantic and Classic* (London: Gollancz, 1972), 183.

[67] The second prologue is in NBE 18. 414–19. Both 1839 prologues, the second orchestrated by Oliver Knussen, are recorded by John Eliot Gardiner (Philips 454 454–2).

bold expansion of the Neapolitan region (compare Faust's Invocation, and 'Judex crederis'), and approaches a clear cadence. There is, however, an abortion of the cadence in the harmonic domain: the melody itself describes a potentially cadential bass, g♯–c♯, but the cello grinds down to G♮, touching but not establishing the upper neighbour A♭/G♯.

The next subsection (B4) gropes towards A major, although for a moment C major is a possible outcome. The bass ascent from G♮ through G♯ to A is a remote reminiscence of 'Scène d'amour' (bars 107–16), which is also the source of the 'pun' between C and c♯ (Romeo's theme, bars 146 and 172). The clarinet enters an octave above the initiating tone of subsection A1 and the Invocation, and falls through d♮″ to c♯″. The attenuated bass supports a cadence in A, but is overtaken by the emphatic entrance of the full orchestra for subsection A′5, where the treble emphatically restores e‴. In this passage a second upper-register fall through d♮″ to c♯″ is disputed by the higher octave. If my reduction at this stage seems sketchy, it is because the effect, 'hysterical reminiscence', is created by textural incompleteness. The return to earlier themes provides a form of coherence for the symphony as a whole, but does nothing to define a thematic and rhythmic profile for the Tomb Scene itself; indeed, it may add a further element of disruption, as in bars 108–12 where the heard metre of Romeo's theme is now 9/8. Certainly this section fails to blossom into exaltation, and the music misses a potential breakthrough, instead collapsing into foreground incoherence. Yet there is no serious challenge to the key of A major. The foreground shows a striking failure of the cadential bass-line to support the fall of the upper line. At bars 185–6, an upper-register descent from e‴ through d‴ to c♯‴ is completed, and the melody is transferred back to the second octave, but the expected b–a″ is delayed: this final step in the fundamental line instead takes place unharmonized, in the original register below middle C, completing a recitative-like passage for violins. The rest is coda.

Ex. 9.8 tries to fit the tomb scene into a theoretical framework widely accepted for nineteenth-century music. Beginning and ending in different keys is matched, for instance, by Chopin (Second Ballade, F to A minor, reversing Berlioz's C♯ minor to A). But the wild transformation of material from the love scene compels us to consider the movement in relation to another; it must be considered a dramatic rather than a tonal gesture (it surely inspired Wagner, in Act III of *Tristan*, to the delirious reprise of one of the loveliest themes of Act II, now fast and in 5/4). The main contribution to the perceived incoherence of the scene is its extreme rhythmic dislocation; this resides less in the occasional change or combination of metres than in the rejection of periodicity. There is, moreover, perceptible co-ordination between rhythm and pitch: in the fast sections, rhythmic impetus is interrupted at points where the principal pitch configurations are especially prominent—at the opening, and bars 74–90, 150, 185, and 204–10. The empty texture is reflected in a lack of directed middle-ground progressions, and still more by the absence for considerable stretches of any clearly directed bass-line; sometimes the bass virtually doubles the treble (a not untypical feature).[68]

Reduction of this movement to a graph is not difficult, but frankly invites suspension of disbelief. This music is not governed by the polyphonic considerations best demonstrated by Schenkerian analysis; it emerges as music of gesture rather than of consistent goal-orientation. Where rhythmic impetus is maintained, it tends to coincide with disruption of the polyphonic dimension. The music asserts, rather than organically develops, its final tonic; the bass arpeggiation covers only the closing stages. My use of a Schenkerian paradigm in this context is partly intended to reveal precisely those qualities in the music which cannot be circumscribed by it. But confinement to one paradigm produces an inadequate analysis of any composition. The music deserves the theoretical risk of involving ourselves in a combination of approaches to music that may do justice to its actual complexity—or its messiness. It is possible to approach the scene as part of a virtual, or covert, opera. Juliet's death-speech is a recitative; one might ask, therefore, why Romeo sings an aria, but Juliet does not. Better not ask why their brief reunion is so inarticulate in its ecstasy; probably Berlioz did not realize, when he saw the play, how dreadfully articulate are Garrick's feeble verses. Juliet may be heard dying in the last six notes of the oboe, which are of disputed origin: they may be related to a configuration with the Neapolitan sixth at the end of the Invocation, but also to the oboe melody before the ball scene, which when it reappears during the festivity marks the moment when the lovers first speak.

Still thinking operatically, we might complain that we receive little insight into the characters at the moment of death. Comparing the endings of Bellini's *Norma* and Verdi's *Il trovatore*, Joseph Kerman points out that we have just heard an aria from Norma, and we know how she feels, whereas at the end of *Il trovatore*, 'the music is adequate to the physical action; it is not adequate . . . for the leftover psychological action'.[69] An instrumental aria for Juliet corresponding to Romeo's invocation, on the other hand, would not be true to the play, and might fatally endanger musical coherence.

For there *is* musical coherence. Quite apart from motivic cross-references, Ex. 9.8 suggests that there may be a shade too much, at the close, to suit the programme. For representational music may be meant to sound incoherent, while appealing directly to the imagination, which in turn is governed by the visual, dramatic, and emotional aspects of the scene. This music addresses us in a puzzling but exhilarating way; but there is no musical substitute for knowing what Berlioz asked us to know, the tragedy of Shakespeare with the dénouement by Garrick; the scene is already over-determined by its programme. Hence Berlioz risks the musical incoherence detected by a large

---

[68] See *MLB* 92–107, and *Roméo*, 54.

[69] Joseph Kerman, *Opera as Drama* (new and rev. edn., London: Faber & Faber, 1989), 222–3.

number of listeners; but where the programme would justify a complete breakdown of musical syntax, and achieves it in some parameters, notably thematic and rhythmic, the parameter of pitch connection remains in force as a source of a musical coherence. Arguably this contradicts the programme and imperils the experience as a dramatic revelation. If there were singing characters, it is doubtful whether any of the critics would have objected to the way the musical notes progress. Whether Berlioz, in different circumstances, would really have preferred to write an opera on the play, he makes a good fist of justifying his symphonic procedure in the foreword to the published score.[70] Nevertheless, in the tomb scene he goes to the brink of dealing with his characters operatically, and in that respect at least, the transition from symphony to opera in the finale is something of a relief.

Ex. 9.8 *Roméo et Juliette,* Tomb scene (reduction)

[70] 'Avant-propos de l'auteur', NBE 18. 2; *Roméo,* 87.

GENRE: THE LAST SYMPHONIC WORKS

What is it that made people—even Berlioz—refer to works as 'symphonies' which are plainly nothing of the kind? One reason must be *Roméo et Juliette*, which is a symphony, and yet is not. It has the teleological thrust one attributes to Beethoven, being directed towards a weighty finale which in symphonic terms may seem simple, even banal, in content, but which climaxes the work with tremendous grandeur: one could say the same of Beethoven's Fifth and, especially, the Ninth. Yet *Roméo* is never understood that way, and discussions of it usually concentrate on the second to fourth movements,

275

excerpts which have dominated its performing history. The right comparison is perhaps not a symphony at all, but Beethoven's C sharp minor quartet, which also has seven movements (Table 9.7); there are grounds for comparison if we divide the first movement of *Roméo*, but fuse the 'Tombeau' and choral finale.

TABLE 9.7 Comparison of *Roméo* with Beethoven, Op. 131

Op. 131	Fugue	Dance	Recit.	Slow (variations)	Scherzo	Lament	Finale
Roméo	Fugue (combats)	Recit. (prologue)	Dance (ball scene)	Slow (love scene)	Scherzo	Convoi funèbre	Tombeau/ Finale

Although he listed *Lélio* among his symphonic works, Berlioz objected to references to *La Damnation* as if it were a symphony.[71] Berlioz's lack of interest in generic purity may have led people to assume that anything he wrote for the concert-hall must be some kind of symphony. Although the symphony concept was well established in Parisian culture thanks to the Société des concerts, it did not appear indigenous, for the swarm of eighteenth-century French symphonies catalogued by Barry S. Brook was by now forgotten.[72] With Félicien David's 'Symphonic odes', the different level of musical invention is less likely to have struck a contemporary audience than the aesthetic parallels: *Le Désert* (1844) and *Christophe Colombe* (1847) appealed to the imagination in much the same way as *Lélio* and *La Damnation*, although the former includes spoken text and the latter imitates an action like a drama, with characters; both are filled with imitation and possess a rich orchestral palette.

Nowadays we are more likely to question the standing of *Roméo et Juliette* as a symphony than to think of including *Lélio* in that category. But there is enough internal evidence to justify the generic confusion. In *Lélio*, only its finale, the potentially independent *La Tempête*, has any symphonic qualities, and Berlioz's informal list ('Symphonies: Fantastique|Mélologue|Harold| Funèbre|Roméo et Juliette') arose from his connecting it to *Symphonie fantastique* (in more formal lists, *Lélio* always comes immediately after the symphony); Berlioz noted that *Lélio* includes—among other things—'morceaux symphoniques' (1842) or 'symphonies' (1851). The plurals suggest a use of the word 'symphony' traditional in the theatre: a piece without voices, included

---

[71] The error made by unsympathetic commentators like Scudo, Wagner, and others has its origin in favourable criticism (see NBE 8b. 458), and is repeated in contrasting the Gounod and Boito *Faust* operas with 'Liszt's and Berlioz's symphonic versions' by Gary Tomlinson in *Metaphysical Song* (Princeton: Princeton University Press, 1999), 105, although Berlioz's version is closer to Gounod and Boito than to its dedicatee, Liszt.

[72] Barry S. Brook, *La Symphonie française dans la second moitié du XVIIIème siècle* (Paris: Université de Paris, Institut de Musicologie, 1962).

within a dramatic work. *Lélio* contains only one, the 'La Harpe éolienne', but *La Tempête*, which includes voices, is among his longest symphonic movements.

La Damnation is another matter. In eventually terming it 'Légende', Berlioz suppressed his original and generically straightforward subtitle, 'Opéra de concert'. Moreover, while nothing can justify calling it 'a symphony', it begins with a symphonic tapestry, the introduction in which orchestral 'tone-painting' is the principal genre: the solo voice is but one strand in the texture, and the fugato but one of its musical techniques. This is, surely, a 'pastoral symphony' in the theatrical or oratorio sense (but without allusions to Christmas). The symphonic anticipation of the next two numbers, and the march which is no mere orchestral transcription but a symphonic 'setting' of the Hungarian material, complete a Part I which is more than half instrumental, and Part II opens with more orchestrally dominated expression. The recitatives and choruses are insufficient to overcome critical prejudice that Berlioz was a composer of symphonies, for they are no less compatible with a symphonic concept than parts of the recently performed *Le Désert* and, indeed, *Roméo et Juliette*, where the 'Convoi funèbre' and finale are purely operatic. As *La Damnation* develops, the picture changes: the scene in Auerbach's cellar is stageable, as is all of Part III, particularly if a split stage— something Berlioz had come across—or some other device makes possible instant changes of scene (see Chapter 10). The instrumental dances in Parts II and III are genre pieces, not essentially symphonic. Part IV again changes generic perspective, sharply reducing the consequentiality one expects in opera. Much the same could be said of *L'Enfance du Christ*, where Parts I and III, aside from the narrative and closing chorus, contain straightforwardly theatrical scenes; and the two fugal overtures ('Marche nocturne' and overture to *La Fuite en Egypte*) can be as easily related to theatrical as to symphonic traditions. I am not aware that anybody ever alluded to *L'Enfance* as a symphony, perhaps because its sacred subject pointed to another genre cultivated by David (*Moïse, Eden*). *La Damnation* might nowadays be perceived as an oratorio, but not in the mid-nineteenth century when the secular oratorios of Handel (*Hercules, Semele*) were forgotten.

Since Berlioz's output involves voices, we might better perceive the symphonic elements in his dramatic works as an invasion of the fantasia—natural, perhaps, to the composer of *Symphonie fantastique*—and a threat to generic stability and, very likely, to one or more of the characters. Scenic and characterization elements are never dissolved into the symphonic, however; for Berlioz, composing dramatically, symphonic fantasia was one of several different means to an end. Berlioz's willingness to allow an overlap between the theatre and the concert-hall reflects part of the spirit of his age. Such divisions were tighter in the eighteenth century where, nevertheless, many topics and even forms appear both in theatre and concert music. In transcriptions, by Liszt and others, operatic music was heard in the salon and recital hall;

overtures migrated to the symphony concert along with operatic excerpts; when he could not hire a concert-hall, Berlioz gave unstaged performances in a theatre (including the première of *La Damnation*). Normally an apostle of authenticity through the letter of the score, Berlioz presented extracts from Gluck and Spontini, the former with chorus singing the solo parts, in large-scale concerts in Paris. With the exception of *Symphonie funèbre et triomphale*, he used theatrical means to realize his symphonic visions: in *Symphonie fantastique* and *Harold*, off-stage players; in the former, bells, and in both, harps; in *Roméo*, solo and choral voices, on and off stage, even before operatic forms become involved. Consequently there is generic overlap between these works and *La Damnation* and *L'Enfance*: which in turn overlap with the operas.

But when it comes to writing for the theatre, there is not much influence from the concert-hall. In *Benvenuto Cellini*, overture and pantomime are conventional in operatic terms, although the overture is an unusually well-developed piece of symphonic writing for its time. The symphonic casting of Perseus, in its original form, is not unprecedented—Rossini's crossing of the Red Sea in *Moïse et Pharaon* (1827) also uses symphonic music to make a magnificent climax—although it is an outstanding example of a dramatic action in which words have only a minimum place. In *Les Troyens*, the 'Chasse royale' which opens Act IV is a magnificent piece of orchestral music, and among Berlioz's richest orchestral fantasias, but depictions of serene countryside, hunting, and storms, while rarely combined in a single movement, are undoubtedly part of French operatic tradition, and if Berlioz knew little of Rameau, and inherited such things from Gluck (Act II of *Orphée*; *Armide*), he was also aware of the continuation of the tradition in Méhul and Lesueur.

Berlioz took no conscious decision to abandon the symphony after 1840, but in the early 1850s, when a symphonic idea occurred to him, he felt obliged on economic grounds to suppress it.[73] He retained his interest in the most important aspect of symphonic music, as he saw it: not musical architecture, but instrumental *expression*. He composed only three more overtures, all of them masterly, but only one, *Le Corsaire*, is not directly related to an opera. *Le Carnaval romain* is an 'ouverture caractéristique', a generic pointer to something more entertaining than symphonic, but unlike many of its contemporaries, which fling operatic themes into an amiable pot-pourri, it is sharply etched in form. The opening gesture is imitative, a promise of contrapuntal development fulfilled only near the end (from bar 356), and the sharp break in continuity which precedes the love-duet theme (cor anglais) in C major (flat III) poses a formal question answered when this is treated in fugato (from bar 304). The melody is given three times with increasingly carnivalesque accompaniments, the third time in close canon; magically, the

---

[73] *Memoirs*, ch. 59.

carnival is shut out (bar 61) for the yearning cadences, only to burst in irresistibly. Nearly 200 bars of the Allegro are transcribed from the opera and form in effect a repeated exposition (written out with variations). This provides a solid basis for quicksilver developments including changes of metre, a harmonic mystery when the music settles onto B flat (bar 298), and two fugatos, in between which the second theme is recapitulated; otherwise development continues until it merges into cadential peroration: 'there is no more exhilarating ending in the repertoire'.[74]

A similar freedom of overall design prevails in *Le Corsaire*, written only a few months later, although it required radical revision before reaching its final form. Berlioz's confidence in his own powers of orchestral training is reflected in what must be one of the most unnerving openings in the repertoire, for the strings' 'tirade of running quavers' and the syncopated woodwind 'patter'.[75] The slow section, also in a flat key (here flat VI), is more fully integrated with the Allegro, in which it functions as a contrasting theme and a topic of development, and the form almost defies analysis.[76] Equally, given its mixed literary associations, it must defy programmatic interpretation, and this time Tovey, calling it 'as salt a sea-piece as has ever been written', is on the mark, despite the absence of the usual signifiers for waves, storms, and for that matter, and to make an obvious comparison, calm seas, prosperous voyages, seagulls, and counterpoint.[77] Finally, the overture *Béatrice et Bénédict* is a masterpiece of thematic blending, providing developments of material understated in the opera, in a rich pattern of sound which in its entirely orthodox form harks back less to Weber (whose *Oberon* is the masterly precedent for such blending) than to Rossini, a last, and at last affectionate, tribute to *opera buffa*.

Berlioz's last symphonic masterpiece, however, is neither an overture nor a symphony, but the funeral march for *Hamlet*. It brings together many Berliozian preoccupations: marching, a marked national character (see Chapter 6), dramatic interpretation, and a sense of tragic inevitability otherwise only achieved in *Les Troyens*. Despite its theatrical origin, this is a concert piece, and one which makes its effect from the deformation of a traditional formal design, a compact sonata form built with strophic units of eleven, then ten bars.[78] Its impact results from the stability evoked by a ritual of mourning. The tread of the basses, made more vigorous but no less grim at the recapitulation, the elegiac melody, and the keening of the wordless chorus are all ritual elements, while agonizing dissonances and unpredictable modulations, mainly within the second theme, engage with the sublime. Where the

---

[74] Del Mar, *Conducting Berlioz*, 134.   [75] Ibid., 135–6.   [76] See *MLB* 192–3

[77] D. F. Tovey, *Essays in Musical Analysis*, vi: *Miscellaneous Notes* (London: Oxford University Press, 1939), 51; on Mendelssohn's sea-pieces see R. Larry Todd, *Mendelssohn: The Hebrides and other Overtures* (Cambridge: Cambridge University Press, 1993); id., 'Of Sea-Gulls and Counterpoint', *19th-Century Music*, 2 (1979), 197–213.

[78] A complete breakdown of its form is given in *MLB* 187.

eschatological masterpieces, 'Lacrimosa' and 'Judex crederis', broke through into the major mode, the *Hamlet* march builds to a mighty climax (bar 85), at which point 'a peal of ordinance is shot off'. The opportunity is there for a grand conclusion, but Berlioz goes beyond the ritual to compose its negation, one of the greatest tragic endings in nineteenth-century symphonic music. The guns shatter the musical discourse; after a silence, the music drags itself back into sound and struggles to reintegrate, but fails: it succeeds only in setting up a potentially endless ostinato (from bar 106), on material derived from the main theme, but in reality little more than a groan. There is no judgement here, and no triumph. Despite the revision of *Le Corsaire*, *Béatrice*, and the Royal Hunt, Berlioz's symphonic life really ends here, with that of his favourite Shakespeare hero.

10 Berlioz Dramatist

INTRODUCTION

'Expression is not the only objective of dramatic music. It would be as crude as it is pedantic to despise the purely sensual pleasure we find in particular aspects of melody, harmony, rhythm, and orchestration, independently of all connection to depiction of the feelings and passions of the drama.'[1] Berlioz's comment, made in the context of a discussion of Gluck's *Alceste*, should encourage us to seek for musical enjoyment in his dramatic works, as well as truthfulness of dramatic expression. But there is no useful truth without quality of invention, and the quality of being enjoyable may enhance the dramatic function of music. Admittedly some of the most beguiling music, like the ballets in *Les Troyens*, might be considered, as Gluck once said, to be *hors d'œuvre*, in that the drama can get along very well without them. But Berlioz is most dramatic when his musical invention is at its highest intensity. Among late eighteenth-century composers, Mozart rather than Gluck might come to mind to demonstrate this point; but one could also use Verdi or Wagner.

Musical enjoyment may be derived from the perception of qualities which run throughout a dramatic work, providing a unique coloration, or 'tinta'. This concept is most developed in Verdi studies, where it counters—relative to Wagner—a perceived lack of musical unity.[2] Stylistic coherence is a reasonable requirement in any kind of drama; 'unity' in only one of its parameters is less obviously essential. 'Tinta' may be connected with Hugo's view of 'local colour' which 'ought not to be on the surface of the drama, but deep down, in the very heart of the work, from where it spreads outwards'.[3] For Gilles de Van, '*tinta* is based on the use of melodic, rhythmic, harmonic, and orchestral analogies specific to an opera and occurring frequently enough to be significant; these kinships are sufficiently clear to be discernible through

---

[1] *A travers chants*, 175–6.

[2] The notion of 'tinta' derives from Verdi himself and was discussed by Abramo Basevi in 1859; see Bent, *Music Analysis in the Nineteenth Century*, ii. 196.

[3] Preface to *Cromwell*, cited from Roger Parker, *The Oxford Illustrated History of Opera* (Oxford: Oxford University Press, 1994), 146.

analysis but not so close as to constitute recurring themes'.[4] Harold S. Powers refers to 'the agglomeration of diverse techniques, conventions, and novelties in several domains'.[5] I have already mentioned contributions to this kind of underlying connection, in the form of certain sprung rhythms and chords on the sharp seventh degree in *Harold en Italie*, and the various exploitations of space in the Requiem. If perceptions of 'tinta' are a musical pleasure, the main reason for seeking it out is its contribution to dramatic expression; and a similar method, of accumulation of particularities, informs the musical characterization of individuals.

In the 1820s Berlioz haunted the musical theatres of Paris, and also the spoken theatre (Comédie-Française). Recent research suggests that popular theatre formed one of the elements of grand opera which coalesced in *Robert le Diable*.[6] Berlioz regarded such entertainment with a disdain earned by his work as a chorister at the Nouveautés; but like Meyerbeer, he remained open to influence from the popular theatre.[7] The *haute vulgarisation* of the Opéra, which killed the repertoire that Berlioz loved the most (Gluck and Spontini), was achieved partly by stealing the musical clothes of *opéra comique*, and developing spectacular effects from popular theatre, in which the experiments of Daguerre also played a part. Thus grand opera in the period of Scribe, Auber, Halévy, and above all Meyerbeer was an eclectic co-ordination of the arts, a collectively authored *Gesamtkunstwerk*, making an impact on the audience by visual as much as musical and poetic means. Berlioz did not necessarily despise these tendencies, nor did he articulate priorities, like Gluck, Wagner, or Lesueur, in theoretical and cod-historical tracts, but his priorities are clear—like Mozart, he privileged music over the other elements—and are not those of the Opéra.

His opera reviews, aimed at a general readership, are not a reliable guide to this aesthetic, since he was compelled to devote more space to plot summary than to the music. Contrary to legend, he generally admired Meyerbeer (Halévy rather less). If, as Katharine Ellis notes, he damned Act II of *Les Huguenots* with faint praise, it was because its interest was largely visual; musical inventiveness would be out of place.[8] Despite widespread mutual back-scratching in the press, and the need to temper opinions for diplomatic reasons, we should not assume that praise of Meyerbeer was drawn from

[4] Gilles de Van (trans. Gilda Roberts), *Verdi's Theater* (Chicago: University of Chicago Press, 1998), 33.

[5] Harold S. Powers, '"La solita forma" and "The Uses of Convention"', *Acta musicologica*, 59 (1987), 67.

[6] Sarah Hibberd, 'Magnetism, Muteness, Magic: *Spectacle* and the Parisian Stage c.1830', Ph.D. thesis (Southampton University, 1999).

[7] An 'unworthy melodrama' at the Porte St Martin may have influenced *La Damnation*: *CG* i. 213; NBE 8b. 455.

[8] Katharine Ellis, *Music Criticism in Nineteenth-Century France: Le Revue et Gazette musical de Paris, 1834–1880* (Cambridge: Cambridge University Press, 1995), 29, 185. Berlioz's reviews of *Les Huguenots* are in *Critique musicale*, ii. 431–8, 587–93, 607–12.

Berlioz reluctantly.[9] There was surely a measure of mutual influence; two years before the production of *Robert*, Meyerbeer admired *Huit scènes de Faust*, and while finishing the posthumously produced *L'Africaine*, he allegedly attended performances of *Les Troyens à Carthage,* 'for my pleasure and my instruction'.[10] Berlioz used examples by Meyerbeer in his *Traité*, and the composers might be seen as vying with each other in the use of the latest developments in instrumental technology, with Meyerbeer, thanks to the resources of the Opéra, usually in the lead, for example in using the bass clarinet and saxhorns. Meyerbeer had a better sense of what the contemporary stage required than Berlioz, who was caviar to the general. But the received idea that Meyerbeer was commercial and Berlioz artistically advanced is too simple. Meyerbeer was highly adventurous, and probably more influential, not least in his concern with the totality of the operatic experience. Berlioz may have puzzled the same audiences precisely because his music demanded too much of their powers of concentrated attention.

Spectacle

Of the main elements of opera, the *mise-en-scène* occupies the most uncertain rhetorical position. It is seldom the work of those whom we regard as an opera's authors (librettist, composer); it is usually lost, beyond some descriptions or, if we are lucky, directions in the librettos and *livrets de mise-en-scène*; and it is the most fluid element in modern productions, even those few which consult the original stage directions.[11] In any case three out of Berlioz's six major dramatic works were not intended to be staged.

But this does not mean that, in his operas, spectacle need not matter. Alban Ramaut plays down what is quintessentially theatrical in Berlioz's operas: 'Berliozian opera is always articulated around three paradoxical invariables: the lack of individual characterizations, the avoidance of spectacle as an independent element, since its powers are given to the orchestra, and the normal time-scale of dramatic events which is transferred from the spaces in which action unfolds to the density of symphonic discourse.'[12] This view is much exaggerated. Berlioz wanted to impress his audiences, and his only opera uncorrupted by the centrality of visual imagery is *Béatrice et Bénédict*. In *Les Francs-juges*, Ferrand and Berlioz clearly intended to deploy every resource

---

[9] For the liveliest description of the Parisian critical scene, see Balzac, *Illusions perdues*.

[10] Cairns, *Servitude*, 703; his source is Boschot.

[11] *Livrets de mise-en-scène* were prepared, and survive, for many works in the Opéra repertoire, as they do for works of Verdi; these include detailed notes on the movement and expression of the actors, as well as information about the sets, intended to guide productions in other theatres, and directors of revivals.

[12] 'L'Opéra berliozien s'articule toujours, en effet, autour de trois constantes paradoxales: l'absence de caractérisation des personnages, la visualisation scénique éludée en tant que telle et réinvestie dans l'orchestre, la durée nécessaire à l'évolution dramatique transférée de l'espace dans lequel se meut l'action à l'épaisseur de la matière symphonique.' Ramaut, *Hector Berlioz, compositeur romantique français*, 133.

to achieve visual impact: a Gothic castle, crowd scenes, a rural idyll, and a dénouement in a vast cavern dominated by a mechanical statue designed to crush people to death. Although the staging of *Benvenuto Cellini* was not innovatory, like that of *Robert le Diable*, the Opéra lavished resources on it; besides its expensive soloists, the cast-list in the libretto for the second tableau (the Carnival) names visible personnel (female/male) for the Parade 1/3; saltimbanques 0/4; soloists (coryphées) in the saltarello, 3/3, corps de danse 12/12; sbires (police), 0/2; seigneurs 0/12; peuple 24/0, and children 24/10—and this does not include the chorus. In Act II, the Pope (Cardinal) entered with four pages (females in breeches) and twelve seigneurs; two other dancers were 'spadassins' (hit-men). None of these people sings. The first act climaxes in one of opera's most glorious crowd scenes; in the final coup at the end of the opera, the cover of the forge blows off and a torrent of liquid metal falls to earth. The end of *La Muette de Portici*, an eruption of Vesuvius, need not have been much more spectacular. For Weimar, Berlioz substituted the still more brilliant and equally unlikely vision of a red-hot metal statue. No wonder the Opéra wanted no more of Berlioz: failure was too expensive.

Les Troyens, besides more formal ballets, includes two crowd scenes and two processions in Act I alone; despite his tart comments on processions in *La Juive*, Berlioz intended taking full advantage of the Opéra's resources in staging, with extras and on-stage musicians (although its requirements pale beside those of *Le Prophète*).[13] Paradoxically this would mean using modern instrumental resources (saxhorns) on stage despite the Opéra's concern for historically informed scenery and costumes. In Act II, the city burns; Act III climaxes in a visual epiphany, when Aeneas flings off his disguise; in Act IV, the 'Chasse royale' requires a stream, turning into a flash flood, a tree struck by lightning, and characters on horseback. The visual beauties of Act IV are part of its dramatic point and, ghosts apart, it is only in this act that Berlioz included supernatural beings in his cast. In Act V, a funeral pyre is raised, and the audience shares Dido's prophetic vision of the Capitol of Rome. The still grander original conception extinguishes the sorrows of Carthage in a procession of Roman conquerors and Virgil himself, singer of arms and the man; this time Berlioz's music is not so rich as to make the scene conceivable without an elaborate spectacle.[14] But Berlioz's priorities lay with epic, not with culinary theatre. At least the revised ending can be staged with more normal resources, even without the vision of Rome, since the symbolism of the Trojan March in triumphal mode, clashing with the inescapable sight of Dido dying, forms a sufficiently ironic counterpoint between what we hear and what we see.

[13] On *La Juive*, see *Critique musicale*, ii. 73–8.
[14] For a discussion of this scene see Kemp, *Les Troyens*, 63–5; the music is in NBE 2c. 888–928.

Characterization

Berlioz's music characterizes at least to the extent of separating the musical language of the different characters, and mirroring their feelings in identifiable elements of his music, supplying to each character a distinct 'tinta'. His dramatic works are not disguised symphonies; they are dominated by voices and vocal forms, and even *Les Troyens* sets out as a number opera, additionally divided into scenes and tableaux.[15] The agonies he suffered when preparing to stage *Benvenuto, Les Troyens à Carthage,* operas by Gluck, and *Béatrice et Bénédict,* are like those of Verdi and Wagner, despite their far greater success in bending theatres to their will. Many problems related to the adequacies, or otherwise, of singers, vocal and histrionic. Like his contemporaries, he worked out a dramatic plan based on arias, duets and ensembles, scenes mixing soloists and chorus, and finales, and aimed always to write effectively for voices as well as instruments. Even scenes requiring musical dissolution, deformation, and fantasy, do not depend on symphonic methods, but remain voice-dominated.

It would probably be fair to say that the surviving music from *Les Francs-juges* shows no particular evidence of a gift for characterization, rather than for selecting appropriate signifiers for each situation. But this more limited objective is a step towards a more articulate characterization, and a second step is taken in *Herminie* and *Cléopâtre*; since the arias cover several moods, the characters begin to seem multi-dimensional. If the music itself is inadequate, characterization will suffer the same fate. If *Herminie*, despite one eminently Berliozian melody (the later *idée fixe*), is relatively conventional, in *Cléopâtre* Berlioz let himself go, having already composed *Huit scènes de Faust*, in which the different simplicities of Brander and Marguerite, and the malice of Mephistopheles, are superbly etched by lyrical numbers, without recitative. An articulate characterization is built out of contrasts between lyrical numbers and details within recitative, although the emotional qualities of an aria may be transferable, as in Gluck, Bellini, and Verdi as well as Berlioz, from one drama to another. Once fixed in a context, these emotions become facets of a complex persona.

The development of a dramatic character may be arrested before the end; or it may continue through, and contribute to, understanding of the very dénouement. Thus Berlioz's Faust, who is not Goethe's, loses individuality during his final recitative (after the 'Invocation'), and is merely a terrified voice in 'La course à l'abîme'; then he disappears in 'Pandemonium' and takes no part in the epilogue on earth and in heaven. On the other hand, Cassandra, and especially Dido, bring about catharsis through their very public suicides; like Faust's, their final speeches are recitative, but their deaths coincide with fateful events, the sack of Troy and the departure of the Trojans to Italy; there is no further scene change and no significant musical material

---

[15] Inconsistencies in defining 'numbers' are noted in 'Overture'.

is introduced following their deaths. The cumulative characterization of their roles, including arias, recitatives, and contributions to ensembles, is consummated in a supreme moment.

Berlioz's powers of characterization have been demonstrated by his musical separation of two roles of similar tessitura, Cassandra and Dido, within one opera.[16] Another comparison could be made between three low-voiced clerics: the Pope (Cardinal) in *Benvenuto*, Lawrence in *Roméo*, and Hubert in *La Nonne sanglante*. The Pope and Hubert both present themselves in D flat, with low-voiced orchestration, but these are entirely different characterizations. The Pope (Ex. 10.1a) is preceded not only by his attendants but by four bassoons, bass clarinet, trombones, and ophicleide, playing his tune; he is marked at once as both menacing and comic. He enters uttering benevolent platitudes in a melody concentrated on a few rhythmic units; it unrolls in grand, classical phraseology and ternary form: (A) twice three bars, then three times two, ending in the dominant; (B) twice three bars, then four, modulating back; (A') as A but ending in the tonic. In the face of Cellini's rebellion and highly efficient blackmail, the pontifical façade breaks down; within the extended sextet, a corrupt human emerges, authoritarian and testy (see below). Berlioz's attempt to join the operatic mainstream is reflected in the symmetrical two-bar phrasing of Hubert's aria, its unambiguous binary design, and perhaps, despite passing tonal inflections, an absence of modulation in the first phrase (Ex. 10.1b). But with Lawrence, freed of constraints within his own domain of 'dramatic symphony', Berlioz had already developed an aria form without reprise and almost without repetition, progressively lengthening from two- through three- to four-bar units. Both arias explore the upper range of the voice towards the end—what aria does not?—but Hubert remains more focused upon his lower register, including a sustained low A♭. This is clearly intended as a good vocal effect, in that a rhetorical line of communication is established between the singer (as it might be Nicolas Levasseur) in his own person, and an admiring audience. A musical dramatist takes advantage of vocal capabilities to enhance characterization within the drama; Hubert's gravity and complacency are symbolized by this solemn resonance.

Lawrence eventually succeeds in pacifying the feuding families by inflaming them with his own passionate conviction. Hubert has already pacified two warring factions with the promise of Agnes's marriage to Rodolphe's hated brother. But he can no more pacify Rodolphe than Lawrence could have persuaded the Capulets to allow a living Romeo to marry Juliet. Hubert is disturbed by the unexpected complication of Rodolphe's love for Agnes, but while sympathetic, he sounds understandably more detached than Lawrence. The aria includes *pertichini*, interruptions from the other character, some vocal, more consisting of wind and string gestures representing Rodolphe's

---

[16] 'Dido's *Monologue* and *Air*', in Kemp, *Les Troyens*, especially 176–80; see also Ch. 7.

movements or internal anguish. Hubert responds by a rerun of his melody, with added orchestral eloquence; what was originally string accompaniment is replaced by trombones and horns. The reprise is further enriched by some modulations, but when Rodolphe sings again, Hubert shushes him, and then fades musically from the scene. Eloquence like Lawrence's, which changes style in response to interruption, would mitigate against dramatic credibility, for Rodolphe rejects Hubert's advice to bow to fate, and thus sets the plot in motion. One could make similar comparisons with the great tenor roles,

Ex. 10.1*a* Entry of the Pope (*Benvenuto Cellini*)

b. Hubert's aria (*La Nonne sanglante*)

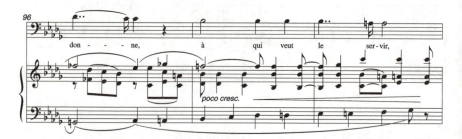

Cellini, Faust, Aeneas, and Benedick, of whom the first is perhaps, as a character, not entirely *réussi*, while the last is witty, but in contrast to Beatrice, scarcely more than one-dimensional.

Building dramatic forms: the *Roméo* finale

Benvenuto Cellini was mostly written before *Les Huguenots* reached the stage, but Berlioz's next dramatic work, *Roméo et Juliette*, contains a warm musical tribute to the grand opera of Rossini and Meyerbeer. Following the hushed end to the tomb scene, the genre 'dramatic symphony' is merged with opera; an operatic version might give individual voices to the lovers' parents and the prince, but the finale nevertheless seems designed for staging. The fanfare and crescendo of the choral entries make a theatre redundant, however, for the music fills the stage of the imagination; an ascending figure (from bar 16) revives the atmosphere of 'combats, tumulte' from the first movement; consternation is signified by a unanimous roar of 'Ciel!' from both families; silence is made palpable by the sustained bass A♭; and the apprehension of a crime ('Quel mystère affreux') is signified by a harmonic 'mystery'. Lawrence's *scena* consists of a series of waves, the last of which carries the warring families with it. The recitative begins simply, but a held oboe note reminds us of the end of the tomb scene, and thus of Juliet's last breath. He moves into higher gear with the *tempo d'inizio*, a freewheeling narrative in C minor over a throbbing ostinato.[17] A descending whimper from the violins, covering a fourth, tritone, or fifth, is added to the accompaniment; the accumulation of texture critically enhances the expression. Turning from narrative to eulogy, Lawrence's Air in E flat is a series of smaller waves, appealing to sentiment, without threat; but these waves successively grow until the last two high E♭s and the extended final phrase.[18] This wave, moreover, dissipates its energy in a brief instrumental coda; Lawrence changes tone abruptly, coming to the expected Allegro ('Où sont ils maintenant, Ces ennemis farouches?'), with no *tempo di mezzo*, but leaping from E flat to B major, tending to support the weighty signification attached to moves down a major third in *Les Troyens*.[19] There is no real form; rather, there is deformation. The orchestral figure hums along confidently, with wind interventions which imply a growing determination. After eulogy, the hell-fire sermon; the listeners are highly inflammable; Lawrence reaches no definite ending, but breaks his orotund phrasing and driving ostinato for more recitative (bar 229). Notwithstanding the grand orchestral roars, prophetic of the fall of Troy, this may be a rhetorical error: no longer carried away by the musical tide, the families retrench to the stubborn stupidity typical of ancient enmity, nearly setting the cycle of violence into motion once more by retreating to the fugal combat in the purely orchestral first movement of the symphony ('Combats,

---

[17] This narrative was considerably reduced on revision: NBE 18. 420–4.
[18] See Rushton, 'Misreading Shakespeare', 214–17.   [19] See 'Overture'.

tumultes': bar 238). The cross-reference is not aimed at formal 'unity', but at a symbolic defeat of the lyrical by the symphonic; an essentially instrumental idea has seized control of the voices. Tonally, Lawrence's attempt to establish B major in one step from E flat was glib, and premature: the symphony's opening B minor must be assimilated into the synthesis at which he is aiming. The families carry the reprise of the first movement as far as its modulation to D major (represented by its dominant, bar 263); Lawrence makes himself heard before the jaunty second theme of the first movement can intervene, and he insists upon D minor (bar 268). Returning to narrative, sentiment, and sermon, is useless: he must pray. But from this point, a sharpward move in tonality has the effect of affirmation, achieved in the third section of the aria ('Grand Dieu, qui voit au fond de l'âme'), a prayer which is also magnificently rhetorical; its essence is the conversion of the D♮ of the B minor/D major area into the D♯ of, at last, an *achieved* B major. The ascending triplets in the bass are a diatonic inversion of the earlier chromatic whimper. Melodic and harmonic impulses converge at the climax ('Comme la paille au gré du vent'), an irresistible triumph of the lyrically ordered.

As Lawrence repeats his prayer (Ex. 10.2), the families fall in behind him, one of the most remarkable passages of the symphony (from bar 358). Halting woodwind, obviously indebted to Beethoven, mark their hesitant *rapprochement*; they stand as if on the edge of an abyss, a doubtful future without the comforting certainties of hatred. The modulation descends with alarming rapidity through a circle of fifths. The D chord whose third, F♯, links to the key of B, stands as the last representative of the opening B minor. In the oath of reconciliation, the broadly conceived line includes a worm of doubt in a chromatic descent based on perfect fifths ('Au livre du pardon'), tangled harmony resolved by the D♮ to D♯ resolution at the vocal peak (bars 402–3). A complete statement with chorus is followed by a short episode and partial restatement.[20] In using a swinging 9/8, Berlioz crowned a tradition represented by the splendid oaths in *Guillaume Tell* and *Les Huguenots*, the style being irresistibly like Meyerbeer's blessing of the daggers (while the violin figure, as Liszt implied, anticipates the Pilgrims in *Tannhäuser*); the first audience for *Roméo* might well have noticed that Berlioz's Catholic reconciliation emulated Catholics planning a massacre, but the reference is surely not intended ironically. Berlioz may have felt that Meyerbeer's music—which he discussed in detail and praised as 'sublime horror'—embodied an equivalent passion to that of Lawrence and the families, and that the more noble dramatic context would do the rest.[21] He surely wished to do no more than justice to the final scene which (he believed) had not been performed since Shakespeare's time. But whatever its relationship to other examples of the genre, the finale of *Roméo et Juliette* is one of the finest passages of grand

[20] This episode was originally longer and included the proposal, more suited to spoken than sung drama, to raise a golden memorial to the lovers. NBE 18. 431–6.

[21] *Critique musicale*, ii. 436.

opera music from the glory years of the genre. Its success is the more ironic because the year of its performance, 1839, had begun with the withdrawal of *Benvenuto Cellini* from the Opéra.

BENVENUTO CELLINI, 'PETIT OPÉRA SEMI-SERIA'

Why did *Benvenuto Cellini* fail so miserably? It is tempting to blame the genre, but the Opéra repertoire was never confined to tragedy, nor to five-act block-busters. An evening's entertainment might mix a shorter or 'petit' opera, or part of an opera, with ballet. When Berlioz observed that 'there are not many ballets whose length [i.e. relative brevity] allows performance alongside my work', he meant alongside a complete performance; scheduling his opera

Ex. 10.2 *Roméo et Juliette*, No. 7 (Finale), from bar 336

depended on the ballerina.[22] There were a few performances of one act, a fate which, notoriously, had already overtaken *Guillaume Tell*.

  Benvenuto conforms with the Opéra repertoire in mingling historical with fictional characters, and in identifiable 'real' sets, one reason for casting Perseus, a Medici commission, in the Coliseum rather than Florence. Louise Bertin's *Esmerelda* (1836) featured Notre-Dame still more extensively; since this is the opera most comparable to *Benvenuto*, and Berlioz had assisted in its preparation, its poor reception was a bad omen. The composers had something in common, including an attraction to enharmony, and the association

---

[22] 'le nombre des ballets dont l'étendue permet de les donner avec mon ouvrage est très petit'. Letter to Liszt, 22 Jan. 1839, *CG* ii. 521.

of the heroine with the oboe. *Esmerelda* is more radical than *Benvenuto* in privileging ensembles, including scenes of revelry and mob violence, over aria. Berlioz felt this was a mistake.[23] His own opera, arguably, suffers from the opposite fault. Opera semi-seria implies a sentimental work, with an escape from jeopardy to a happy ending, as in *La gazza ladra* and *La sonnambula*.[24] *Benvenuto* started life as an *opéra comique* and despite the death of a minor personage, and a 'message' about art and society, it embraces comedy more wholeheartedly than was usual at the Opéra. Nevertheless, there were precedents. In *Robert le diable*, the air for Raimbaut ('Ah! L'honnête homme') is turned into a duet by the mocking asides of Bertram: the style is comic, the import sinister. Similar asides by Fieramosca turn what Teresa and Cellini clearly believe to be a love duet into a comic trio. Despite complaints about informal language in the libretto, the failure of *Benvenuto Cellini* cannot wholly be attributed to its difference from standard repertoire and complaints that it was an 'opéra bouffe' seem disingenuous.

It was standard critical practice to blame failure on the libretto, for which Berlioz must take his share of the responsibility—or, since the libretto has many virtues, the credit.[25] If it was a subject out of its time, that could also be said of *Les Troyens*, where, however, the one author (preferable to a committee) was the composer, by now vastly more experienced through conducting and reviewing operas. Throughout *Les Troyens*, musical and dramatic threads work together consistently. It would be difficult to maintain that with any version of *Benvenuto Cellini*. Nevertheless, it has variety, incident, and lively characterization; and perusal of the early reviews suggests that the failure was mainly attributable to the qualities of the music which generated such epithets as 'learned' and 'exhausting': 'For the rest, we acknowledged the effort, the work, the science, and not ten bars of music made for us.'[26] The prejudice concerning Berlioz's symphonic proclivities, or his orchestral dispositions in the Requiem, is not wholly responsible for a perception that in *Benvenuto*, there was not enough routine work for the normal listener to grasp.

Characters and music: Act I

Today we can profitably scan the score of *Benvenuto* in search of 'purely sensual pleasure'; it is less consistently rewarding to relate the music to the drama. Yet it starts with a scene which mingles musical inventiveness of high order with engaging comedy. The opening fugato ('learned', of course)

---

[23] *Critique musicale*, ii. 595–600.

[24] I would exclude tragedies of realistic or sentimental ambience (but see Emanuele Senici, 'Verdi's Luisa, a Semiserious Alpine Virgin', *19th-Century Music*, 22 (Fall, 1998), 144–68).

[25] On the libretto, see NBE 1a, p. xii. While Barbier and de Wailly were called in to prepare new text for a possible Paris revival in 1856, Berlioz had presumably made the changes necessary for the Weimar version.

[26] Bloom, *Berlioz,* Benvenuto Cellini. *Dossier de Presse parisienne, passim*: cited, 37; see also NBE 1a, pp. xv–xvii.

sharply characterizes fussy, pompous Balducci. His growing peevishness is marked by a stretto in the minor (122/43), the entries mounting by fifths.[27] Can Berlioz have equated Balducci with his teacher Reicha, who wrote several fugues, whose boldness of method does not prevent them being tedious? At the climax, when Balducci invokes the Pope—while questioning his judgement—the chain of suspensions is the product of studying strict counterpoint (124/77–84). Then Berlioz introduces Balducci's personal motive, an ostinato grumble, agitated but immobile (125/94); among other sections eventually removed from the score, it permeates his aria, in which he actually sings this originally instrumental idea (128/139). Even without the aria, he is unforgettably limned as a descendant of Bartolo, confining his ward (in this case, his daughter) to the house; the forging scene adds a layer of malice, also omitted in Weimar ('Vous! un homme de génie!', 1149/107).

The serenaders, twangling guitars off-stage, pelt Balducci with flour and Teresa with flowers and a *billet*; she anticipates Cellini's arrival in her aria. Teresa proves no mere sop to conventional love interest. If the opera's real theme is the artist as hero, Cellini's standing is not yet apparent, and hers is the first rounded characterization. It helps that her aria has two movements, and embodies conflicts of love and family duty, and apprehensions of disaster and happiness, raising her above run-of-the-mill sentimental lovers; this characterization is achieved by the musical 'pleasure' Berlioz legitimized. Her own motive, as Miriam Lensky has shown, is covert, appearing as a descending scale, usually part-chromatic, to form a 'personal tinta'.[28] It first appears in the Largo (153/175), when she is showered with blooms. She does not sing, but the beautifully etched wind phrase against a high tremolo, closed with delicate pizzicato chords, certainly refers to her, not Balducci; and it does not, as one might infer, refer only to Cellini's image of her, for it recurs when she is left alone (165/2). As she thinks of the risks they are taking, the brief middle-register 'canto' (violas, cellos, 167/15), with its anxious chromaticism and shifting rhythm, is the first of many such heart-stopping moments in Berliozian drama. In 'Entre l'amour et le devoir', substituted for the aria which became *Rêverie et caprice*, she ponders the frustration of being young and dependent: 'What you wish for, you must fear, and place no trust even in hope.' The solo oboe which is Berlioz's nearly invariable response to sympathetic femininity (compare *Le Roi Lear* and *Roméo*, II) leads the cantabile, a simple ternary form with coda. The main section is a melody with the simplest of accompaniments, but in the middle section intricate patterns—low string shudders, violin triplets which might refer to Cellini, and appoggiaturas on the second beats echoed by wind (from 189/26)—fall like the shadows of butterflies; the keys range from D sharp minor through to D major—Berlioz's favourite 'pun'—and although the return strategy is conventional, the fer-

---

[27] References are in the form page/bar number in NBE1; this is to assist navigation through the different versions.

[28] Lensky, 'Characterization in the Dramatic Works of Hector Berlioz', 127–37.

mata on the dominant is a grinding minor ninth (191/45). Teresa shows her mettle more directly when she shakes off this mood for a cabaletta ('When I'm your age, grandma, then I'll be good') with giddy coloratura, glittering harp, and a cadenza which Berlioz no doubt wrote to forestall something improvised and worse.

The artist-hero first appears only as a dashing lover, to a vigorous strain from his serenade which might have been, but is not, a personal motive, for it is apparently a noise in the street (Cellini identifies it as the carnival). He tries to calm her with a phrase almost too melting (217/23–6). The tonality, originally E, has reached C; it drops the same interval to A flat for the duet. These major third shifts do not appear to signal any dramatic change, as they do elsewhere in Berlioz, but they are ubiquitous in this scene, where Cellini seduces Teresa from her duty. At first she demurs, but since her answering phrase echoes his, like Zerlina's 'vorrei et non vorrei' in the locus classicus of seductions, 'Là ci darem la mano', we infer that while words express doubt, the *voice*, always more to be believed in opera, is already in the grip of Cellini's fascination. Cellini is not planning any brutal Don Juan seduction; if his words ('So far from you, sad and banished, my soul loses all hope') seem over the top, the exquisite melodic sequence argues for his sincerity (219/39; see Ex. 4.1*a*). This elegant sentiment is mingled with farce. Berlioz originally polluted Teresa's response with Fieramosca's surreptitious entrance (221/50); but wiser councils prevailed even before the first performance. Fieramosca now enters after Teresa's stanza (227/86), so that the first words he overhears are abuse of himself. Cellini has not prevailed by sentiment; he tries instead, with more success, to point out that if she does not elope with him, she will have to marry Fieramosca. This is underpinned with a matching version of the arpeggio motive with which it begins; instead of four crotchets the rhythm is three demisemiquavers (the second filling in the interval of a third), a demisemiquaver rest, and two quavers. This violence affects, or is effected by, harmony as well: A flat minor is represented as G sharp minor in the progression g♯, G♮, C♮, G♯, c♯, A, V/A. Teresa's response passes through G♭, C♭, G♮, c, and A♭, to close in F minor. Such drastic chord changes bespeak a more than normal agitation.[29]

This trio is planned on an enormous scale and with such thematic richness that it may well have disturbed the critics as too complex to assimilate in the theatre; the farcical element is quickly exhausted. First the cantabile returns as a canonic duet (repeated in *Le Carnaval romain*). Then another burst of fury at Fieramosca (239/134) leads to a new key area, F major, in which Berlioz introduces a flood of new ideas. The Allegro 3/4 bars ($\downarrow$. = 56) correspond to the 9/8 bars ($\downarrow$. = 168), but present entirely different moods. In the first 3/4, Cellini offers a third possibility: neither Fieramosca nor death, but

---

[29] Cellini's speech has two 'puns' [g♯–G♮ and C♮–c♯] and Teresa adds another (C♭–c); both have two more drops of a major third [Cellini, C♮–G♯ and c♯–A; Teresa, C♭–G♮ and c–A♭).

elopement. The 9/8 exposes in whispers the plan to escape under the cover of the carnival. The new tune at bar 229, significantly, is the first which Teresa herself introduces; it marks a revival of her doubts ('Is it not an offence against religion to desert my father?'—for her mother is dead). This theme is used in the overture, as the lyrical melody in the Allegro, and at the heart of the overture it is given to the oboe; our prior hearings add emotional focus to the trio. Cellini cunningly suggests that for her to enter a convent, or marry Fieramosca, would itself be blasphemy; he persuades her by falling in with her tune, but ripening its expression through modulation to flat VI (D flat). This time Teresa takes the music down another major third, to A (262/272), and the key duly reverts to F, completing a major-third circle. The 9/8 is repeated; Teresa wants to get her instructions clear and Fieramosca must overhear all the details of the rendezvous which he missed before. This is highly entertaining; but then Cellini recovers Teresa's melody (273/357), she repeats it, and the first 3/4 melody (the lovers) is combined with the 9/8 (Fieramosca). Berlioz saw no need to cut this immense ensemble, revising only details; unfortunately it is not a finale, and in context, since more farcical humiliation for Fieramosca is piled on to end the first tableau, the trio may be too clever for the good of the opera.

Seekers after *Tristan* anticipations may have overlooked the opening bars added to the second scene for Weimar (339/2–5), but their veiled but sensuous atmosphere is quickly dissipated by the sentimentality of Cellini's Romance, which, since we have already seen Cellini the lover, we do not need.[30] He is established as a man of action and an artist when he refuses a drink and leads the chorus of 'ciseleurs', but this scene also contains some dispensable plotting and shows a less appealing side to Cellini's cronies, in dealing with the innkeeper.[31] The Carnival rebuilds momentum from its witty combination of three melodic strands (Balducci, Teresa, and the whispering of Ascanio and Cellini), before the surpassingly brilliant Saltarello. The final action scene is less known than the Saltarello, thanks to the *Carnaval romain* overture, but is no less fine in its blend of jollity, farce, and perplexity, and, for poor Pompeo, tragedy. In such grand ensembles, Berlioz is in his element; motives from *Les Francs-juges* and the Resurrexit are reworked and developed in flickering, inconstant modulations; the climax is splendidly weighty and offers a chance for Teresa and Ascanio to soar above the chorus. Fieramosca's arrest and Ascanio's adroit spiriting away of Teresa are events hardly noticed in the music, and after Cellini's exit, the last prevailing impres-

---

[30] For an analysis, see *MLB* 175–8.

[31] The singing style Berlioz uses for the innkeeper bears marks of the Jewish characterizations deplorably developed by Wagner in the roles of Mime and Beckmesser; see Barry Millington, 'Nuremberg Trial: Is there anti-Semitism in *Die Meistersinger*', *Cambridge Opera Journal*, 3 (1991), 247–60. But contrary to Fauquet (*L'Avant-scène opéra*, 92), and my review of Bloom, *The Life of Berlioz* (*Music and Letters*, 80 (1999), 450), Cellini's reference to 'juif mesquin' is directed at Balducci (NBE 2b. 434), and presumably intended metaphorically.

sion is massive *futility*—rather like the *Don Giovanni* sextet, in which the character with most vital energy is also absent.

The final act

In the second act (in Weimar, the third), we face one of the most complicated textual problems in any major opera (see NBE 1c).[32] Weimar reduces the two tableaux to one. Whereas revisions to the 'Paris 1' version made before the first performances left the story-line intact, the slicker 'Weimar' version simplifies the plot and changes events around so as to compel the relocation of several musical numbers; Berlioz had to insist that arias threatened with being cut were repositioned and retained, thus fortuitously avoiding subversion of number-opera in favour of Wagnerian continuity.[33] The Paris time-sequence is more realistic, and Ascanio's aria is more effective for coming immediately after the events he satirizes; in the Weimar version he has to remind us of what happened before the interval. In the Paris versions Balducci enters twice, both times equally shocked at finding his daughter in Cellini's workshop; the final tableau was padded out with episodes involving Fieramosca's feeble plots—though the defeated reminiscence of his aria is worth having (1097/120). The gap between the passages with greatest musical momentum, the sextet in which Cellini is given a day (in Weimar an hour) to cast his statue or be hanged, and the forging scene itself, remain a problem in both versions; and Weimar reduces each of these grand scenes by substantial cuts.

The prayer of Teresa and Ascanio and Cellini's return and narrative make a picturesque start to the act, but the versions quickly diverge, with the Weimar sequence introducing Ascanio's aria before Cellini's return. When the lovers decide to run away, regardless of Perseus awaiting completion, the ideal artist-as-hero loses face; Cellini as lover and adventurer, swashbuckling no doubt, is a considerably less interesting conception. The slow movement in F sharp minor was cut from the duet for Weimar, a considerable loss musically and in characterization, especially of Teresa. Berlioz might have spared his tenor, and retained the expressive essence of the duet, by pruning both movements, for the vigorous syncopation of the Allegro sounds exhausting.[34] Balducci, Fieramosca, and eventually the Pope arrive for the quintet, sextet, and finale, a witty and abrasive sequence which makes expert use of two principal motives: the solemn Pope theme which opens the sextet, and a curling

---

[32] The NBE editor, Hugh Macdonald, deserves our thanks for making navigation through three versions, if not easy, at least possible. The Weimar sequence is contained in the Choudens score (1886), republished as a miniature score by Kalmus (No. 513). See also Thomasin K. La May, 'A New Look at the Weimar Versions of Berlioz's *Benvenuto Cellini*', *Musical Quarterly*, 65 (1979), 559–72.

[33] See his letters to Liszt, *CG* iv. 179 and 182–9 (the latter consisting mainly of musical notation); Cairns, *Servitude*, 495.

[34] For Cellini especially, the inclusion of the whole duet makes the last act particularly strenuous. Berlioz had already made a few cuts in the first movement of the duet before the first performance.

6/8 melody (Ex. 10.3). First, Fieramosca and Balducci complain to the Pope, shaking but never quite upsetting his tonal orientation to D flat major, and he retains that key in addressing Cellini (to 867/88). Cellini's mendacious denial of any wrong-doing breaks at once into the final key of the ensemble; again, the leap is down a major third (written as A major, 867/92). The tempo increases and the metre changes to 6/8, where the curling theme is introduced (Ex.10.3*a*); its first association, therefore, is with Cellini's admission that the statue is not yet forged. A repetition closes in F sharp minor (873/122 and 877/142). We lose sight of this melody in the ensuing passage, which includes Cellini's threat to break the mould of Perseus unless the Pope accedes to his demands: he wants indulgence, Teresa, and to cast his own statue ('Rien que celà!'). This passage of some 160 bars was replaced by about ninety in Weimar. Berlioz cut a fugato for Pope and woodwind ('Ah! ça, démon!', 897/267), calling it 'mesquin' and 'in the style of the meanest opéra comique'—too harsh a verdict, since it incisively exposes the papal morals.[35] The versions merge at 'pendu!', as Cellini sings the Pope's tune 'ironically'— what indulgence!—since if he fails he will be hanged. Weimar picks up the curling theme at the start of the substitute passage (921/416, Ex. 10.3*b*). In the Paris versions this theme instead becomes the main theme of the finale (935/3), which was cut in Weimar. Paired statements for the Pope and Cellini (Ex. 10.3*c*) are repeated after an episode for all six voices to a cadence (944/50). The remainder resumes the mixture of 4/4 and 6/8 heard in the sextet, subjects the theme to fragmentation, and climaxes with reiterated *opera buffa* cadences. The orchestral coda (955/116) empties the stage; it repeats the paired statements of the theme, at last in a high register, before the Pope's theme mutters a disgruntled farewell.[36]

In the Weimar version Cellini, with one hour to finish his work and papal guards watching, sings an aria. In Paris a new series of episodes follows, and Ascanio's aria intervenes before 'Sur les monts les plus sauvages', a better aria than Cellini's Romance but hardly less gratuitous. We have seen him willing to abandon his art for love, and now he wants to quit and wander in the hills. The form is elaborate, the melodic and harmonic development masterly, but the sentiment weakens the character and distracts from the dramatic goal. The forging scene regenerates the opera, especially in the Paris version where its first grand strophe is given twice (to 1141/69). This part-canonic expansion of a simple, even banal, motive captures the workmanlike energy, the heat, the risk, and the sheer effort of the massive undertaking of casting a huge statue. If the temperature drops before the last reprise of the guild hymn, such rounding-off is normal in operas in which the serious message is not, perhaps, too serious.

---

[35] *CG* iv. 234.

[36] The only 'complete' recording of the opera (by Colin Davis for Philips) cobbles the versions of the sextet together, it has to be said with some success.

Ex. 10.3 *Benvenuto Cellini*, Sextet and finale

a. Sextet

b. Sextet, Weimar only

c. Finale

The hero and his problems

The modern archetype of a mixed genre, Mozart's *Don Giovanni*, was well known in Paris in Italian and French.[37] David Cairns finds much in common between it and *Benvenuto Cellini*, and not only because both include death by duel, an escape by the cornered and morally equivocal 'hero' just before the interval, and a climax involving a statue.[38] Although Cellini is the title-role, in both operas one or both tenor arias might be omitted to advantage. Both operas are fundamentally comedies, but appear to have a serious message (what it may be is more disputable). Another resemblance is that both have exceptionally good openings, and the episodic nature of what follows, particularly in their second acts, tends to diminish momentum.

So what is this opera saying? Joël-Marie Fauquet says that for Berlioz, Cellini is 'not a sixteenth-century sculptor but a brother in arms'.[39] In 1838, Liszt had already identified the subject and its creator, though Macdonald points out that Berlioz made no such claim.[40] To take the artist as a dramatic hero was novel, although it could be paralleled in the novels of Balzac (the artist in *La Rabouilleuse*, the musician in *Gambara*). The parallels between operatic hero and composer are identified by François Piatier as a rebellious attitude to patronage; artistic exaltation; combativeness and spleen; and a shared interest in technical innovation. Cellini, the model for a considerable amount of romantic art, is represented as lover, provocateur of authority (the Pope), and creator.[41] Such a complex pattern makes difficult the identification of as clear a musical characterization for Cellini as that of Teresa, or one-dimensional persons like Fieramosca, the Pope, and Balducci. Adolphe Nourrit, a friend of Berlioz and the first Raoul in *Les Huguenots*, whom he must surely have had in mind for the role, had lost his vocal confidence; the cynical indifference of his replacement, Gilbert Duprez, did much to kill the opera's chances. Admittedly the role is taxing, even with the Weimar cuts and without the more extended cadenza to 'Sur les monts'; like Aeneas, Fauquet suggests, Cellini requires 'two tenors in one'.[42]

Contemporary witnesses bear out the jaundiced account in Berlioz's memoirs (chapter 48) concerning inadequate performance, critical rejection, and public perceptions: Berlioz had misread his audience, which surely did not share the prejudice of many established musicians and of the management. I

---

[37] Berlioz reviewed the Opéra production at length (*Journal des Débats*, 15 Nov. 1835; *Critique musicale*, ii. 345–51; trans. Julian Rushton, *W. A. Mozart: Don Giovanni* (Cambridge: Cambridge University Press, 1981), 131–6). See Katharine Ellis, 'Rewriting *Don Giovanni*, or "The Thieving Magpies"', *Journal of the Royal Musical Association*, 119 (1994), 212–50.

[38] Cairns, *Servitude*, 116.

[39] 'Les Voix de Persée', *L'Avant-scène opéra*, 142 (*Benvenuto Cellini*), 85.

[40] Liszt, 'The Perseus of Benvenuto Cellini' (see Ch. 4, n. 1); Macdonald, NBE 1a, p. xix.

[41] Piatier, *Benvenuto Cellini ou le mythe de l'artiste*, 61–78; 24–30; 120.

[42] On requirements for head and chest voice in this aria, see Fauquet, 'Les Voix de Persée', 88–91, and Ch. 7 above (n. 7). Berlioz wrought vengeance on the whole race of star tenors in his 'Étude astronomique' (*Soirées*, sixth evening).

have singled out a number of what seem to me faults with Berlioz's most incompletely realized work. But the central problem is one Gluck allegedly identified in a Rameau opera: 'puzza di musica': it stinks of music. If Rameau can recover from this superfluity, so should *Benvenuto Cellini*. The most interesting, and musically the richest, French opera between *Guillaume Tell* and *Les Troyens* is also 'Le seul opéra romantique française'.[43] It is natural, for Berlioz's supporters then and now, to blame the libretto, and certainly neither version is other than flawed. But what really caused the downfall of *Benvenuto Cellini* was the music; it was too good for its performers and its public.[44]

CONCERT OPERA: DRAMATIC LEGEND

Had Berlioz been offered a more definite commission for *La Nonne sanglante*, and thus temporarily exhausted his interest in 'Gothic' subjects, *La Damnation de Faust* might never have been written. However, one need not assume that Berlioz's *Nonne* would necessarily have succeeded any better than Gounod's (1854), for which the libretto was considerably reworked. Where their versions overlap, Berlioz's surviving music is finer, but so broadly conceived that each of the three numbers appears over-long. And if Berlioz's work had been staged in the late 1840s, it would soon have come up against competition from Meyerbeer (*Le Prophète*). On the whole, therefore, it is difficult to regret the demise of *La Nonne*, since instead we have *La Damnation* and, eventually, *Les Troyens*, a work which would certainly never have existed had Berlioz become the darling of the Opéra. In *La Nonne sanglante*, Berlioz seems to have worked deliberately at a lower temperature than he preferred; whereas his wholehearted commitment is unmistakable in every bar of *La Damnation*.

Each number of Berlioz's *Huit scènes de Faust* presupposes the dramatic context of Goethe's *Faust*, Part I. For nearly every number, the score includes the spoken lines from Nerval's translation immediately before and after the lyric. Only the ninth lyric, the chorus of soldiers, was removed from its original context and appended to Marguerite's Romance; in a brief but prophetic musical overlap, drumbeats are heard behind the final phrase on the cor anglais. By this juxtaposition of characters, Berlioz hoped to enhance the effect of both.[45] This was one of many ideas refined in *La Damnation*, the first dramatic work for whose text he was essentially responsible.[46]

---

[43] Fauquet, 'Les Voix de Persée', 86; he too refers to an 'excess of music', 88.

[44] For an admirably upbeat assessment of this opera from another perspective, see Gary Schmidgall, *Literature as Opera* (New York: Oxford University Press, 1977), 151–77.

[45] 'Although in Goethe's play this *Chœur de soldats* comes several scenes earlier than Marguerite's *Romance*, I have nevertheless linked these pieces together; I consider the contrast resulting from the juxtaposition of two such different characters can enhance the effect of both of them.' NBE 5. 96.

[46] On the division of authorship in the text, NBE 8b. 501; for a critical appraisal, see Katherine Reeve, '*The Damnation of Faust*, or the Perils of Heroism in Music', in Bloom, *Studies*, 148–88.

The most superficial acquaintance with *La Damnation* should have fore-stalled the common observation that it is essentially an expansion of *Huit scènes*. All nine lyrics are included, and the eight scenes retain their original texts with no more than minor modifications; the five solo songs are virtually unchanged except for their instrumentation. Yet only the two songs in Auerbach's cellar retain their original context, and the reordering of these scenes is a good measurement of Berlioz's departure from Goethe's plan (see Table 10.1). The existence of *Huit scènes* exerted an influence over the even-tual design of *La Damnation*, but only in so far as all of them somehow had to be incorporated. When he set out for Germany in the autumn of 1845, Berlioz took an unfinished text by Almire Gandonnière. They evidently met to discuss the work in Paris, and only one short letter survives: Berlioz con-firms a meeting, and says the recitatives must be cut to the bare minimum.[47] Although he wrote three lyrics, most of Gandonnière's work consists of recitative designed to provide revised contexts for the lyrics of *Huit scènes*, starting with the original No. 2, 'Ronde de paysans', which is the first to be heard. He supplied the recitative surrounding the original No. 1, the Easter Hymn, including the entrance of Mephistopheles, and the scene in Auerbach's cellar, his first lyric being the drinking song. After the songs of the rat and the flea, he added Faust's expression of disgust, and the following scene by the Elbe (which has no direct precedent in Goethe), including 'Voici des roses' and Faust's recitative on waking up.

Berlioz is believed to have first referred to *La Damnation* as 'drame de con-cert' in three acts.[48] Probably he always intended Mephistopheles to appear earlier than in Goethe. The original plan was perhaps to characterize the world-weary Faust by his negative reaction to the 'Ronde de paysans', then, following some unknown link, to return him to his study where he contem-plates suicide, but repents on hearing the Easter Hymn. In Vienna, Berlioz composed his *Marche de Rákóczy* for Budapest, and decided to present it to Paris, but within a larger work, perhaps feeling that on its own, its national-ist associations would have no meaning. Berlioz is therefore responsible for Faust's visit to Hungary; this required no alteration to the words of 'Ronde de paysans', but Berlioz wrote new recitative before the March, and the open-ing lines of Part II which refer back Part I. By 13 March, he referred to his 'grand opéra de Faust (opéra de concert en 4 actes)'.[49] Berlioz's defence for taking Faust to Hungary may seem disingenuous, and the March is often considered gratuitous; but it does add something for Faust to despise before succumbing to the blandishments of the Easter Hymn, and so develops the concept of Faust as afflicted less by surfeit of knowledge than by ennui.[50] The

[47] *Memoirs*, ch. 54; *CG* ii. 283–4.
[48] On an albumleaf, present whereabouts unknown, dated 12 Jan. 1846; NBE 8b. 485.
[49] *CG* ii. 325.
[50] On Berlioz's defence see NBE 8a. 2; Henry Barraud calls the march 'gratuitous', *L'Avant-scène opéra*, 22, 25. See also *MLB* 261.

TABLE 10.1 Nine scenes from *Faust*

Goethe	*Huit scènes* (1829)	*La Damnation* (1846)
(Faust's study) Bells and Easter Hymn: 'Christ ist erstanden!'	No. 1 'Chants de la Fête de Pâques'	Part II scene 4 (Nord de l'Allemagne. Faust seul dans son cabinet de travail) Chant de la Fête de Pâques
(Outside the city gate) Soldiers: 'Burgen mit hohem|Mauern und Zinnen'	*See No. 7*	Part II scene 8 (Final): Chœur de soldats
(The same) Peasants beneath the lime-trees: 'Der Schäfer putze sich zum Tanz'	No. 2 Paysans sous les tilleuls. Danse et chant.	Part I scene 2 (Plaines de Hongrie) 'Ronde de paysans'
(Faust's study) Spirits: 'Schwindet, ihr dunkeln|Wölbungen droben!'	No. 3 'Concert de sylphes' (sextet)	Part II scene 7 (Bosquets et prairies du bord de l'Elbe) Chœur de gnomes et de sylphes. Songe de Faust
(Auerbach's cellar in Leipzig): 'Es war ein Ratt' im Kellernest'	No. 4 'Écot de joyeux compagnons' (Histoire d'un Rat)	Part II scene 6 (Cave d'Auerbach) Chanson de Brander
(The same): 'Es war einmal ein König|Der hatt' einen grossen Floh'	No. 5 'Chanson de Méphistophélès' (Histoire d'une Puce)	(The same) Chanson de Méphistophélès
(Evening: a small, neat room) 'Es war ein König in Thule'	No. 6 'Le Roi de Thulé', 'Chanson gothique'	Part III scene 11 (Le soir dans la chambre de Marguerite) 'Le Roi de Thulé', Chanson gothique
(Gretchen am Spinnrade allein): 'Meine Ruh' ist hin'	No. 7 Romance de Marguerite and Chœur de soldats	Part IV scene 15 (Chambre de Marguerite) Romance 'D'amour l'ardente flamme'
(Night: street in front of Gretchen's house) 'Was macht du mir|Vor Liebchens Tür'	No. 8 Sérénade de Méphistophélès	Part III scene 12 (Une rue devant la maison de Marguerite) Sérénade de Méphistophélès

resulting four-part scheme has the advantage that each part opens with a monologue, the first three for Faust and the last for Marguerite, closely followed by Faust's invocation to nature. Another gain is the orchestral development of Faust's first monologue, which mingles the pastoral fugato with ideas from both the 'Ronde de paysans' and the March, in a glorious sunrise, one of the work's finest inspirations.

From the scene in Faust's study through to the end of Part II, Berlioz evidently left the agreed design intact. Events are piled up swiftly. In Goethe the Easter Hymn is not connected to Mephistopheles' entrance, and Gandonnière, or Berlioz, made a significant alteration to Nerval's translation; after rejecting suicide, Faust claims 'la terre m'a reconquis' (Nerval), but 'le ciel m'a reconquis' (Berlioz). This return to thoughts of heaven suggests a level of self-deception which a return to earth would not imply. Hence the immediate apparition of Mephistopheles, with a sulphurous snarl and a tonal wrench by a tritone from F to B major—chords to be magnificently juxtaposed in the opening and closing bars of 'Pandemonium'. Berlioz further altered Part II by supplying words for Faust during the Easter Hymn and the chorus of gnomes and sylphes, the two movements most extensively revised in form and substance. Faust does not sing at all in *Huit scènes*; here he can form a complementary musical relationship with choruses which powerfully affect his feelings. Hearing Faust's voice within them emphasizes the significant absence of any similar relationship between Faust and the peasants and Hungarian soldiers of Part I. Faust's detached philosophical stance is undone by the Easter Hymn in a welter of nostalgia; the sylphes' chorus is transformed into a voluptuous dream with a specific object, Marguerite. Berlioz also detached the full-length chorus of soldiers from Marguerite's Romance, to form a rousing finale. Revising the instrumentation (the original is accompanied only by drumbeats and a fanfare), he followed it with the students' Latin song to his own text; the gloriously anarchic superimposition of these choruses makes a climax equivalent in weight to the Hungarian March at the end of Part I. The students' song begins resolutely in D minor 2/4, against the soldiers' B flat major, 6/8, but while the students stick to their metre, their tonality is eventually assimilated. Faust (and Mephistopheles) sing along with the students; Faust is thus consciously distanced from the military. But, significantly, Faust finally joins the soldiers' line, singing triplets (bars 201, 203) as if aware that they are all on the same mission, hunting for girls. And while the feckless youths will be happy with prostitutes, the devil's plan is that Faust will destroy an innocent girl.

Gandonnière provided the opening to Part III, including Faust's aria and Marguerite's opening words, up to 'Le Roi de Thulé'. From that point forward, if he wrote anything else, it was not used; but he had supplied contexts for seven of the nine numbers, excluding only the Serenade and Romance, which now appear in reverse order from the *Huit scènes* (and Goethe). On one level Part III is more operatic that the rest, because besides two strophic songs (ballad and serenade), there is a true aria (Faust's 'Merci, doux crépuscule'), a love duet, and an action trio with choral intervention, culminating in a static ensemble at the exact moment when action is inevitable, as in many an act ending (as with Don Giovanni, we do not see Faust escape). Yet on another level Part III is less operatic than cinematic. Whereas the magical orchestral transformations of Part II, variations of each other, allow time to change the set while expertly leading to the mood and key of the next scene, the scene changes in Part III are instantaneous. We are asked to understand that the first and last scenes, in Marguerite's bedroom, are continuous despite being divided by the scene in the street (see Table 10.2). Thus the invocation, 'Menuet des follets', and Serenade are performed simultaneously with 'Le Roi de Thulé' and the love duet.[51] That we must *understand* the scenes as occurring simultaneously is made clear by the echo of 'Le Roi de Thulé' which begins the resumed scene in the bedroom, before Faust emerges from behind the curtains and launches the love duet. In the trio (bars 31–4), Mephistopheles ironically sings 'En raillant Marguerite, Ils appellent sa mère', to a motive from the noisy serenade which rouses the neighbours and leads to the break-up of the love scene at the critical moment (see Exx. 6.9 and 10.4).

If we ignore the opening fanfare in B flat, Berlioz planned Part III as a move away from, and recovery of, the key of F. Further ironies may be read into his use of the tritone. The virtually atonal opening of Mephistopheles' invocation describes the tritone F to B. In the bedroom, the love duet in E

TABLE 10.2 Simultaneity in *La Damnation*, Part III

Marguerite			[F]		E	F
		Pre-echo of Ballad (G)	Enters (C minor): pre-echo Romance (B) Ballad (G or F)	Echo of Ballad (G)	Love duet	Trio
Faust	F				E	F
	Aria	Dialogue	hidden	Dialogue	Duet	Trio
Mephisto		(G♭)	F/D	D	B	F
		Pre-echo of Serenade	Invocation	Menuet des follets: 2nd pre-echo of Serenade	Serenade	Trio

[51] The period between Mephistopheles leaving the bedroom and returning—Marguerite's entrance, her ballad, her encounter with Faust, and the duet—requires nearly fifteen minutes' music, split by the ten minutes or so of the street scene. The times are near enough to be comparable, and would have corresponded more closely before Berlioz made cuts in Mephistopheles' evocation and the serenade.

collapses into the key of F, but Mephistopheles' personal plot goes from B (serenade, Satanic) directly to F (trio, mundane). Marguerite anticipates phrases from the Romance in B, whereas the Romance itself is in F. This scheme became tangled, however, when Berlioz decided to transpose 'Le Roi de Thulé' down to F. The preceding chromatic modulation was readily adjusted, but the ballad is still anticipated and echoed by wind instruments playing in G (see Table 10.2).[52] One might rationalize this by suggesting that the pre-echo and post-echo are heard only by the audience, not the characters. But who, in a musical drama, hears what?[53] Mephistopheles apparently *does* hear the pre-echo, for he immediately says 'Je l'entends'. But if the clarinet represents Marguerite humming a phrase or two as she approaches her room, why does she then sing the ballad a tone lower?

Techniques of anticipation and recollection seem to have preoccupied Berlioz when he was revising and piecing together *La Damnation*, following his return to France in the spring of 1846. When the Ronde and the March are anticipated during the first scene, the wonderful crescendo prepares a strategy for later use. The technique of pre-echo, as opposed to the commoner reminiscence, forms part of the 'tinta' of *La Damnation*.[54] Within Part III, anticipations are mostly connected with Marguerite. When she anticipates the Romance, she is also recollecting the dream visited on her by Mephistopheles, in which she anticipates meeting Faust. Her recitative description ('qu'il était beau') is of the man whose absence, in the Romance itself, she will lament, evoking in the same music his walking, his carriage, his seductive voice ('Sa marche que j'admire, Son port si gracieux, Sa voix enchanteresse'). Thus the Romance itself recollects something we have heard as an anticipation, and takes on a different emotional shade, as the end of the affair (in Goethe it precedes Mephistopheles' serenade and the eminently operatic scene with Marguerite's soldier-brother Valentine, whom Berlioz omits). Having crudely tacked the soldiers' chorus onto the end of the Romance in *Huit scènes*, and begun Part III with fanfares, Berlioz more subtly uses his poetic transition to the soldiers' song after the Romance as a multiple reminiscence, of the fanfare and chorus (both from 1829), and of the students' Latin song. Like Faust with the two other choruses from *Huit scènes*, Marguerite sings over this alien music; and the final entry of the cor anglais completes one of nineteenth-century music's most delicately balanced

---

[52] On the modulation, see *MLB* 38–9.

[53] Nearly every discussion of operatic aesthetics touches on this point. See among others Edward T. Cone, 'The World of Opera and its Inhabitants', in *Music: A View from Delft*, 125–38; David Rosen, 'Cone and Kivy's "World of Opera"', *Cambridge Opera Journal*, 4 (1992), 61–74; Peter Kivy, 'Composers and "Composers": A Response to David Rosen', ibid., 179–86.

[54] Miriam Lensky, 'Berlioz's Symbolic Use of Anticipation Technique in *La Damnation de Faust*', in Jeff Bernard, Gloria Withalm (eds.), *Signs, Music, Society—Proceedings of a Transdisciplinary Colloqium, Vienna, March 1999* (forthcoming).

ironies when its string accompaniment, thanks to a form of metric modulation, forms a pizzicato reminiscence of the drumbeat.[55]

Genre

What is the form of a 'concert opera'—since 'dramatic legend' clearly prescribes nothing? For much of the time it is little different from staged opera. But Berlioz had recently composed a dramatic symphony; and the orchestra has a personality rarely heard in contemporary opera, giving rise to fantasia-like forms in which vocal dominance is not unequivocally established, as in three of Faust's monologues and the 'Course à l'abîme'. Faust's aria (the third monologue) is voice-dominated, but in a continuously developing form; until the closing repetition ('Seigneur, seigneur!') melodic reprise lies below the surface, although sections are defined by tonality and text. The magnificently defiant 'Invocation à la nature' is still more cohesive, giving the impression of a single huge musical section, but the orchestra appears alien to the voice, even when it acts as an echo.[56] In contrast to the through-composed arias of Faust and Mephistopheles and the scenes involving Marguerite, the strophic songs, all taken over from *Huit scènes*, are diegetic; they require music even in a spoken performance. The Serenade of *Huit scènes* could be played on stage, to the accompaniment of a guitar, amplified in *La Damnation* to pizzicato strings. The scenes for Marguerite suggest a character more firmly based in her environment than Faust. She enters with her thoughts disordered, a thread of orchestral melody failing to exert formal control, but as she dismisses her dream the orchestra gathers itself for the phrases anticipated from the Romance; this allows us to hear the strophic ballad, 'Le Roi de Thulé', as a sublimation of her own yearning for an ideal lover.

She and Faust meet ostensibly as equals, but on operatic territory, in music with clear formal subdivisions, territory which Mephistopheles visits only ironically and Faust, otherwise, not at all. Berlioz himself condemned Faust: 'This is not another transcendent *grand amour* like Romeo's, not a Shakespearean love. Faust *condescends* to love Marguerite; he protects her [*sic*]. Romeo raises himself to Juliet's love, she is his equal.'[57] Faust moves more naturally within a supernatural realm, quickly accepting his 'guide infernal' with whom, unlike ordinary people, he can empathize, or thinks he can (calling Mephistopheles 'pauvre démon'—essentially a phrase from Goethe—suggests insensitivity to danger). Faust's sexual urgency prohibits closure in the duet (see Ex. 6.9); his pollution of Marguerite is signified by pollution of the operatic domain, which belongs to ordinary people, but on which the supernatural impinges.[58] With Mephistopheles' entry, the voices

---

[55] See *MLB* 140. [56] On these arias, see *MLB* 234–53. [57] *CG* v. 222; see Ch. 6, n. 36.
[58] In her fascinating discussion, Reeve ('*The Damnation*', 179–83), I think, misunderstands my comment (*MLB* 229) on the operatic domain being Marguerite's rather than Faust's. I did not intend to suggest that she was not his victim. Faust's assumption of an operatic musical style, although within his scope (as Reeve remarks, p. 180), is nevertheless part of a diabolical plot.

lose control to the driving figure in the middle (baritonal, Mephistophelian) register of the orchestra (Ex. 10.4). The duet and two-movement trio have an Italian formal solidity, but in this central section the symphonic appears to take over, as it did in Faust's first two monologues. He fights to restore opera (from bar 57) with a free-flowing melodic line which drifts into conventionality. The best interpretation one can put on the closing 6/8 is that the banality of an operatic ensemble here freezes time to evoke a surreal horror.[59]

Ex. 10.4 *La Damnation de Faust*, Part III (trio; follows Ex. 6.9)
(upper strings omitted)

[59] David Cairns writes: 'Do not accuse *The Damnation of Faust* of gross unnevenness . . . without considering whether Berlioz used banality for dramatic purposes (as I am sure he did in the finale to Part 3).' 'Berlioz and Criticism: Some Surviving Dodos', *Musical Times*, 10 (1963), 550.

Other original features include the anticipations woven into a whole section rather than a recitative. One is the symphonic introduction to Part I. In Part II, 'Voici des roses', 'Chœur de Gnomes et de Sylphes', and 'Ballet des sylphes' form a linked triptych based on a single theme—hardly a symphonic process and incidentally one of many formal achievements which Berlioz disdained to use again; the aria anticipates the chorus, and the delicate waltz is both a reminiscence and an integral prolongation of its last tonic harmony. In Part III, the coda to 'Menuet des follets', an afterthought, transforms the melody of the *next* piece, the Serenade—which, however, has already been heard before Marguerite's entrance.

The most obvious element to distinguish dramatic 'legend' from dramatic 'symphony' is consistent vocal characterization; another—with one exception (see below)—is the absence of external commentary like the *Roméo et Juliette* prologue. Formal fluidity is another; yet another is the exploitation of material from everyday life, to which the nearest approach in *Roméo* is the happy chorus of Capulets, at the start of the love scene, singing a metrically altered reminiscence of the ball music (Ex. 2.1). Part III of *La Damnation* opens with a fanfare, used in No. 7 of *Huit scènes* during the soldiers' chorus. It is repeated in Part IV to symbolize Marguerite's alienation from society, through her sinful love of Faust. Perhaps to assure us that the character overhears this music, Berlioz quoted a traditional fanfare published in 1825.[60] Of course, the signification does not depend on actual quotation, and he could not depend on its being recognized. Mephistopheles hears and comments on the hunting horns in Part IV which accompany Faust signing the pact; they signify not only that Mephistopheles is hunting Faust, but a general indifference of human society, anticipating Auden's sharp observations on tragedy ('Musée des Beaux Arts').[61]

The salvation of Faust

The role of Faust was entirely new in 1846, and he is 'on stage' (as it were) all the time, apart from the street scene in Part III, Marguerite's Romance, and her apotheosis. This quintessentially French Faust continued a tradition established in the 1820s by three translations of Goethe, the superb Delacroix lithographs, and related theatrical enterprises such as Castil-Blaze's *Robin des bois* (based on *Der Freischütz*), Meyerbeer's *Robert le diable*, and Bertin's *Fausto* (Théâtre Italien, 1831), a skilled exercise in an Italian style mingled with the influence of Weber and, perhaps, of Berlioz himself.[62]

What of the fate of this hero, who is self-evidently not Goethe's? Little justifies his reputation as philosopher and scientist, Mephistopheles' epithet 'fier esprit', or the gloating reception in 'Pandemonium'. Reeve's analysis of Faust as a musically defined hero interrogates our received notions of the heroic within nineteenth-century culture, which can encompass a Tristan as well as an Aeneas or Siegfried. She argues cogently that it is wrong to find him 'an unworthy match for his literary model'; elsewhere I have tried to show how his role coheres on the musical level.[63] Mephistopheles' strategy is to render Faust unable to act for himself, but he already finds it difficult to reach any conclusion; his first solo is abandoned in the key of B flat, leaving the orchestra to recover the tonic, D, and his second, arguably the only monologue in which he is in control of the situation, still drifts into recitative, following which he fails to carry through his intended suicide (see Ex. 4.8*a*, *b*). His later solos gain in coherence, but both require orchestral postludes. In 'Merci, doux crépuscule', the postlude includes reminiscences of the aria; it represents his curiosity, as he roams among Marguerite's belongings, and his mingled delight and insecurity. When the orchestra concludes Faust's 'Invocation à la nature' with a new and sombre winding theme and an alienating modal cadence, it suggests the monumental indifference of the phenomena to which he is reaching out for fulfilment: forests, rocks, torrents, the wild and shining world of nature.

---

[60] See NBE 8b. 455.

[61] 'About suffering they were never wrong,|The Old Masters.' W. H. Auden, *Collected Poems* (London: Faber & Faber, 1976), 179.

[62] Bertin uses only one of the scenes published by Berlioz in 1829, the Easter Hymn, where she anticipates *La Damnation* by superimposing the voice of Faust. Several Delacroix lithographs are reproduced in *L'Avant-scène opéra*, 22.

[63] Reeve, '*The Damnation*', 149; *MLB* 228–34.

Equally symbolic of a breakdown of purpose in Part IV is the abandonment of continuity; each movement stands splendidly isolated from its neighbours. An exception to this severe separation is 'Course à l'abîme', completed—but in B major, not its opening C minor—by the first chord of 'Pandemonium', at the moment of Faust's disappearance. The end of *Robert le diable* is a precedent for this extraordinary moment; Bertram goes to hell in B major, and the music is wrenched, rather than modulating, to F major for the heaven-on-earth happy ending, with the church prepared for Robert's wedding. This sequence hardly supports Wagner's epigram, 'effects without cause', and its sources lie in scenic effects Berlioz witnessed in 1828 in the Porte St Martin *Faust*, where a split stage showed heaven and hell. In a concert opera, Berlioz could not combine these opposites, despite the example of Lesueur's *La Mort d'Adam*, nor could even he combine heavenly and hellish music. The split stage, and the problem of its musical representation, surfaced again at the end of *Les Troyens*.

From this point, Berlioz himself seems infirm of purpose, questioning his own title, although in his foreword, he used Faust's damnation to distance himself from Goethe. The 'Epilogue on earth' ('Alors, l'enfer se tut') which separates 'Pandemonium' from heaven is the one passage comparable to the Prologue in *Roméo*, in which the singers comment on, rather than participating within, the action. This belated attempt at a new generic perspective strikes a jarring note, whereas the operatic finale of *Roméo* was anticipated by earlier sections involving choruses of Capulets. That hell should fall silent seems unlikely; and the boiling lakes of flame and grinding teeth were better left to the imagination. Possibly, however, the failure of tone came in 'Pandemonium' itself, which Jacques Barzun compares to a middle-class party in which the devils try 'to romp and be gay', producing 'a hymn to odious desolation . . . Berlioz shows us that Hell is dullness, stupidity, and weakness of will'.[64] One moment of beauty shines through: in 'La course à l'abîme', the solo oboe represents Faust's image of Marguerite's suffering, and within 'Pandemonium' itself, two isolated oboe notes—G♮, the dominant pitch of 'La course', but now in a B major context (bars 14 and 22)—remind us of the cause of Faust's sacrifice at the moment in which Mephistopheles declares his victory.

The demonic triviality of 'Pandemonium' may be appropriate punishment for Faust, but constitutes purgatory rather than damnation. Certainly the angels in Marguerite's apotheosis encourage her to hope: 'Conserve l'espérance, Et souris au bonheur.' Perhaps the angels are only trying to cheer Marguerite up; as Reeve observes, her reception into heaven is accomplished without offering her any choice, at the cost of 'her sexuality, her humanity, her very life', a price expressed in the austere beauty of the orchestral continuum.[65] The cryptic allusion to hope, however, is explained by Berlioz's origi-

---

[64] *Berlioz and the Romantic Century*, i. 494.   [65] Reeve, '*The Damnation*', 166.

nal text, performed before he decided that Part IV was too long, and cut nearly half of 'Pandemonium' and several bars from 'Le ciel'. The omitted text runs: 'L'Éternel te pardonne, et sa vaste clémence Un jour sur Faust aussi peut-être s'étendra.' This can only refer to Goethe's Part II, of which Berlioz was aware (it was published after the composition of *Huit scènes*). What hopes were Marguerite to entertain, if not for Faust's eventual redemption? The cut was surely not made merely to remove these words, as it extends several bars further back; it was surely made in the interests of proportion and musical progression. Twenty bars (hardly Berlioz at the top of his form) were replaced by the present bar 35, and their removal produced the beautiful sequence from B flat minor to D flat major.[66]

La Damnation de Faust is Berlioz's most glitteringly inventive work and his greatest challenge to conventionality, both in its treatment of Faust himself, and in its methods of representation.[67] Contrasting it with Wagner's overture and Liszt's symphony, Hugo Wolf says that 'Berlioz failed to achieve an organic work of art', but continues by calling it 'a fragmentary mosaic, a haphazard structure replete with the most beautiful details, but without a clearly conscious aim'.[68] Unlike some of Berlioz's critics, Wolf was not chauvinistic; he says the same of Schumann's *Faust*. It is hardly self-evident that this subject, any more than Don Juan, is best served by an 'organic work of art'; but it would be idle to deny the generic problem of a 'concert opera'. When performed in the theatre, it seems clearly not to have been designed for the stage, whereas the formality of concert-hall presentation (particularly in evening dress) stultifies emotion and dims the magic. There is an openness about Berlioz's work which suits its theme; its freshness of invention and brilliance of execution may not match Liszt's symphony in fidelity to Goethe and thematic coherence, or Gounod's opera as theatrical entertainment, but it is hardly philistine to find Berlioz's work the most enjoyable of the three.

L'ENFANCE DU CHRIST: ORATORIUM EINER ZUKUNFTSMUSIKER?[69]

Berlioz's generic title is 'Trilogie sacrée', not oratorio; the genre of *L'Enfance du Christ* is not as straightforward as might appear. Like *La Damnation*, it is not meant to be staged, but it includes stage directions. Yet it has seldom aroused controversy, perhaps because, if only by sleight of hand, it contrives to appear homogeneous. This is partly a function of 'tinta', appearing literally as limitation of orchestral colour: after the first scene of Part I (*Le Songe d'Hérode*), the orchestra's fundamental sonority of strings and high woodwind

---

[66] See NBE 8b. 546–9.

[67] For a further overview, see *L'Avant-scène opéra*, 22, the essays by Joseph-Marie Bailbé ('Berlioz et les tentations de Faust', 8–12) and David Cairns ('Le mal d'isolement', 14–17).

[68] *The Music Criticism of Hugo Wolf*, trans. and ed. Henry Pleasants (New York: Holmes & Meier, 1978), 197–201.

[69] Richard Pohl called it 'Oratorio by a Musician of the Future': *Hektor Berlioz: Studien und Erinnerungen* (Leipzig, 1884), 58.

choir is undisturbed by any brass, even horns; timpani fall silent until well into Part III; there is otherwise no percussion. Homogeneity is also obtained through a more consistent interaction of performers and audience. The narrator (solo tenor), who is external to the action, initiates both prologue and epilogue, and his interventions in Parts II (*La Fuite en Egypte*) and III (*L'Arrivée à Saïs*) remind us of the antiquity of events, even of religious belief. This does nothing to blunt the emotional impact of scenes which function on a human, and more nearly operatic, plane.

The overall design of *L'Enfance* is Berlioz's most lucid, balancing symmetry and asymmetry. The 'sacred trilogy' is mirrored by the short central triptych, *La Fuite en Egypte*, with which composition began; within the larger outer parts, the ferocity of Herod matches that of the anti-Semitic inhabitants of Saïs; each part gets under way with a minor-key orchestral fugato. Less symmetrically, the prologue and epilogue are respectively a recitative and unaccompanied chorus; in Part I the 'Marche nocturne' follows the Prologue, and in Part III the fugue turns into a narration. All three parts end with an angelic chorus, heard from afar and singing a Hebrew word, but in Part I the angels have a long speech and 'Hosanna' is ornate, where the other entries are simple to the point of musical attenuation. The chorus plays a variety of roles: in Part I they are soothsayers (men only), while in Parts II and III mixed voices sing the evergreen 'Adieu des bergers' and the more varied music of the Ishmaelite family. In the Epilogue, the chorus joins the narrator as representatives of the present day, while the instruments fall silent.

Silence, indeed, is a major contribution to a sense of *temporal* space, as distinct from the physical space implied in the Requiem. Part I includes a measured seven-bar silence, dividing the opposed scenes of Herod in Jerusalem, and the holy family in Bethlehem (see Ex. 6.4). In Part III, the domestic scene ends by assuring us of the safety of the holy family through the gentlest of F major cadences, pizzicato; the following bars create a stillness suggestive of the passing of ages through isolated string notes, *arco*, each with a fermata and separated by unmeasured silences, reminiscent of Romeo's entrance to the tomb. At a deep structural level the progression is quite simple, moving from the perfect fifth A♭/D♭ by contrary motion to B♭: when this resolves back, the F major chord already seems centuries away from the previous one. Driving the tonality ever flatward, the narrator reminds us of Christ's sacrifice; the last orchestral cadence, in A flat minor with flat (modal) leading-note in the bass, is a sacred equivalent to the cadence in Faust's equally heartfelt 'Invocation à la nature'.[70]

These cross-references with Berlioz's other works are pertinent because the critical success of *L'Enfance* was accompanied by perception of a change in Berlioz's style. Recent criticism tends to accept his refutation of this notion,

---

[70] The tonalities here (A flat minor, E major) appear in the Prologue (bars 8, 15), although it is framed by F minor and C major. Berlioz composed Part I after Part III; in this instance a long-range tonal link may have been intended.

and suggests instead a belated tribute to his pious teacher.[71] However, Lesueur's Old Testament Latin oratorios are poles apart from the methods, style, and intention of *L'Enfance*; his marching shepherds, in *Oratorio de Noël* (No. 5), sing the 'Laudamus' of the Mass, with a Noël added to Lesueur's own merry tune, to make a huge movement out of just eight words; this has no influence on Berlioz's F sharp minor fugue for the same incident (and Lesueur was not capable of Berlioz's rich mixture of fugue and sonata form, in this and the 'Marche nocturne', an atmospheric masterpiece, for all that the title may be derived from Lesueur's *Ossian*). Lesueur's interest in modality is a more general influence. The three fugal introductions all use flattened leading-notes, implying the Aeolian mode, and Herod shows a penchant for the Phrygian flat supertonic. Berlioz always qualifies the modes by functional harmony from the major-minor system, but modality undoubtedly contributes to the work's 'tinta'.

In this, the first of three dramatic works which effectively terminated Berlioz's career, it is clear that he was content to express feelings and situations in formal patterns essentially unchanged over his lifetime. A 'Zukunftsmusiker', like Liszt or Wagner, is on the look-out for new harmonies and ways of presenting ideas; reverence for the past is coupled with practical criticism—and, from Wagner, theoretical criticism. Berlioz's musical language was as personal and original as theirs, but he found new reserves in such traditional patterns as recitative and aria. Indeed, one might argue that unlike Wagner, he simply did not trouble to disguise these rhetorical modes. Recitative is in any case appropriate for a narrator ('récitant'). In the Prologue the orchestra supports the mood of the words more than their details, although it shudders when 'the mighty trembled' (bar 10). The string entry, tremolo, and simultaneous harmonic change from flats to sharps (a♭–E, bar 15) mark the change of rhetorical mode from narrative to exhortation. From bar 21 the tone is allowed to soften, and the accompaniment returns to woodwind, when the narration refers to the divine warning to Christ's parents. The unaccompanied recitative of the two Romans during the March updates *recitativo semplice*, rare in Berlioz, to convey information quickly.

The third recitative, for Herod, is the first that is personally expressive, in the operatic tradition of *recitativo obbligato*. The scene begins with a searing orchestral passage whose primal harmonic upheaval (initially through ascending fifths) is articulated by a short motive, like the forging scene of *Benvenuto Cellini*. The trombones make their first appearance in a sustaining rather than motivic role, but Berlioz omits the horns which were active during the preceding March, an example of his preference for primary rather than blended colours. Herod's aria is generally accepted as among Berlioz's finest, perhaps because it offers insight into a disturbed mind. The verse—'O misère des rois, Régner et ne pas vivre! A tous donner des lois, Et désirer de

---

[71] For instance, Holoman, *Berlioz*, 27.

suivre Le chevrier au fond des bois'—reverts to the improbable pastoral nostalgia of Cellini's 'Sur les monts', but Herod's aria is not as escapist; Berlioz neglects such pastoral markers as the 6/8 metre and Romance texture, which he reserves, along with bird or animal sounds, for the scene in Bethlehem. Berlioz's words place the central affect first and allow it to dominate: Herod's fantasy of escape from himself is real enough for words, but not for music. Few will sympathize with his complaint ('How unhappy I am, being rich and powerful'), but it makes for original musical imagery and an ironic contrast with the Bethlehem scene, in which there are real animals, and life is not easy at all.

The scene begins in F minor with a three-flat signature; the aria drops the A♭, but periodically restores it as a Phrygian flat second. The introduction travels through a tonal sequence compatible with G minor, and prepares a V–i cadence, so the first flat second, in an F minor chord where D major is expected (bar 36), makes a peculiarly gloomy impression just before the vocal entry.[72] Herod himself begins with a Phrygian motive, but the modality of the orchestra is inherently unstable, for the bassoon counterpoint passes through A♮ in the same bar (39; also 41 and 47, and oboe in 49). Herod's thoughts, sleeping and waking, return to the prophetic dream of his overthrow; his struggle to control them takes the form of an aspiration, more searching than the parallel textual conceit about turning goatherd, towards diatonic tonality. He first accepts the extra flats, heading for A flat major (bar 43), but then moves—precisely at 'le chevrier au fond des bois'—to B flat major, where a tonal G minor aria 'ought' to go (bars 53–4). The following passage remains within the norms of a G minor aria: orchestral oscillation (bars 54–6) between the dominant (D major) and B♭, for Herod's plea to the night, and the turn to D minor by way of an augmented sixth (horn: A♭ = G♯), lead to prolonged D minor harmony (bars 62–6). Herod's grand phrases ('O nuit profonde'. . . 'Et que ton voile effleure') restore his high E♭ (67, last heard in 49) and the likely outcome is still B flat major; instead the E♭ is taken as the flat second in D minor for two modal cadences (bars 70, 74). A retransition repeats the orchestral introduction, but in D minor, ending with a regular cadence to bar 83. Herod sings against this passage, intermittently, as if listening; the melody, first boldly sung by cellos but now more plaintive on solo oboe and bassoon, represents his dream, and the throbbing accompaniment is a physiological manifestation of fear, using Berlioz's personal 'fate' motive.[73] Returning to the opening text, Herod again strives to conquer the Phrygian gloom by using his opening phrase in an upward sequence, developed by the orchestra; and he may seem to be overcoming forces hostile to his peace at bars 96–7, when A♭ leads to a chord of G *major*, a tonal promise fulfilled by the C minor implications of bar 98. At the same time, however, the dream motive reappears

---

[72] Bar numbers are taken from NBE 11, counting throughout the scene; the aria begins at bar 27.

[73] See 'Overture' and Ex. 10.5.

(cor anglais, bassoons, horns), without the throbbing accompaniment, but against an inexorably falling bass scale. At last Herod himself sings the dream motive; it has conquered his mind, and at 'interminable nuit' he falls back to the Phrygian cadence of the introduction. In the orchestral postlude the dream motive is heard in yet another instrumental colour, unison upper strings, with three manifestations of terror in the layered accompaniment: tremolo (cellos, basses), the 'fate' rhythm (ominous in trombones), and a measured woodwind trill. Ending with two more Phrygian cadences, the aria banishes the possible comfort of tonality.

The next scene is from the world of opera. Narration of Herod's dream (the motive softly in the clarinet) leads to the cabalistic dance; as the dream is interpreted the motive begins on a solo trombone, but inverted, a rare event in Berlioz. The original form is restored for the third phrase, and the A flat cadence (bar 115) repeats Herod's own cadence (bar 38). This cross-reference confirms the truth of the dream, and its warm sonority may remind the audience that the threat to Herod is God's gift to the righteous; the scene in Bethlehem duly establishes the key of A flat major. Berlioz's dramatic works contain many such economies, but few more potent. The following recitative is a fine example of the musically sinister, closing with three wind instruments alternating major chords of F and A, over a pedal (bars 127–9). The oboe swells like a bagpipe; the flute and clarinet in octaves, both below the oboe, are in their most hollow registers; Weber would have been proud of his disciple.

After the savage chorus, culminating in the brief (optional) appearance of cornets for the final fling of the brass (Ex. 6.5), silence brings us to the beautiful Bethlehem duet (No. 5). This and the familiar numbers of Part II require no further exegesis. Berlioz himself favoured Herod's music, perhaps feeling ashamed of the success of the 'Adieu des bergers', which he improvised during a party.[74] *La Fuite en Egypte* consists of three gems, the most successful with early audiences being 'Le repos de la sainte famille', originally subtitled 'Légende et pantomime' as though Berlioz thought of silent actors playing out the narrative; the setting by an oasis may explain its pastoral references (6/8, occasional Romance texture, measured flute trill and scales like water), but the evocation of benign peace is achieved through simple, unforgettable melodies and clean declamation. The major-mode ending in a new texture (entry of the angelic choir) is more subtly handled than at the end of the Requiem's Offertoire, because wistful alternation of modes permeates the whole movement. No wonder, at this point, that Berlioz concluded he had written a complete work, and published it.

At the opening of Part III the fugal theme of Part II is presented in raw wind colour, and the texture thinly covers a wide range, a musical metaphor for exposure to the elements. In another masterly compression, at bars 112–14, Berlioz presents a theme which we surely hear as related to the fugue

---

[74] See NBE 11, p. x.

theme, with its third and fourth notes reversed (D–G–B♭–A instead of D–G–A–B♭). This proves to be the main theme of the following duet (No. 11), in the implied key, again G minor. The duet itself gains from an almost under-stated character. The violas run their thread of lamentation through sections of dialogue, accompanied by strings, but are silent when Joseph knocks at the doors in Saïs, when the accompaniment is for woodwind. This systematic orchestration becomes deformed at the nadir of the family's fortunes, follow-ing a second rejection by the anti-Semitic inhabitants; tremendous effort is needed to achieve a third and decisive stanza, in which Joseph addresses God directly, at the top of his own vocal tessitura and in A flat and E flat minor (Ex. 10.5). There follows an athematic passage based on Berlioz's fate motive

Ex. 10.5 *L'Enfance du Christ*, Part III, duet

(from bar 173). In recitative accompanied by hollow minor thirds, Joseph persuades the exhausted Mary to raise her voice. The harmonies—diminished sevenths, minor mode, enharmonic modulation—play their part, as does silence, but the music would still be potent if reduced to its rhythmic dimension. This is the only scene in Part III to include timpani; otherwise there are strings and woodwind instruments including a cor anglais, by this date hardly an exotic instrument (although its use as a member of the woodwind choir is as Berliozian as its solo use in Marguerite's Romance was in 1829). When the duet resumes, the viola tessitura reaches an extreme point; the singers require a great effort to reach a continuous motion, unbroken by exhausted pauses; the necessary pitch of desperation is eventually achieved by forcing the key up from F to the repeated G minor cadences.

The paterfamilias emerges—preferably, for verisimilitude, not sung by whoever sang Herod, for his music has the nobility of a traditional French operatic priest. Although he soon reaches his hospitable stride (Allegro in march tempo, No. 12, bar 25), the violas continue their lament as far as bar 63, increasingly within the textural range of the other strings; at bar 45 the violas seem to resolve into the voice part just as it introduces a phrase ('Que de leurs pieds meurtris') which in turn becomes a fugue subject. The animation of the Ishamaelite family is effected by combined simple and compound rhythms, and the ending of this fugue, in harmonic indeterminacy (bar 136), leads to another fugato of Mendelssohnian lightness, during which the young Ishmaelites and their servants prepare food and beds for the refugees. All this is wonderfully touching, and done with the subtlest of musical and dramatic continuity; it is a pity that Berlioz then falls back into explanatory dialogue and chamber music (No. 13, trio for two flutes and harp). Despite many lovely touches in the last domestic chorus (No. 14), notably the woodwind interplay from bar 66 which recalls the Bethlehem duet, it is left to the epilogue to restore an atmosphere in which a wider significance overcomes charm.

Why, to me, is *L'Enfance du Christ* less fascinating than Berlioz's other large-scale works? Its overall plan is among his best, unless we feel the omniscient evangelist presiding over a dramatic presentation is a flaw in Bach's Passions. Besides the sensitive balance of symmetry with asymmetry, thematic integration is handled with unsurpassed delicacy. The questions it raises, but which *La Damnation* or *Les Troyens* avoid, are of tone, and emerge from the details which do not derive from the strictly biblical narrative. The Bethlehem scenes are exquisite descendants of medieval Madonna and Child paintings, untainted by sentimentality. I can swallow the soothsayers: their music broadens Berlioz's range. But would Roman soldiers bring (explicitly) Jewish soothsayers to the Jewish king? Why must they interrupt the wonderful 'Marche nocturne' with piffling detail ('Polydorus! Je te croyais déjà, soldat, aux bords du Tibre')? Berlioz was perhaps thinking of scenes in Shakespeare when we learn something useful, or gain insight, from minor characters, but the narrator has already mentioned Herod's crime, and unlike the sentries' scene in *Les Troyens*, this offers no new viewpoint, has no independent music, and is not even comic. And is not the immaculately crafted salon music, the trio for two flutes and harp, more seriously out of place even than the 'Marche hongroise'? And is not the family where the refugees find shelter, poor but abundantly supplied with milk and grapes, and just happening to be headed by a fellow carpenter, hopelessly cosy? This is not only to carp at Berlioz the dramatist, since the music itself cannot be absolved from matching these situations to perfection; almost throughout, dramatic doubts which I would like to banish are drowned in musical enjoyment. While *L'Enfance du Christ* is the work of an artist increasingly retrospective in mood, and, in the light of contemporary music by Liszt and Wagner, hardly the work of a 'musician of the future', it is still Berlioz the composer at the top of his form, ready to embark on *Les Troyens*.

LES TROYENS, TRAGÉDIE LYRIQUE

For Berlioz, *Les Troyens* was always a single five-act opera, and he adhered to this plan despite its division in performances during his lifetime, and publication for long after.[75] Yet the separation of *La Prise de Troie* (which can well be divided into three acts) and *Les Troyens à Carthage* makes some sense, in dramatic terms as well as those of theatrical practicality, and would have made more had Berlioz added a third opera—*Les Troyens en Italie*, perhaps, for which a French precedent exists, complete with an apparition of Dido's ghost.[76] Dido might have died with dignity, to her own music; the apotheosis of the 'Marche troyenne' could have been reserved for the taking of Latium. But this is a quasi-Wagnerian fantasy; in Paris in the 1850s it was courageous enough to undertake a single work in five acts, contrived to maintain at least a surface resemblance to grand opera. Berlioz displayed some insouciance with respect to market trends in a genre already past its zenith.[77] As with *Benvenuto Cellini*, he placed music first and compressed enough into his five acts for two normal grand operas. Indeed, *Les Troyens* is so alienated from contemporary operatic mores that the best generic description is one already antiquated by the time of Gluck, 'Tragédie lyrique'.[78]

[75] The performances at the Théâtre Lyrique in 1863 were of *Les Troyens à Carthage*. The publisher Choudens never issued the full score, and nearly all vocal scores are divided into two operas.

[76] *Énée et Lavinie*, by Fontenelle, set by Colasse (1690) and Dauvergne (1758). For the subdivision of Act I of *La Prise de Troie*, see NBE 2c. 788–9.

[77] See William L. Croston, *French Grand Opera: An Art and a Business* (1948; repr. New York: Da Capo Press, 1972); Anselm Gerhard, *Die Verstädterung der Oper*, trans. Mary Whittall as *The Urbanization of Opera* (Chicago: Chicago University Press, 1998); and a recent and subtle interpretation of the genre, particularly its visual aspect, Cormac Newark, 'Staging Grand Opéra: History and the Imagination in Nineteenth-Century Paris', D.Phil. thesis (University of Oxford, 1999).

[78] Jean-Michel Brèque, 'La Grande Tragédie lyrique selon Berlioz', *L'Avant-scène opéra*, 32.

At another interpretative level, of spirit rather than genre, *Les Troyens* firmly rejects grand opera. Paul Robinson, in an admirable essay, defines its 'distinctive flavour' through 'its single-minded devotion to an idea . . . *Les Troyens* is a musical embodiment of the Hegelian idea of history', an idea he shrewdly locates in a compositional trait, a contribution to its 'tinta', the activity of the melodic bass-line he calls the 'historical bass'.[79] There is a paradox here, since whereas grand opera can usually be related to an historical event, the story of *Les Troyens* is unfashionably mythological, with scenes and forms which emerged from Berlioz's reading of Virgil, so that for 'authentic' staging, archaeology must replace history. He continued to omit connective plot-tissue, while permitting himself more recitative than in *La Damnation*, and retaining many conventional operatic landmarks such as arias, duets, and larger ensembles, many involving chorus and principals. Nevertheless within these forms he mostly eschewed conventional formulae, for instance in finales.

An unconventional aspect of *Les Troyens* is the close musical connection between discontinuous numbers, and even whole acts, achieved by careful disposition of keys and motives.[80] He begins by an extension of his anticipation technique, since the misplaced rejoicing of the liberated Trojans (No. 1) prepares the motives of Cassandra's doom-laden aria (No. 2). He stages, but also subverts, ritual scenes typical of the operatic grandiose. As the Act I finale, the 'Marche troyenne' passes away to leave Cassandra alone on stage; the act ends in agonized B flat minor, the opening tonality of Act II, in which her prophecies are fulfilled. The destruction of Troy is signalled by tonal instability: the closing key of Act II, C minor, is virtually unprepared and contradicts the one-flat key-signature.[81] Between Acts II and III much time passes before the Trojans reach Carthage, yet the keys are linked (C minor to E flat major), and an arpeggio motive from the second-act finale (bars 252–4) anticipates the opening motive of Act III. The only finale in traditional mould is that of Act III, a mighty ensemble involving the principals, but it ends with a fade-out, signifying the departure of the army, based on the chromatic motive which opens Act IV. At this point, the connective system breaks down. Act IV ends with the most devastating of possible reversals; the close of the love duet in G flat is succeeded by the motives of doom; Mercury summons Aeneas to 'Italie'. The tonality, typically, plunges an enharmonic major third to D, but a moment later the act ends asserting E minor. Continuity is fractured by every possible binary opposition, and there is no link to Act V, which opens in B flat major with the sailor's nostalgic song. The tonal chasm

---

[79] Paul Robinson, 'The Idea of History: Hector Berlioz's *Les Troyens*', in *Opera and Ideas*, 103–54, cited 105, 109, and on the 'historical bass', 125–7.

[80] These points are considered in more detail in 'The musical structure' in Kemp, *Les Troyens*, 119–49, and 'Overture'.

[81] A probable model is the still more extreme ending of Act II of *Der Freischütz*, where Weber abandons his key-signature, implies closure in C minor, and finally dives into F sharp minor.

between these acts represents Aeneas's fateful decision to obey the gods and leave for Italy, and his actual departure is marked by another—B flat major to A minor—before the second tableau, reflecting the shift in perspective from the Trojans to Dido. That such connections have some dramatic meaning is implied when the last two tableaux, which present Dido's tragedy, are tonally linked by a standard dominant to tonic relationship, the A flat of Dido's aria to the C sharp minor of the funeral ceremony, as well as the dactylic 'fate' rhythm.

The numbers into which Berlioz carefully measured out his epic vision grow increasingly meaningless as it proceeds. The first acts to be composed were the first and fourth. In these the number structure is generally secure, as it is for much of Act III, although No. 25 melts into No. 26, the reprise of the 'Marche troyenne' in the minor mode. But Acts II and V become increasingly continuous, at least within their separate tableaux. In Act V, numbers are formed into larger groups through recurring motives; the syncopation from No. 39 (from bar 19) recurs after the sentries' duet to bring Aeneas on stage (No. 41), and Nos. 42–4 are structured by three allusions to the 'Marche troyenne'. In the final tableau, the division into numbers is virtually meaningless. But throughout the five acts, intentionally or otherwise, Berlioz drew disparate scenes together by a network of identifiable allusions and cross-references, covering tonality and tonal progression (notably down a major third/diminished fourth: the first three numbers are in G, E flat, and B), motivic shapes, and motivic rhythms. The 'fate' rhythm already used in *L'Enfance du Christ* (see Ex. 10.5, bar 173) is hammered home at crucial points such as the entry of the ghost of Hector (No. 12, bar 66), and is combined with the reprise of the funeral ceremony within No. 50 (from bar 17). The surging scale which introduces Cassandra is coupled with a Berlioz fingerprint, a dotted rhythm with lower neighbour-note, in her first aria, and thereby anticipates the fall of Troy at the beginning of Act II; in Act IV these elements recur in the free-flowing and expressive middle-register melodies of the Quintet, when Dido fatally yields to her adulterous love, and in Mercury's appearance. In Act III, Ascanius's speech (No. 27) is replete with cross-references, starting with the Carthaginian anthem (bars 1–4). A rerun of the keys in the first part of Act I occurs when Dido cadences in G, Narbal enters with dire news in E flat, and the finale ends in B. Through such features *Les Troyens* attains its greatest originality and vitality, and consistently resists the clichés of grand opera.

The libretto; the characters

Where Berlioz the author of critical prose is usually admired, Berlioz the poet arouses more temperate admiration. In *Les Troyens*, the eighteenth-century origins of his verse style are at least consistent with the Gluckian inspiration of his declamation. Many passages would not seem out of place in post-Racine tragedy, including circumlocution and misplaced epithets. Aeneas enters in the utmost agitation (No. 7) but with sufficient composure to say 'Du peuple et des soldats, O roi, la foule S'enfuit et roule Comme un torrent'; the Trojan generals, equally agitated (No. 39) on seeing the ghost of Hector, add 'dont l'œuil courroucé luit'.[82] But some passages maintain the high standard reached by Faust's 'Invocation' and the Shakespeare-inspired love duet, and there are many carefully crafted lyrics alongside the textual elements which 'are nothing but respect for the conventional'.[83]

The importance of a text for music lies more in its structure than in verbal detail, important though this can be, since the chief mark of identification for an operatic character must be musical. Nevertheless I cannot accept the view that 'in their musical handling, these persons remain more "musical forms", moments of pure music, than individuals taking part in an action', though there might be something to be said for the view that they are less people than aspects of a heroic vision.[84] In so far as his epic intentions determine the detail, it is true that Berlioz's characters are not in control of their destinies. But people caught up in a web of events determined by the will of gods, whose presence is palpable and who occasionally intervene, are still individuals; portraying them in the round, Berlioz achieved models of operatic characterization. The distinction between Cassandra and Dido, whose vocal tessitura is close enough for the roles to be taken by one performer (preferably not on the same night), may seem to break down during Dido's tormented recitative in Act V (No. 46). But this is because the characterizations intersect. Both women are in the grip of impotent fury at what fate has decreed; even so Dido's recitative (No. 46) is markedly less dependent on diminished sevenths than Cassandra's (No. 3), aiming more often, within a tonally fluctuating context, at dominant sevenths and triads. While both women commit suicide nobly, in public, Cassandra does so as part of a collective act, whereas Dido's suicide is enacted very much alone. The ritual context explains the topical similarity in the surrounding music, pointing to a social, rather than personal, connection between these female victims.[85] In more intimate scenes, their most characteristic musical patterns are markedly different; Dido and her court favour 6/8 metre, which Cassandra never uses, and their principal melodic shapes are subtly and consistently differentiated.[86] Within the epic structure, moreover, the women have mutually exclusive aims. Cassandra appears as a ghost in Act V, to urge Aeneas to desert Dido and proceed to Italy, and thus helps bring about Dido's tragedy.

Aeneas is no one's favourite hero; in every treatment of this story, his treatment of Dido appears unforgivable. At least Berlioz's Aeneas, if not forgiven, can be understood; through an accumulated richness of detail, his perplexed

[82] Rushton, 'Berlioz's Roots in 18th-century French Opera', *Berlioz Society Bulletin*, 50 (1965), no. 3; see also A. R. W. James, 'Berlioz the poet?', in Kemp, *Les Troyens*, 67–75.

[83] Ramaut, *Hector Berlioz, compositeur romantique français*, 94.

[84] Ibid. 83–4; see also 101.   [85] On this parallel, see 'Overture', 121.

[86] See Rushton, 'Dido's Monologue and Air', in Kemp, *Les Troyens*, 176–80.

sense of destiny, at war with his own desires, is true to Virgil. But Berlioz's Dido is less obviously the victim of Venus, and more of a generalized *fatum*, than Virgil's. The characterization of Aeneas is achieved by orchestral and vocal, as well as verbal, means.[87] The problems of this role include the difficulty of finding a tenor capable of doing justice both to its heroic, and to its tender, aspects.[88] *Les Troyens* may not be grand opera, but in its emphasis on the voice, it is emphatically operatic—a view at odds with the critical opinion that privileges Berlioz the orchestral, over the vocal, composer.

A fourth characterization, confined to the Trojan acts, bears this out. Choroebus, whose duet with Cassandra (No. 3) is the culmination of the first tableau, brings his own musical qualities to the score. The ebullient syncopations of his personal motive surge up in the last bars of No. 2, and again during No. 3 after Cassandra's 'C'est le temps de mourir, et non pas d'être heureux', to begin a transition to the first of his short arias, the E major 'cavatine' ('Reviens à toi'). The subsequent recitative (from bar 101) is dominated by Cassandra and by a new, violent motive which is eventually regularized as the theme of the formal duet. From bar 165 the motive fades in an atonal chain of diminished sevenths, intensified by dissonant appoggiaturas from the oboe (Ex. 10.6). When Choroebus sings, he associates the chromatic descent with his perception of Cassandra as deranged, and soothingly repeats his cavatina. Even in its first statement, however, the string accompaniment is not as regular as it looks; in the repeat, the oboe persists in its wailing and Cassandra mutters her dissent. The violent motive reappears with aching tenderness (bar 210; its resemblance to the first phrase of the *idée fixe* in *Symphonie fantastique*, emphasized by the pause and *sforzando*, is hard to read meaningfully unless as autobiography). Choroebus responds to Cassandra's calmer plea for him to leave Troy by a new andante ('Mais le ciel et la terre'), a radiant vision as remote from the reality of their situation as its F major is from the main tonal centres of the scene. The disarmingly simple melody is freely developed with a partial reprise, embedded in topical references of some complexity: the peaceful flow of a smooth minuet; the ravishing muted-violin line, which evades categorization as accompaniment, heterophony, or counterpoint; pastoral imagery in the oboe and string trills; and a pedal which supports Berlioz's favourite indirect key-relation, the flat mediant (A♭). Amid the turbulence of the epic scenes, the intimate moments of *Les Troyens* include some of its finest music, quite apart from their function as contrast and sources of insight into the characters whom tragedy is about to destroy; and without such insight, there is no tragedy, only disaster.

When a male character is characterized through lyricism, and a female through vehement recitative, the inversion of nineteenth-century norms is palpable. Merely to join them in a duet is unlikely to reconcile them.

---

[87] Lensky, 'Characterization in the Dramatic Works of Hector Berlioz', 177–219.

[88] Robinson makes this point: *Opera and Ideas*, 103. See also Joël-Marie Fauquet, 'Vienne une Cassandre, vienne une Didon', *L'Avant-scène opéra*, 137–42.

Ex. 10.6 *Les Troyens*, Act I (No. 3), from bar 165

Cassandra's prophecies, while true, are fated not to be believed, and the duet has the delicate task of conveying this without antagonism between these affianced lovers, whose objective is one another's happiness and safety. All the preceding measured music ('Malheureux roi', 'Reviens à toi', 'Mais le ciel et la terre'), is in 3/4, in slow to medium tempos; the recitative which introduced the theme shown in Ex. 10.6 (from bar 101), and the duet itself, based on the same theme, are also in 3/4, but Allegro. The tonality lies as far as possible from 'Mais le ciel' (B from F), but is the key of Choroebus's entrance, and close to the E major of 'Reviens à toi'. The form of the ensemble is strophic, which hardly suits Cassandra at all. Thus the fiery B major of Choroebus's entrance (although in 4/4) and the recurrence of his motive after the third strophe (bar 379) and in the coda (bar 505) might suggest that the duet takes place on his ground; and in that last recitative Cassandra admits partial defeat ('A tant de douleurs je succombe!'). But she leads the duet; it uses her theme; in the second strophe, Choroebus imitates her music. She succumbs only to the realization that she will never get through to him; her gory vision of his death is true, and further words are pointless. In the duet, therefore, she takes control of his ground, talking a language he might understand. When he does not, in the fourth stanza, she accepts the inevitable, although she nearly destroys the duet in doing so, in two phrases which seem intended to resolve in a remote region, probably C minor (the 'pun' partner of B major), at 'à ton funeste amour', bars 465–8; but the orchestra does not follow her. The late-flowering of the home dominant, F sharp major, at her capitulation to destiny ('Eh bien! violà ma main'), is bitterly ironic, given its erotic connotation elsewhere in Berlioz. One assumes that Choroebus ('Viens, viens!', the words of Faust seducing Marguerite) will take the suggestion of their dying together metaphorically.

Ritual, romance, and tragedy

The rest of Act I mainly unfolds as a ritual, unprecedented in its wealth of musical colour. Berlioz's determination to achieve the 'historical' accuracy of grand opera led him to fill the libretto with classical and mythological allusions, placing a Proustian value on place-names; the antique sistrum (No. 4), the entirely modern saxhorns, and the third ballet in Act IV (see Chapter 6), follow at a distance the preoccupation of musicians under the French revolution with antique brass and percussion.[89] Berlioz was a master of the *cortège*, of which No. 4 ('Marche et Hymne') is a splendid example.[90] But percussion colour takes second place, in assessing its impact, to its harmonic vagaries: never far from its melodic and harmonic centre, C, it mixes major and minor and their relations while tonicizing at least nine pitches. The opening move to a D flat chord brings closure on A flat as early as bar 9; C is heard as V/F minor (bar 19) and tonic (bar 23); the next cadence is E minor (bar 33). The middle section is more fluid and less prone to cadence, but the grandiose chord-progression e–C–d–B♭ ('Dieu de l'Olympe, Dieu des mers!') is followed by a reference to G minor (bars 48–50), then by a sequence to a G flat cadence (bar 58). Another sequence returns to C as V/F minor (from 65). Enharmonic treatment of D♭ as C♯ (bars 71–3) pulls the music back for a reprise; 'Dieu de l'Olympe' begins a fourth higher (bar 103), but is varied and extended in the progression a–F–D–b–G, finally reaching the home dominant.

Ritual wrestling (No. 5) abruptly gives way to a funeral rite. Andromache's mime is both slow march and an aria for clarinet, interrupted by another brass-and-percussion-based ritual, in which Priam and Hecuba bless their grandson, and hardly disturbed by Cassandra's intervention (which includes, from bar 81, the oboe wailing from Ex. 10.6). Evidently we are witnessing a well-planned series of tableaux, to be completed by another joyous cortège, but it is rudely fractured. The scene with the Greek spy Sinon breaks the rigid structure of dramatically static musical numbers, but consists of the plot-filling Berlioz was usually anxious to avoid. It was later omitted. The scene adds to the catalogue of associations between disaster and B flat minor (bar 24: 'death!'), and from bar 119 introduces a sinuous bass-line which is not only part of the opera's historical 'tinta' but anticipates the representation of serpents in No. 7; otherwise it is surprisingly free of cross-references. Moreover it shows Priam taking the lead by ordering the destruction of the Scaean gate to admit the wooden horse, and his rejection, face to face, of Cassandra's advice.[91]

The disruption following the Andromache scene was originally marked by tonal disorientation: No. 6 modulates from A minor to F sharp minor, and the Sinon scene takes off from E minor. No. 7, however, Aeneas's shocked and shocking announcement of the death of Laocoon, reverses the keys of No. 6, starting in F sharp minor and ending in A major; the octet ('Châtiment effroyable') in F sharp minor rounds off a group of three numbers which

---

[89] See the glossary of names and catalogue of 'antique and obsolete instruments' in Kemp, *Les Troyens*, 196–212; David Charlton, 'New Sounds for Old: Tam-tam, Tuba curva, Buccin', *Soundings*, 3 (1973), 39–47.

[90] See Guiomar, *Le Masque et le fantasme*, on cortèges, from 319; see also Ramaut, *Berlioz, compositeur romantique français*, 33.

[91] This scene is sometimes restored in modern performances, including Dutoit's recording (Decca 443 693-2), orchestrated by Hugh Macdonald; the surviving score is in NBE 1c. 875–86. Berlioz did not entirely succeed in removing allusions to it; Aeneas in No. 9 blames Pallas Athene for the death of Laocoon, an explanation which emerges from Sinon's story.

Berlioz did not design, but which results from cutting the Sinon scene. For the octet, perhaps in emulation of his own 'Judex crederis', Berlioz wrote a fugue in which the subject systematically ends a tone lower, to reach C minor in bar 31 (the fugue subject itself, in F sharp, climaxes on a G♮ supported by a fully orchestrated chord of C major). The sublime is not a common feature of grand opera, but Berlioz wasted none of his experience in achieving it here. The role of Cassandra stands out as the ensemble winds to its grim conclusion, and in No. 9 she cuts through the climax of misplaced delight, perfectly illustrating Guiomar's 'aesthetic of the cry' as 'a break within the context'.[92]

Cassandra's lament (No. 10) intrudes on the ritual, and for an aria it is short and peculiarly disorganized, reflecting her inability to control the inevitable tragedy. It reaches no kind of closure and spills over into No. 11, the grand finale with 'Marche troyenne'. The first distant fanfare is answered by the strings, unmistakably, with the 'death motive', repeated in bars 62–3 (Cassandra: 'L'ennemi vient et la ville est ouverte!').[93] There are precedents for this finale; in Cherubini's *Médée*, the heroine raves at Jason's wedding cortège, and Berlioz was impressed by the grand marches in Spontini's *Olympie* and Meyerbeer's *Le Prophète*. Berlioz's way of uniting three groups of stage instruments (two of brass, peripatetic; one of oboes and harps, stationary), then disrupting them, recalls the central finale of *Don Giovanni*. Yet he contrives to be original. Even if we ignore Cassandra and the tearing orchestral gestures which support her against the crowd, the interlocking thematic units performed by the cortège of chorus and stage instruments never fully cohere.

The exposition (approach) is given to the first brass group, with half the chorus. It includes the main theme A (see Ex. 6.1); a hymn-like motive (B, bar 29) which does not recur; a secondary march motive (A', bar 50); and its important sequel (C, bar 62). The first reprise of A marks a preliminary climax (bar 74), with the tentative addition of the second brass group; a formal unit closes at bar 86. In what could be considered the 'trio' section, the oboe and harp group takes over (bar 87). Its pastoral drone, already used in No. 1, accompanies the chorus in a G minor melody (D, which shares figures with C); the first band accompanies. The second band, which so far has made little impact, intervenes coarsely (bar 100); oboes and chorus accept its modulation to F and continue unperturbed, to the second band's 'oompah' accompaniment and joyous whoops from the first band. At bar 115, the massed forces are all on stage and the second band presents a more concise but complete formal unit bounded by theme A, in which the central part is mingled with the 'trio' material, now accompanying theme C (to which the

---

[92] 'le cri est discontinu sur le contexte', *Le Masque et le fantasme*, 176. Guiomar classifies cries as expression of internal fantasy; external-sounding menace (including the diabolic); cry of the witness to the universe (Cassandra) and of the universe to the witness; ambiguous or polyreferential cries (ibid., 165–6).

[93] See Ch. 6 n. 4.

second band adds its oompah). The return to A (bar 141) is heralded by the first band, and this formal unit is closed when the second band leaves the stage (bar 151). From here, the material continues in a more desultory sequence, without returning to the opening theme. If the wooden horse has appeared (at *c*.bar 115), it should now be leaving the stage.[94] As chorus and oboes take up theme C again, the people with the horse hear a clash of armour from inside; the march stops; but Cassandra's hopes are dashed by the moronic cry 'présage heureux', and the procession moves on. The chorus and second band, now off-stage, have a new motive ('Fiers sommets de Pergame', bar 168), albeit one easily related to the others. The first band fades into the distance with A1 and C. This is not the sustained and exhilarating confusion of the finale to Part II of *La Damnation*; the march's brilliance is finally kept at an ironic arm's length. The focus is on Cassandra, who ends the act with a storm of despair.

Act II explodes ritual, and with it musical formality, but the destruction is again distanced, perceived at first through Aeneas's window. The musical imagery suffices; disaster has never been more effectively made musical (not even by Wagner, whose calamities always contain the seeds of redemption). Ascanius scurries about, fearing to wake his father, to whom Hector's ghost speaks in a sepulchral chromatic descent, another wonderful application of systematic composition to a theatrical situation. Pantheus and others burst in; Ascanius returns, his previous music miraculously transformed in the new context (compare p. 226 of the score, from bar 60, with p. 209, bars 37–9); Choroebus's arrival wrenches the tonality to A minor from F. Aeneas defies Hector, who has told him to escape, by going into battle, first leading a brief ensemble with a phrase of strenuous tessitura and pitch dislocation (within B flat major, G♭, F♯, G♮, with bass B♮), which breaks through by resolving the melodic pitches (G♮, G♭, F) in a phrase simple—indeed, banal—enough for everyone to take up the Virgilian cry: 'Le salut des vaincus est de n'en plus attendre!' The still centre of the act, the prayer in Locrian mode, prepares for bereaved Cassandra's entrance; she too takes the lead, but in mass suicide, made convincing by the ecstatic choral apotheosis ('Complices de sa gloire')—like the end of Part III of *La Damnation*, a passage in which Berlioz's dramatic requirements triumphantly overcome the risk of banality. The machinery of grand opera can offer nothing at once so harrowing and so elevating as this short second act.

To pass from Troy to Carthage is to leave romantic chaos for classical order. Rather than Napoleon III, Dido's court contains memories of Charles X, whose coronation in 1825, of which Berlioz must have heard reports from Lesueur, was castigated by Chateaubriand as bad theatre; it evoked the *ancien régime* image, here peculiarly perverted, of a king 'beneficently receiv-

---

[94] Berlioz finally decided that the horse should remain unseen. On this see Kemp's analysis, from which I differ in identifying only one section as a formal 'trio': *Les Troyens*, 157–61.

ing the arts, agriculture and commerce into his care'.[95] Superficially the first scene restores the comfort of ritual, but numerous details limn the personality, at once noble and nervous, of the Queen, and the fragility of her empire. Her first recitative closes in B flat (317/25), and strings pick up the key of G flat from nowhere in a scurrying figure reminiscent of Ascanius, syncopated when not in semiquavers. There is no need for stage business here, but it sets the equivocal mood of the aria ('Chers Tyriens') in which it continues as a plaintive commentary (see Ex. 4.1b). The anthem glows with confidence, but the tiny and fascinating ballet movements are more equivocal; No. 20 (building-workers) fades away, No. 21 (sailors) punctuates, with eerie flickers from two piccolos, a melody which might hardly float, were it not syncopated, and No. 22 (field-workers), led by a 'robust old man', is an exquisite pastorale with more than a hint of melancholy.

The lyrical part of the duet (No. 24) is led by Anna, but throughout it there runs an orchestral thread, mainly in the violins, which continually harps on the motive which opens the scene, and traces the inner thoughts of Dido; its contour inverts a passage in 'Chers Tyriens' (compare 319/48 with 365/1). By the time Dido has prepared to receive the Trojans in her second air ('Errante sur les mers', see Ex. 7.6), the portrait is complete; her justifiable fury in Act V, with its stylistic cross-reference to Cassandra, affects us so powerfully because it seems to depart from a hitherto almost saintly character. It is in Act IV that Dido appears most fulfilled. Once past the solos for Anna and Narbal, repeated in a somewhat artificial combination (especially as Anna's air is barely half the length of Narbal's), this is one of the loveliest acts in all opera, Berlioz's response to Act II of his beloved Gluck's *Orfeo*. It unrolls in discrete movements, connected with minimal recitative and a brief formal narrative, Aeneas's comment on the fate of Andromache, which is also Dido's cue to accept, in the quintet, that a widow may remarry. The septet is among Berlioz's most delicate miniatures, doubly systematic, with its upper pedal and intermediate sound, like waves gently breaking.[96] This collective response to a night whose beauty is essentially a musical creation is sensitively linked to the love duet (see Chapter 6), and the act could end as an unblemished idyll, the epic forgotten, were it not for the shattering entrance of Mercury.

Mercury prepares us for a final act with a new and tragic musical ambience, moving in generally faster tempos; two arias in 6/8 evoke the atmosphere of Act IV like reflections in a broken mirror. This is the only act to fall into three tableaux. The first two are structured towards the great aria of departure for Aeneas, and Dido's simpler aria of resignation; the third tableau is virtually a

---

[95] Benjamin Walton, '"Quelque peu théâtral": the Coronation of Charles X', in 'Romanticisms and Nationalisms in Restoration France', Ph.D. thesis (University of California (Berkeley), forthcoming). The opening of the Carthaginian anthem 'Gloire à Didon' resembles one of Lesueur's many settings of 'Domine salvum fac regem'.

[96] See *MLB* 138.

continuous finale, although Berlioz divided it into four numbers. The heart-broken nostalgia of the sailor Hylas and the comic duet of sentries, like the poem of the love duet, are tributes to Shakespeare, viewing great events through the eyes of common humanity, which suffers, sometimes stoically, often with humour. Aeneas's aria is a show-stopper, rather unfortunately as its grandiose A flat major conclusion should audibly be juxtaposed to the low D♮ which introduces the Trojan ghosts (another tribute to Shakespeare: *Richard III*).[97] The duet for Dido and Aeneas was an afterthought, intruding on a magnificent farewell which he can only utter in her absence; confronted with her, he is tongue-tied, at least musically (perhaps Berlioz did not wish to let him off too lightly). This duet ('Errante sur tes pas') marks the lovers' complete breakdown in mutual understanding by progressive deformation towards recitative.

Dido, deserted, deserves some of the finest music in mid-century opera, beginning with the mourning cellos of the A minor ensemble which opens the second tableau. After her frenzied recitative, culminating in the wordless cries she emits when alone, Dido's monologue forms a masterpiece of Gluckian pathos. In the aria ('Adieu, fière cité') her serene acceptance of destiny generates a haunting line which is nevertheless modelled closely on the text. As so often in Berlioz's highest pathos, the accompaniment is centred on woodwind with a plaintive string commentary, this time for violas. Dido is beyond despair. As she enters the ritual in the final tableau she claims, haltingly, to be calm (728/15), and the orchestra does not gainsay her, as Gluck's does in *Iphigénie en Tauride*.[98] Instead the brass adds the fate rhythm to the melody of the preceding ritual procession (No. 49, 'Cérémonie funèbre'). With her prophecy, the choral outbursts, and her death, the music can only match the action; to impose order would be to mitigate the Carthaginian disaster. The anathema pronounced upon the race of Aeneas hits a characteristic flat seventh (A♭, No. 52 bar 10), but since the Trojan March itself promptly follows its usual harmonic course, from B flat to A flat, the chorus is mocked, and its curse degenerates into an exuberant counterpoint as the march swings jauntily into its melodies D and A. The march was promisingly developed before Aeneas's departure (from 645/4), but its raw reprise in the final scene, overwhelming Dido's death, is not so much perfunctory as cruel. While music (and scenery) proclaim the glory of Rome, the hearts and minds of the listeners will be with Dido. Berlioz built this tragic paradox into his ending, rather than concluding with the death-shudder he risked in *Cléopâtre*, to maintain his epic-historical vision. But he knew modern Rome; he had walked among its ruins. Reading this scene in its political context, and that of grand opera,

---

[97] Roger Savage, 'Dido dies again', in Michael Burden (ed.), *A Woman Scorn'd: Responses to the Dido Myth* (London: Faber & Faber, 1998), 28. The Andante of the aria is analysed in *MLB* 159–65.

[98] The scene where Orestes claims 'Le calme rentre dans mon cœur', but the stabbing viola rhythm contradicts him.

Anselm Gerhard asserts that Berlioz had in mind the newly established and—for the moment—brilliant empire of Napoleon III.[99] But the hollow orchestral triumph over Dido's dying voice also conveys the ironic message that no empire lasts for ever.

[99] Gerhard, *The Urbanization of Opera*, 397–9.

Postscript

BÉATRICE ET BÉNÉDICT

Berlioz had abandoned major compositional ambitions both before and after *Les Troyens*. Yet, in his last years, he experienced remission of a debilitating illness only when musically active; he might have been expected to go on composing, if only trifles, as therapy. An opera on *Much Ado about Nothing* without the main plot might appear to epitomize the trifling, but it fulfilled a long-standing ambition to make something out of Shakespeare's comedy, stimulated by the scintillating war of words between the title-roles. It may seem odd that Berlioz was not attracted to the supremely operatic Don John plot, Claudio's renunciation of Hero, and the vengeful alliance of Beatrice and Benedick; one earlier plan changed all the characters except these two.[1] One might regret a real *Much Ado* opera by Berlioz, just as one might regret his *Antony and Cleopatra*, but it is better to develop our understanding of what we have.

Taken on its own terms, *Béatrice et Bénédict* is as enjoyable and satisfying as any of Berlioz's major works. The inspiration familiar to audiences from its overture (the only late Berlioz in many conductors' repertoire) wells up in several fast numbers (Nos. 5 and 7 in Act I, 9 and 15 in Act II), although the final duet feels underdeveloped given the overture's resourceful treatment of its theme. There are many charming comic touches—in the music, as well as the dialogue, largely a translation of Shakespeare—to which Berlioz added the heavier comedy of Kapellmeister Somarone. His 'grotesque epithalamium' (No. 6) is Berlioz's last diatribe against the abuse of fugue, and his drinking song satirizes another overrated genre. Hero and Claudio remain, but there is no potential tragedy, and Claudio has no independent musical personality. Besides her striking double aria, Hero is heard in the delicate Nocturne, which might be compared with the two 6/8 duets in *Les Troyens* (part of the duet for Anna and Dido, texturally similar to the Nocturne, and

---

[1] NBE 3. 299–300; see also Rushton, 'Berlioz's Swan-Song: Towards a Criticism of *Béatrice et Bénédict*'.

339

the love duet). But the most remarkable aspect of these beautiful passages is their dissimilarity: none would fit the context of another.

Berlioz's comic gift was already apparent in *Benvenuto Cellini*. *Béatrice* is less ambitious in the scope of its ensembles, but more pointed, and the comedy is not without shadows. The first duet between Beatrice and Benedick (No. 4) is elegant, but slows their raillery, better suited to the electric tempo of No. 15 in which it has a new context, marriage; the best part of No. 4 is the final allegro, sung aside. The greatest numbers are the two trios, which mark Berlioz's most advanced contemplation of the polarity of male and female. For the other men, Benedick's objections to marriage are a joke; the rattling dialogue, mock solemnity, and patter-singing of the G major trio in Act I (No. 5) are worthy to rank with the masterpieces of Italian *opera buffa*. The opera was first completed early in 1862; Marie Berlioz died in June. After the première (August 1862), Berlioz inserted the A flat major trio for the women into Act II. The situation does not correspond to that of Act I; unlike Benedick, Beatrice joins this trio after being told of Benedick's love for her. Hero and Ursula tease Beatrice, who is not yet openly 'converted' to marriage. Their gentler raillery and Beatrice's agitated response do more than make clear, if her formidable aria did not, that she loves Benedick; Hero's apology (for such it appears to be, from the music rather than the words) is the epitome of sisterly tenderness. Many musical, as well as verbal, signals, suggest that Berlioz, however he may be considered to have behaved to his two wives in their lifetimes, now paid them tribute by emphasizing how much greater, in marriage, is the price paid by the female.[2] Coinciding with the end of his servitude in journalism, *Béatrice et Bénédict* is not an unfitting end to his greatness.

POSTERITY

Tom Wotton, in his perceptive Berlioz study, suggested that '*The Trojans* is Berlioz's finest work, though the *Te Deum* (containing perhaps his grandest number) runs it close'.[3] This view may appear as eccentric today as it probably did in 1935, or would have done in 1860, yet it raises serious points about critical reception. Berlioz's impact on other composers comes mainly from his symphonies, including the partly vocal *Roméo et Juliette*, ancestor of Franck's *Psyché*, for all its post-Wagnerian eroticism. *Harold en Italie* spawned Tchaikovsky's *Manfred* and Rimsky-Korsakov's *Antar*, despite the latter's insistence that his work was a suite, whereas *Symphonie fantastique* and *Harold* were 'incontestable symphonies'.[4] *Symphonie fantastique*, virtually quoted at the start of the 'Mephistopheles' movement in Liszt's *Faust Symphony*, has an assured place in the history of the programmatic invasion

---

[2] This matter is more fully discussed in 'Berlioz's Swan-Song'.

[3] Wotton, *Hector Berlioz*, 151.

[4] N. A. Rimsky-Korsakov, *My Musical Life* (New York: Knopf, 1923, repr. London: Eulenburg, 1974), 92.

of the concert repertoire by the theatrical and the subjective. The repertoire of concert overtures and symphonic poems, in which the orchestra speaks with its own voice, has Berliozian ancestry, as does the legion of later composers who think orchestrally, in mixed and layered timbres, rather than colourfully 'orchestrating' something fully articulate in monochrome.

Although his openly dramatic works have artistic progeny, they are usually perceived as relatively conventional in form, and even *Les Troyens* has never been considered as essential as *Symphonie fantastique* within historical overviews of the period.[5] Cornelius's *Der Barbier von Bagdad*, which contributed to Liszt's downfall in Weimar, was the work of Berlioz's faithful translator; its pale exoticism suggests Félicien David, but its witty ensembles bespeak an acolyte of *Benvenuto Cellini*. Donald J. Grout suggests that Ernest Reyer's *Sigurd* is modelled on *Les Troyens*.[6] Otherwise Berlioz's dramatic works receive discriminating praise, rather than claims for canonical status, although *La Damnation de Faust* has been among his best-known works since the 1870s. Berlioz's concentration of drama into tableaux, omitting musically uninspiring connections, affected Musorgsky, who once called him music's 'super-thinker', and Rimsky-Korsakov, though he found Berlioz 'unusual, "dishevelled" and, in any event, far from technically perfect'; his reputation in late nineteenth-century Russia riled Stravinsky.[7] Richard Strauss listed *Les Troyens* and *Benvenuto Cellini* among operas to be included in an ideal repertoire, and *L'Enfance du Christ*, a favourite work of Elgar, influenced Tippett in designing *A Child of our Time*.[8] The French opera composers of the next generation—Saint-Saëns, Bizet, Massenet—may have owed more to Berlioz's general example than to his actual works. The finest pages in the title-role of Gounod's *Faust* contain reminiscences of Berlioz's conception of the role, and his *Roméo et Juliette* sets the prologue in choral recitative, less austerely than Berlioz, but surely a direct tribute.[9] Berlioz, standing for independent forms and lively coloration, was a bold alternative for younger composers to the senior composers who took more conventional operatic paths—Auber, Halévy, Thomas. But these younger composers also assimilated such foreign invaders as Meyerbeer, Donizetti, Verdi, and eventually Wagner. This grafting of materials into a thoroughly French eclecticism was nothing new—Berlioz himself assimilated the residue of earlier invasions, from Gluck and Spontini—

[5] Exceptions are the space devoted to *Les Troyens* by Donald J. Grout in *A Short History of Opera* (New York: Columbia University Press, 1947), 318–23, and by Georg Knepler in *Musikgeschichte des 19tes Jahrhunderts* (Berlin: Henschelverlag, 1961), 290–315.

[6] Grout, *Short History*, 414–15.

[7] Alexandra Orlova, *Musorgsky's Days and Works: A Biography in Documents* (Ann Arbor: UMI Research Press, 1983), 282; Rimsky-Korsakov, *My Musical Life*, 124; Igor Stravinsky and Robert Craft, *Conversations with Igor Stravinsky* (London: Faber & Faber, 1959), 28–9.

[8] Michael Kennedy, *Richard Strauss: Man, Musician, Enigma* (Cambridge: Cambridge University Press, 1999), 366, and *Portrait of Elgar* (3rd edn., Oxford: Clarendon Press, 1987), 68; Ian Kemp: *Tippett, the Composer and his Music* (London: Eulenburg, 1984), 150.

[9] On Gounod's *Roméo* prologue, see Steven Huebner, *The Operas of Charles Gounod* (Oxford: Oxford University Press, 1990), 155.

but it distanced these composers from the primary colours of Berlioz's orchestra, and the neo-classic sensibility which increasingly preoccupied him.

A later generation yet, including Debussy whose attitude to Berlioz was at best ambivalent, continued to benefit from Berlioz's romantic idealism: his uncompromising search for forms peculiar to his subject or artistic aim, his equally uncompromising high-mindedness, and his gestural and colouristic rhetoric.[10] While people continued to regard Berlioz as an under-trained composer, unable to write coherent harmony which would work in 'black and white', transcribed for piano, his idealism could still be perceived as a noble eccentricity, an example to relish out of the classroom, although others fatuously declared him 'not a musician'. The idealism of his greatest works is marked by their generic eccentricity; Berlioz worked out schemes for his own works without conforming to traditional, or audience, expectations. If Wagner referred to Berlioz's 'Faust symphony' and Debussy, reviewing a staged version of *La Damnation*, to the 'music for *Roméo et Juliette*', as if it were incidental, we should not be surprised.[11]

One might put such difficulties in reception down to Berlioz's impractical idealism. It should perhaps be added, therefore, that the main element of impracticality is conceptual. On the technical level, there is little that is impractical even in his most demanding scores. As a chorus singer and percussionist, he experienced the wrong end of the stick before becoming a conductor, and he learned the craft of musical direction with the perfectionism he seems to have put into all his undertakings, including journalism and his ventures into theatrical poetry. In *Les Francs-juges* and *Benvenuto Cellini* the most impractical element is the libretto. As his own librettist, Berlioz became more practical, the scenic ambitions of *Les Troyens* notwithstanding; he aided the integration of the visual and musical by poetry which may be old-fashioned, but is thoroughly fitted for music. His fury at cuts in *Les Troyens à Carthage* imposed by the Théâtre Lyrique was surely fuelled by the implied slight to his professionalism.

Critical evaluation should not be brushed off with a *de gustibus non est disputandum*, although there will always be those who dislike Berlioz—or Mahler, Vaughan Williams, and others with marked individuality and high ideals; there exist people who dislike Bach and Mozart. More puzzling than blanket incomprehension are highly partial views of his output, and of his career as a whole. Wotton's preferences may be compared to this conclusion: 'With *Symphonie fantastique*, Berlioz created a work which has to overshadow all his later compositions.'[12] The reputation of this symphony

[10] See *Debussy on Music: The Critical Writings*, collected and introduced by François Lesure, ed. and trans. Richard Langham Smith (Ithaca, NY: Cornell University Press, 1977), 67–8.

[11] *Selected Letters of Richard Wagner*, trans. and ed. Stewart Spencer and Barry Millington (London: Dent, 1987), 268. *Debussy on Music*, 193.

[12] Berger, *Phantastik als Konstruktion*, 190; it is his final sentence. ('Berlioz hat mit der "Symphonie fantastique" ein Werk geschaffen, das alle seine späteren Kompositionen überschatten musste.')

certainly exceeds that of anything else Berlioz composed; and he may never have surpassed its purely musical originality. Nevertheless, it remains a work of brilliant youth, rather than a mature masterpiece. With due deference to *Harold, Benvenuto*, and the Requiem, I think it would be truer to suggest that Berlioz reached the height of his powers in *Roméo et Juliette*, a conceptually problematic work in which many people have located his greatest music: it is his *Idomeneo*, his *Fidelio*, his *Euryanthe*. After *Roméo*, Berlioz did not experience any creative decline; the evidence of his manuscripts, even of later works which he performed frequently, suggests increased mastery of material, with *L'Enfance du Christ* and *Béatrice et Bénédict* remarkably free of indecisiveness and revision; these works may represent a reduction in ambition, not in achievement. Yet Wolfgang Dömling also privileges the instrumental music, denying Berlioz's vocal works equivalent standing: 'The cardinal point of Berlioz's output is the new conception of the symphony; the symphonic works, which at the same time are dramatic, stand as signposts of his creativity—despite the Requiem, despite *Benvenuto Cellini* and *Les Troyens*.'[13] 'Signpost', where 'foundation' would be uncontroversial, privileges that singularity, also isolated by Rudolf Bockholdt, in which Berlioz most resists classification adjacent to Austro-German musical traditions. One might be tempted to postulate a modern German view of Berlioz, inflected by differences of language, culture, and a preference virtually unchanged since Schumann for 'abstract' music; only Berlioz's perceived emphasis on contrast and effect, which for most of the previous century and a half was read negatively, is now read positively.[14] Dömling asks rhetorically 'Did Berlioz really want to become an opera composer?' and strives to answer 'no'.[15] But the weight of evidence is against him, from the 1820s to the end when, having suppressed a symphony in the early 1850s because of the cost of mounting performances, he nevertheless risked money to perform a dramatic work, *L'Enfance du Christ*, and wrote his last two operas when he did not need, other than from artistic necessity, to write anything at all.

French discourse about Berlioz's music tends towards philosophical meditation, and interpretation of Berlioz as a man of letters, but writers such as Michel Guiomar and the French contributors to *L'Avant-scène opéra* give the large vocal works their due (hardly anybody gives Berlioz's smaller works their due, except for *Les Nuits d'été*). Anglo-American scholarship has taken the lead in biographical research and in editing Berlioz's scores, although the New Berlioz Edition is published from Germany, and in ridding us of misconceptions—although my sifting of indexes and ephemeral publications

---

[13] 'Der Angelpunkt in Berlioz' Oeuvre ist der neue Begriff von "Symphonie"; die symphonischen Werke, die zugleich dramatische sind, stellen die Wegmarken in seinem Schaffen dar—trotz *Requiem*, trotz *Benvenuto Cellini* und der *Troyens*.' Dömling, *Zeit*, 238.

[14] Dömling, *Zeit, passim*; the section on critical history (129–49) is a useful summary. On Bockholdt, see *MLB* 24–5; elsewhere in *Berlioz-Studien* he deals sensitively with word–music issues.

[15] Dömling, *Zeit*, 126.

(such as notes with recordings) confirms a strikingly high error-count in comments made in passing on Berlioz's life and music (he would not have been surprised).[16] Common to these musicological traditions is the aim of musical and dramatic understanding of Berlioz's work, and of the contexts in which it was created. Contextual understanding is initially served by biographies and interdisciplinary studies, while much light on Berlioz's musical world comes from the recent musicological interest in grand opera, and on Berlioz's journalism.[17] Contextual studies have been a primary focus of recent musicology, if not of this book. Nevertheless, it seems appropriate to conclude by addressing, if not answering, a pair of questions which bear on interpretation of his entire life and output.

BERLIOZ CONSERVATIVE OR RADICAL? SUCCESS OR FAILURE?

Present-day Berlioz studies vary between interpretation of his career as a triumph or a disaster, just as critical assessments of the music divide on whether he is best represented as a progressive or a conservative figure. The view of his career as something triumphant requires rejection of Berlioz's self-image, particularly in the later stages of the *Memoirs*, which can be read as embittered special pleading, subject to correction through sceptical historical investigation of documents; and these in turn can lead to unexpected confirmation of his centrality in Parisian musical life. His concert-giving activities over a long period are certainly impressive, both in self-promoted and national events. Additional positive factors are his reputation abroad; his ubiquity in musical journalism; his perceived influence on others (Liszt, David); the importance to the next generation of the *Grand Traité*; his eventual entry into the Legion of Honour and the Institute.[18] Yet there are many reasons to understand, even to concur with, Berlioz's self-image. His uniqueness won him an early reputation as an eccentric; Ralph Locke places both Berlioz and Debussy as 'in some ways marginal, or at least highly controversial, in their time', as distinct from their present reputations.[19] Berlioz was excluded where he most desired to belong—the teaching faculty of the Conservatoire, the opera houses (except for *Benvenuto Cellini*), and the Société des concerts. Musical

[16] One example: a wide-ranging and often-cited study of Parisian performance and audiences states that Habeneck promoted Berlioz at the Société des concerts on more than one occasion. But there was only *Rob Roy*; the next performance of Berlioz by the Société, in 1849, was conducted by Girard. James H. Johnson, *Listening in Paris* (Berkeley and Los Angeles: University of California Press, 1995), 260. The truth would have emerged from accurate reading of the ostensible secondary source, Holoman, *Berlioz*.

[17] On context, besides the main biographies (Barzun, Cairns, Holoman, Bloom), and Dömling, *Zeit*, see John Crabbe, *Hector Berlioz, Rational Romantic*. Work on grand opera and journalism is cited above.

[18] Although the list given here is my own, this view is broadly espoused by leading scholars such as Peter Bloom and D. Kern Holoman.

[19] Ralph Locke, 'The French Symphony', ch. 7 of D. Kern Holoman (ed.), *The Nineteenth-Century Symphony* (New York: Schirmer, 1997), 163.

success in mid-nineteenth-century France was measured in terms of opera and of virtuosity; Berlioz was not a successful opera composer, and he was not an instrumental virtuoso; the counter-argument that he was a virtuoso conductor only emphasizes his oddity. The monster concerts which so impressed audiences and caricaturists won him no permanent position. David Cairns says that their success was 'built on sand'; his interpretation of the evidence leads him to conclude that Berlioz's life was 'tragic—but for us at least, worth the cost'.[20] He never fitted into the cultural establishment, and he was passed over in favour of palpably inferior musicians for teaching and conducting posts and, indeed, the Institute; his election after three failures exactly mirrors his earlier wrestling with the Prix de Rome, and the irony that he eventually succeeded Adolphe Adam will not have escaped him. Opinion today is similarly divided on the virtues of his journalism, and on his repeated complaints about being dependent on it. There is a potential contradiction here, as he could surely not have done so well something that he entirely disliked. However, to be an innovative composer and conductor is surely enough for one professional career, even in a century of polymaths, and other composers who also wrote prose—Schumann, Liszt, Wagner—were not compelled, like Berlioz, to review any old rubbish that came their way; nor did they have to temper their artistic outrage in the interests of an employer, like Berlioz at the *Journal des Débats*.

What seems certain is that Berlioz felt bitter because he had fought for recognition up to the successful première of *Roméo and Juliette*, and yet thereafter he had to fight just as hard, and with less success, at least until *L'Enfance du Christ*. In the 1840s, his operatic undertakings came to nothing and *La Damnation de Faust* attracted little public interest; his successes after 1850, at home and abroad, must be weighed against his massive disappointment over *Les Troyens*. Berlioz blamed the public for seeking novelty rather than quality, for being more excited about the newest grand opera, and the newest virtuoso, than about Beethoven or revivals of Gluck and Spontini. If he nevertheless himself espoused novelty, it was based on what he rightly considered as high artistic ideals and a belief in the enduring value of serious art, for which means must be fashioned for particular expressive or dramatic ends. Berlioz wanted the public behind him, but although his works sometimes had considerable appeal, he resisted falling back on successful formulas, hoping always to lead the public to admiration of higher art; his rhetorical attitude would nowadays be called élitist.

To suggest that Berlioz simply fell behind the times is too simple. The young disciple of Weber and Beethoven, composers who in 1820s Paris were decidedly 'progressive', never betrayed his earlier love for the masters of neoclassical French opera. Problems in interpreting his career have always arisen from the one-sided perception of Berlioz as a brazen Romantic, a wild man

---

[20] Cairns, *Servitude*, 306, 779.

of 'unfortunate tendencies'. No doubt the establishment perceived him as a radical, composing music difficult to perform and assimilate, and believed his influence to be pernicious, even if his style was not actually the result of incompetence. Having been through the Conservatoire mill in respect to counterpoint, and trained with Lesueur in dramatic composition and word-setting, he could maintain that his innovations had a solid foundation in technique. His unusual handling of polyphony was not the result of inexperience, and if anything he became more individualistic in his later works—not that anything is weirder than the frenetic transition in the first movement of *Symphonie fantastique* (Ex. 9.6), or 'Songe d'une nuit de Sabbat', but his handling of simpler things becomes increasingly unconventional.[21]

At the same time, Berlioz came to deplore certain developments in contemporary music, and eventually parted company with his old ally Liszt; even at the height of Liszt's Berlioz promotions in Weimar, one wonders how much Berlioz relished conducting the première of Liszt's E flat piano concerto (1855). While composing *Les Troyens*, he compared Wagner's theories concerning the primacy of poetry to Gluck's, and praised the latter for not living up to them.[22] With *Tristan*, it is apparent from marginal jotting in the score Wagner gave him that he simply could not swallow the altered chords and the polyphonically induced false relations.[23] Berlioz's own affection for fugato and melody-dominated textures, and his musical forms, with their strophic tendencies, are hardly modernistic; they refreshed symphonic and operatic discourse alike, precisely because of their apparently poor fit with routine generic expectations. Berlioz's status as an orchestral innovator, for whom quality, distance, and direction of sound and colour take on expressive significance, is secure, although his warmest admirers may treasure still more his melodic invention and dramatic sensibility. His significance in the history of transformation of themes, and of programmatic music, is likewise assured; but his rhetorical developments, of beginnings and endings, of thematic apotheosis and combination, are viewed more equivocally. The apotheosis of Romeo's love song, and other brilliant climaxes, are called crude by those who probably relish the gloriously inflated climaxes in Chopin and Liszt's piano music; the abundant and visible virtuosity, and the evanescent quality of piano tone, make acceptable what raises eyebrows when a melody is sung by trombones; Debussy detected a note of irony.[24] In the primacy of melody, often overlooked because for Berlioz, melody did not imply symmetry, he is

---

[21] See for instance the analyses of *Prière de matin* and other pieces: *MLB* 92–5.

[22] Letter of 12 Aug. 1856 to Princess Carolyne Sayn-Wittgenstein, *CG* v. 352.

[23] F-Pn Rés V^m 3.5. These notes were discovered and reported by Alfred Ernst: 'Wagner, corrigé par Berlioz', *Le Ménestrel*, 50 (1884, 28 Sept.), 348–9. Camille Benoit responded in four articles which appear to have escaped the bibliographical net ('Le système harmonique de Wagner (A propos des annotations de *Tristan* par Berlioz))', *Le Ménestrel*, 50 (1884, 5 and 12 Oct., 2 and 9 Nov.), 364, 372–3, 388–9, 395–7. See also Berlioz's review of the *Tristan* prelude, *A travers chants*, 327.

[24] See *Roméo*, 75–7, *Debussy on Music*, 303.

more easily related to French and Italian than to German traditions. His formal advances (programme symphony, dramatic symphony, orchestral song) were outgrowths of existing possibilities (overtures and symphonies, dramatic cantatas, orchestrated romances and concert arias), rather than seismic shifts in the understanding of what music can do, like Schumann's piano works and Wagner's music dramas. No more than they did Berlioz depend on classical models, and nor was he an imitator; more than most, he exemplifies Dahlhaus's dictum that 'In the language of eighteenth-century aestheticians, *imitatio* was replaced and superseded by *aemulatio*'.[25] Berlioz is not often understood in that light because, unlike say Schumann, or Brahms, he emulated what is no longer common currency—French revolutionary music, Lesueur's church music, Gluck's, Méhul's, Spontini's, and Weber's operas. But if Berlioz was less of an innovator than he might appear to those without knowledge of these predecessors, he is no less truly original, and his skill in emulation enabled him to evade a potentially more crushing influence. The trajectory of his career from a period of confronting Beethoven, in his dramatic symphonies, to the admitted and perhaps evasive retrenchment of the choral and operatic works, is a realignment of priorities which should certainly not be construed as a failure. Berlioz turned from Beethoven back to his own roots; Dahlhaus's election of Berlioz as 'our star witness for a break with tradition in French music' could not be more misguided.[26] Berlioz's last works elevate nostalgia to the highest artistic level, and break out of nineteenth-century moulds by recovering the past; they are not intrinsically inferior, just because they do not conform to a Hegelian (and Germano-centric) teleology. Berlioz's artistic defeat continues to shine with undiminished glory.

[25] Carl Dahlhaus, trans. J. Bradford Robinson, *Nineteenth-Century Music* (Berkeley and Los Angeles: University of California Press, 1989), 27.
[26] Ibid. 24.

Select Bibliography

WORKS BY BERLIOZ

A travers chants. Études musicales, adorations, boutades, et critiques (Paris: Michel Lévy, 1862). Critical edn., ed. Léon Guichard (Paris: Gründ, 1971). Trans. Elizabeth Csicsery-Rónay as *The Art of Music and Other Essays* (Bloomington and Indianapolis: Indiana University Press, 1994).

Correspondance générale de Hector Berlioz (Paris: Flammarion), vol. i: *1803–32*, ed. Pierre Citron (1972); ii: *1832–42*, ed. Frédéric Robert (1975); iii: *1842–50*, ed. Citron (1978); iv: *1851–5*, ed. Citron, Yves Gérard, Hugh Macdonald (1983); v: *1855–9*, ed. Macdonald, Lesure (1989); vi: *1859–63*, ed. Macdonald, Lesure (1995).

Critique musicale 1823–1863, ed. H. Robert Cohen and Yves Gérard (Paris: Buchet/Chastel), vol. i: *1823–34* (1996); vol. ii: *1835–6* (1998).

Grand Traité d'Instrumentation et d'orchestration modernes 1st edn. (Paris: Schonenberger, 1843); 2nd edn. (1855); trans. M. Cowden Clarke as *A Treatise Upon Modern Instrumentation and Orchestration* (London: Novello, 1856).

Hector Berlioz: Cauchemars et passions (anthology), ed. Gérard Condé (Paris: J.-C. Lattès, 1981).

Les Grotesques de la musique (Paris: Bourdilliat, 1859). Critical edn., ed. Léon Guichard (Paris: Gründ, 1969).

Les Musiciens et la musique, ed. André Hallays (Paris: Calman-Lévy, 1903). Excerpts trans. in Rushton, *W. A. Mozart: Don Giovanni* (Cambridge: Cambridge University Press, 1981); David Brown, *Glinka* (London: Oxford University Press, 1974).

Les Soirées de l'orchestre (Paris: Michel Lévy, 1852). Critical edn., ed. Léon Guichard (Paris: Gründ, 1968). Trans. Jacques Barzun as *Evenings with the Orchestra* (Chicago: University of Chicago Press, 1956; repr. 1999).

Mémoires d'Hector Berlioz (Paris: Michel Lévy, 1870). Critical edn., ed. Pierre Citron (Paris: Flammarion, 1969; repr. 1991 with addenda and corrigenda); trans. David Cairns as *The Memoirs of Hector Berlioz* (London: Gollancz, 1969).

NBE: Hector Berlioz, *New Edition of the Complete Works*, gen. ed. Hugh Macdonald (Kassel: Bärenreiter, 1969–[2003]).

OBE: Hector Berlioz, *Werke*, ed. Malherbe and Weingartner (Leipzig: Breitkopf & Härtel, 1900–7).

GENERAL BIBLIOGRAPHY

Adam International Review, 34th year, issues 331–3 (1969).

Avant-scène opéra, L', 142 (*Benvenuto Cellini*) (1991); 22 (*La Damnation de Faust*) (1995); 128–9 (*Les Troyens*) (1990).

BANKS, PAUL, 'Coherence and Diversity in the *Symphonie Fantastique*', *19th-century Music*, 8 (Summer 1984), 37–43.

——'Berlioz's "Marche au supplice" and *Les Francs juges*: A Re-examination', *Musical Times*, 130 (Jan. 1989), 16–19.

BARZUN, JACQUES, *Berlioz and the Romantic Century*, 2 vols. (Boston: Little, Brown, 1950; 2nd edn., New York: Columbia University Press, 1969).

BENT, IAN (ed.), *Music Analysis in the Nineteenth Century*, vol. ii: *Hermeneutic Approaches* (Cambridge: Cambridge University Press, 1994).

——*Music Theory in the Age of Romanticism* (Cambridge: Cambridge University Press, 1996).

BERGER, CHRISTIAN, *Phantastik als Konstruktion: Hector Berlioz' 'Symphonie fantastique'. Kieler Schriften zur Musikwissenschaft*, xxvii (Kassel: Bärenreiter, 1983).

BLOOM, PETER A. 'Orpheus's Lyre Resurrected: A *Tableau musical* by Berlioz', *Musical Quarterly*, 61 (1975), 189–211.

——'A Return to Berlioz's *Retour à la vie*', *Musical Quarterly*, 64 (1978), 354–85.

——'Berlioz and the Prix de Rome of 1830', *Journal of the American Musicological Society*, 34 (1981), 279–304.

——(ed.), *Music in Paris in the Eighteen-Thirties* (Stuyvesant, NY: Pendragon Press, 1987).

——(ed.), *Berlioz Studies* (Cambridge: Cambridge University Press, 1992).

——(ed.), *Hector Berlioz,* Benvenuto Cellini. *Dossier de Presse parisienne (1838): Critique de l'Opéra français du XIXème Siècle 3* (n.p.: Musik-Edition Galland, 1995).

——*The Life of Berlioz* (Cambridge: Cambridge University Press, 1998).

——(ed.), *The Cambridge Companion to Berlioz* (Cambridge: Cambridge University Press, 2000).

BOCKHOLDT, RUDOLF, 'Eigenschaften des Rhythmus im instrumentalen Satz bei Beethoven und Berlioz', *Bericht über den internationalen musikwissenschaftlichen Kongress Bonn 1970* (Kassel: Bärenreiter, 1972), 29–32.

——'Die idée fixe der Phantastischen Symphonie', *Archiv für Musikwissenschaft*, xxx (1973), 190–207.

——*Berlioz-Studien* (Tutzing: Schneider, 1979).

BONDS, MARK EVAN, *After Beethoven: Imperatives of Originality in the Symphony* (Cambridge, Mass.: Harvard University Press, 1996).

BOSCHOT, ADOLPHE, *L'Histoire d'un romantique*, i: *La Jeunesse d'un romantique: Hector Berlioz, 1803–1831*; ii: *Un romantique sous Louis-Philippe: Hector Berlioz, 1831–1842*; iii: *Le Crépuscule d'un romantique: Hector Berlioz, 1842–1869* (Paris: Plon, 1906, 1908, 1913).

CAIRNS, DAVID, *Responses* (London: Secker & Warburg, 1973).

——'Spontini's Influence on Berlioz', in D. B. Weiner and W. R. Keyler (eds.), *From Parnassus: Essays in Honor of Jacques Barzun* (New York: Harper & Row, 1976), 25–41.

——*Berlioz*, vol. i: *The Making of an Artist, 1803–1832* (London: André Deutsch, 1989; 2nd rev. edn., London: Allen Lane, the Penguin Press, 1999); vol. ii: *Servitude and Greatness* (London: Allen Lane, the Penguin Press, 1999).

COLLET, ROBERT, 'Berlioz: Various Angles of Approach to his Work', *The Score and IMA Magazine*, 10 (Dec. 1954), 6–19.

Select Bibliography

CONE, EDWARD T. (ed.), *Berlioz: Fantastic Symphony* (Norton Critical Scores) (New York: Norton and London: Chappell, 1971).

——'A Lesson from Berlioz', in *The Composer's Voice* (Berkeley: University of California Press, 1974).

——*Music: A View from Delft*, ed. Robert P. Morgan (Chicago: University of Chicago Press, 1989).

CRABBE, JOHN, *Hector Berlioz, Rational Romantic* (London: Kahn & Averill, 1980).

DAHLHAUS, CARL, 'Allegro frenetico. Zum Problem des Rhythmus bei Berlioz', *Melos* 3/3 (1977), 212–14.

——'Studien zu romantischen Symphonien. Form und Thematik im ersten Satz der *Harold-Symphonie* von Berlioz', *Jahrbuch des Staatlichen Instituts für Musikforschung* 1972 (1973), 116–19.

DEL MAR, NORMAN, *Conducting Berlioz* (Oxford: Clarendon Press, 1997).

DÖMLING, WOLFGANG, 'Die Symphonie fantastique und Berlioz' Auffassung von Programmusik', *Die Musikforschung*, 28 (1975), 260–83.

——'En songeant au temps . . . à l'espace', *Archiv für Musikwissenschaft*, 33 (1976), 241–60.

——*Hector Berlioz. Die symphonisch-dramatischen Werker* (Stuttgart: Reclam, 1979).

——*Hector Berlioz: Symphonie fantastique* (*Meisterwerke der Musik*, 19) (München: Fink, 1985).

——*Hector Berlioz und seine Zeit* (Laaber: Laaber-Verlag, 1986).

FRIEDHEIM, PHILIP, 'Radical Harmonic Procedures in Berlioz', *Music Review*, 21 (1960), 282–96.

——'Berlioz and Rhythm', *Music Review*, 37 (1976), 5–44.

GONNARD, HENRI, *La Musique modale en France de Berlioz à Debussy* (Paris: Honoré-Champion, 2000).

GRUNFELD, FREDERIC V., '"Not two flutes, you scoundrels! Two piccolos! Two piccolos! Oh, what brutes!"', *Horizon*, 12/4 (Autumn 1970), 103–11.

GUIOMAR, MICHEL, *Le Masque et le fantasme: L'Imagination de la matière sonore dans la pensée musicale de Berlioz* (Paris: Librairie José Corti, 1970).

HEIDLBERGER, FRANK, *Hector Berlioz. Les Troyens à Carthage. Dossier de presse parisienne (1863). Critique de l'Opéra français du XIXème Siècle 4* (Musik-Edition Lucie Galland, 1995).

HOLOMAN, D. KERN, 'The Present State of Berlioz Research', *Acta Musicologica*, 47 (1975), 31–67.

——'Reconstructing a Berlioz Sketch', *Journal of the American Musicological Society*, 28 (1975), 125–30.

——'Berlioz au Conservatoire: Notes biographiques', *Revue de Musicologie*, 62 (1976), 289–92.

——*The Creative Process in the Autograph Documents of Hector Berlioz c.1818–1840* (Ann Arbor: UMI Studies in Musicology, 1980).

——'The Berlioz Sketchbook Recovered', *19th-Century Music*, 7 (1984), 282–317.

——*Catalogue of the Works of Hector Berlioz*. NBE 25 (Kassel: Bärenreiter, 1987).

——*Berlioz* (Cambridge, Mass.: Harvard University Press and London: Faber, 1989).

——(ed.), *The Nineteenth-Century Symphony* (New York: Schirmer, 1997).

HOPKINSON, CECIL, *A Bibliography of the Musical and Literary Works of Hector Berlioz* (Edinburgh Bibliographical Society, 1951; 2nd rev. edn. Tunbridge Wells: Richard Macnutt, 1981).

IRONFIELD, SUSAN, 'Creative Developments of the "Mal d'Isolement" in Berlioz', *Music and Letters*, 59 (1978), 33–48.

KEMP, IAN (ed.), *Hector Berlioz: Les Troyens* (Cambridge Opera Handbook) (Cambridge: Cambridge University Press, 1988).

KOHRS, KLAUS HEINRICH, '*La Veillée de David*. Hector Berlioz über Jean-François Le Sueur', *Biographische konstellation und künstlerisches Handeln. Frankfurter Studien* (Mainz: Schott, 1997), 61–80.

LANGFORD, JEFFREY, 'Berlioz, Cassandra, and the French Operatic Tradition', *Music and Letters*, 62 (1981), 310–17.

——'The "Dramatic Symphonies" of Berlioz as an Outgrowth of the French Operatic Tradition', *Musical Quarterly*, 69 (1983), 85–103.

——'Musical-Dramatic Parallels in the Operas of Hector Berlioz', *Studies in the History of Music*, 2: Music and Drama (New York: Broude Brothers, 1988), 152–70

LANGFORD, JEFFREY, and GRAVES, JANE DENKER, *Hector Berlioz: A Guide to Research* (New York and London: Garland, 1989).

LENSKY, MIRIAM, 'Characterization in the Dramatic Works of Hector Berlioz', Ph.D. thesis (University of Leeds, 1998).

LISZT, FRANZ, 'Berlioz und seine "Harold-Symphonie"', *Neue Zeitschrift für Musik* (1855), repr. *Gesammelte Schriften*, iv, ed. Lisa Ramann (1882) (Wiesbaden, 1978), 1–102. Partial trans. in Strunk *Source Readings in Music History*, rev. edn., ed. Leo Treitler (New York and London: Norton, 1998), 1159–74.

——*Lettres d'un bachelier ès musique*, trans. Charles Suttoni as *An Artist's Journey* (Chicago: University of Chicago Press, 1989).

LOCKE, RALPH P., 'Cutthroats and Casbah Dancers, Muezzins and Timeless Sands: Musical Images of the Middle East', *19th-Century Music*, 22 (1998), 20–53.

——'Paris: Centre of Intellectual Ferment', in Alexander Ringer (ed.), *Man and Music: The Early Romantic Era. Between Revolutions: 1789 and 1848* (London: Macmillan, 1990), 32–83.

MACDONALD, HUGH, 'Berlioz's Self-borrowings', *Proceedings of the Royal Musical Association*, 92 (1965–6), 27–44.

——'A Critical Edition of Berlioz's Les Troyens', Ph.D. (University of Cambridge, 1968).

——*Berlioz Orchestral Music* (London: BBC, 1969).

——'Berlioz's Orchestration: Human or Divine?', *Musical Times*, 110 (1969), 255–8.

——*Berlioz* (The Master Musicians) (London: Dent, 1982).

——'Berlioz's *Messe solennelle*', *19th-Century Music*, 16 (Spring 1993), 267–85.

MAUS, FRED EVERETT, 'Intersubjectivity and Analysis: Schumann's Essay on the *Fantastic Symphony*', in Ian Bent (ed.), *Music Theory in the Age of Romanticism* (Cambridge: Cambridge University Press, 1996), 125–38.

MONGRÉDIEN, JEAN, *Jean-François Le Sueur, contribution à l'étude d'un demi-siècle de musique française (1780–1830)*, 2 vols. (Berne: Peter Lang, 1980).

——*J.-F. Le Sueur: A Thematic Catalogue of his Complete Works* (New York: Pendragon Press, 1980).

——*La Musique en France des Lumières au Romantisme, 1789–1830* (Paris: Flammarion, 1986).

NOSKE, FRITZ, *French Song from Berlioz to Duparc* (New York: Dover, 1970), trans. Rita Benton from *La Mélodie française de Berlioz à Duparc* (Amsterdam: North Holland Publishing Company, 1954).

PERL, BENJAMIN, 'L'Orchestre dans les opéras de Berlioz et de ses contemporains', Thèse de Doctorat de 3ème Cycle (Université des Sciences Humaines de Strasbourg, 1989).

PIATIER, FRANÇOIS, *Hector Berlioz: Benvenuto Cellini ou le mythe de l'artiste* (Collections les Grands Opéras) (Paris: Aubier Montagne, 1979).

PRIMMER, BRIAN, *The Berlioz Style* (London: Oxford University Press, 1973).

RAMAUT, ALBAN, *Hector Berlioz, compositeur romantique français* (n.p.: Actes Sud, 1993).

RATNER, LEONARD G., *Romantic Music: Sound and Syntax* (New York: Schirmer Books, 1992).

REEVE, KATHERINE KOLB, 'The Poetics of the Orchestra in the Writings of Hector Berlioz', thesis (Yale University, 1978).

Revue Musicale, La, 233 (*Hector Berlioz 1803–1869*) (1956).

Revue de Musicologie, La, 63 (Colloque Hector Berlioz, Paris 1975) (1977).

ROBINSON, PAUL, *Opera and Ideas: From Mozart to Strauss* (Ithaca, NY: Cornell University Press, 1985).

ROSEN, CHARLES, *The Romantic Generation* (London: HarperCollins, 1996).

RUSHTON, JULIAN, 'The Genesis of Berlioz's "La damnation de Faust"', *Music and Letters*, 56 (1975), 129–46.

——'Berlioz through the Looking-Glass', *Soundings* (University College Cardiff Press), 6 (1977), 51–66.

——'Berlioz's Swan-Song: Towards a Criticism of *Béatrice et Bénédict*', *Proceedings of the Royal Musical Association*, 109 (1982–3), 105–18.

——*The Musical Language of Berlioz* (Cambridge Studies in Music) (Cambridge: Cambridge University Press, 1983).

——'The Overture to *Les Troyens*', *Music Analysis,* 4 (1985), 119–44.

——*Berlioz: Roméo et Juliette* (Cambridge Music Handbook) (Cambridge: Cambridge University Press, 1994).

——'Misreading Shakespeare: Two Operatic Scenes of Berlioz', in Holger Klein and Christopher Smith (eds.), *The Opera and Shakespeare* (*Shakespeare Yearbook*, 4: Lewiston, NY: Edwin Mellon Press, 1994), 213–27.

——'Berlioz and *Irlande*: From Romance to Mélodie', in Patrick F. Devine and Harry White (eds.), *Irish Musical Studies* (the Maynooth International Musicological Conference 1995), part 2 (Dublin: Four Courts Press, 1996), 224–40.

——'Ecstasy of Emulation: Berlioz's *Messe solennelle* and his Debt to Lesueur', *Musical Times*, 140/1868 (Autumn 1999), 11–18.

SCHACHER, THOMAS, *Idee und Erscheinungsform des Dramatischen bei Hector Berlioz* (Hamburger Beiträge zur Musikwissenchaft, 33) (Hamburg: Verlag der Musik-alienhandlung Karl Dieter Wagner, 1987).

SCHUMANN, ROBERT, 'Symphonie von H. Berlioz', *Gesammelte Schriften* (Leipzig: Georg Wigands Verlag, 1854), 118–51. Trans. in Edward T. Cone, *Berlioz: Fantastic Symphony* (New York: Norton and London: Chappell, 1971), 220–48, and Ian Bent, *Music Analysis in the Nineteenth Century*, vol. ii: *Hermeneutic Approaches* (Cambridge: Cambridge University Press, 1994), 161–94.

TEMPERLEY, NICHOLAS, 'The *Symphonie fantastique* and its Program', *Musical Quarterly*, 57 (1971), 593–608.

Tovey, Donald Francis, *Essays in Musical Analysis*, iv: *Illustrative Music* (London: Oxford University Press, 1937); vi: *Miscellaneous Notes* (1939).

Wotton, Tom S., *Hector Berlioz* (London: Oxford University Press, 1935).

Wright, Michael G. H., *A Berlioz Bibliography: Critical Writing on Hector Berlioz from 1825 to 1986* (Farnborough: Saint Michael's Abbey Press, n.d. [1986]).

Index of Berlioz's Musical Works

Note: individual sections of multi-movement works may also be mentioned in sections dealing with the work as a whole, picked out in bold; generic descriptions: romance = strophic song; mélodie = through composed song; entries in **bold** refer to a music example, table, or substantial discussion

'Absence' (mélodie, H.85), see *Nuits d'été*
'Adieu Bessy' (romance, H.46), see *Irlande*
Albumleaves, various, 49, 67, 107, 111 n. 28
'Amitié, reprends ton empire' (romance, H.10), 9, **115–19**, 185
'Arabe jaloux, L'', *see* 'Maure jaloux'
'Aubade' (mélodie, H.78), 41
'Au bord d'une rivière' (romance, H.132), 64
'Au cimetière' (mélodie, H.86), see *Nuits d'été*

'Ballet des ombres, Le' (chorus with piano, H.37), 26; used in *Benvenuto Cellini*, 38; 44, 60, 73, 81; used in *Roméo*, 82; **121–4**, 133, 165, 185
Béatrice et Bénédict (opera, H.138), **65–6**, 93, 190, 283, 285, 289, **339–40**, 343
    Act I. Overture, 142, 279–80; Hero's aria, 187; men's trio, 98; duo-nocturne, 152;
    Act II. Chœur à boire, 165 and n., Aria (Beatrice), 187; Scherzo-duettino, 142
'Belle Isabeau, La' (ballad, H.94), 50, 67, 134, 179
'Belle voyageuse, La' (romance, H.42), see *Irlande*
Benvenuto Cellini (Opéra semi-seria, H.76), 35, **37–40**, 53, 57, 66; borrowings in, 71–2; 81, 154, 187–8, 204, 249–50; staging, 284–5; **291–303**, 341–3; characterization, 286–9, 295–7, 302–3; first version, 141, 249;
    Act I. Overture, 38, 78, 87, 100, **106**, 141, 217, 244 n., 278, 298; Introduction, 145; Balducci's aria, 187; Teresa 's aria 'Ah! Que l'amour . . .' (rejected), 47, **78–9**, 187; 'Entre l'amour . . .', 187, 296–7; Love Duet/trio, **75–8**, 86, 295–8; second tableau Romance, 166, 187; Fieramosca's aria, 188; Le Carnaval, 38, 44, 82–3, 122 n.; pantomime, 106.
    Act II. Prayer and Cellini's narrative, 132, 206; duet, 154, 299; Quintet, sextet, finale,

286, 299–300; Ascanio's aria, 187–8; Cellini: 'Sur les monts', 167, 187, 318; Workers' chorus, 143–4; Finale, 278, 300, 317
Beverley (cantata, lost, H.19), 8–11

'Canon libre à la quinte' (vocal duet, H.14), 9, 107, 169, 181
'Captive, La' (romance, H.60), 30, 34–5, 143, 149, 174, 178; orchestral version, **53–4**; 57, 67, 185
Carnaval romain, Le (overture, H.95), 47, 50, 81–2, 160, 197, 278–9, 297
'Champs, Les' (romance, H.67), 35, 55, 72, **179–81**
'Chanson à boire' (chorus, H.43), see *Irlande*
'Chanson des pirates' (lost, H.34), 32
'Chanson de brigands' (chorus), see *Lélio* No.2
'Chanson du pêcheur' (ballad), see *Lélio* No.1
'Chansonette de M. Léon de Wailly' (romance, H.73), 38, 73, 165 n.
'Chant des Bretons, Le' (chorus, *Fleurs des Landes* No.5, H.71), 37, 55, 185–6
Chant des chemins de fer (cantata, H.110), 49, 55, 165, 216, **218–19**, 220
'Chant guerrier' (chorus, H.41), see *Irlande*
'Chant sacré' (chorus, H.44), see *Irlande*
'Chasseur danois, Le' (romance, H.104), 50, 67, 179
Cheval arabe, Le (cantata, lost, H.12), 7
Cinq mai, Le (cantata, H.74), 33–5, 37, 44, 67, 165, 185
Cléopâtre (cantata, H.36), 17–18, **26**, 30, 81, 140, 199, 266, 285, 336; reused, 30, 33, 38, 71, 73, **75**, **78**, 86; Méditation, 32, 83, **139–41**
Corsaire, Le (*Ouverture du Corsaire*, H.101), 50, 101, 160, 216, 241 n., 278–80
'Coucher du soleil, Le' (romance, H.39), see *Irlande*
Cri de guerre de Brisgaw, Le (intermezzo, unfinished, H.23C), 36

Damnation de Faust, La (dramatic legend, H.111), 6, 25, 39, 47, **50–3**, 61, 66, 100, 112, 134, 161, 188, 218, 239–40, 251, 264, 276–8, **303–15**, 342; technique of anticipation, **250–1**, 308–9; genre, 309–13; characterization, 285, 289; composition of, 303–8; fate of Faust, 313–15
    Part I. Plaines de Hongrie, 93–4, 247; Hungarian March (*Marche de Rácóczy*), 52, 143–4, 277, 304
    Part II. Nord de l'Allemagne, 58, **93–5**, 277, 313; Chant de la Fête de Pâques, 142; entry of Mephistopheles, 141; interlude, 250; Chanson d'un rat–Amen, 193–4, 197, 225; 'Voici des roses', **95–7**, 189; Chœur de gnomes et de sylphes, 96; Ballet des sylphes, 81, 97; Finale, 22, 306, 334
    Part III. Air de Faust, 95, 154, 309, 313; Marguerite's entrance, 154; Le Roi de Thulé, 144, **172–6**, 180, 250–1; Menuet de follets, 131, **145**; Love duet, **154–6**, 331; Trio and finale, 131, 219, **309–12**, 334;
    Part IV. Romance, 140, 154, **181–4**, 251; Invocation à la nature, 3, 93, 95, 99, 139, 235, 272, 313, 316; Recitative, 313; La course à l'abîme, 89, 142–3. 314; Pandaemonium, 142, 269, 314–5: Epilogue (Le Ciel), 49, 142–3, 314–5
'Dans l'alcôve sombre' (romance, unfinished), 35, 102
'Dépit de la bergère, Le' (romance, H.7), 8, 65, 112, 114, 167, 172, 180
Dernier Jour de monde, Le (projected oratorio, H.61), 34

'Élégie en prose' (mélodie, H.47), see *Irlande*
Enfance du Christ, L' (Sacred trilogy, H.130), 6, 57–8, **60–1**, 100, 175, 277–6, **315–24**, 341, 343; instrumentation, 315–6, 323; modality, 144
    Part I. Le Songe d'Hérode. Marche nocturne, 81, **130**, 277; Air d'Hérode,113, 188, **317–19**; Soothsayers, chorus, **134–7**, 144–5; scene in Bethlehem, 175, 188, 316
    Part II. La Fuite en Egypte, 58, 241, 319. Overture, 250, 277; Adieu des bergers, 144, 175, 188.
    Part III. L'Arrivée à Saïs. Introduction, 250; Duet, 188, **319–23**; Trio (flutes and harp), 144; Epilogue, 6, 60
Episode de la vie d'un artiste, see *Symphonie fantastique* and *Lélio*
Erigone (intermezzo, fragmentary, H.77), 41, 46
Estelle et Némorin (opera, lost, H.17), 8–9, 84

Faust, see *Huit scènes de Faust, Damnation de Faust*

Fête musicale funèbre (projected, H.72), 34, 45, 216–7
Feuillets d'album (three songs, H.121), 55, 67; see also *Les Champs, Chant des chemins de fer, Zaïde*
'Flea song' ('Chanson de Méphistophélès'), see *Huit scènes de Faust*
Fleurs des landes (five songs, H.124), 55, 67, 179; see also 'Le Matin', 'Petit Oiseau', 'Le Trébuchet', 'Le Jeune Pâtre breton', 'Le Chant des Bretons'
Francs-juges, Les (opera, fragmentary, H.23), 8, **11–13**; 1829 version, 12–13, 24–6; 36, 57, 133, 143, 187, 283, 285, 343; Overture, 12, 23, 44, 133, 217, 237–8, **241–6**. Opening chorus, **89–92**; Trio pastoral, 172; 'Marche des gardes', 12, 25; reused in later works, 28–9, 36, 38, 44 n., 45, 48, 58, 73, 83, 298
Freyschütz, Le (recitatives to Weber's *Der Freischütz*, H.89), 48, 57, 93
Fugue (H.22), 8, 107
Fuite en Egypte, La ('Mystère en style ancien', H.128), see *L'Enfance du Christ*

Grande messe des morts (Requiem, H.75), 6, 30, **40–1**, 44, 81, 142, **203–15**, 216, 224, 239, 282, 295, 316, 343; orchestral forces, 57, 203, 209; text, 204, 212, 220; form and tonality, 204–6, 214
    Introit: Requiem, Kyrie, 122, **205–6**, 241–2; Sequence. 'Dies irae', 'Tuba mirum', 203, 206, **209–10**, 229; 'Quid sum miser', 209; 'Rex tremendae', 89, 196, **212–14**, 235; 'Quaerens me', 61, 220; 'Lacrimosa', 201 n., 209–10, 219, 229, 234, 236, 280; Offertoire, 44, 75, 83, 110, 112, **210–11**, 212, 225, 319; 'Hostias', **205–7**, **214–15**; Sanctus, 'Hosanna', 112, 211, 221, 225; Agnus Dei/'Amen', 194, 205, 212, **215**
Grande symphonie funèbre et triomphale (H.80), **45**, 47, 161, **216–18**, 249, 278; Marche funèbre, 119, **128–9**, 217; Oraison funèbre, 73; Apothéose, 53, **128–9**, 144

Hamlet, see *Tristia*
Harold en Italie (Symphony with solo viola, H.68), 3, 6, 30, 35, **36–7**, 57, 75, 81, 126, 153; programme, 160–1; 204, **247–9**, 252–3, 266–9, 282, 340; *idée fixe*, 73–5, 79, 240, 248, 267. 'Harold aux montagnes', 119, 143, 267; 'Marche des pèlerins', **36–7**, 132, 206, 211, 267, 278; 'Sérénade', 143, **248–9**; 'Orgie de brigands', 131, 134, 142, 268–9, 278
'Harpe éolienne, La', see *Lélio*
'Hélène' (Ballade, H.40), see *Irlande*
Herminie (cantata, H.29), **17–22**, **24**, 92, 113, 285; re-used, 26, 28, 78, **84–6**, 258, 260, 264

Huit scènes de Faust (H.33), **25–6**, 35, 50–1, 57, 72, 121, 166–7, 178, 264, 283, 285, **303–6**, 309, 315. 'Chant de la Fête de Pâques', 61, 142; 'Chœur de sylphes (sextet), 28, 96, 197; 'Le Roi de Thulé', 144, **172–6**, 180; 'Romance'/'Chœur de soldats', 140, 172, 174, **181–4**, 308, 312, 323; 'Sérénade', 149, 172

'Hymne à la France' (chorus, *Vox Populi* No. 2, H.97), 55, 216, 220

'Hymne pour la consécration du nouveau tabernacle' (chorus, H.135), 65

'Hymne pour l'élévation' (harmonium, H.100), 49, 58, 225

'Île inconnue, L'' (mélodie, H.87), see *Nuits d'été*

Impériale, L' (cantata, H.129), **58–60**, 75, 85–6, 131, 216, **218–20**

Irlande (*Neuf mélodies irlandaises*, song cycle, H.38), **25–7**, 33, 35, 44, 55, 67, 119–20, 165 n., 166–7, 178; 'Le coucher du soleil', **176–9**; 'Hélène', 169, 176 'Chant guerrier', 178; 'La Belle Voyageuse', **120–1**, 134, 172, 174–6; 'Chant sacré', 48; 'L'Origine de la harpe', 172, 174, 176; 'Adieu Bessy', 72, 176, 178–9; 'Élégie en prose', 106, 176, 178, 181; choruses, 185

'Je crois en vous' (romance, H.70), 35; used in *Benvenuto Cellini*, 38; sketches, **102–6**; 165 n., 179

'Jeune Pâtre breton, Le' (romance, *Fleurs des Landes* No.4, H.65), 35–6, 55, 174, 179

'Je vais donc quitter . . .' (romance, lost, H.6), 9, 28, 83, **167–9**, 251, 257

Jugement dernier, Le (projected opera-oratorio, H.61), 28

Lear, see *Roi Lear, Le*

Lélio (Mélologue, H.55), **30–3**, 57, 62, 160, 276–7; recycling in, 71–3. 'Chanson du pêcheur', 25, 165; 'Chœur d'ombres', 83, 140; 'Scène de brigands', 185, 268–9; 'Chant de bonheur', 75–8, **86–8**, 113; 'Les Derniers Souvenirs' ('La Harpe éolienne'), 62, 277; *La Tempête*, 29–30, 72, 78, 127, 165 n., 237, 241, 246, 267, 276–7

'Marche au supplice', see *Symphonie fantastique*

'Marche des gardes', see *Les Francs-juges*

'Marche funèbre', see *Tristia*

Marche de Rákóczy ('Marche hongroise', H.109), see *La Damnation de Faust*

Marche religieuse des Mages (lost, H.27), 23, 33, 37

Mass, see *Messe solennelle*

'Matin, Le' (romance, *Fleurs des Landes* No.1, H.125), 55, 175, 180

'Maure jaloux, Le' ('L'Arabe jaloux', romance, H.9), 9, **113–6**, 118–9, 143, 168–9

'Méditation religieuse' (chorus, H.56), see *Tristia*

'Menace de Francs, La' (chorus, *Vox Populi* No.1, H.117), 53, 55, 216

Messe solennelle (H.20), 8, **10–11**, 40, 72–3, 81, 98, 100, **107–12**, **192–202**; reused, 201; 'Introduction', 56 n.; Kyrie/Christe, 51, 81; as fugue, **110–12**; 216, 256; adapted in Requiem, 41, 75, 83, **209–11**. 'Gloria in excelsis . . . Laudamus te', 38, 47, 82; 'Gratias . . . Qui tollis', 28, 75, 82, **89–90**, 120, 172, 221, **258–63**, 264–6; 'Quoniam', **108–10**, 209, 225, 233. 'Credo in unum Deum', 73; 'Incarnatus', 120; 'Crucifixus', 73, 139, **199**; 'Resurrexit', 3, 4, 9, 23, 28; reused, 34, 39, 41, 56, 83, 131; two versions, **202–3**; 227, 298. 'Motet pour l'offertoire', 9; **Sanctus**, 221; 'O salutaris', 109; 'Agnus Dei', 73, 113; used in Te Deum, **227–9**; 'Domine salvum', 216

'Montagnard exilé, Le' (H.15), 9, 118–9, 169, 172, 181

Mort d'Orphée, La (cantata, H.25), 4, 14, **17–22**; performance, 23; 24–5, 41, 72–3, 93, 108, 113, 140, 172; reused in *Lélio*, 33, 75, **86–7**, 113

'Mort d'Ophélie, La' (Ballade, H.92), see *Tristia*

'Nessun maggior piacere' (song, H.114), 49, 52

Neuf mélodies, see *Irlande*

'Nocturne' (vocal duet, H.31), 24

Nonne sanglante, La (opera, fragmentary, H.91), 48, 50, 53, 57–8, 63–4, 133, 188, 303; Bass aria, **286–8**; Duet and ballad, 4, **134–8**

Nuits d'été, Les (song cycle, H.81), 44, **45–6**, 53, 60, 62, 67, 81, 98, 165–6, 169, **180–5**, 239, 343; 'Villanelle', 166, 186; 'Le Spectre de la rose', 153–4, 165; 'Sur les Lagunes', 165; 'Absence', 53, 55, 166

'Origine de la harpe, L'' (romance, H.45), see *Irlande*

Orphée, see *Mort d'Orphée, La*

Passage de la mer rouge, La (oratorio, lost, H.18), 8, 9–11

'Petit Oiseau' (romance, *Fleurs des Landes* No.2: H.126), 55, 175, 180

'Pleure, pauvre Colette' (romance, H.11), 9, 114, 169

Potpourri concertante (H.1), 6

Prise de Troie, La, 324

'Prière du matin' (chorus, H.112), 50, 67, 179, 186, 346 n.·

Index of Berlioz's Musical Works

Quartetto e coro dei maggi (chorus, H.59), 31, 33
Quintets (H.2–3), 5

Receuil de romances (H.8), 6
Requiem, see *Grande messe des morts*
Resurrexit (H.20B), see *Messe solennelle*
Retour à la vie, Le, see *Lélio*
Retour de l'armée d'Italie, 34–5; used in
  Harold, 37, 131, 268
Rêverie et caprice (romance, violin and
  orchestra, H.88), 47, **78–9**, 187, 296
Richard en Palestine, 24, 84
Rob-Roy MacGregor, Intrata di (overture,
  H.54), 30–1, 344 n.; reused in *Harold*, 36,
  72–5; 143, 241–2
Roi Lear, Grande Ouverture du (H.53), 30–1,
  36, 44, 79, 157, 160, 239, 241, **245–7**, 267,
  296
'Romance de Marie Tudor' (song, lost, H.66),
  35
Roméo et Juliette (dramatic symphony, Op.17:
  H.79), 4, 6, **41–4**, 47, 51 n., 57, 60–1, 112,
  161, 167, 253, 269, **275–6**, 278, 340, 342–3
  Introduction, Prologue, 133, 155–8, 212,
  240–1, 251, 271, 312, 314; 'Strophes', 161,
  165, 188; 'Scherzetto', 165 n.; 'Roméo
  seul', **149–51**, 153, 296; 'Grande Fête chez
  Capulet', 75, **79–81**, 131–2, 134, 142, 170,
  271, 346; 'Scène d'amour', 99, 145,
  149–53, 184, 238, 270–2, 312; Scherzo,
  'La reine Mab', 82, 122 n., 146; Second
  Prologue, 157, 271; 'Convoi funèbre', 132,
  271, 177; 'Roméo au tombeau des
  Capulets', 140, 235, 257, **269–75**; Finale,
  58, 157, 219, 277, **289–91**, 314; aria, 113,
  188, 286–7

'Sara la baigneuse' (Ballade, H.69), 37, 53, 57,
  67, 149, 186
Sardanapale (cantata, H.50), 17–18, **27**, 29, 57,
  81, 149; reused, 34, 42–3, 58, 64, **72–5**,
  79–82, 85–6, 131, 170, 219–20
Scène héroïque (cantata, H.21), 4, 8, 11, **13–17**,
  23; revised, 36; 64, 72–3, 143, 216–17, 227;
  Recitative and aria, 59, **89–92**; Finale, 36
Sérénade agreste à la madone (harmonium,
  H.98), 49
sketchbook of 1832–6 (H.62), 34, **101–6**, 192–3
'Spectre de la rose, Le' (mélodie, H.83), see
  Nuits d'été
'Sur les Lagunes' (mélodie, H.84), see *Nuits
  d'été*
Symphonie fantastique (H.48), 6, 12, **28–9**,
  30–1, 35, 52, 57, 81, 178, 237, **251–66**,
  340–3; form and Beethoven, 159, 251–3;
  programme, 62, 155–61, 212, 238, 247,
  251–2, 254–6; *idée fixe*, 73, 78, **84–6**, 113,
  131–2, 153, 256–7, 260, 263, 266, 328

Rêveries, passions, **83–5**, 124, 168–9, 217,
  257–9, 346; *Largo*, 227 n., 241–2, 244–5;
  'Un bal', 43, 131; 'Scène aux champs',
  73–5, 82–3, 127, 139, 153, 214, 238,
  259–63, 278; 'Marche au supplice', 36, 73,
  129–30; 'Songe d'une nuit de Sabbat',
  40–1, 99, 132–4, **254–7**, 269, 271, 278, 346
Symphonie funèbre, see *Grande Symphonie
  funèbre et triomphale*

'Tantum ergo' (chorus, H.142), 67, 185–6
Te Deum (H.118), 6, 50, 53, **55–7**, 203, 216–8,
  220–36, 340; text, 220–3; tonality, form,
  223–4; 'Te Deum laudamus', 107, **225–6**;
  Prélude, 223–4; 'Tu Christe', 131; 'Te ergo
  quæsumus', 61, 73, 113, **227–9**; 'Judex
  crederis', 100, 107, 139, 142, 143 n., 198,
  229–36, 259, 272, 280; Marche, 107, 223–4,
  235
Tempête, Ouverture de La (H.52), see *Lélio*
'Temple universel, Le' (chorus, H.137), 65, 186
Toccata (harmonium, H.99), 49
'Toi qui l'aimas' (romance, H.16), 9, 120, **169–71**
'Trébuchet, Le' (duet, *Fleurs des Landes* No.3,
  H.113), 50, 55, 149
Tristia (H.119), 33, 55, 67. 'Méditation
  religieuse', 33; 'La Mort d'Ophélie', 49, 57,
  67, 179; 'Marche funèbre' (*Hamlet*), 49, 57,
  143, 239, 266, **279–80**
Troyens, Les (H.133), 6–7, 34, 48, 58, **61–5**, 66,
  126–7, 144–5, 166–7, 188–9, 250, 303,
  324–37, 340, 343; staging, 284; characterization, 285–6, 326–31; tonality and form,
  230, 289, 325–6; thematic cross reference,
  251; ballets, 281
  Act I. Cassandra, 'Malheureux Roi', 188,
  331; Duet, **328–31**; Hymne, 332; Ballet,
  127, 142; Pantomime (Andromaque), 63,
  127, 332, 'Sinon scene', 332; Cassandra,
  'Non, je ne verrai pas', 75, **77**, **82**, 188–9,
  333; Finale (Marche troyenne), **127–9**, 250,
  333–4
  Act II. First tableau, **127**, 131, 243; Second
  tableau, 131, 140, 144
  Act III. 334–5. Anthem, 189; 'Chers Tyriens',
  77, **81–2**, 189; Duet (Dido, Anna), 152;
  'Errante sur les mers', **189–91**; Marche
  troyenne in minor mode, 250; Finale, 22,
  131, 152, 219
  Act IV. 127, 152, 335. Chasse royale, **127–8**,
  278, 280; March, **130**; Ballets, 142, **145–8**;
  Chant d'Iopas, 99, 167, 175; Duet (Dido,
  Aeneas), **152–3**, 154
  Act V. 335–6. Duet (sentries), 66, 324; Aria
  (Aeneas), 189; Dido: monologue and
  'Adieu, fière cité', 81, 140, 189; Cérémonie
  funèbre, 127, 132, 140; finale, 314
Troyens à Carthage, Les, 66, 283, 285, 324, 342

Variations for guitar (lost, H.30), 24
'Veni Creator' (chorus, H.141), 67, 186
'Villanelle' (romance), H.82, see *Nuits d'été*
Vox Populi (H.120), 55, 67; see La Menace des
  Francs and Hymne à la France

Waverley, Grande Ouverture de (H.26), 14,
  22–3, 36, 44, 143, 160, 217, **237–47**, 258

'Zaïde' (bolero, H.107), 50, 55, 143, 179

General Index

Adam, Adolphe (composer, 1803–56) 27, 217, 345
Auber, Daniel-François-Esprit (composer, 1782–1871) 35, 48, 62, 282, 341; *La muette de Portici* 63, 158, 284
Bach, J. S. 64, 192, 342; Passions, 225, 323; Mass, 264
Barbier, Auguste (librettist of *Benvenuto Cellini*, 1805–82) 37 n., 295 n.
Barzun, Jacques 28, 160, 254, 271, 314
Beethoven, Ludwig van (1770–1827) general and influence on Berlioz 7, 25, 64, 72, 122, 126–8, 144, 158, 192, 258, 290, 345, 347; Overtures 237–8, 241–3, 266; *Coriolan* 31; 'Emperor' concerto, 28; Symphonies, 240–4, 252–3, 266–8; *Eroica* 4, 23, 240; Fifth 23, 124, 160, 244, 273; *Pastoral* 127, 159–60; Seventh 36; Ninth 37, 42, 131, 275; *Missa Solemnis* 100, 108, 195; *Fidelio* 264, 343; C♯ minor quartet 276
Bellini, Vincenzo (1801–35) 193, 264; *Norma* 273, 285; *La sonnambula* 295
Béranger, Pierre-Jean (poet, 1780–1857) 33, 35, 179
Berger, Christian 256, 342

BERLIOZ, LOUIS-HECTOR (1803–69):
Aesthetics 23, 82–3; words and music 84–97, 113; sacred music 108–9, 192; theatre music 281–3; catalogues of his works 50, 53, 57; compositional methods 3–4, 8, 101–7; recycling 3–4, 71–84; critical evaluation of 344–7; early influences 4–6; early studies 7–11, 14; influence on later composers and critical reception 340–4; and politics 3, 45, 52–3; and the Prix de Rome 14–24, 107–8, 149, 169
Prose works: *Euphonia* 49, *Grand Traité* 49, 57, 208 n., 214, 283, 344

Bertin, Louise (composer, 1805–77) 169; *Esmerelda*, 13 n., 133, 294; *Fausto*, 313
Bizet, Georges (1838–75) 45, 341
Brahms, Johannes (1833–97) 72, 347
Bruckner, Anton (1822–96) 143 n., 217, 220
Byron, Lord (1788–1824) 25, 48; *Childe Harold* 36–7; 50, 149, 160

Cairns, David 13, 73, 236, 264, 302, 310 n., 345
Catel, Charles-Simon (composer, theorist, 1773–1830) 5, 107
Charles X, King of France 27, 197 n., 216, 334
Chateaubriand, François-René (1768–1848) 29 n., 83, 238, 334
Cherubini, Luigi (1760–1842) 7–8; Communion march 23, 127, 137–9; Masses, 194–5; Requiem 40, 193; *Médée*, 7, 333; as pedagogue 107–8, 112
Chopin, Frédéric 6, 62 n., 126, 241, 272, 346
Cone, Edward T. 132 n., 160–1, 204, 205 n., 208, 214, 229, 271, 308 n.

D'Alembert, Jean le Rond, theorist 5, 115
David, Félicien (composer, 1810–76) 45, 143, 145 n., 276–7, 341, 344
Debussy, Claude 239, 246, 341–2, 344, 346
Delacroix, Eugène (1798–1863) 149, 313
Dömling, Wolfgang 160, 212, 214, 254, 258, 343
Du Boys, Albert (poet, translator) 9, 32 n., 119–20
Dubœuf, Estelle (Berlioz's first love) 28, 159
Duparc, Henri (1848–1933) 45, 166

Elgar, Edward 72, 341
Elliot, J. H. 134, 270

Fauquet, Joël-Marie 298 n., 302–3
Fauré, Gabriel (1845–1924) 45, 166
Ferrand, Humbert (poet, librettist, 1805–68)
 4, 11–14, 18, 26–7, 29, 32, 71; 'Chant du
 brigand' 32; and *Les Francs-juges* 11–13,
 36, 133, 283; and *Scène héroïque* 13–14
Florian, Jean-Pierre-Claris de (author,
 1755–94) 9, 28, 83–4, 114, 167 169, 258
Franck, César (1822–90), *Psyché* 152–3, 340

Gandonnière, Almire (librettist of *la
 Damnation de Faust*) 50–2, 95, 304–6
Garrick, David (actor, playwright, 1717–79)
 270, 273
Gautier, Théophile (poet, 1811–72) 45–6;
 Mlle de Maupin 149, 154
Gerhard, Anselm 133 n., 337
Gerono, Hyacinth (1797–1868) 7, 107, 112–5
Gilbert, Alphonse (composer) 17 n., 18, 22
Gilbert, David, 79–81
Gluck, Christoph Willibald (1714–87),
 general and influence on Berlioz 7, 12–14,
 35, 63, 72; 126–7, 139, 144, 189, 264, 278,
 281–2, 285, , 324, 341, 345–7; his aesthetic
 83 n., 303; *Orfeo* 278, 335; *Alceste* 281,
 Iphigénie en Tauride 336
Goethe, Johann Wolfgang (1749–1832) 25–6,
 154, 187; *Faust* 25, 28–9, 32, 49, 52, 134 n.,
 141–2, 172, 175, 285, 303–15; *Le pêcheur*
 25, 32
Gounet, Thomas (1801–69) 11 n., 26, 32 n.,
 36, 166
Gounod, Charles (1818–93), *Faust* 172, 269,
 276 n., 341; *Roméo et Juliette* 132; *La
 Nonne sanglante* 303
Guérin, Léon (poet) 35, 102
Guiomar, Michel 132, 207 n., 333, 343

Habeneck, François-Antoine (conductor,
 1781–1849) 23, 240
Halévy, Fromental (1799–1862) 8 n., 35, 62,
 282, 341; *La Juive* 63, 144, 284
Handel, George Frederick 72, 277; *Messiah*
 264
Hanslick, Eduard 83, 125, 240
Haydn, Franz Joseph 45, 139, 192, 220
Heine, Heinrich (poet, 1797–1856) 207, 210
Hepokoski, James 239, 246
Hoffmann, E.T.A. (writer and composer,
 1776–1822) 29 n., 125
Holoman, D. Kern 64, 102
Huber, Ferdinand (composer, 1791–1863) 31
 n., 35
Hugo, Victor (poet, 1802–85) 13, 25, 29 n.,
 32, 34–5, 57, 102, 133, 148, 192, 281; *Les
 Orientales* 34, 37, 149

Kemp, Ian 42–4, 79–81, 152 n.

Lesueur (Le Sueur), Jean-François
 (1760–1837, composer and Berlioz's
 teacher) 5, 14, 23, 25, 40, 60, 64, 144, 216,
 260, 278, 282, 317, 334–5, 346–7; his
 aesthetics 122, 224; on fugue 192–4; as
 teacher of Berlioz 7–11, 18, 83, 107–8,
 113–15, 120, 122, 125–6, 204; prosody (*In
 media nocte*) 99; *Oratorio de Noël* 11, 110,
 188, 196, 317; *Ossian* 12, 317; *La Mort
 d'Adam* 314; Masses 194–201; *Troisème
 Messe solennelle* 10, 195
Lewis, Matthew (*The Monk*) 48, 133
Liszt, Franz (1811–86) 32, 53, 63–4, 71, 126,
 148, 250, 277, 290; and *Benvenuto Cellini*
 302; 317, 324, 341, 344–6; transcription of
 Symphonie fantastique 263; *Faust*
 symphony 141, 276 n., 315, 340

Macdonald, Hugh 9, 67, 81, 208 n., 214–15,
 238, 263, 299 n., 302, 332 n.
Mahler, Gustav (1860–1911) 45, 81, 128, 131,
 240, 342
Martini (Schwarzendorf), Jean-Paul Egide
 (composer, 1741–1816) *Plaisir d'amour*
 arr. Berlioz (H.134) 65, 166
Méhul, Nicolas-Etienne (1763–1817) 7,
 12–13, 53, 134, 278, 347
Mendelssohn, Felix (1809–47) 25, 119, 126,
 225; 'Italian' symphony 37, 267
Meyerbeer, Giacomo (1791–1864) 25, 35, 48,
 62, 125, 134, 341; *Les Huguenots* 44, 63,
 282, 289–90, 302; *Le Prophète* 63, 284, 303,
 333; *Robert le diable* 63, 166, 282–4, 295,
 313–4
Micznik, Vera 126
Michaelis, Christian Friedrich 139
Mongrédien, Jean 8, 99 n., 108, 192, 194 n.,
 196 n.
Moore, Thomas 25–6, 31–3, 172, 176
Mozart, Wolfgang Amadè (1756–91) 66, 72,
 112 n., 127, 144, 192, 240, 281, 342;
 Idomeneo 343; *Don Giovanni* 139, 193 n.,
 297, 299, 302, 307, 333; *Così fan tutte* 153;
 Requiem 40, 71–2, 83, 139, 193 n., 194,
 206; Te Deum 220; G minor symphony
 268
Musorgsky, Modest (1839–81) 341

Napoleon Bonaparte 4, 33–5, 40, 56, 144,
 197 n., 235
Napoleon III 53, 56, 58, 63, 223, 334, 337
Nerval, Gérard de (poet, translator, 1808–55)
 25, 50, 141, 172–4, 303, 306
Noske, Fritz 127, 167 n., 176
Nourrit, Adolphe (tenor, 1802–39) 144 n.,
 302

Orléans, monarchy, 30, 45, 51, 216; Duc d', 48

Paganini, Niccolò (1782–1840) 6, 36, 41
Piatier, François 302
Pohl, Richard (critic, 1826–96) 64, 315 n.
Prévost, Eugène-Prosper (composer, 1809–72) 17 n., 22, 26, 89

Ramaut, Alban 83, 283, 327
Rameau, Jean-Philippe 64, 189, 278, 303; harmonic theory 5, 8, 107, 112–9, 122, 225
Ratner, Leonard G. 126, 128 n., 131
Récio, Marie (Berlioz's second wife) 47, 53, 55
Reeve, Katherine 240, 309 n., 313
Reicha, Antonín (composer, theorist, Berlioz's counterpoint teacher, 1770–1836) 7–8, 12 n., 14, 252; on French prosody, 88–9, 95, 167; counterpoint teaching 107–8, 112; fugues, 296
Richault, Simon (publisher) 53, 55, 58, 67
Rimsky-Korsakov, Nikolai Andreyevich (1844–1908) 340–1
Robinson, Paul 152 n., 153, 325
Rossini, Gioacchino (1792–1868) 7, 14, 23, 62; overtures 82, 241; 264, 279, 289; *Guillaume Tell* 266, 290, 294, 303; *Moïse* 278; *La gazza ladra* 295
Rouget de Lisle, Claude-Joseph (1760–1836) 53

Saint-Saëns, Camille (1835–1921) 143, 153, 341
Schacher, Thomas 205 n., 213, 229, 237 n., 238
Schenker, Heinrich 100, 112 n., 205 n., 271, 273
Schubert, Franz (1797–1828), *Erlkönig* arr. Berlioz (H.136) 65; 72, 98, 154, 185; C major symphony 267
Schumann, Robert (1810–56) 6, 72, 119, 122, 160, 241, 270, 343, 345–7; review of *Symphonie fantastique* 158–9, 252, 257–8; *Faust*, 315
Scott, Sir Walter (1771–1832) 24–5, 31, 143, 238
Scribe, Eugène (librettist, 1791–1861) 48, 53, 63, 282
Shakespeare, William 25–6, 133, 139, 172, 187, 323; *Hamlet* 31–2, 49, 83, 121; *King Lear* 157, 245; *The Merchant of Venice,*
153, 327; *Much Ado about Nothing* 65–6, 339; *Richard III* 336; *Romeo and Juliet* 41–2, 83, 132, 153, 270–4
Smithson, Harriet (Berlioz's first wife) 23–4, 29, 33, 47, 62, 159, 161, 270
Société des Concerts du Conservatoire 23, 238, 240, 243, 276, 344 n.
Spontini, Gaspare (1774–1851) 7; *La Vestale* 13; 25, 35, 63, 126, 207, 278, 282; *Olympie* 333; 341, 345, 347
Strauss, Richard 270, 341
Stravinsky, Igor 100, 159, 341

Tchaikovsky, Pyotr Il'yitch 30, 131, 340
Thomas, Ambroise (composer, 1811–96) 37, 341
Tomlinson, Gary 276 n.
Tovey, Donald F. 3, 112 n., 157, 279

Verdi, Giuseppe (1813–1901) 6, 64, 72, 127, 264, 281, 283 n., 285, 341; *Don Carlos* 63; *Macbeth* 73; *Otello*, 65, 141, 157; *Il trovatore* 63, 273; Requiem, 205–6, 214, 256; Te Deum 220
Viardot, Pauline 53
Vigny, Alfred de (poet, 1797–1863) 37 n., 45
Virgil (*Aeneid*) 63, 159, 187, 284, 325, 328

Wagner, Richard (1813–83) 64, 119, 126–7, 148, 153, 205 n., 217, 250, 281–2, 285, 314, 317, 324, 334, 341–2, 345–7; *Faust* overture 315; *Die Meistersinger* 298 n.; *Der Ring* 127, 143 n., 226; *Tannhäuser* 62, 73, 290; *Tristan* 149–50, 272, 298, 346
Wailly, Léon de (librettist of *Benvenuto Cellini*) 37 n., 295 n.
Walton, Benjamin 335 n.
Weber, Carl Maria von (1786–1826) 7, 14, 22–3, 319, 345, 347; overtures 237–8; *Abu Hassan* 66 n., 147; *Chasse de Lützow* arr. Berlioz (H.63) 35; *Euryanthe* 13, 66 n., 343; *Der Freischütz* 25, 66 n., 99, 122, 144, 241, 325 n.; as *Robin des bois* 13, 313; adapted by Berlioz 48; *Oberon* 25, 66. 241–3, 279
Wolf, Hugo 157, 315
Wotton, Tom 53, 340, 342